The Modern Library College Editions

SHELLEY
Selected Poetry and Prose

MODERN LIBRARY COLLEGE EDITIONS

The Selected
POETRY AND PROSE OF
Percy Bysshe Shelley

Edited, with an Introduction, by
CARLOS BAKER
Associate Professor of English, Princeton University

THE MODERN LIBRARY · NEW YORK

The text of Shelley's poetry in this edition is substantially that of the first editions. Occasional emendations on the authority of later editors have been made. In addition, a small number of silent changes in punctuation, etc., have been introduced for the sake of clarity.

Acknowledgment is made to The Clarendon Press, Oxford, for the use of their edition of Shelley's Literary and Philosophical Criticism edited by John Shawcross, who based his edition upon the Essays and Letters of Shelley, edited by Mary Shelley, Shelley Memorials, edited by Lady Shelley, and Shelley's Prose Works, edited by H. Buxton Forman.

Random House IS THE PUBLISHER OF

THE MODERN LIBRARY

BENNETT A. CERF · DONALD S. KLOPFER · ROBERT K. HAAS

Manufactured in the United States of America

INTRODUCTION

by Carlos Baker

"HAD you never heard of Shelley?" said Mr. Bons to the boy in Forster's "Celestial Omnibus." Hanging his head, the boy said no. "But is there no Shelley in the house?" The boy's mother rose to the question. "Dear Mr. Bons, we aren't such Philistines as that. Two at the least. One a wedding present, and the other, smaller print, in one of the spare rooms." Mr. Bons smiled. "I believe," said he, "we have seven Shelleys."

Mr. Bons' figure was correct. The wedding-present Shelley and the spare-room Shelley may safely be ignored. But there are at least seven others who are worth paying some attention to: the radical reformer, the classical Hellenist, the romantic humanist, the lyricist, the philosophical poet, the tragedian of human corruption, and the unorthodox theist, as "god-intoxicated" as the German mystic Novalis, but much more firmly grounded in a hard-won idealistic system of thought.

With the possible exception of William Hazlitt, Shelley is the most consistent radical in the English romantic movement. His reforming zeal earned him the distrust of reactionary elements in the Regency period, and the admiration of such Olympian revolutionaries of his own and later times as Byron and Bernard Shaw. *Queen Mab,* the earliest of his long poems, reflects his devotion to books like William Godwin's *Political Justice* and Holbach's atheistic and materialistic treatise, the *Système de la Nature.* With fierce youthful enthusiasm, Shelley embraces a majority of the religious and secular heresies which nineteenth-century Englishmen inherited from their "enlightened" forebears in England and France. The poem thunders ominously against the worship of Jehovah, who for Shelley is a figure comparable to Blake's Nobodaddy. It rather stridently opposes the Christian Church, its dogmas, its priesthood, and its historical record. On the secular side, its catalog of evils includes war, slavery, wealth, prostitution, commerce, and custom. And like all of Shelley's poetry, *Queen Mab* cries out against the tyranny of all earthly kings whatsoever. But through the educated optimism of the prophetic fairy queen, Shelley also anticipates a future historic time when the lion will lie down with the lamb and the infant can safely undertake games beside the den of the cockatrice. Assuming man's possible perfectibility once he has overthrown his literally enthralling institutions, Shelley sums up his program in Voltaire's directive: *"Ecrasez l'infâme."* The poet of *Queen Mab* would make the world safe for the millennium through the removal of all environmental abominations. After that, in another phrase of Voltaire's, *"il faut cultiver nos jardins."*

From 1814 onward, though Shelley's reforming purposes remained as strong as ever, his tone altered, and his didacticism became less oppressive. While he still gladly assumed the moral duty of reminding men of what they might be, his hopes for the wholesale overturn of existing social institutions became less sanguine. *The Revolt of Islam,* his longest and least successful poem, is an idealized allegory of the French Revolution in which two rebel leaders named Laon and Cythna nearly succeed in converting Islam to a new order where the social law of love prevails. Their martyrdom, apparently inevitable under the present world dispensation, shows that the world will not be ready to receive such saints until it can reform itself from the inside out.

To provide an outline of this process of internal revolution for mankind's moral edification is the central problem of Shelley's lyrical drama on the Titan. The point of *Prometheus Unbound,* like that of T S. Eliot's latter-day *Waste Land,* is that when love fails all is lost unless love can be revived. Chained to his lonely rock in the Caucasus, Prometheus is an image for man's mind enslaved to hatred and fear, and tortured by all the ills that mentality is heir to. The furies which harass Prometheus are cousins-german to those in Eliot's *Family Reunion,* though they move across a lonely mountainside instead of hiding behind the drawing-room curtains. Indeed it is a kind of family reunion—of the mind of man with the principle of divine love—toward which Shelley's heroic drama steadily moves. Only the elimination of Jupiter, the hate principle, can prepare the way for Prometheus' reunion with Asia, the love principle, and unbind the mind of man from a 3000-year thralldom which he has imposed upon himself. Blake had a phrase for the chains of Prometheus: in his angry lyric, "London," he called them "mind-forged manacles." But neither Blake nor Shelley supposed that so miraculous an about-face on the part of man was in immediate (or even predictable) prospect. Behind the insistent hopefulness of Shelley's drama, the conditional IF bulks large as life. He is not so much proclaiming that man is free as he is setting forth the only conditions under which genuine freedom is to be attained. "IF", in a word, is another name for the double-edged "law of Demogorgon". If the mind of man, now conditionally purged, should again allow hate to assume supremacy, Jupiter will reassert his dominion, and the chains will once again clamp Prometheus to his lonely rock.

Shelley's broadly ethical consideration of the problem of human welfare in *Prometheus Unbound* did not mean, of course, that he had abandoned his post as watchdog of European liberty. From popular hymns like his revised version of "God Save the King" to the carefully argued prose of his *Philosophical View of Reform*, Shelley's later political works are all occasional. The occasions were those on which he thought he saw liberty threatened, liberty destroyed, or liberty triumphant. He had early resolved to cry down oppression and to salute all positive acts of reform or revolution in the Europe of his time. *The Masque of Anarchy* is a popular allegory on the infamous Peterloo massacre, where mounted dragoons bloodily broke up a workers' rally outside the manufacturing city of Manchester. *Swellfoot the Tyrant* amusingly combines Sophocles and Aristophanes with Punch and Judy in a shilling satire on the marital misadventures of George IV and his hapless Queen Caroline. On the positive side, one could count the "Ode to Liberty", celebrating the Spanish popular revolution of 1820, or the "Ode to Naples", Shelley's salute to the Neapolitan uprising against Austrian rule. In *Hellas*, as in these serious odes, the poet assumed the high style of *Prometheus Unbound* to praise the modern Greeks for their attempt to throw off Turkish domination in that painfully misrun revolution which claimed Byron's life in 1824. For Shelley the nineteenth-century political outlook was dark but not hopeless. Whatever poetry could do to enlarge the hope or dispel the darkness Shelley set himself to accomplish.

This task was not so hard as it might have been if Shelley had lacked a model. Luckily he carried in his mind's eye and used as an instrument of measurement on all things modern a blueprint of earthly perfection as embodied in that ancient City of Light, Athens in the age of Pericles. If Keats had traveled widely in imaginary realms of gold where Homer ruled, Shelley as classical Hellenist could have written a full-length Baedeker on the intellectual life of Greece from Homer to Aristotle. Incessant reading in the original language, coupled with close study of classical models at school, at college, and during his "Attic winter" with

Hogg and Peacock had made him a respectable Hellenist even in a time when these were far more numerous, on a per capita basis, than they are today. He undertook extensive translations from the dialogues of Plato. He "imitated" Aeschylus and Sophocles and Aristophanes. He took the great Socrates as one of his heroes. He set down eloquent descriptive notes on the Greek sculpture in Florence, grew ecstatic over the stonework of Phidias, and saw his earthly paradises enhanced with "Praxitelean shapes."

In the classical revival which is one of the distinguishing events of the romantic age, Shelley's role is therefore significant. Few of his contemporary poets knew the civilization of ancient Greece so well as he. Sometimes, as in the celebrated closing chorus of *Hellas,* he invests the rugged old peninsula and the waters round it with a dreamlike quality. But this is the result of excessive love rather than the idyllic ignorance of the amateur. "What the Greeks were," he cried, "was a reality, not a promise." He deeply believed that modern Europe owed all the best that it was or could hope to be to "the influence and inspiration of those glorious generations."

What the "holy city of Byzantium" was for William Butler Yeats, the Athenian city-state was for Shelley. Here, in defiance of the weathering of time, stood the "monuments of unageing intellect." Here lived in perpetuity the philosopher-kings of a nobler civilization. Yeats' image for the flux of things, "the dolphin-torn, the gong-tormented sea", is comparable to Shelley's "tide of war" in one of the semi-choruses of *Hellas.* For like Byzantium,

> Greece and her foundations are
> Built below the tide of war,
> Based on the crystalline sea
> Of thought and its eternity;
> Her citizens, imperial spirits,
> Rule the present from the past;
> On all this world of men inherits
> Their seal is set.

Much of the esthetic behind Yeats' best and strongest poetry is summarized in the Byzantium lyrics; Shelley's own esthetic position is well illustrated in what he says of the literature of ancient Greece. "Homer embodied the ideal perfection of [infant Greece] in human character; nor can we doubt that those who read his verses were awakened to an ambition of becoming like to Achilles, Hector, and Ulysses. . . . The sentiments of the auditors must have been refined and enlarged by a sympathy with such great and lovely impersonations, until from admiring they imitated, and from imitation they identified themselves with the objects of their admiration." In the time of the great Greek tragedians, this process was intensified. The works of Aeschylus and Sophocles are "as mirrors in which the spectator beholds himself . . . stripped of all but that ideal perfection and energy which everyone feels to be the internal type of all that he loves, admires, and would become." This esthetic process—the awakening and enlargement of sympathetic perception, the growing desire (at once ethical and emotional) to imitate, and the willed development of imitation to the stage of self-identification—lies at the foundation of all Shelley's visionary poetry. Yeats understood the matter perfectly.

Shelley's nearly absolute devotion to the Hellenic ideal for man is an indication of the extent of his romantic humanism. Though he was always the champion of the oppressed against the oppressors, and always supported the theoretical right of the people to self-government, he had little faith in the dependability of the common man. Such faith, indeed, was rare in his country and his time. But uncommon man, man as moral leader, man as philosopher-king, man as poet-thinker, claimed his veneration and his allegiance. Not men in general, but deep-browed men like Socrates and Plato, Shakespeare and Spenser, were worthy of being described, in the famous phrase of Protagoras, as "the measure of all things."

He always revered greatness; it was his conception of what was great which changed subtly as he matured. As a youth under the intellectual dominance of the Enlightenment, he was seduced by the materialistic doctrine of necessitarianism, as naturalistic a philosophy as any we know today. According to this doctrine, mind is a function of matter, and man is inexorably controlled, whether he knows it or not, by the same laws that govern the material universe. In the early pamphlet, A Refutation of Deism, one of the disputants flatly asserts that "the laws of motion and the properties of matter suffice to account for every phenomenon, or combination of phenomena" in the knowable world. But Shelley could not long pay more than intellectual lip service to a position so thoroughly opposed to his native and temperamental idealism. By 1818, and probably before that, he had completely reversed his field of vision. Now he vigorously asserted the priority of mind over matter, urging his good friend Maria Gisborne to accept a kind of optimism "in which we are our own gods." In *Prometheus Unbound,* man is defined as "one harmonious soul of many a soul, whose nature is its own divine control." Even the Renaissance humanism of Pico and Sir Thomas More went no further than this.

With his reverence for greatness and his growing belief that man under proper moral guidance could be the master of his own destiny, Shelley combined a supreme faith in the sanative powers of poetry. For him poetry was always the outgrowth of some constructive ethical program, usually supported by an idealistic metaphysic. His definition of the term was broad enough to include most of the great imaginative systems of thought from Plato to Spinoza. Had he anticipated Carlyle in writing a book on heroes, hero-worship, and the heroic in history, he would have emphasized the hero as poet, whom he felt to be the strongest force for mental rehabilitation that human history knows.

A Defence of Poetry is perhaps Shelley's most extended contribution to the literature of hero-worship. Its central idea, which is Shelley's explanation of the manner in which poetry acts to produce the moral improvement of man, is likewise the central idea of Shelley's humanism. "The great secret of morals," says the essayist, "is love; or a going out of our own nature, and an identification of ourselves with the beautiful which exists in thought, action, or person, not our own. A man, to be greatly good, must imagine intensely and comprehensively. . . . The great instrument of moral good is the imagination; and poetry administers to the effect [moral good] by acting upon the cause [imagination]. Poetry enlarges the circumference of the imagination by replenishing it with thoughts of ever new delight, which have the power of attracting and assimilating to their own nature all other thoughts. . . . Poetry strengthens the faculty which is the organ of the moral nature of man [imagination] in the same manner as exercise strengthens a limb."

If the great secret of moral good is love, and the great instrument of moral good is the imagination, and the great strengthener of the imagination is poetry, we possess the theorem by which Shelley would prove the importance of poets in the stabilization and development of human morality. From Plato onward, says Shelley, a chorus of the greatest writers have successively celebrated "the dominion of love, planting as it were trophies in the

human mind of that sublimest victory over sensuality and force."
These writers are the true heroes of the Western tradition, and
the central reason for Shelley's humanism.

. . . .

During the nineteenth century Shelley's lyrics far outshone his
longer poems in popularity. Generally speaking, if one had heard
of Shelley at all, he knew "The Cloud" or the "Ode to the West
Wind" or "To a Skylark"—that perennial triumvirate in whose
name the more massive achievement of Shelley as symbolic
thinker was ordinarily forgotten. The apparently innocuous rhe-
torical beauty of these poems charmed the eye and pleased the
ear. Taken together with some of the love-poetry and the "Hymn
to Intellectual Beauty", they helped to establish a stereotype of
Shelley as Ariel or as Angel, a fleet-footed, rosy-fingered messenger from another world who never stayed in one place long
enough to invite or permit intellectual analysis or appraisal.
Among the anthologists, Brooke and Palgrave thought nothing
of extracting songs from the more extended works. In demon-
strating the superficial beauties of the poet, they felt safe in
ignoring the context of philosophic poetry to which many of the
lyrics owed their origin and their point. Arnold and Swinburne
were agreed that Shelley was a lyricist; little else in the canon
claimed serious attention. Near the end of the Victorian period,
W. B. Yeats ironically said that the popularity of "The Cloud"
was owing to the ease with which it could be understood: Shelley's more important poems, since they required of readers a real
expenditure of imaginative energy, went by the board.

This obvious imbalance between the known and the unknown
Shelley has not been redressed in the present century. The schol-
arly literature on Shelley is enormous, but much more of it has
been devoted to literary source-hunting and biographical fact-
hunting than to the attempt to see Shelley plain, steadily, and
whole. Santayana, among the professional philosophers, has offered a perceptive essay, Croce a series of insights, and Whitehead
an appreciation of the poet's scientific acumen. Among the more
widely influential poet-critics of the past forty years, however, it
has been fashionable to use the worst of Shelley as a means of
suggesting that his best is not much better.

If the imbalance is to be adjusted, the lyricist must give ground
before that too little known Shelley, the visionary philosophical
poet. This side of his work, proportionately far the most extensive,
belongs in the line of descent from the myth-making Plato.

through Dante and Milton, up to Blake and Coleridge, and on to the later Yeats. Shelley may well have descended from his great predecessors in other ways: in breadth of vision, in sustained quality of performance, in technical mastery of his various media. Wherever one ranks him, his most energetic and protracted effort as philosopher-poet lay in the ordering and projection of his vast cosmology, his serious and profound explanation of the way the world is put together. "The course of his philosophical growth," as Professor Lionel Trilling has observed, "is his claim to greatness and to the attention of our generation."

Shelley seems to have understood the difficulties of the problem in symbolic communication which he set for himself. He knew from experience too much about the limitations of the public intellect (which has never shown a strong appetite for complex and erudite symbolism, though it regularly employs simpler images in daily communication) to suppose that his system would be received with universal acclaim. If he resembled Blake in believing that he must create his own system or be enslaved by another man's, he went farther than Blake in his attempts to reach the public ear. In the end he was obliged to admit that his success had not been noteworthy. "I can compare my experience in this respect," he glumly wrote, "to nothing but a series of wet blankets." Yet he persisted in his determination not to cheapen the quality of his most important work or to diminish, for public purposes, the magnitude of his vision. At the time of his death he was working on the best poem he ever did, but *The Triumph of Life* is also one of his most difficult works, embracing what is best in all seven Shelleys. If it is now possible to understand what he meant his poetry to be and to do, something like poetic justice has begun to operate in Shelley's posthumous career.

. . . .

The conception of tragedy in Shelley's thought is worth restatement if only to counteract the widespread notion that sentimental optimism denied him the tragic view of human life. In the first place it is a mistake to suppose that his mature intellectual position was either unduly sentimental or immoderately optimistic. No one who has read through his letters during the period 1819–1822 could properly accuse him of optimism about the course of human affairs in Europe, in England, or in general. If his poetry of the same period exhibits something like optimism, it is because one of Shelley's theories about the higher kind of poetry was that it ought to hold up before the mind's eye certain "idealisms of moral excellence" in order to suggest to men what they might achieve if they dared. Always between the lines, and often in their very language, the perceptive reader will find evidence of Shelley's tragic sense of the gap between what is and what ought to be.

The tragic situation in Shelley arises from either of two sources: a corrupt and corrupting social environment ruled by custom and superstition; or the individual's failure, through spiritual obliquity or simple desperation, to keep to his moral ideals. According to Shelley, the proper response even to the worst injuries is kindness, forbearance, and "a resolution to convert the injurer . . . by peace and love." Shelley never willingly sanctioned an act of violence. Any form of vengeance, any assertion of the *lex talionis,* seemed to him a pernicious error. Yet corrupt society is always forcing the individual's hand, with the result that he either forgets his ideals or sacrifices them to the exigencies of the moment. A degree of moral deformity inevitably results. The act of violence is never without a deleterious effect on the doer. Shelley defines tragedy as the result of any situation which produces moral deformity.

The case of Beatrice Cenci illustrates the point. In the old yellow book on the misfortunes of the Cenci family, Shelley found all the moral deformity he could use, as well as some which he felt obliged to delete in the interests of getting his play performed on the London stage. As Shelley presents her, Beatrice is at first a kind of saint, devoted to all the highest ideals of human conduct. Then the change is catalogued. Under the vindictive brutality of her psychotic father, and within the corrupt social environment of her native city, she is rapidly converted into an efficient murderess, destroying her father and defying the legal system which brings her to trial. Her moral duty was clear—to hold out for her ideals, to be of the stuff of sainthood. Had she done so, said Shelley, she would not have been a tragic figure.

This conception of tragedy is neither Aristotelean nor Shakespearean, though it contains elements of both. It lays emphasis, however, on spiritual or moral corruption as the supreme error which flesh is heir to. Shelley and Blake took as their goal the fullest possible development of the human personality to a complete and rounded whole. If this goal were to be achieved, to paraphrase Mr. T. S. Eliot, it would cost not less than everything. Such an attitude is of course at odds with the spirit of acceptance or compromise which is the essence of a "realistic" ethic. Moral realism assumes a basic resistance in the nature of things, a fundamental disability in all humankind. This is the doctrine of accepted imperfection; we make the best of the best bargain we are able to make. Unalterably opposed to such a bargain-counter conception of human destiny, Shelley and Blake would not willingly settle for anything less than perfection. The abrogation of personal integrity must therefore strike them both as a tragic loss to the individual potential.

The voluntary (or involuntary) surrender of personal integrity in exchange for non-spiritual values is the theme of Shelley's last poem, *The Triumph of Life*. Using the stanza form of the *Divine Comedy*, with Rousseau as substitute for Dante's Virgil, Shelley pictures the life of this world as a cold inferno set in the midst of unapprehended paradise. Nearly all the great personages in history pass down the dusty roadway, following the triumphal chariot of the Worldly Life. Like barbarian prisoners in a Roman triumphus, they are in chains. "In the battle Life and they did wage," Rousseau explains, "She remained conqueror." The notable exceptions, absentees from the procession, are the sacred few who could not tame their spirits to the Worldly Life's omnipotence. These are of Athens and Jerusalem—Socrates and Jesus Christ. It is a measure, the final one, of Shelley's tragic view of life that his sacred few, though sacred, should be so few.

If Jesus and Socrates are his ultimate earthly heroes, his deepest allegiance is reserved for a supernal power in which all such heroes share, even the lesser men among them. Shelley's religion is unorthodox and individualistic in the extreme, but also strong and constant. It should be thought of, not as the antagonist of his humanism, but as the universal setting in which his humanism flourished. Like a true evangelical, he never desisted from the attempt to make others understand the spiritual truths he knew. Professor Notopoulos calls him a natural Platonist. He was also a natural theist. Even in the callow days of his professed atheism, he recognized the existence of a supreme and beneficent Force. By 1816 he attempted to define it as Intellectual Beauty. Afterwards he came to think of it more exactly as cosmic love, the constant "One" in a world of flux where the many change and pass.

His recurrent symbol for this spiritual energy is the idealized figure of a woman. Speaking of Thomas Hardy's invented deity, the "President of the Immortals", G. K. Chesterton called Hardy anthropomorphic through sheer atheism. Of Shelley it might be said that he was gynecomorphic through exuberant theism. In the "Hymn", the goddess has not yet taken form. Capable though it is of producing an ecstatic response, Intellectual Beauty is only "the awful shadow of some unseen Power". By the time of *Prometheus Unbound,* however, the Power has been incarnated in Asia, wife of the Titan. In later poems she assumes other names and other forms: the Witch of Atlas, the Lady of the Garden in "The Sensitive Plant", Emilia in *Epipsychidion,* Urania in *Adonais,* and the rainbow-goddess Iris in *The Triumph of Life.*

The rationale for this symbol is partly Shelleyan and partly Platonic. For the young Shelley, woman seemed to be the completing agent for man, the necessary complementary force by which his fullest self-realization was made possible. As his theism developed, he transferred his "completing agent" concept to a non-earthly plane. The woman-symbol, which had for him extremely complex mythological as well as highly personal associations, was conveniently carried over. Following imaginatively the counsel which Diotima gave Socrates in Plato's *Symposium,* Shelley sought to elevate his thinking through the forms of knowledge up to the contemplation of Divine Ideas and finally to "the vision of one single science." In the end, his single science, the great agency making for unification in a divided world, was the doctrine of cosmic love. Only by understanding it could man reach the height of his manifest destiny. Shelley used his woman-symbol as a means of suggesting the outlines of a power which might otherwise have been indescribable. Evidently he was not wholly successful in projecting his idea. A number of his biographers have assumed, with varying degrees of unimaginative obtuseness, that Shelley's goddesses are very little more than disguised compliments to earthly mistresses.

Shelley's theism is too complicated and detailed to be adequately explained in an introduction. The careful reading of *Epipsychidion, Adonais, The Triumph of Life* and *A Defence of Poetry* shows how he put it to work. The whole broad structure rests on the faith that there is available to the perceptive and imaginative man an inexhaustible reservoir of spiritual energy, not unlike what Blake apotheosized in his Los-symbol. In two impassioned stanzas of *Adonais,* the elegy for Keats, Shelley attempts to define his meaning. First, it is the "plastic stress" of the one supreme Spirit which sweeps through the dull, dense world and tortures the unwilling dross toward its own magnificent likeness. Second, it is that "sustaining Love" which burns bright or dim through the realm of being according to the imaginative capabilities of its various recipients. All creatures and things are as mirrors reflecting "the fire for which all thirst". The state of grace in Shelleyan theology is the near approach to the Supreme Likeness; the state of sin is a turning away from the Supreme Good. But the Supreme Love is always available to those who earnestly seek it. This is all that "gives grace and truth to life's unquiet dream." It is more than enough.

It might have been E. M. Forster, but it was actually Alfred Stieglitz, who used to say that if there were two doors, the first labeled, "This Way to See God", and the second, "This Way to Hear a Lecture About God", everyone would rush to the second door. No one would dare to face the implications of entering the first. The difference between Shelley and other people (excluding Dante, Milton, Blake, and many religious mystics) is that he would rush directly to door Number One. His most difficult and in many ways his best poetry is an attempt to relate symbolically what he found on the other side of that door.

BIOGRAPHICAL NOTE

SHELLEY's life (1792–1822) is easily summarized. The biographies listed below will of course be consulted by anyone concerned with the events of his career in any detail. An excellent introduction for the uninitiated student is Ernest Bernbaum's essay in the revised edition of his standard *Guide Through the Romantic Movement*. Born at Field Place, Sussex, where his father Timothy was a country squire, Shelley got his public schooling (which he profoundly disliked) at Syon House Academy and Eton. His freer and happier life at University College, Oxford, was permanently interrupted by his expulsion in the spring of 1811 for alleged contumacy in connection with a pamphlet called *The Necessity of Atheism* on which he collaborated with his good friend Thomas Jefferson Hogg. He soon married Harriet Westbrook, a school friend of one of his sisters, after a hasty elopement which both of the contracting parties had occasion to repent a few years later. The first three years of his marriage read like a political travelogue, but he wrote extensively and read intensively during journeyings which took him into Ireland, Wales, Scotland, and the south of England.

The shaky foundations of his marriage fell to the ground in 1814 when he left England with Mary Godwin, daughter of his revered philosopher friend, William Godwin, and her step-sister, Claire Clairmont. His wife Harriet committed suicide by drowning in 1816, and the poet married the girl with whom he had conducted a liaison. The rest of Shelley's life was spent on the Continent, at first in Switzerland, where he began a six-year friendship with Lord Byron, and afterwards in Italy, where Shelley and Mary lost two young children by sickness and where the bereaved mother nearly collapsed. All of Shelley's most memorable poetry and prose was done in the four-year period, 1818–1822, a length of time roughly equivalent to the four last years of Keats both in intensity of application and in degree of productivity. On July 8, 1822, he was drowned with two companions in a sailing accident in the Gulf of Spezia. Like Keats he was buried in the Protestant Cemetery in Rome.

BIBLIOGRAPHICAL NOTE

THE modern standard biography of Shelley is Newman I. White, *Shelley*, 2 volumes, New York, 1940. The late Professor White revised and shortened the larger book as *Portrait of Shelley*, New York, 1945. Edmund Blunden's *Shelley: A Life Story*, London, 1946, is a brilliant and readable narrative. Two very searching studies of the youthful Shelley are A. M. D. Hughes, *The Nascent Mind of Shelley*, Oxford, 1947, and K. N. Cameron, *The Young Shelley*, New York, 1950.

Among critical books of interest to the general reader or the specialist, the following are recommended: Ellsworth Barnard, *Shelley's Religion*, Minneapolis, 1936; Joseph Barrell, *Shelley and the Thought of His Time*, New Haven, 1947; O. W. Campbell, *Shelley and the Unromantics*, London, 1924; Carl Grabo, *The Magic Plant*, Chapel Hill, 1936; B. P. Kurtz, *The Pursuit of Death*, New York, 1933; James A. Notopoulos, *The Platonism of Shelley*, Durham, 1949; Melvin T. Solve, *Shelley's Theory of Poetry*, Chicago, 1927; Floyd Stovall, *Desire and Restraint in Shelley*, Durham, 1931; and *Shelley's Major Poetry: The Fabric of a Vision*, Princeton, 1948, by the editor of this volume of selections.

Contents

PREFACES AND ESSAYS

Narrative Poems
and Lyrical Dramas

From QUEEN MAB

(CANTO VI)

'THROUGHOUT these infinite orbs of mingling light,
Of which yon earth is one, is wide diffused
A Spirit of activity and life,
That knows no term, cessation, or decay;
That fades not when the lamp of earthly life,
Extinguished in the dampness of the grave,
Awhile there slumbers, more than when the babe
In the dim newness of its being feels
The impulses of sublunary things,
And all is wonder to unpractised sense: 10
But, active, steadfast, and eternal, still
Guides the fierce whirlwind, in the tempest roars,
Cheers in the day, breathes in the balmy groves,
Strengthens in health, and poisons in disease;
And in the storm of change, that ceaselessly
Rolls round the eternal universe, and shakes
Its undecaying battlement, presides,
Apportioning with irresistible law
The place each spring of its machine shall fill;
So that when waves on waves tumultuous heap   20
Confusion to the clouds, and fiercely driven
Heaven's lightnings scorch the uprooted ocean-fords,
Whilst, to the eye of shipwrecked mariner,
Lone sitting on the bare and shuddering rock,
All seems unlinked contingency and chance:
No atom of this turbulence fulfils
A vague and unnecessitated task,
Or acts but as it must and ought to act.
Even the minutest molecule of light,
That in an April sunbeam's fleeting glow   30
Fulfils its destined, though invisible work,
The universal Spirit guides; nor less,
When merciless ambition, or mad zeal,
Has led two hosts of dupes to battle-field,

3

That, blind, they there may dig each other's graves
And call the sad work glory, does it rule
All passions: not a thought, a will, an act,
No working of the tyrant's moody mind,
Nor one misgiving of the slaves who boast
Their servitude, to hide the shame they feel,   40
Nor the events enchaining every will,
That from the depths of unrecorded time
Have drawn all-influencing virtue, pass
Unrecognized or unforeseen by thee,
Soul of the Universe! eternal spring
Of life and death, of happiness and woe,
Of all that chequers the phantasmal scene
That floats before our eyes in wavering light,
Which gleams but on the darkness of our prison,
    Whose chains and massy walls   50
    We feel, but cannot see.

'Spirit of Nature! all-sufficing Power,
Necessity! thou mother of the world!
Unlike the God of human error, thou
Requir'st no prayers or praises; the caprice
Of man's weak will belongs no more to thee
Than do the changeful passions of his breast
To thy unvarying harmony: the slave,
Whose horrible lusts spread misery o'er the world,
And the good man, who lifts, with virtuous pride,   60
His being in the sight of happiness
That springs from his own works; the poison-tree,
Beneath whose shade all life is withered up,
And the fair oak, whose leafy dome affords
A temple where the vows of happy love
Are registered, are equal in thy sight:
No love, no hate thou cherishest: revenge
And favouritism, and worst desire of fame
Thou know'st not: all that the wide world contains
Are but thy passive instruments, and thou   70
Regard'st them all with an impartial eye,
Whose joy or pain thy nature cannot feel,
    Because thou hast not human sense,
    Because thou art not human mind.

'Yes! when the sweeping storm of time
Has sung its death-dirge o'er the ruined fanes
And broken altars of the almighty Fiend
Whose name usurps thy honours, and the blood
Through centuries clotted there, has floated down
The tainted flood of ages, shalt thou live   80
Unchangeable! A shrine is raised to thee,
　　Which nor the tempest-breath of time,
　　Nor the interminable flood
　　Over earth's slight pageant rolling,
　　　Availeth to destroy,—
The sensitive extension of the world.
　　That wondrous and eternal fane,
Where pain and pleasure, good and evil join,
To do the will of strong necessity,
　　And life, in multitudinous shapes,   90
Still pressing forward where no term can be,
　　Like hungry and unresting flame
Curls round the eternal columns of its strength.'

VIII

THE FAIRY

'THE Present and the Past thou hast beheld:
It was a desolate sight. Now, Spirit, learn
　　The secrets of the Future.—Time!
Unfold the brooding pinion of thy gloom,
Render thou up thy half-devoured babes,
　　And from the cradles of eternity,
Where millions lie lulled to their portioned sleep
By the deep murmuring stream of passing things,
Tear thou that gloomy shroud.—Spirit, behold
　　　Thy glorious destiny!'   10

　　　Joy to the Spirit came.
Through the wide rent in Time's eternal veil,
Hope was seen beaming through the mists of fear:
　　　Earth was no longer Hell;
　　　Love, freedom, health, had given
Their ripeness to the manhood of its prime,

    And all its pulses beat
Symphonious to the planetary spheres:
    Then dulcet music swelled
Concordant with the life-strings of the soul;   20
It throbbed in sweet and languid beatings there,
Catching new life from transitory death,—
Like the vague sighings of a wind at even,
That wakes the wavelets of the slumbering sea
And dies on the creation of its breath,
And sinks and rises, fails and swells by fits:
    Was the pure stream of feeling
    That sprung from these sweet notes,
And o'er the Spirit's human sympathies
With mild and gentle motion calmly flowed.   30

    Joy to the Spirit came,—
    Such joy as when a lover sees
The chosen of his soul in happiness,
    And witnesses her peace
Whose woe to him were bitterer than death,
    Sees her unfaded cheek
Glow mantling in first luxury of health,
    Thrills with her lovely eyes,
Which like two stars amid the heaving main
    Sparkle through liquid bliss.   40

Then in her triumph spoke the Fairy Queen:
'I will not call the ghost of ages gone
To unfold the frightful secrets of its lore;
    The present now is past,
And those events that desolate the earth
Have faded from the memory of Time,
Who dares not give reality to that
Whose being I annul. To me is given
The wonders of the human world to keep,
Space, matter, time, and mind. Futurity   50
Exposes now its treasure; let the sight
Renew and strengthen all thy failing hope.
O human Spirit! spur thee to the goal
Where virtue fixes universal peace,
And midst the ebb and flow of human things,

Show somewhat stable, somewhat certain still,
A lighthouse o'er the wild of dreary waves.

'The habitable earth is full of bliss;
Those wastes of frozen billows that were hurled
By everlasting snowstorms round the poles,   60
Where matter dared not vegetate or live,
But ceaseless frost round the vast solitude
Bound its broad zone of stillness, are unloosed;
And fragrant zephyrs there from spicy isles
Ruffle the placid ocean-deep, that rolls
Its broad, bright surges to the sloping sand,
Whose roar is wakened into echoings sweet
To murmur through the Heaven-breathing groves
And melodize with man's blest nature there.

'Those deserts of immeasurable sand,   70
Whose age-collected fervours scarce allowed
A bird to live, a blade of grass to spring,
Where the shrill chirp of the green lizard's love
Broke on the sultry silentness alone,
Now teem with countless rills and shady woods,
Cornfields and pastures and white cottages;
And where the startled wilderness beheld
A savage conqueror stained in kindred blood,
A tigress sating with the flesh of lambs
The unnatural famine of her toothless cubs,   80
Whilst shouts and howlings through the desert rang,
Sloping and smooth the daisy-spangled lawn,
Offering sweet incense to the sun-rise, smiles
To see a babe before his mother's door,
        Sharing his morning's meal
    With the green and golden basilisk
        That comes to lick his feet.

'Those trackless deeps, where many a weary sail
Has seen above the illimitable plain
Morning on night, and night on morning rise,   90
Whilst still no land to greet the wanderer spread
Its shadowy mountains on the sun-bright sea,
Where the loud roarings of the tempest-waves

So long have mingled with the gusty wind
In melancholy loneliness, and swept
The desert of those ocean solitudes,
But vocal to the sea-bird's harrowing shriek,
The bellowing monster, and the rushing storm,
Now to the sweet and many-mingling sounds
Of kindliest human impulses respond.   100
Those lonely realms bright garden-isles begem,
With lightsome clouds and shining seas between,
And fertile valleys, resonant with bliss,
Whilst green woods overcanopy the wave,
Which like a toil-worn labourer leaps to shore,
To meet the kisses of the flow'rets there.

'All things are recreated, and the flame
Of consentaneous love inspires all life:
The fertile bosom of the earth gives suck
To myriads, who still grow beneath her care,   110
Rewarding her with their pure perfectness:
The balmy breathings of the wind inhale
Her virtues, and diffuse them all abroad:
Health floats amid the gentle atmosphere,
Glows in the fruits, and mantles on the stream:
No storms deform the beaming brow of Heaven,
Nor scatter in the freshness of its pride
The foliage of the ever-verdant trees;
But fruits are ever ripe, flowers ever fair,
And Autumn proudly bears her matron grace,   120
Kindling a flush on the fair cheek of Spring,
Whose virgin bloom beneath the ruddy fruit
Reflects its tint, and blushes into love.

'The lion now forgets to thirst for blood:
There might you see him sporting in the sun
Beside the dreadless kid; his claws are sheathed,
His teeth are harmless, custom's force has made
His nature as the nature of a lamb.
Like passion's fruit, the nightshade's tempting bane
Poisons no more the pleasure it bestows: 130
All bitterness is past; the cup of joy
Unmingled mantles to the goblet's brim,
And courts the thirsty lips it fled before.

'But chief, ambiguous Man, he that can know
More misery, and dream more joy than all;
Whose keen sensations thrill within his breast
To mingle with a loftier instinct there,
Lending their power to pleasure and to pain,
Yet raising, sharpening, and refining each;
Who stands amid the ever-varying world, 140
The burthen or the glory of the earth;
He chief perceives the change, his being notes
The gradual renovation, and defines
Each movement of its progress on his mind.

'Man, where the gloom of the long polar night
Lowers o'er the snow-clad rocks and frozen soil,
Where scarce the hardiest herb that braves the frost
Basks in the moonlight's ineffectual glow,
Shrank with the plants, and darkened with the night;
His chilled and narrow energies, his heart, 150
Insensible to courage, truth, or love,
His stunted stature and imbecile frame,
Marked him for some abortion of the earth,
Fit compeer of the bears that roamed around,
Whose habits and enjoyments were his own:
His life a feverish dream of stagnant woe,
Whose meagre wants, but scantily fulfilled,
Apprised him ever of the joyless length
Which his short being's wretchedness had reached;
His death a pang which famine, cold and toil 160
Long on the mind, whilst yet the vital spark
Clung to the body stubbornly, had brought:
All was inflicted here that Earth's revenge
Could wreak on the infringers of her law;
One curse alone was spared—the name of God.

'Nor where the tropics bound the realms of day
With a broad belt of mingling cloud and flame,
Where blue mists through the unmoving atmosphere
Scattered the seeds of pestilence, and fed
Unnatural vegetation, where the land 170
Teemed with all earthquake, tempest and disease,
Was Man a nobler being; slavery
Had crushed him to his country's blood-stained dust;

Or he was bartered for the fame of power,
Which all internal impulses destroying,
Makes human will an article of trade;
Or he was changed with Christians for their gold,
And dragged to distant isles, where to the sound
Of the flesh-mangling scourge, he does the work
Of all-polluting luxury and wealth,   180
Which doubly visits on the tyrants' heads
The long-protracted fulness of their woe;
Or he was led to legal butchery,
To turn to worms beneath that burning sun,
Where kings first leagued against the rights of men,
And priests first traded with the name of God.

'Even where the milder zone afforded Man
A seeming shelter, yet contagion there,
Blighting his being with unnumbered ills,
Spread like a quenchless fire; nor truth till late   190
Availed to arrest its progress, or create
That peace which first in bloodless victory waved
Her snowy standard o'er this favoured clime:
There man was long the train-bearer of slaves,
The mimic of surrounding misery,
The jackal of ambition's lion-rage,
The bloodhound of religion's hungry zeal.

'Here now the human being stands adorning
This loveliest earth with taintless body and mind;
Blessed from his birth with all bland impulses,   200
Which gently in his noble bosom wake
All kindly passions and all pure desires.
Him, still from hope to hope the bliss pursuing
Which from the exhaustless lore of human weal
Dawns on the virtuous mind, the thoughts that rise
In time-destroying infiniteness, gift
With self-enshrined eternity, that mocks
The unprevailing hoariness of age,
And man, once fleeting o'er the transient scene
Swift as an unremembered vision, stands   210
Immortal upon earth: no longer now
He slays the lamb that looks him in the face,
And horribly devours his mangled flesh,

Which, still avenging Nature's broken law,
Kindled all putrid humours in his frame,
All evil passions, and all vain belief,
Hatred, despair, and loathing in his mind,
The germs of misery, death, disease, and crime.
No longer now the wingèd habitants,
That in the woods their sweet lives sing away,   220
Flee from the form of man; but gather round,
And prune their sunny feathers on the hands
Which little children stretch in friendly sport
Towards these dreadless partners of their play.
All things are void of terror: Man has lost
His terrible prerogative, and stands
An equal amidst equals: happiness
And science dawn, though late upon the earth;
Peace cheers the mind, health renovates the frame;
Disease and pleasure cease to mingle here,   230
Reason and passion cease to combat there;
Whilst each unfettered o'er the earth extend
Their all-subduing energies, and wield
The sceptre of a vast dominion there;
Whilst every shape and mode of matter lends
Its force to the omnipotence of mind,
Which from its dark mine drags the gem of truth
To decorate its Paradise of peace.'

IX

'O HAPPY Earth! reality of Heaven!
To which those restless souls that ceaselessly
Throng through the human universe, aspire;
Thou consummation of all mortal hope!
Thou glorious prize of blindly-working will!
Whose rays, diffused throughout all space and time,
Verge to one point and blend for ever there:
Of purest spirits thou pure dwelling place!
Where care and sorrow, impotence and crime,
Languor, disease, and ignorance dare not come: 10
O happy Earth, reality of Heaven!

'Genius has seen thee in her passionate dreams,
And dim forebodings of thy loveliness

Haunting the human heart, have there entwined
Those rooted hopes of some sweet place of bliss
Where friends and lovers meet to part no more.
Thou art the end of all desire and will,
The product of all action; and the souls
That by the paths of an aspiring change
Have reached thy haven of perpetual peace,   20
There rest from the eternity of toil
That framed the fabric of thy perfectness.

'Even Time, the conqueror, fled thee in his fear;
That hoary giant, who, in lonely pride,
So long had ruled the world, that nations fell
Beneath his silent footstep. Pyramids,
That for millenniums had withstood the tide
Of human things, his storm-breath drove in sand
Across that desert where their stones survived
The name of him whose pride had heaped them there.   30
Yon monarch, in his solitary pomp,
Was but the mushroom of a summer day,
That his light-wingèd footstep pressed to dust:
Time was the king of earth: all things gave way
Before him, but the fixed and virtuous will,
The sacred sympathies of soul and sense,
That mocked his fury and prepared his fall.

'Yet slow and gradual dawned the morn of love;
Long lay the clouds of darkness o'er the scene,
Till from its native Heaven they rolled away: 40
First, Crime triumphant o'er all hope careered
Unblushing, undisguising, bold and strong;
Whilst Falsehood, tricked in Virtue's attributes,
Long sanctified all deeds of vice and woe,
Till, done by her own venomous sting to death,
She left the moral world without a law,
No longer fettering Passion's fearless wing,
Nor searing Reason with the brand of God.
Then steadily the happy ferment worked;
Reason was free; and wild though Passion went   50
Through tangled glens and wood-embosomed meads,

Gathering a garland of the strangest flowers,
Yet like the bee returning to her queen,
She bound the sweetest on her sister's brow,
Who meek and sober kissed the sportive child,
No longer trembling at the broken rod.

'Mild was the slow necessity of death:
The tranquil Spirit failed beneath its grasp,
Without a groan, almost without a fear,
Calm as a voyager to some distant land,   60
And full of wonder, full of hope as he.
The deadly germs of languor and disease
Died in the human frame, and Purity
Blessed with all gifts her earthly worshippers.
How vigorous then the athletic form of age!
How clear its open and unwrinkled brow!
Where neither avarice, cunning, pride, nor care,
Had stamped the seal of grey deformity
On all the mingling lineaments of time.
How lovely the intrepid front of youth!   70
Which meek-eyed courage decked with freshest grace;
Courage of soul, that dreaded not a name,
And elevated will, that journeyed on
Through life's phantasmal scene in fearlessness,
With virtue, love, and pleasure, hand in hand.

'Then, that sweet bondage which is Freedom's self,
And rivets with sensation's softest tie
The kindred sympathies of human souls,
Needed no fetters of tyrannic law:
Those delicate and timid impulses   80
In Nature's primal modesty arose,
And with undoubted confidence disclosed
The growing longings of its dawning love,
Unchecked by dull and selfish chastity,
That virtue of the cheaply virtuous,
Who pride themselves in senselessness and frost.
No longer prostitution's venomed bane
Poisoned the springs of happiness and life;
Woman and man, in confidence and love,

Equal and free and pure together trod   90
The mountain-paths of virtue, which no more
Were stained with blood from many a pilgrim's feet.

'Then, where, through distant ages, long in pride
The palace of the monarch-slave had mocked
Famine's faint groan, and Penury's silent tear,
A heap of crumbling ruins stood, and threw
Year after year their stones upon the field,
Wakening a lonely echo; and the leaves
Of the old thorn, that on the topmost tower
Usurped the royal ensign's grandeur, shook   100
In the stern storm that swayed the topmost tower
And whispered strange tales in the Whirlwind's ear.

'Low through the lone cathedral's roofless aisles
The melancholy winds a death-dirge sung:
It were a sight of awfulness to see
The works of faith and slavery, so vast,
So sumptuous, yet so perishing withal!
Even as the corpse that rests beneath its wall.
A thousand mourners deck the pomp of death
To-day, the breathing marble glows above   110
To decorate its memory, and tongues
Are busy of its life: to-morrow, worms
In silence and in darkness seize their prey.

'Within the massy prison's mouldering courts,
Fearless and free the ruddy children played,
Weaving gay chaplets for their innocent brows
With the green ivy and the red wall-flower,
That mock the dungeon's unavailing gloom;
The ponderous chains, and gratings of strong iron,
There rusted amid heaps of broken stone   120
That mingled slowly with their native earth:
There the broad beam of day, which feebly once
Lighted the cheek of lean Captivity
With a pale and sickly glare, then freely shone
On the pure smiles of infant playfulness:
No more the shuddering voice of hoarse Despair
Pealed through the echoing vaults, but soothing notes

Of ivy-fingered winds and gladsome birds
And merriment were resonant around.

'These ruins soon left not a wreck behind: 130
Their elements, wide scattered o'er the globe,
To happier shapes were moulded, and became
Ministrant to all blissful impulses;
Thus human things were perfected, and earth,
Even as a child beneath its mother's love,
Was strengthened in all excellence, and grew
Fairer and nobler with each passing year.

'Now Time his dusky pennons o'er the scene
Closes in steadfast darkness, and the past
Fades from our charmèd sight. My task is done: 140
Thy lore is learned. Earth's wonders are thine own,
With all the fear and all the hope they bring.
My spells are passed: the present now recurs.
Ah me! a pathless wilderness remains
Yet unsubdued by man's reclaiming hand.

'Yet, human Spirit, bravely hold thy course,
Let virtue teach thee firmly to pursue
The gradual paths of an aspiring change:
For birth and life and death, and that strange state
Before the naked soul has found its home,   150
All tend to perfect happiness, and urge
The restless wheels of being on their way,
Whose flashing spokes, instinct with infinite life,
Bicker and burn to gain their destined goal:
For birth but wakes the spirit to the sense
Of outward shows, whose unexperienced shape
New modes of passion to its frame may lend;
Life is its state of action, and the store
Of all events is aggregated there
That variegate the eternal universe;   160
Death is a gate of dreariness and gloom,
That leads to azure isles and beaming skies
And happy regions of eternal hope.
Therefore, O Spirit! fearlessly bear on:
Though storms may break the primrose on its stalk,

Though frosts may blight the freshness of its bloom,
Yet Spring's awakening breath will woo the earth
To feed with kindliest dews its favourite flower,
That blooms in mossy banks and darksome glens,
Lighting the greenwood with its sunny smile.   170

'Fear not then, Spirit, Death's disrobing hand,
So welcome when the tyrant is awake,
So welcome when the bigot's hell-torch burns;
'Tis but the voyage of a darksome hour,
The transient gulf-dream of a startling sleep.
Death is no foe to Virtue: earth has seen
Love's brightest roses on the scaffold bloom,
Mingling with Freedom's fadeless laurels there,
And presaging the truth of visioned bliss.
Are there not hopes within thee, which this scene   180
Of linked and gradual being has confirmed?
Whose stingings bade thy heart look further still,
When, to the moonlight walk by Henry led,
Sweetly and sadly thou didst talk of death?
And wilt thou rudely tear them from thy breast,
Listening supinely to a bigot's creed,
Or tamely crouching to the tyrant's rod,
Whose iron thongs are red with human gore?
Never: but bravely bearing on, thy will
Is destined an eternal war to wage   190
With tyranny and falsehood, and uproot
The germs of misery from the human heart.
Thine is the hand whose piety would soothe
The thorny pillow of unhappy crime,
Whose impotence an easy pardon gains,
Watching its wanderings as a friend's disease:
Thine is the brow whose mildness would defy
Its fiercest rage, and brave its sternest will,
When fenced by power and master of the world.
Thou art sincere and good; of resolute mind,   200
Free from heart-withering custom's cold control,
Of passion lofty, pure and unsubdued.
Earth's pride and meanness could not vanquish thee,
And therefore art thou worthy of the boon
Which thou hast now received: Virtue shall keep
Thy footsteps in the path that thou hast trod,

And many days of beaming hope shall bless
Thy spotless life of sweet and sacred love.
Go, happy one, and give that bosom joy
  Whose sleepless spirit waits to catch   210
  Light, life and rapture from thy smile.'

  The Fairy waves her wand of charm.
Speechless with bliss the Spirit mounts the car,
  That rolled beside the battlement,
Bending her beamy eyes in thankfulness.
  Again the enchanted steeds were yoked,
  Again the burning wheels inflame
The steep descent of Heaven's untrodden way.
  Fast and far the chariot flew:
  The vast and fiery globes that rolled   220
  Around the Fairy's palace-gate
Lessened by slow degrees and soon appeared
Such tiny twinklers as the planet orbs
That there attendant on the solar power
With borrowed light pursued their narrower way.

  Earth floated then below:
  The chariot paused a moment there;
    The Spirit then descended:
The restless coursers pawed the ungenial soil,
Snuffed the gross air, and then, their errand done,   230
Unfurled their pinions to the winds of Heaven.

  The Body and the Soul united then,
A gentle start convulsed Ianthe's frame:
Her veiny eyelids quietly unclosed;
Moveless awhile the dark blue orbs remained:
She looked around in wonder and beheld
Henry, who kneeled in silence by her couch,
Watching her sleep with looks of speechless love,
    And the bright beaming stars
    That through the casement shone.   240
        [1812–1813; unauthorized publ. 1821]

ALASTOR

OR

THE SPIRIT OF SOLITUDE

PREFACE

THE poem entitled *Alastor* may be considered as allegorical of one of the most interesting situations of the human mind. It represents a youth of uncorrupted feelings and adventurous genius led forth by an imagination inflamed and purified through familiarity with all that is excellent and majestic, to the contemplation of the universe. He drinks deep of the fountains of knowledge, and is still insatiate. The magnificence and beauty of the external world sinks profoundly into the frame of his conceptions, and affords to their modifications a variety not to be exhausted. So long as it is possible for his desires to point towards objects thus infinite and unmeasured, he is joyous, and tranquil, and self-possessed. But the period arrives when these objects cease to suffice. His mind is at length suddenly awakened and thirsts for intercourse with an intelligence similar to itself. He images to himself the Being whom he loves. Conversant with speculations of the sublimest and most perfect natures, the vision in which he embodies his own imaginations unites all of wonderful, or wise, or beautiful, which the poet, the philosopher, or the lover could depicture. The intellectual faculties, the imagination, the functions of sense, have their respective requisitions on the sympathy of corresponding powers in other human beings. The Poet is represented as uniting these requisitions, and attaching them to a single image. He seeks in vain for a prototype of his conception. Blasted by his disappointment, he descends to an untimely grave.

The picture is not barren of instruction to actual men. The Poet's self-centred seclusion was avenged by the furies of an irresistible passion pursuing him to speedy ruin. But that Power which strikes the luminaries of the world with sudden darkness and extinction, by awakening them to too exquisite a perception of its influences, dooms to a slow and poisonous decay those meaner spirits that dare to abjure its dominion. Their destiny is more abject and inglorious as their delinquency is more contemptible and pernicious. They who, deluded by no generous

18

error, instigated by no sacred thirst of doubtful knowledge, duped by no illustrious superstition, loving nothing on this earth, and cherishing no hopes beyond, yet keep aloof from sympathies with their kind, rejoicing neither in human joy nor mourning with human grief; these, and such as they, have their apportioned curse. They languish, because none feel with them their common nature. They are morally dead. They are neither friends, nor lovers, nor fathers, nor citizens of the world, nor benefactors of their country. Among those who attempt to exist without human sympathy, the pure and tender-hearted perish through the intensity and passion of their search after its communities, when the vacancy of their spirit suddenly makes itself felt. All else, selfish, blind, and torpid, are those unforeseeing multitudes who constitute, together with their own, the lasting misery and loneliness of the world. Those who love not their fellow-beings live unfruitful lives, and prepare for their old age a miserable grave.

"The good die first,
And those whose hearts are dry as summer dust,
Burn to the socket!"

December 14, 1815.

Nondum amabam, et amare amabam, quaerebam quid amarem, amans amare.   *The Confessions of St. Augustine.*

EARTH, ocean, air, belovèd brotherhood!
If our great Mother has imbued my soul
With aught of natural piety to feel
Your love, and recompense the boon with mine;
If dewy morn, and odorous noon, and even,
With sunset and its gorgeous ministers,
And solemn midnight's tingling silentness;
If autumn's hollow sighs in the sere wood,
And winter robing with pure snow and crowns
Of starry ice the grey grass and bare boughs;   10
If spring's voluptuous pantings when she breathes
Her first sweet kisses, have been dear to me;
If no bright bird, insect, or gentle beast
I consciously have injured, but still loved
And cherished these my kindred; then forgive
This boast, belovèd brethren, and withdraw
No portion of your wonted favour now!

Mother of this unfathomable world!
Favour my solemn song, for I have loved
Thee ever, and thee only; I have watched   20
Thy shadow, and the darkness of thy steps,
And my heart ever gazes on the depth
Of thy deep mysteries. I have made my bed
In charnels and on coffins, where black death
Keeps record of the trophies won from thee,
Hoping to still these obstinate questionings
Of thee and thine, by forcing some lone ghost
Thy messenger, to render up the tale
Of what we are. In lone and silent hours,
When night makes a weird sound of its own stillness, 30
Like an inspired and desperate alchymist
Staking his very life on some dark hope,
Have I mixed awful talk and asking looks
With my most innocent love, until strange tears
Uniting with those breathless kisses, made
Such magic as compels the charmèd night
To render up thy charge: . . . and, though ne'er yet
Thou hast unveiled thy inmost sanctuary,
Enough from incommunicable dream,
And twilight phantasms, and deep noon-day thought, 40
Has shown within me, that serenely now
And moveless, as a long-forgotten lyre
Suspended in the solitary dome
Of some mysterious and deserted fane,
I wait thy breath, Great Parent, that my strain
May modulate with murmurs of the air,
And motions of the forests and the sea,
And voice of living beings, and woven hymns
Of night and day, and the deep heart of man.

There was a Poet whose untimely tomb   50
No human hands with pious reverence reared,
But the charmed eddies of autumnal winds
Built o'er his mouldering bones a pyramid
Of mouldering leaves in the waste wilderness:—
A lovely youth,—no mourning maiden decked
With weeping flowers, or votive cypress wreath,
The lone couch of his everlasting sleep:—
Gentle, and brave, and generous,—no lorn bard

Breathed o'er his dark fate one melodious sigh:
He lived, he died, he sung, in solitude.   60
Strangers have wept to hear his passionate notes,
And virgins, as unknown he passed, have pined
And wasted for fond love of his wild eyes.
The fire of those soft orbs has ceased to burn,
And Silence, too enamoured of that voice,
Locks its mute music in her rugged cell.

By solemn vision, and bright silver dream,
His infancy was nurtured. Every sight
And sound from the vast earth and ambient air,
Sent to his heart its choicest impulses.   70
The fountains of divine philosophy
Fled not his thirsting lips, and all of great,
Or good, or lovely, which the sacred past
In truth or fable consecrates, he felt
And knew. When early youth had passed, he left
His cold fireside and alienated home
To seek strange truths in undiscovered lands.
Many a wide waste and tangled wilderness
Has lured his fearless steps; and he has bought
With his sweet voice and eyes, from savage men,   80
His rest and food. Nature's most secret steps
He like her shadow has pursued, where'er
The red volcano overcanopies
Its fields of snow and pinnacles of ice
With burning smoke, or where bitumen lakes
On black bare pointed islets ever beat
With sluggish surge, or where the secret caves
Rugged and dark, winding among the springs
Of fire and poison, inaccessible
To avarice or pride, their starry domes   90
Of diamond and of gold expand above
Numberless and immeasurable halls,
Frequent with crystal column, and clear shrines
Of pearl, and thrones radiant with chrysolite.
Nor had that scene of ampler majesty
Than gems or gold, the varying roof of heaven
And the green earth lost in his heart its claims
To love and wonder; he would linger long
In lonesome vales, making the wild his home,

Until the doves and squirrels would partake   100
From his innocuous hand his bloodless food,
Lured by the gentle meaning of his looks,
And the wild antelope, that starts whene'er
The dry leaf rustles in the brake, suspend
Her timid steps to gaze upon a form
More graceful than her own.

                    His wandering step,
Obedient to high thoughts, has visited
The awful ruins of the days of old:
Athens, and Tyre, and Balbec, and the waste
Where stood Jerusalem, the fallen towers   110
Of Babylon, the eternal pyramids,
Memphis and Thebes, and whatsoe'er of strange
Sculptured on alabaster obelisk,
Or jasper tomb, or mutilated sphynx,
Dark Æthiopia in her desert hills
Conceals. Among the ruined temples there,
Stupendous columns, and wild images
Of more than man, where marble daemons watch
The Zodiac's brazen mystery, and dead men
Hang their mute thoughts on the mute walls around,   120
He lingered, poring on memorials
Of the world's youth, through the long burning day
Gazed on those speechless shapes, nor, when the moon
Filled the mysterious halls with floating shades
Suspended he that task, but ever gazed
And gazed, till meaning on his vacant mind
Flashed like strong inspiration, and he saw
The thrilling secrets of the birth of time.

    Meanwhile an Arab maiden brought his food,
Her daily portion, from her father's tent,   130
And spread her matting for his couch, and stole
From duties and repose to tend his steps:—
Enamoured, yet not daring for deep awe
To speak her love:—and watched his nightly sleep,
Sleepless herself, to gaze upon his lips
Parted in slumber, whence the regular breath
Of innocent dreams arose: then, when red morn

Made paler the pale moon, to her cold home
Wildered, and wan, and panting, she returned.

The Poet wandering on, through Arabie   140
And Persia, and the wild Carmanian waste,
And o'er the aërial mountains which pour down
Indus and Oxus from their icy caves,
In joy and exultation held his way;
Till in the vale of Cashmire, far within
Its loneliest dell, where odorous plants entwine
Beneath the hollow rocks a natural bower,
Beside a sparkling rivulet he stretched
His languid limbs. A vision on his sleep
There came, a dream of hopes that never yet   150
Had flushed his cheek. He dreamed a veilèd maid
Sate near him, talking in low solemn tones.
Her voice was like the voice of his own soul
Heard in the calm of thought; its music long,
Like woven sounds of streams and breezes, held
His inmost sense suspended in its web
Of many-coloured woof and shifting hues.
Knowledge and truth and virtue were her theme,
And lofty hopes of divine liberty,
Thoughts the most dear to him, and poesy,   160
Herself a poet. Soon the solemn mood
Of her pure mind kindled through all her frame
A permeating fire: wild numbers then
She raised, with voice stifled in tremulous sobs
Subdued by its own pathos: her fair hands
Were bare alone, sweeping from some strange harp
Strange symphony, and in their branching veins
The eloquent blood told an ineffable tale.
The beating of her heart was heard to fill
The pauses of her music, and her breath   170
Tumultuously accorded with those fits
Of intermitted song. Sudden she rose,
As if her heart impatiently endured
Its bursting burthen: at the sound he turned,
And saw by the warm light of their own life
Her glowing limbs beneath the sinuous veil
Of woven wind, her outspread arms now bare,

Her dark locks floating in the breath of night,
Her beamy bending eyes, her parted lips
Outstretched, and pale, and quivering eagerly.   180
His strong heart sunk and sickened with excess
Of love. He reared his shuddering limbs and quelled
His gasping breath, and spread his arms to meet
Her panting bosom: . . . she drew back a while,
Then, yielding to the irresistible joy,
With frantic gesture and short breathless cry
Folded his frame in her dissolving arms.
Now blackness veiled his dizzy eyes, and night
Involved and swallowed up the vision; sleep,
Like a dark flood suspended in its course,   190
Rolled back its impulse on his vacant brain.

    Roused by the shock he started from his trance—
The cold white light of morning, the blue moon
Low in the west, the clear and garish hills,
The distinct valley and the vacant woods,
Spread round him where he stood. Whither have fled
The hues of heaven that canopied his bower
Of yesternight? The sounds that soothed his sleep,
The mystery and the majesty of Earth,
The joy, the exultation? His wan eyes   200
Gaze on the empty scene as vacantly
As ocean's moon looks on the moon in heaven.
The spirit of sweet human love has sent
A vision to the sleep of him who spurned
Her choicest gifts. He eagerly pursues
Beyond the realms of dream that fleeting shade;
He overleaps the bounds. Alas! Alas!
Were limbs and breath and being intertwined
Thus treacherously? Lost, lost, for ever lost,
In the wide pathless desert of dim sleep,   210
That beautiful shape! Does the dark gate of death
Conduct to thy mysterious paradise,
O Sleep? Does the bright arch of rainbow clouds,
And pendent mountains seen in the calm lake,
Lead only to a black and watery depth,
While death's blue vault, with loathliest vapours hung,
Where every shade which the foul grave exhales
Hides its dead eye from the detested day,

Conducts, O Sleep, to thy delightful realms?
This doubt with sudden tide flowed on his heart,   220
The insatiate hope which it awakened, stung
His brain even like despair.

                        While daylight held
The sky, the Poet kept mute conference
With his still soul. At night the passion came,
Like the fierce fiend of a distempered dream,
And shook him from his rest, and led him forth
Into the darkness.—As an eagle grasped
In folds of the green serpent, feels her breast
Burn with the poison, and precipitates
Through night and day, tempest, and calm, and cloud,   230
Frantic with dizzying anguish, her blind flight
O'er the wide aëry wilderness: thus driven
By the bright shadow of that lovely dream,
Beneath the cold glare of the desolate night,
Through tangled swamps and deep precipitous dells,
Startling with careless step the moonlight snake,
He fled. Red morning dawned upon his flight,
Shedding the mockery of its vital hues
Upon his cheek of death. He wandered on
Till vast Aornos seen from Petra's steep   240
Hung o'er the low horizon like a cloud;
Through Balk, and where the desolated tombs
Of Parthian kings scatter to every wind
Their wasting dust, wildly he wandered on,
Day after day a weary waste of hours,
Bearing within his life the brooding care
That ever fed on its decaying flame.
And now his limbs were lean; his scattered hair
Sered by the autumn of strange suffering
Sung dirges in the wind; his listless hand   250
Hung like dead bone within its withered skin;
Life, and the lustre that consumed it, shone
As in a furnace burning secretly
From his dark eyes alone. The cottagers,
Who ministered with human charity
His human wants, beheld with wondering awe
Their fleeting visitant. The mountaineer,
Encountering on some dizzy precipice

That spectral form, deemed that the Spirit of wind
With lightning eyes, and eager breath, and feet   260
Disturbing not the drifted snow, had paused
In its career: the infant would conceal
His troubled visage in his mother's robe
In terror at the glare of those wild eyes,
To remember their strange light in many a dream
Of after-times; but youthful maidens, taught
By nature, would interpret half the woe
That wasted him, would call him with false names
Brother, and friend, would press his pallid hand
At parting, and watch, dim through tears, the path   270
Of his departure from their father's door.

  At length upon the lone Chorasmian shore
He paused, a wide and melancholy waste
Of putrid marshes. A strong impulse urged
His steps to the sea-shore. A swan was there,
Beside a sluggish stream among the reeds.
It rose as he approached, and with strong wings
Scaling the upward sky, bent its bright course
High over the immeasurable main.
His eyes pursued its flight.—'Thou hast a home,   280
Beautiful bird; thou voyagest to thine home,
Where thy sweet mate will twine her downy neck
With thine, and welcome thy return with eyes
Bright in the lustre of their own fond joy.
And what am I that I should linger here,
With voice far sweeter than thy dying notes,
Spirit more vast than thine, frame more attuned
To beauty, wasting these surpassing powers
In the deaf air, to the blind earth, and heaven
That echoes not my thoughts?' A gloomy smile   290
Of desperate hope wrinkled his quivering lips.
For sleep, he knew, kept most relentlessly
Its precious charge, and silent death exposed,
Faithless perhaps as sleep, a shadowy lure,
With doubtful smile mocking its own strange charms.

  Startled by his own thoughts he looked around.
There was no fair fiend near him, not a sight
Or sound of awe but in his own deep mind.

A little shallop floating near the shore
Caught the impatient wandering of his gaze.   300
It had been long abandoned, for its sides
Gaped wide with many a rift, and its frail joints
Swayed with the undulations of the tide.
A restless impulse urged him to embark
And meet lone Death on the drear ocean's waste;
For well he knew that mighty Shadow loves
The slimy caverns of the populous deep.

The day was fair and sunny, sea and sky
Drank its inspiring radiance, and the wind
Swept strongly from the shore, blackening the waves.   310
Following his eager soul, the wanderer
Leaped in the boat, he spread his cloak aloft
On the bare mast, and took his lonely seat,
And felt the boat speed o'er the tranquil sea
Like a torn cloud before the hurricane.

As one that in a silver vision floats
Obedient to the sweep of odorous winds
Upon resplendent clouds, so rapidly
Along the dark and ruffled waters fled
The straining boat.—A whirlwind swept it on,   320
With fierce gusts and precipitating force,
Through the white ridges of the chafèd sea.
The waves arose. Higher and higher still
Their fierce necks writhed beneath the tempest's scourge
Like serpents struggling in a vulture's grasp.
Calm and rejoicing in the fearful war
Of wave ruining on wave, and blast on blast
Descending, and black flood on whirlpool driven
With dark obliterating course, he sate:
As if their genii were the ministers   330
Appointed to conduct him to the light
Of those belovèd eyes, the Poet sate
Holding the steady helm. Evening came on,
The beams of sunset hung their rainbow hues
High 'mid the shifting domes of sheeted spray
That canopied his path o'er the waste deep;
Twilight, ascending slowly from the east,
Entwined in duskier wreaths her braided locks

O'er the fair front and radiant eyes of day;
Night followed, clad with stars. On every side   340
More horribly the multitudinous streams
Of ocean's mountainous waste to mutual war
Rushed in dark tumult thundering, as to mock
The calm and spangled sky. The little boat
Still fled before the storm; still fled, like foam
Down the steep cataract of a wintry river;
Now pausing on the edge of the riven wave;
Now leaving far behind the bursting mass
That fell, convulsing ocean: safely fled—
As if that frail and wasted human form   350
Had been an elemental god.

                    At midnight
The moon arose: and lo! the ethereal cliffs
Of Caucasus, whose icy summits shone
Among the stars like sunlight, and around
Whose caverned base the whirlpools and the waves
Bursting and eddying irresistibly
Rage and resound for ever.—Who shall save?—
The boat fled on,—the boiling torrent drove,—
The crags closed round with black and jaggèd arms,
The shattered mountain overhung the sea,   360
And faster still, beyond all human speed,
Suspended on the sweep of the smooth wave,
The little boat was driven. A cavern there
Yawned, and amid its slant and winding depths
Ingulfed the rushing sea. The boat fled on
With unrelaxing speed.—'Vision and Love!'
The Poet cried aloud, 'I have beheld
The path of thy departure. Sleep and death
Shall not divide us long!'

                    The boat pursued
The windings of the cavern. Daylight shone   370
At length upon that gloomy river's flow;
Now, where the fiercest war among the waves
Is calm, on the unfathomable stream
The boat moved slowly. Where the mountain, riven,
Exposed those black depths to the azure sky,
Ere yet the flood's enormous volume fell

Even to the base of Caucasus, with sound
That shook the everlasting rocks, the mass
Filled with one whirlpool all that ample chasm;
Stair above stair the eddying waters rose,   380
Circling immeasurably fast, and laved
With alternating dash the gnarled roots
Of mighty trees, that stretched their giant arms
In darkness over it. I' the midst was left,
Reflecting, yet distorting every cloud,
A pool of treacherous and tremendous calm.
Seized by the sway of the ascending stream,
With dizzy swiftness, round, and round, and round,
Ridge after ridge the straining boat arose,
Till on the verge of the extremest curve,   390
Where, through an opening of the rocky bank,
The waters overflow, and a smooth spot
Of glassy quiet mid those battling tides
Is left, the boat paused shuddering.—Shall it sink
Down the abyss? Shall the reverting stress
Of that resistless gulf embosom it?
Now shall it fall?—A wandering stream of wind,
Breathed from the west, has caught the expanded sail,
And, lo! with gentle motion, between banks
Of mossy slope, and on a placid stream,   400
Beneath a woven grove it sails, and, hark!
The ghastly torrent mingles its far roar,
With the breeze murmuring in the musical woods.
Where the embowering trees recede, and leave
A little space of green expanse, the cove
Is closed by meeting banks, whose yellow flowers
For ever gaze on their own drooping eyes,
Reflected in the crystal calm. The wave
Of the boat's motion marred their pensive task,
Which nought but vagrant bird, or wanton wind,   410
Or falling spear-grass, or their own decay
Had e'er disturbed before. The Poet longed
To deck with their bright hues his withered hair,
But on his heart its solitude returned,
And he forbore. Not the strong impulse hid
In those flushed cheeks, bent eyes, and shadowy frame
Had yet performed its ministry: it hung
Upon his life, as lightning in a cloud

Gleams, hovering ere it vanish, ere the floods
Of night close over it.

                The noonday sun   420
Now shone upon the forest, one vast mass
Of mingling shade, whose brown magnificence
A narrow vale embosoms. There, huge caves,
Scooped in the dark base of their aëry rocks,
Mocking its moans, respond and roar for ever.
The meeting boughs and implicated leaves
Wove twilight o'er the Poet's path, as led
By love, or dream, or god, or mightier Death,
He sought in Nature's dearest haunt some bank,   430
Her cradle and his sepulchre. More dark
And dark the shades accumulate. The oak,
Expanding its immense and knotty arms,
Embraces the light beech. The pyramids
Of the tall cedar overarching, frame
Most solemn domes within, and far below,
Like clouds suspended in an emerald sky,
The ash and the acacia floating hang
Tremulous and pale. Like restless serpents, clothed
In rainbow and in fire, the parasites,
Starred with ten thousand blossoms, flow around   440
The grey trunks, and, as gamesome infants' eyes,
With gentle meanings, and most innocent wiles,
Fold their beams round the hearts of those that love,
These twine their tendrils with the wedded boughs
Uniting their close union; the woven leaves
Make net-work of the dark blue light of day,
And the night's noontide clearness, mutable
As shapes in the weird clouds. Soft mossy lawns
Beneath these canopies extend their swells,
Fragrant with perfumed herbs, and eyed with blooms   450
Minute yet beautiful. One darkest glen
Sends from its woods of musk-rose, twined with jasmine,
A soul-dissolving odour, to invite
To some more lovely mystery. Through the dell,
Silence and Twilight here, twin-sisters, keep
Their noonday watch, and sail among the shades,
Like vaporous shapes half seen; beyond, a well,
Dark, gleaming, and of most translucent wave,

Images all the woven boughs above,
And each depending leaf, and every speck   460
Of azure sky, darting between their chasms;
Nor aught else in the liquid mirror laves
Its portraiture, but some inconstant star
Between one foliaged lattice twinkling fair,
Or painted bird, sleeping beneath the moon,
Or gorgeous insect floating motionless,
Unconscious of the day, ere yet his wings
Have spread their glories to the gaze of noon.

   Hither the Poet came. His eyes beheld
Their own wan light through the reflected lines   470
Of his thin hair, distinct in the dark depth
Of that still fountain; as the human heart,
Gazing in dreams over the gloomy grave,
Sees its own treacherous likeness there. He heard
The motion of the leaves, the grass that sprung
Startled and glanced and trembled even to feel
An unaccustomed presence, and the sound
Of the sweet brook that from the secret springs
Of that dark fountain rose. A Spirit seemed
To stand beside him—clothed in no bright robes   480
Of shadowy silver or enshrining light,
Borrowed from aught the visible world affords
Of grace, or majesty, or mystery;—
But undulating woods, and silent well,
And leaping rivulet, and evening gloom
Now deepening the dark shades, for speech assuming,
Held commune with him, as if he and it
Were all that was; only—when his regard
Was raised by intense pensiveness—two eyes,
Two starry eyes, hung in the gloom of thought,   490
And seemed with their serene and azure smiles
To beckon him.

        Obedient to the light
That shone within his soul, he went, pursuing
The windings of the dell. The rivulet;
Wanton and wild, through many a green ravine
Beneath the forest flowed. Sometimes it fell
Among the moss with hollow harmony

Dark and profound. Now on the polished stones
It danced, like childhood laughing as it went:
Then, through the plain in tranquil wanderings crept,   500
Reflecting every herb and drooping bud
That overhung its quietness.—'O stream!
Whose source is inaccessibly profound,
Whither do thy mysterious waters tend?
Thou imagest my life. Thy darksome stillness,
Thy dazzling waves, thy loud and hollow gulfs,
Thy searchless fountain, and invisible course
Have each their type in me; and the wide sky
And measureless ocean may declare as soon
What oozy cavern or what wandering cloud   510
Contains thy waters, as the universe
Tell where these living thoughts reside, when stretched
Upon thy flowers my bloodless limbs shall waste
I' the passing wind!'

            Beside the grassy shore
Of the small stream he went; he did impress
On the green moss his tremulous step, that caught
Strong shuddering from his burning limbs. As one
Roused by some joyous madness from the couch
Of fever, he did move; yet not like him
Forgetful of the grave, where, when the flame   520
Of his frail exultation shall be spent,
He must descend. With rapid steps he went
Beneath the shade of trees, beside the flow
Of the wild babbling rivulet; and now
The forest's solemn canopies were changed
For the uniform and lightsome evening sky.
Grey rocks did peep from the spare moss, and stemmed
The struggling brook: tall spires of windlestrae
Threw their thin shadows down the rugged slope,
And nought but gnarlèd roots of ancient pines   530
Branchless and blasted, clenched with grasping roots
The unwilling soil. A gradual change was here,
Yet ghastly. For, as fast years flow away,
The smooth brow gathers, and the hair grows thin
And white, and where irradiate dewy eyes
Had shone, gleam stony orbs:—so from his steps
Bright flowers departed, and the beautiful shade

Of the green groves, with all their odorous winds
And musical motions. Calm, he still pursued
The stream, that with a larger volume now   540
Rolled through the labyrinthine dell; and there
Fretted a path through its descending curves
With its wintry speed. On every side now rose
Rocks, which, in unimaginable forms,
Lifted their black and barren pinnacles
In the light of evening, and, its precipice
Obscuring the ravine, disclosed above,
Mid toppling stones, black gulfs and yawning caves,
Whose windings gave ten thousand various tongues
To the loud stream. Lo! where the pass expands   550
Its stony jaws, the abrupt mountain breaks,
And seems, with its accumulated crags,
To overhang the world: for wide expand
Beneath the wan stars and descending moon
Islanded seas, blue mountains, mighty streams,
Dim tracts and vast, robed in the lustrous gloom
Of leaden-coloured even, and fiery hills
Mingling their flames with twilight, on the verge
Of the remote horizon. The near scene,
In naked and severe simplicity,   560
Made contrast with the universe. A pine,
Rock-rooted, stretched athwart the vacancy
Its swinging boughs, to each inconstant blast
Yielding one only response, at each pause
In most familiar cadence, with the howl,
The thunder and the hiss of homeless streams
Mingling its solemn song, whilst the broad river,
Foaming and hurrying o'er its rugged path,
Fell into that immeasurable void
Scattering its waters to the passing winds.   570

   Yet the grey precipice and solemn pine
And torrent were not all;—one silent nook
Was there. Even on the edge of that vast mountain,
Upheld by knotty roots and fallen rocks,
It overlooked in its serenity
The dark earth, and the bending vault of stars.
It was a tranquil spot, that seemed to smile
Even in the lap of horror. Ivy clasped

The fissured stones with its entwining arms,
And did embower with leaves for ever green,   580
And berries dark, the smooth and even space
Of its inviolated floor, and here
The children of the autumnal whirlwind bore,
In wanton sport, those bright leaves, whose decay,
Red, yellow, or ethereally pale,
Rivals the pride of summer. 'Tis the haunt
Of every gentle wind, whose breath can teach
The wilds to love tranquillity. One step,
One human step alone, has ever broken
The stillness of its solitude:—one voice   590
Alone inspired its echoes;—even that voice
Which hither came, floating among the winds,
And led the loveliest among human forms
To make their wild haunts the depository
Of all the grace and beauty that endued
Its motions, render up its majesty,
Scatter its music on the unfeeling storm,
And to the damp leaves and blue cavern mould,
Nurses of rainbow flowers and branching moss,
Commit the colours of that varying cheek,   600
That snowy breast, those dark and drooping eyes.

The dim and hornèd moon hung low, and poured
A sea of lustre on the horizon's verge
That overflowed its mountains. Yellow mist
Filled the unbounded atmosphere, and drank
Wan moonlight even to fulness: not a star
Shone, not a sound was heard; the very winds,
Danger's grim playmates, on that precipice
Slept, clasped in his embrace.—O, storm of death!
Whose sightless speed divides this sullen night: 610
And thou, colossal Skeleton, that, still
Guiding its irresistible career
In thy devastating omnipotence,
Art king of this frail world, from the red field
Of slaughter, from the reeking hospital,
The patriot's sacred couch, the snowy bed
Of innocence, the scaffold and the throne,
A mighty voice invokes thee. Ruin calls
His brother Death. A rare and regal prey

He hath prepared, prowling around the world;   · 620
Glutted with which thou mayst repose, and men
Go to their graves like flowers or creeping worms,
Nor ever more offer at thy dark shrine
The unheeded tribute of a broken heart.

When on the threshold of the green recess
The wanderer's footsteps fell, he knew that death
Was on him. Yet a little, ere it fled,
Did he resign his high and holy soul
To images of the majestic past,
That paused within his passive being now,   630
Like winds that bear sweet music, when they breathe
Through some dim latticed chamber. He did place
His pale lean hand upon the rugged trunk
Of the old pine. Upon an ivied stone
Reclined his languid head, his limbs did rest,
Diffused and motionless, on the smooth brink
Of that obscurest chasm;—and thus he lay,
Surrendering to their final impulses
The hovering powers of life. Hope and despair,
The torturers, slept; no mortal pain or fear   640
Marred his repose, the influxes of sense,
And his own being unalloyed by pain,
Yet feebler and more feeble, calmly fed
The stream of thought, till he lay breathing there
At peace, and faintly smiling:—his last sight
Was the great moon, which o'er the western line
Of the wide world her mighty horn suspended,
With whose dun beams inwoven darkness seemed
To mingle. Now upon the jagged hills
It rests, and still as the divided frame   650
Of the vast meteor sunk, the Poet's blood,
That ever beat in mystic sympathy
With nature's ebb and flow, grew feebler still:
And when two lessening points of light alone
Gleamed through the darkness, the alternate gasp
Of his faint respiration scarce did stir
The stagnate night:—till the minutest ray
Was quenched, the pulse yet lingered in his heart.
It paused—it fluttered. But when heaven remained
Utterly black, the murky shades involved   660

An image, silent, cold, and motionless,
As their own voiceless earth and vacant air.
Even as a vapour fed with golden beams
That ministered on sunlight, ere the west
Eclipses it, was now that wondrous frame—
No sense, no motion, no divinity—
A fragile lute, on whose harmonious strings
The breath of heaven did wander—a bright stream
Once fed with many-voicèd waves—a dream
Of youth, which night and time have quenched for ever,   670
Still, dark, and dry, and unremembered now.

O, for Medea's wondrous alchemy,
Which wheresoe'er it fell made the earth gleam
With bright flowers, and the wintry boughs exhale
From vernal blooms fresh fragrance! O, that God,
Profuse of poisons, would concede the chalice
Which but one living man has drained, who now,
Vessel of deathless wrath, a slave that feels
No proud exemption in the blighting curse
He bears, over the world wanders for ever,   680
Lone as incarnate death! O, that the dream
Of dark magician in his visioned cave,
Raking the cinders of a crucible
For life and power, even when his feeble hand
Shakes in its last decay, were the true law
Of this so lovely world! But thou art fled
Like some frail exhalation, which the dawn
Robes in its golden beams,—ah! thou hast fled!
The brave, the gentle, and the beautiful,
The child of grace and genius. Heartless things   690
Are done and said i' the world, and many worms
And beasts and men live on, and mighty Earth
From sea and mountain, city and wilderness,
In vesper low or joyous orison,
Lifts still its solemn voice:—but thou art fled—
Thou canst no longer know or love the shapes
Of this phantasmal scene, who have to thee
Been purest ministers, who are, alas!
Now thou art not. Upon those pallid lips
So sweet even in their silence, on those eyes   700
That image sleep in death, upon that form

Yet safe from the worm's outrage, let no tear
Be shed—not even in thought. Nor, when those hues
Are gone, and those divinest lineaments,
Worn by the senseless wind, shall live alone
In the frail pauses of this simple strain,
Let not high verse, mourning the memory
Of that which is no more, or painting's woe
Or sculpture, speak in feeble imagery
Their own cold powers. Art and eloquence,   710
And all the shows o' the world are frail and vain
To weep a loss that turns their lights to shade.
It is a woe 'too deep for tears,' when all
Is reft at once, when some surpassing Spirit,
Whose light adorned the world around it, leaves
Those who remain behind, not sobs or groans,
The passionate tumult of a clinging hope;
But pale despair and cold tranquillity,
Nature's vast frame, the web of human things,
Birth and the grave, that are not as they were.   720

[1815; publ. 1816]

JULIAN AND MADDALO

A CONVERSATION

PREFACE

The meadows with fresh streams, the bees with thyme,
The goats with the green leaves of budding Spring,
Are saturated not—nor Love with tears.—VIRGIL's *Gallus*.

COUNT MADDALO is a Venetian nobleman of ancient family and of
great fortune, who, without mixing much in the society of his
countrymen, resides chiefly at his magnificent palace in that city.
He is a person of the most consummate genius, and capable, if he
would direct his energies to such an end, of becoming the redeemer of his degraded country. But it is his weakness to be
proud: he derives, from a comparison of his own extraordinary
mind with the dwarfish intellects that surround him, an intense
apprehension of the nothingness of human life. His passions and
his powers are incomparably greater than those of other men;

and, instead of the latter having been employed in curbing the former, they have mutually lent each other strength. His ambition preys upon itself, for want of objects which it can consider worthy of exertion. I say that Maddalo is proud, because I can find no other word to express the concentered and impatient feelings which consume him; but it is on his own hopes and affections only that he seems to trample, for in social life no human being can be more gentle, patient, and unassuming than Maddalo. He is cheerful, frank, and witty. His more serious conversation is a sort of intoxication; men are held by it as by a spell. He has travelled much; and there is an inexpressible charm in his relation of his adventures in different countries.

Julian is an Englishman of good family, passionately attached to those philosophical notions which assert the power of man over his own mind, and the immense improvements of which, by the extinction of certain moral superstitions, human society may be yet susceptible. Without concealing the evil in the world, he is for ever speculating how good may be made superior. He is a complete infidel, and a scoffer at all things reputed holy; and Maddalo takes a wicked pleasure in drawing out his taunts against religion. What Maddalo thinks on these matters is not exactly known. Julian, in spite of his heterodox opinions, is conjectured by his friends to possess some good qualities. How far this is possible the pious reader will determine. Julian is rather serious.

Of the Maniac I can give no information. He seems, by his own account, to have been disappointed in love. He was evidently a very cultivated and amiable person when in his right senses. His story, told at length, might be like many other stories of the same kind: the unconnected exclamations of his agony will perhaps be found a sufficient comment for the text of every heart.

I RODE one evening with Count Maddalo

Upon the bank of land which breaks the flow
Of Adria towards Venice: a bare strand
Of hillocks, heaped from ever-shifting sand,
Matted with thistles and amphibious weeds,
Such as from earth's embrace the salt ooze breeds,
Is this; an uninhabited sea-side,
Which the lone fisher, when his nets are dried,

Abandons; and no other object breaks
The waste, but one dwarf tree and some few stakes   10
Broken and unrepaired, and the tide makes
A narrow space of level sand thereon,
Where 'twas our wont to ride while day went down.
This ride was my delight. I love all waste
And solitary places; where we taste
The pleasure of believing what we see
Is boundless, as we wish our souls to be:
And such was this wide ocean, and this shore
More barren than its billows; and yet more
Than all, with a remembered friend I love   20
To ride as then I rode;—for the winds drove
The living spray along the sunny air
Into our faces; the blue heavens were bare,
Stripped to their depths by the awakening north;
And, from the waves, sound like delight broke forth
Harmonizing with solitude, and sent
Into our hearts aëreal merriment.
So, as we rode, we talked; and the swift thought,
Winging itself with laughter, lingered not,
But flew from brain to brain,—such glee was ours,   30
Charged with light memories of remembered hours,
None slow enough for sadness: till we came
Homeward, which always makes the spirit tame.
This day had been cheerful but cold, and now
The sun was sinking, and the wind also.
Our talk grew somewhat serious, as may be
Talk interrupted with such raillery
As mocks itself, because it cannot scorn
The thoughts it would extinguish:—'twas forlorn,
Yet pleasing, such as once, so poets tell,   40
The devils held within the dales of Hell
Concerning God, freewill and destiny:
Of all that earth has been or yet may be,
All that vain men imagine or believe,
Or hope can paint or suffering may achieve,
We descanted, and I (for ever still
Is it not wise to make the best of ill?)
Argued against despondency, but pride
Made my companion take the darker side.
The sense that he was greater than his kind   50

Had struck, methinks, his eagle spirit blind
By gazing on its own exceeding light.
Meanwhile the sun paused ere it should alight,
Over the horizon of the mountains:—Oh,
How beautiful is sunset, when the glow
Of Heaven descends upon a land like thee,
Thou Paradise of exiles, Italy!
Thy mountains, seas, and vineyards, and the towers
Of cities they encircle!—it was ours
To stand on thee, beholding it: and then,   60
Just where we had dismounted, the Count's men
Were waiting for us with the gondola.—
As those who pause on some delightful way
Though bent on pleasant pilgrimage, we stood
Looking upon the evening, and the flood
Which lay between the city and the shore,
Paved with the image of the sky . . . the hoar
And aëry Alps towards the North appeared
Through mist, an heaven-sustaining bulwark reared
Between the East and West; and half the sky   70
Was roofed with clouds of rich emblazonry
Dark purple at the zenith, which still grew
Down the steep West into a wondrous hue
Brighter than burning gold, even to the rent
Where the swift sun yet paused in his descent
Among the many-folded hills: they were
Those famous Euganean hills, which bear,
As seen from Lido thro' the harbour piles,
The likeness of a clump of peakèd isles—
And then—as if the Earth and Sea had been   80
Dissolved into one lake of fire, were seen
Those mountains towering as from waves of flame
Around the vaporous sun, from which there came
The inmost purple spirit of light, and made,
Their very peaks transparent. 'Ere it fade,'
Said my companion, 'I will show you soon
A better station'—so, o'er the lagune
We glided; and from that funereal bark
I leaned, and saw the city, and could mark
How from their many isles, in evening's gleam,   90
Its temples and its palaces did seem
Like fabrics of enchantment piled to Heaven.

I was about to speak, when—'We are even
Now at the point I meant,' said Maddalo,
And bade the gondolieri cease to row.
'Look, Julian, on the west, and listen well
If you hear not a deep and heavy bell.'
I looked, and saw between us and the sun
A building on an island; such a one
As age to age might add, for uses vile,   100
A windowless, deformed and dreary pile;
And on the top an open tower, where hung
A bell, which in the radiance swayed and swung;
We could just hear its hoarse and iron tongue:
The broad sun sunk behind it, and it tolled
In strong and black relief.—'What we behold
Shall be the madhouse and its belfry tower,'
Said Maddalo, 'and ever at this hour
Those who may cross the water, hear that bell
Which calls the maniacs, each one from his cell,   110
To vespers.'—'As much skill as need to pray
In thanks or hope for their dark lot have they
To their stern maker,' I replied. 'O ho!
You talk as in years past,' said Maddalo.
' 'Tis strange men change not. You were ever still
Among Christ's flock a perilous infidel,
A wolf for the meek lambs—if you can't swim
Beware of Providence.' I looked on him,
But the gay smile had faded in his eye.
'And such,' he cried, 'is our mortality,   120
And this must be the emblem and the sign
Of what should be eternal and divine!—
And like that black and dreary bell, the soul,
Hung in a heaven-illumined tower, must toll
Our thoughts and our desires to meet below
Round the rent heart and pray—as madmen do
For what? they know not,—till the night of death
As sunset that strange vision, severeth
Our memory from itself, and us from all
We sought and yet were baffled.' I recall   130
The sense of what he said, although I mar
The force of his expressions. The broad star
Of day meanwhile had sunk behind the hill,
And the black bell became invisible,

And the red tower looked gray, and all between
The churches, ships and palaces were seen
Huddled in gloom;—into the purple sea
The orange hues of heaven sunk silently.
We hardly spoke, and soon the gondola
Conveyed me to my lodging by the way.   140

    The following morn was rainy, cold and dim:
Ere Maddalo arose, I called on him,
And whilst I waited with his child I played;
A lovelier toy sweet Nature never made,
A serious, subtle, wild, yet gentle being,
Graceful without design and unforeseeing,
With eyes—Oh speak not of her eyes!—which seem
Twin mirrors of Italian Heaven, yet gleam
With such deep meaning, as we never see
But in the human countenance: with me   150
She was a special favourite: I had nursed
Her fine and feeble limbs when she came first
To this bleak world; and she yet seemed to know
On second sight her ancient playfellow,
Less changed than she was by six months or so;
For after her first shyness was worn out
We sate there, rolling billiard balls about,
When the Count entered. Salutations past—
'The word you spoke last night might well have cast
A darkness on my spirit—if man be   160
The passive thing you say, I should not see
Much harm in the religions and old saws
(Tho' I may never own such leaden laws)
Which break a teachless nature to the yoke:
Mine is another faith'—thus much I spoke
And noting he replied not, added: 'See
This lovely child, blithe, innocent and free;
She spends a happy time with little care,
While we to such sick thoughts subjected are
As came on you last night—it is our will   170
That thus enchains us to permitted ill—
We might be otherwise—we might be all
We dream of happy, high, majestical.
Where is the love, beauty, and truth we seek
But in our mind? and if we were not weak

Should we be less in deed than in desire?'
'Ay, if we were not weak—and we aspire
How vainly to be strong!' said Maddalo:
'You talk Utopia.' 'It remains to know,'
I then rejoined, 'and those who try may find   180
How strong the chains are which our spirit bind;
Brittle perchance as straw . . . We are assured
Much may be conquered, much may be endured,
Of what degrades and crushes us. We know
That we have power over ourselves to do
And suffer—what, we know not till we try;
But something nobler than to live and die—
So taught those kings of old philosophy
Who reigned before Religion made men blind;
And those who suffer with their suffering kind   190
Yet feel their faith, religion.' 'My dear friend,'
Said Maddalo, 'my judgement will not bend
To your opinion, though I think you might
Make such a system refutation-tight
As far as words go. I knew one like you
Who to this city came some months ago,
With whom I argued in this sort, and he
Is now gone mad,—and so he answered me,—
Poor fellow! but if you would like to go
We'll visit him, and his wild talk will show   200
How vain are such aspiring theories.'

'I hope to prove the induction otherwise,
And that a want of that true theory, still,
Which seeks a "soul of goodness" in things ill
Or in himself or others, has thus bowed
His being—there are some by nature proud,
Who patient in all else demand but this—
To love and be beloved with gentleness;
And being scorned, what wonder if they die
Some living death? this is not destiny   210
But man's own wilful ill.'

     As thus I spoke
Servants announced the gondola, and we
Through the fast-falling rain and high-wrought sea
Sailed to the island where the madhouse stands.
We disembarked. The clap of tortured hands,

Fierce yells and howlings and lamentings keen,
And laughter where complaint had merrier been,
Moans, shrieks, and curses, and blaspheming prayers
Accosted us. We climbed the oozy stairs
Into an old courtyard. I heard on high,   220
Then, fragments of most touching melody,
But looking up saw not the singer there.
Through the black bars in the tempestuous air
I saw, like weeds on a wrecked palace growing,
Long tangled locks flung wildly forth, and flowing,
Of those who on a sudden were beguiled
Into strange silence, and looked forth and smiled
Hearing sweet sounds.—Then I: 'Methinks there were
A cure of these with patience and kind care,
If music can thus move . . . but what is he   230
Whom we seek here?' 'Of his sad history
I know but this,' said Maddalo: 'he came
To Venice a dejected man, and fame
Said he was wealthy, or he had been so;
Some thought the loss of fortune wrought him woe;
But he was ever talking in such sort
As you do—far more sadly—he seemed hurt,
Even as a man with his peculiar wrong,
To hear but of the oppression of the strong,
Or those absurd deceits (I think with you   240
In some respects, you know) which carry through
The excellent impostors of this earth
When they outface detection—he had worth,
Poor fellow! but a humorist in his way'—
'Alas, what drove him mad?' 'I cannot say:
A lady came with him from France, and when
She left him and returned, he wandered then
About yon lonely isles of desert sand
Till he grew wild—he had no cash or land
Remaining,—the police had brought him here—   250
Some fancy took him and he would not bear
Removal; so I fitted up for him
Those rooms beside the sea, to please his whim,
And sent him busts and books and urns for flowers,
Which had adorned his life in happier hours,
And instruments of music—you may guess
A stranger could do little more or less

For one so gentle and unfortunate:
And those are his sweet strains which charm the weight
From madmen's chains, and make this Hell appear   260
A heaven of sacred silence, hushed to hear.'—
'Nay, this was kind of you—he had no claim,
As the world says'—'None—but the very same
Which I on all mankind were I as he
Fallen to such deep reverse; his melody
Is interrupted—now we hear the din
Of madmen, shriek on shriek, again begin;
Let us now visit him; after this strain
He ever communes with himself again,
And sees nor hears not any.' Having said   270
These words we called the keeper, and he led
To an apartment opening on the sea—
There the poor wretch was sitting mournfully
Near a piano, his pale fingers twined
One with the other, and the ooze and wind
Rushed through an open casement, and did sway
His hair, and starred it with the brackish spray;
His head was leaning on a music book,
And he was muttering, and his lean limbs shook;
His lips were pressed against a folded leaf   280
In hue too beautiful for health, and grief
Smiled in their motions as they lay apart.
As one who wrought from his own fervid heart
The eloquence of passion, soon he raised
His sad meek face and eyes lustrous and glazed
And spoke—sometimes as one who wrote, and thought
His words might move some heart that heeded not,
If sent to distant lands: and then as one
Reproaching deeds never to be undone
With wondering self-compassion; then his speech   290
Was lost in grief, and then his words came each
Unmodulated, cold, expressionless,—
But that from one jarred accent you might guess
It was despair made them so uniform:
And all the while the loud and gusty storm
Hissed through the window, and we stood behind
Stealing his accents from the envious wind
Unseen. I yet remember what he said
Distinctly: such impression his words made.

'Month after month,' he cried, 'to bear this load   300
And as a jade urged by the whip and goad
To drag life on, which like a heavy chain
Lengthens behind with many a link of pain!—
And not to speak my grief—O, not to dare
To give a human voice to my despair,
But live and move, and, wretched thing! smile on
As if I never went aside to groan,
And wear this mask of falsehood even to those
Who are most dear—not for my own repose—
Alas! no scorn or pain or hate could be   310
So heavy as that falsehood is to me—
But that I cannot bear more altered faces
Than needs must be, more changed and cold embraces,
More misery, disappointment, and mistrust
To own me for their father . . . Would the dust
Were covered in upon my body now!
That the life ceased to toil within my brow!
And then these thoughts would at the least be fled;
Let us not fear such pain can vex the dead.

'What Power delights to torture us? I know   320
That to myself I do not wholly owe
What now I suffer, though in part I may.
Alas! none strewed sweet flowers upon the way
Where wandering heedlessly, I met pale Pain,
My shadow, which will leave me not again—
If I have erred, there was no joy in error,
But pain and insult and unrest and terror;
I have not as some do, bought penitence
With pleasure, and a dark yet sweet offence,
For them,—if love and tenderness and truth   330
Had overlived hope's momentary youth,
My creed should have redeemed me from repenting;
But loathèd scorn and outrage unrelenting
Met love excited by far other seeming
Until the end was gained . . . as one from dreaming
Of sweetest peace, I woke, and found my state
Such as it is.—

                    'O Thou, my spirit's mate
Who, for thou art compassionate and wise,

Wouldst pity me from thy most gentle eyes
If this sad writing thou shouldst ever see— 340
My secret groans must be unheard by thee,
Thou wouldst weep tears bitter as blood to know
Thy lost friend's incommunicable woe.

'Ye few by whom my nature has been weighed
In friendship, let me not that name degrade
By placing on your hearts the secret load
Which crushes mine to dust. There is one road
To peace and that is truth, which follow ye!
Love sometimes leads astray to misery.
Yet think not though subdued—and I may well 350
Say that I am subdued—that the full Hell
Within me would infect the untainted breast
Of sacred nature with its own unrest;
As some perverted beings think to find
In scorn or hate a medicine for the mind
Which scorn or hate have wounded—O how vain!
The dagger heals not but may rend again . . .
Believe that I am ever still the same
In creed as in resolve, and what may tame
My heart, must leave the understanding free, 360
Or all would sink in this keen agony—
Nor dream that I will join the vulgar cry;
Or with my silence sanction tyranny;
Or seek a moment's shelter from my pain
In any madness which the world calls gain,
Ambition or revenge or thoughts as stern
As those which make me what I am; or turn
To avarice or misanthropy or lust . . .
Heap on me soon, O grave, thy welcome dust!
Till then the dungeon may demand its prey, 370
And Poverty and Shame may meet and say—
Halting beside me on the public way—
"That love-devoted youth is ours—let's sit
Beside him—he may live some six months yet."
Or the red scaffold, as our country bends,
May ask some willing victim, or ye friends
May fall under some sorrow which this heart
Or hand may share or vanquish or avert;
I am prepared—in truth with no proud joy—

To do or suffer aught, as when a boy   380
I did devote to justice and to love
My nature, worthless now! . . .

                        'I must remove
A veil from my pent mind. 'Tis torn aside!
O, pallid as Death's dedicated bride,
Thou mockery which art sitting by my side,
Am I not wan like thee? at the grave's call
I haste, invited to thy wedding-ball
To greet the ghastly paramour, for whom
Thou hast deserted me . . . and made the tomb
Thy bridal bed . . . But I beside your feet   390
Will lie and watch ye from my winding sheet—
Thus . . . wide awake tho' dead . . . yet stay, O stay!
Go not so soon—I know not what I say—
Hear but my reasons . . . I am mad, I fear,
My fancy is o'erwrought . . . thou art not here . . .
Pale art thou, 'tis most true . . . but thou art gone,
Thy work is finished . . . I am left alone!—

        .   .   .   .   .   .

   'Nay, was it I who wooed thee to this breast,
Which, like a serpent, thou envenomest
As in repayment of the warmth it lent?   400
Didst thou not seek me for thine own content?
Did not thy love awaken mine? I thought
That thou wert she who said, "You kiss me not
Ever, I fear you do not love me now"—
In truth I loved even to my overthrow
Her, who would fain forget these words: but they
Cling to her mind, and cannot pass away.

        .   .   .   .

   'You say that I am proud—that when I speak
My lip is tortured with the wrongs which break
The spirit it expresses . . . Never one   410
Humbled himself before, as I have done!
Even the instinctive worm on which we tread
Turns, though it wound not—then with prostrate head
Sinks in the dust, and writhes like me—and dies?
No: wears a living death of agonies!
As the slow shadows of the pointed grass

Mark the eternal periods, his pangs pass,
Slow, ever-moving,—making moments be
As mine seem—each an immortality!

.   .   .   .

'That you had never seen me—never heard   420
My voice, and more than all had ne'er endured
The deep pollution of my loathed embrace—
That your eyes ne'er had lied love in my face—
That, like some maniac monk, I had torn out
The nerves of manhood by their bleeding root
With mine own quivering fingers, so that ne'er
Our hearts had for a moment mingled there
To disunite in horror—these were not
With thee, like some suppressed and hideous thought
Which flits athwart our musings, but can find   430
No rest within a pure and gentle mind . . .
Thou sealedst them with many a bare broad word,
And searedst my memory o'er them,—for I heard
And can forget not . . . they were ministered
One after one, those curses. Mix them up
Like self-destroying poisons in one cup,
And they will make one blessing which thou ne'er
Didst imprecate for, on me,—death.

.   .   .   .   .   .

                                        'It were
A cruel punishment for one most cruel,
If such can love, to make that love the fuel   440
Of the mind's hell; hate, scorn, remorse, despair:
But *me*—whose heart a stranger's tear might wear
As water-drops the sandy fountain-stone,
Who loved and pitied all things, and could moan
For woes which others hear not, and could see
The absent with the glance of phantasy,
And with the poor and trampled sit and weep,
Following the captive to his dungeon deep;
Me—who am as a nerve o'er which do creep
The else unfelt oppressions of this earth,   450
And was to thee the flame upon thy hearth,
When all beside was cold—that thou on me
Shouldst rain these plagues of blistering agony—
Such curses are from lips once eloquent

With love's too partial praise—let none relent
Who intend deeds too dreadful for a name
Henceforth, if an example for the same
They seek . . . for thou on me lookedst so, and so—
And didst speak thus . . . and thus . . . I live to show
How much men bear and die not!   460

.   .   .   .

                        'Thou wilt tell.
With the grimace of hate, how horrible
It was to meet my love when thine grew less;
Thou wilt admire how I could e'er address
Such features to love's work . . . this taunt, though true,
(For indeed Nature nor in form nor hue
Bestowed on me her choicest workmanship)
Shall not be thy defence . . . for since thy lip
Met mine first, years long past, since thine eye kindled
With soft fire under mine, I have not dwindled
Nor changed in mind or body, or in aught   470
But as love changes what it loveth not
After long years and many trials.

                        'How vain
Are words! I thought never to speak again,
Not even in secret,—not to my own heart—
But from my lips the unwilling accents start,
And from my pen the words flow as I write,
Dazzling my eyes with scalding tears . . . my sight
Is dim to see that charactered in vain
On this unfeeling leaf which burns the brain
And eats into it . . . blotting all things fair   480
And wise and good which time had written there.

'Those who inflict must suffer, for they see
The work of their own hearts, and this must be
Our chastisement or recompense—O child!
I would that thine were like to be more mild
For both our wretched sakes . . . for thine the most
Who feelest already all that thou hast lost
Without the power to wish it thine again;
And as slow years pass, a funereal train
Each with the ghost of some lost hope or friend   490

Following it like its shadow, wilt thou bend
No thought on my dead memory?

                    .   .   .   .

                                        'Alas, love!
Fear me not . . . against thee I would not move
A finger in despite. Do I not live
That thou mayst have less bitter cause to grieve?
I give thee tears for scorn and love for hate;
And that thy lot may be less desolate
Than his on whom thou tramplest, I refrain
From that sweet sleep which medicines all pain.
Then, when thou speakest of me, never say   500
"He could forgive not." Here I cast away
All human passions, all revenge, all pride;
I think, speak, act no ill; I do but hide
Under these words, like embers, every spark
Of that which has consumed me—quick and dark
The grave is yawning . . . as its roof shall cover
My limbs with dust and worms under and over,
So let Oblivion hide this grief . . . the air
Closes upon my accents, as despair
Upon my heart—let death upon despair!'   510

    He ceased, and overcome leant back awhile;
Then rising, with a melancholy smile
Went to a sofa, and lay down, and slept
A heavy sleep, and in his dreams he wept
And muttered some familiar name, and we
Wept without shame in his society.
I think I never was impressed so much;
The man who were not, must have lacked a touch
Of human nature . . . then we lingered not,
Although our argument was quite forgot,   520
But calling the attendants, went to dine
At Maddalo's; yet neither cheer nor wine
Could give us spirits, for we talked of him
And nothing else, till daylight made stars dim;
And we agreed his was some dreadful ill
Wrought on him boldly, yet unspeakable,
By a dear friend; some deadly change in love

Of one vowed deeply which he dreamed not of;
For whose sake he, it seemed, had fixed a blot
Of falsehood on his mind which flourished not   530
But in the light of all-beholding truth;
And having stamped this canker on his youth
She had abandoned him—and how much more
Might be his woe, we guessed not—he had store
Of friends and fortune once, as we could guess
From his nice habits and his gentleness;
These were now lost . . . it were a grief indeed
If he had changed one unsustaining reed
For all that such a man might else adorn.
The colours of his mind seemed yet unworn;   540
For the wild language of his grief was high,
Such as in measure were called poetry;
And I remember one remark which then
Maddalo made. He said: 'Most wretched men
Are cradled into poetry by wrong,
They learn in suffering what they teach in song.'

    If I had been an unconnected man
I, from this moment, should have formed some plan
Never to leave sweet Venice,—for to me
It was delight to ride by the lone sea;   550
And then, the town is silent—one may write
Or read in gondolas by day or night,
Having the little brazen lamp alight,
Unseen, uninterrupted; books are there,
Pictures, and casts from all those statues fair
Which were twin-born with poetry, and all
We seek in towns, with little to recall
Regrets for the green country. I might sit
In Maddalo's great palace, and his wit
And subtle talk would cheer the winter night   560
And make me know myself, and the firelight
Would flash upon our faces, till the day
Might dawn and make me wonder at my stay:
But I had friends in London too: the chief
Attraction here, was that I sought relief
From the deep tenderness that maniac wrought
Within me—'twas perhaps an idle thought—
But I imagined that if day by day

I watched him, and but seldom went away,
And studied all the beatings of his heart   570
With zeal, as men study some stubborn art
For their own good, and could by patience find
An entrance to the caverns of his mind,
I might reclaim him from his dark estate:
In friendships I had been most fortunate—
Yet never saw I one whom I would call
More willingly my friend; and this was all
Accomplished not; such dreams of baseless good
Oft come and go in crowds or solitude
And leave no trace—but what I now designed   580
Made for long years impression on my mind.
The following morning, urged by my affairs,
I left bright Venice.

               After many years
And many changes I returned; the name
Of Venice, and its aspect, was the same;
But Maddalo was travelling far away
Among the mountains of Armenia.
His dog was dead. His child had now become
A woman; such as it has been my doom
To meet with few,—a wonder of this earth,   590
Where there is little of transcendent worth,—
Like one of Shakespeare's women: kindly she,
And, with a manner beyond courtesy,
Received her father's friend; and when I asked
Of the lorn maniac, she her memory tasked,
And told as she had heard the mournful tale:
'That the poor sufferer's health began to fail
Two years from my departure, but that then
The lady who had left him, came again.
Her mien had been imperious, but she now   600
Looked meek—perhaps remorse had brought her low.
Her coming made him better, and they stayed
Together at my father's—for I played,
As I remember, with the lady's shawl—
I might be six years old—but after all
She left him.' . . . 'Why, her heart must have been tough:
How did it end?' 'And was not this enough?
They met—they parted.'—'Child, is there no more?'

'Something within that interval which bore
The stamp of *why* they parted, *how* they met: 610
Yet if thine agèd eyes disdain to wet
Those wrinkled cheeks with youth's remembered tears,
Ask me no more, but let the silent years
Be closed and cered over their memory
As yon mute marble where their corpses lie.'
I urged and questioned still, she told me how
All happened—but the cold world shall not know.

[1818–19; publ. 1824]

PROMETHEUS UNBOUND[1]

A LYRICAL DRAMA

IN FOUR ACTS

Audisne haec, amphiarae, sub terram abdite?

DRAMATIS PERSONÆ

PROMETHEUS	APOLLO	HERCULES
DEMOGORGON	MERCURY	THE PHANTASM OF JUPITER
JUPITER	PANTHEA } Ocean-ides.	THE SPIRIT OF THE EARTH
THE EARTH	IONE	THE SPIRIT OF THE MOON
OCEAN	ASIA	SPIRITS OF THE HOURS

SPIRITS.   ECHOES.   FAUNS.   FURIES.

ACT I

SCENE—*A Ravine of Icy Rocks in the Indian Caucasus.* PROME-
THEUS *is discovered bound to the Precipice.* PANTHEA *and*
IONE *are seated at his feet. Time, night. During the Scene,
morning slowly breaks.*

Prometheus. Monarch of Gods and Dæmons, and all Spirits
But One, who throng those bright and rolling worlds
Which Thou and I alone of living things
Behold with sleepless eyes! regard this Earth
Made multitudinous with thy slaves, whom thou

[1] The Preface Shelley wrote for *Prometheus Unbound* appears on page 442 of the present edition.

Requitest for knee-worship, prayer, and praise,
And toil, and hecatombs of broken hearts,
With fear and self-contempt and barren hope;
Whilst me, who am thy foe, eyeless in hate,
Hast thou made reign and triumph, to thy scorn,   10
O'er mine own misery and thy vain revenge.
Three thousand years of sleep-unsheltered hours,
And moments aye divided by keen pangs
Till they seemed years, torture and solitude,
Scorn and despair,—these are mine empire:—
More glorious far than that which thou surveyest
From thine unenvied throne, O Mighty God!
Almighty, had I deigned to share the shame
Of thine ill tyranny, and hung not here
Nailed to this wall of eagle-baffling mountain,   20
Black, wintry, dead, unmeasured; without herb,
Insect, or beast, or shape or sound of life.
Ah me! alas, pain, pain ever, for ever!

No change, no pause, no hope! Yet I endure.
I ask the Earth, have not the mountains felt?
I ask yon Heaven, the all-beholding Sun,
Has it not seen? The Sea, in storm or calm,
Heaven's ever-changing Shadow, spread below,
Have its deaf waves not heard my agony?
Ah me! alas, pain, pain ever, for ever!   30

The crawling glaciers pierce me with the spears
Of their moon-freezing crystals, the bright chains
Eat with their burning cold into my bones.
Heaven's wingèd hound, polluting from thy lips
His beak in poison not his own, tears up
My heart; and shapeless sights come wandering by,
The ghastly people of the realm of dream,
Mocking me: and the Earthquake-fiends are charged
To wrench the rivets from my quivering wounds
When the rocks split and close again behind: 40
While from their loud abysses howling throng
The genii of the storm, urging the rage
Of whirlwind, and afflict me with keen hail.
And yet to me welcome is day and night,
Whether one breaks the hoar frost of the morn,

Or starry, dim, and slow, the other climbs
The leaden-coloured east; for then they lead
The wingless, crawling hours, one among whom
—As some dark Priest hales the reluctant victim—
Shall drag thee, cruel King, to kiss the blood   50
From these pale feet, which then might trample thee
If they disdained not such a prostrate slave.
Disdain! Ah no! I pity thee. What ruin
Will hunt thee undefended through wide Heaven!
How will thy soul, cloven to its depth with terror,
Gape like a hell within! I speak in grief,
Not exultation, for I hate no more,
As then ere misery made me wise. The curse
Once breathed on thee I would recall. Ye Mountains,
Whose many-voicèd Echoes, through the mist   60
Of cataracts, flung the thunder of that spell!
Ye icy Springs, stagnant with wrinkling frost,
Which vibrated to hear me, and then crept
Shuddering through India! Thou serenest Air,
Through which the Sun walks burning without beams!
And ye swift Whirlwinds, who on poisèd wings
Hung mute and moveless o'er yon hushed abyss,
As thunder, louder than your own, made rock
The orbèd world! If then my words had power,
Though I am changed so that aught evil wish   70
Is dead within; although no memory be
Of what is hate, let them not lose it now!
What was that curse? for ye all heard me speak.

First Voice (*from the Mountains*).

Thrice three hundred thousand years
    O'er the Earthquake's couch we stood:
Oft, as men convulsed with fears,
    We trembled in our multitude.

Second Voice (*from the Springs*).

Thunderbolts had parched our water,
    We had been stained with bitter blood,
And had run mute, 'mid shrieks of slaughter,   80
    Thro' a city and a solitude.

Third Voice (from the Air).

I had clothed, since Earth uprose,
  Its wastes in colours not their own,
And oft had my serene repose
  Been cloven by many a rending groan.

Fourth Voice (from the Whirlwinds).

We had soared beneath these mountains
  Unresting ages; nor had thunder,
Nor yon volcano's flaming fountains,
  Nor any power above or under
  Ever made us mute with wonder.   90

First Voice.

But never bowed our snowy crest
As at the voice of thine unrest.

Second Voice.

Never such a sound before
To the Indian waves we bore.
A pilot asleep on the howling sea
Leaped up from the deck in agony,
And heard, and cried, 'Ah, woe is me!'
And died as mad as the wild waves be.

Third Voice.

By such dread words from Earth to Heaven
My still realm was never riven: 100
When its wound was closed, there stood
Darkness o'er the day like blood.

Fourth Voice.

And we shrank back: for dreams of ruin
To frozen caves our flight pursuing
Made us keep silence—thus—and thus—
Though silence is as hell to us.

The Earth. The tongueless Caverns of the craggy hills
Cried, 'Misery!' then; the hollow Heaven replied,
'Misery!' And the Ocean's purple waves,
Climbing the land, howled to the lashing winds,   110
And the pale nations heard it, 'Misery!'
    Prometheus. I heard a sound of voices: not the voice
Which I gave forth. Mother, thy sons and thou
Scorn him, without whose all-enduring will
Beneath the fierce omnipotence of Jove,
Both they and thou had vanished, like thin mist
Unrolled on the morning wind. Know ye not me,
The Titan? He who made his agony
The barrier to your else all-conquering foe?
Oh, rock-embosomed lawns, and snow-fed streams,   120
Now seen athwart frore vapours, deep below,
Through whose o'ershadowing woods I wandered once
With Asia, drinking life from her loved eyes;
Why scorns the spirit which informs ye, now
To commune with me? me alone, who checked,
As one who checks a fiend-drawn charioteer,
The falsehood and the force of him who reigns
Supreme, and with the groans of pining slaves
Fills your dim glens and liquid wildernesses:
Why answer ye not, still? Brethren!
    The Earth.   They dare not.   130
    Prometheus. Who dares? for I would hear that curse again.
Ha, what an awful whisper rises up!
'Tis scarce like sound: it tingles through the frame
As lightning tingles, hovering ere it strike.
Speak, Spirit! from thine inorganic voice
I only know that thou art moving near
And love. How cursed I him?
    The Earth.   How canst thou hear
Who knowest not the language of the dead?
    Prometheus. Thou art a living spirit, speak as they.
    The Earth. I dare not speak like life, lest Heaven's fell King 140
Should hear, and link me to some wheel of pain
More torturing than the one whereon I roll.
Subtle thou art and good, and though the Gods
Hear not this voice, yet thou art more than God,
Being wise and kind: earnestly hearken now.
    Prometheus. Obscurely through my brain, like shadows dim,

Sweep awful thoughts, rapid and thick. I feel
Faint, like one mingled in entwining love;
Yet 'tis not pleasure.
   The Earth.   No, thou canst not hear:
Thou art immortal, and this tongue is known   150
Only to those who die.
   Prometheus.   And what art thou,
O, melancholy Voice?
   The Earth.   I am the Earth,
Thy mother; she within whose stony veins,
To the last fibre of the loftiest tree
Whose thin leaves trembled in the frozen air,
Joy ran, as blood within a living frame,
When thou didst from her bosom, like a cloud
Of glory, arise, a spirit of keen joy!
And at thy voice her pining sons uplifted
Their prostrate brows from the polluting dust,   160
And our almighty Tyrant with fierce dread
Grew pale, until his thunder chained thee here.
Then, see those million worlds which burn and roll
Around us: their inhabitants beheld
My spherèd light wane in wide Heaven; the sea
Was lifted by strange tempest, and new fire
From earthquake-rifted mountains of bright snow
Shook its portentous hair beneath Heaven's frown;
Lightning and Inundation vexed the plains;
Blue thistles bloomed in cities; foodless toads   170
Within voluptuous chambers panting crawled:
When Plague had fallen on man, and beast, and worm,
And Famine; and black blight on herb and tree;
And in the corn, and vines, and meadow-grass,
Teemed ineradicable poisonous weeds
Draining their growth, for my wan breast was dry
With grief; and the thin air, my breath, was stained
With the contagion of a mother's hate
Breathed on her child's destroyer; ay, I heard
Thy curse, the which, if thou rememberest not,   180
Yet my innumerable seas and streams,
Mountains, and caves, and winds, and yon wide air,
And the inarticulate people of the dead,
Preserve, a treasured spell. We meditate
In secret joy and hope those dreadful words,

But dare not speak them.

    Prometheus.   Venerable mother!
All else who live and suffer take from thee
Some comfort; flowers, and fruits, and happy sounds,
And love, though fleeting; these may not be mine.
But mine own words, I pray, deny me not.   190

    The Earth. They shall be told. Ere Babylon was dust,
The Magus Zoroaster, my dead child,
Met his own image walking in the garden.
That apparition, sole of men, he saw.
For know there are two worlds of life and death:
One that which thou beholdest; but the other
Is underneath the grave, where do inhabit
The shadows of all forms that think and live
Till death unite them and they part no more;
Dreams and the light imaginings of men,   200
And all that faith creates or love desires,
Terrible, strange, sublime and beauteous shapes.
There thou art, and dost hang, a writhing shade,
'Mid whirlwind-peopled mountains; all the gods
Are there, and all the powers of nameless worlds,
Vast, sceptred phantoms; heroes, men, and beasts;
And Demogorgon, a tremendous gloom;
And he, the supreme Tyrant, on his throne
Of burning gold. Son, one of these shall utter
The curse which all remember. Call at will   210
Thine own ghost, or the ghost of Jupiter,
Hades or Typhon, or what mightier Gods
From all-prolific Evil, since thy ruin
Have sprung, and trampled on my prostrate sons.
Ask, and they must reply: so the revenge
Of the Supreme may sweep through vacant shades,
As rainy wind through the abandoned gate
Of a fallen palace.

    Prometheus.   Mother, let not aught
Of that which may be evil, pass again
My lips, or those of aught resembling me.   220
Phantasm of Jupiter, arise, appear!

Ione.

My wings are folded o'er mine ears:
   My wings are crossèd o'er mine eyes:

Yet through their silver shade appears,
  And through their lulling plumes arise,
A Shape, a throng of sounds;
  May it be no ill to thee
O thou of many wounds!
Near whom, for our sweet sister's sake,
Ever thus we watch and wake.   230

Panthea.

The sound is of whirlwind underground.
  Earthquake, and fire, and mountains cloven;
The shape is awful like the sound,
  Clothed in dark purple, star-inwoven.
A sceptre of pale gold
  To stay steps proud, o'er the slow cloud
His veinèd hand doth hold.
Cruel he looks, but calm and strong,
Like one who does, not suffers wrong.

Phantasm of Jupiter. Why have the secret powers
  of this strange world   240
Driven me, a frail and empty phantom, hither
On direst storms? What unaccustomed sounds
Are hovering on my lips, unlike the voice
With which our pallid race hold ghastly talk
In darkness? And, proud sufferer, who art thou?
  Prometheus. Tremendous Image, as thou art must be
He whom thou shadowest forth. I am his foe,
The Titan. Speak the words which I would hear,
Although no thought inform thine empty voice.
  The Earth. Listen! And though your echoes must be mute, 250
Gray mountains, and old woods and haunted springs,
Prophetic caves, and isle-surrounding streams,
Rejoice to hear what yet ye cannot speak.
  Phantasm. A spirit seizes me and speaks within:
It tears me as fire tears a thunder-cloud.
  Panthea. See, how he lifts his mighty looks; the Heaven
Darkens above.
  Ione.   He speaks! O shelter me!
  Prometheus. I see the curse on gestures proud and cold,
And looks of firm defiance, and calm hate,

And such despair as mocks itself with smiles,   260
Written as on a scroll: yet speak! Oh speak!

Phantasm.

Fiend, I defy thee! with a calm, fixed mind,
   All that thou canst inflict I bid thee do;
Foul Tyrant both of Gods and Human-kind,
   One only being shalt thou not subdue.
Rain then thy plagues upon me here,
Ghastly disease, and frenzying fear;
And let alternate frost and fire
Eat into me, and be thine ire
Lightning, and cutting hail, and legioned forms   270
Of furies, driving by upon the wounding storms.

Ay, do thy worst. Thou art omnipotent.
   O'er all things but thyself I gave thee power,
And my own will. Be thy swift mischief sent
   To blast mankind, from yon ethereal tower.
Let thy malignant spirit move
In darkness over those I love:
On me and mine I imprecate
The utmost torture of thy hate;
And thus devote to sleepless agony,   280
This undeclining head while thou must reign on high.

But thou, who art the God and Lord: O, thou
   Who fillest with thy soul this world of woe,
To whom all things of Earth and Heaven do bow
   In fear and worship: all-prevailing foe!
I curse thee! let a sufferer's curse
Clasp thee, his torturer, like remorse;
Till thine Infinity shall be
A robe of envenomed agony;
And thine Omnipotence a crown of pain,   290
To cling like burning gold round thy dissolving brain.

Heap on thy soul, by virtue of this Curse,
   Ill deeds, then be thou damned, beholding good;
Both infinite as is the universe,
   And thou, and thy self-torturing solitude.

An awful image of calm power
Though now thou sittest, let the hour
Come, when thou must appear to be
That which thou art internally;
And after many a false and fruitless crime   300
Scorn track thy lagging fall through boundless space
    and time.

Prometheus. Were these my words, O Parent?
The Earth.   They were thine.
Prometheus. It doth repent me: words are quick and vain;
Grief for awhile is blind, and so was mine.
I wish no living thing to suffer pain.

The Earth.

Misery, Oh misery to me,
  That Jove at length should vanquish thee.
Wail, howl aloud, Land and Sea,
  The Earth's rent heart shall answer ye.
Howl, Spirits of the living and the dead,   310
Your refuge, your defence lies fallen and vanquishèd.

First Echo.

Lies fallen and vanquishèd!

Second Echo.

Fallen and vanquishèd!

Ione.

Fear not; 'tis but some passing spasm,
  The Titan is unvanquished still.
But see, where through the azure chasm
  Of yon forked and snowy hill
Trampling the slant winds on high
  With golden-sandalled feet, that glow
Under plumes of purple dye,   320
Like rose-ensanguined ivory,
  A Shape comes now,

Stretching on high from his right hand
A serpent-cinctured wand.

Panthea. 'Tis Jove's world-wandering herald, Mercury.

Ione.

And who are those with hydra tresses
    And iron wings that climb the wind,
Whom the frowning God represses
    Like vapours steaming up behind,
Clanging loud, an endless crowd—   330

Panthea.

These are Jove's tempest-walking hounds,
    Whom he gluts with groans and blood,
When charioted on sulphurous cloud
    He bursts Heaven's bounds.

Ione.

Are they now led, from the thin dead
On new pangs to be fed?

Panthea.

The Titan looks as ever, firm, not proud.

First Fury. Ha! I scent life!
Second Fury.   Let me but look into his eyes!
  Third Fury. The hope of torturing him smells like a heap
Of corpses to a death-bird after battle.   340
  First Fury. Darest thou delay, O Herald! take cheer, Hounds
Of Hell: what if the Son of Maia soon
Should make us food and sport—who can please long
The Omnipotent?
  Mercury.   Back to your towers of iron,
And gnash, beside the streams of fire and wail,
Your foodless teeth, Geryon, arise! and Gorgon,
Chimæra, and thou Sphinx, subtlest of fiends

Who ministered to Thebes Heaven's poisoned wine,
Unnatural love, and more unnatural hate:
These shall perform your task.
 First fury.   Oh, mercy! mercy! 350
We die with our desire: drive us not back!
 Mercury. Crouch then in silence.
          Awful Sufferer!
To thee unwilling, most unwillingly
I come, by the great Father's will driven down,
To execute a doom of new revenge.
Alas! I pity thee, and hate myself
That I can do no more: aye from thy sight
Returning, for a season, Heaven seems Hell,
So thy worn form pursues me night and day,
Smiling reproach. Wise art thou, firm and good, 360
But vainly wouldst stand forth alone in strife
Against the Omnipotent; as yon clear lamps
That measure and divide the weary years
From which there is no refuge, long have taught
And long must teach. Even now thy Torturer arms
With the strange might of unimagined pains
The powers who scheme slow agonies in Hell,
And my commission is to lead them here,
Or what more subtle, foul or savage fiends
People the abyss, and leave them to their task. 370
Be it not so! there is a secret known
To thee, and to none else of living things,
Which may transfer the sceptre of wide Heaven,
The fear of which perplexes the Supreme:
Clothe it in words, and bid it clasp his throne
In intercession; bend thy soul in prayer,
And like a suppliant in some gorgeous fane,
Let the will kneel within thy haughty heart:
For benefits and meek submission tame
The fiercest and the mightiest.
 Prometheus.   Evil minds 380
Change good to their own nature. I gave all
He has; and in return he chains me here
Years, ages, night and day: whether the Sun
Split my parched skin, or in the moony night
The crystal-wingèd snow cling round my hair:
Whilst my belovèd race is trampled down

By his thought-executing ministers.
Such is the tyrant's recompense: 'tis just:
He who is evil can receive no good;
And for a world bestowed, or a friend lost,   390
He can feel hate, fear, shame; not gratitude:
He but requites me for his own misdeed.
Kindness to such is keen reproach, which breaks
With bitter stings the light sleep of Revenge.
Submission, thou dost know I cannot try:
For what submission but that fatal word,
The death-seal of mankind's captivity,
Like the Sicilian's hair-suspended sword,
Which trembles o'er his crown, would he accept,
Or could I yield? Which yet I will not yield.   400
Let others flatter Crime, where it sits throned
In brief Omnipotence: secure are they:
For Justice, when triumphant, will weep down
Pity, not punishment, on her own wrongs,
Too much avenged by those who err. I wait,
Enduring thus, the retributive hour
Which since we spake is even nearer now.
But hark, the hell-hounds clamour: fear delay:
Behold! Heaven lowers under thy Father's frown.

    Mercury. Oh, that we might be spared: I to inflict   410
And thou to suffer! Once more answer me:
Thou knowest not the period of Jove's power?
    Prometheus. I know but this, that it must come.
    Mercury.   Alas!
Thou canst not count thy years to come of pain?
    Prometheus. They last while Jove must reign: nor
        more, nor less
Do I desire or fear.
    Mercury.   Yet pause, and plunge
Into Eternity, where recorded time,
Even all that we imagine, age on age,
Seems but a point, and the reluctant mind
Flags wearily in its unending flight,   420
Till it sink, dizzy, blind, lost, shelterless;
Perchance it has not numbered the slow years
Which thou must spend in torture, unreprieved?
    Prometheus. Perchance no thought can count them, yet
        they pass.

Mercury. If thou might'st dwell among the Gods the while
Lapped in voluptuous joy?
 Prometheus.   I would not quit
This bleak ravine, these unrepentant pains.
 Mercury. Alas! I wonder at, yet pity thee.
 Prometheus. Pity the self-despising slaves of Heaven,
Not me, within whose mind sits peace serene,   430
As light in the sun, throned: how vain is talk!
Call up the fiends.
 Ione.   O, sister, look! White fire
Has cloven to the roots yon huge snow-loaded cedar;
How fearfully God's thunder howls behind!
 Mercury. I must obey his words and thine; alas!
Most heavily remorse hangs at my heart!
 Panthea. See where the child of Heaven, with wingèd feet,
Runs down the slanted sunlight of the dawn:
 Ione. Dear sister, close thy plumes over thine eyes
Lest thou behold and die: they come: they come   440
Blackening the birth of day with countless wings,
And hollow underneath, like death.
 First Fury.   Prometheus!
 Second Fury. Immortal Titan!
 Third Fury.   Champion of Heaven's slaves!
 Prometheus. He whom some dreadful voice invokes is here,
Prometheus, the chained Titan. Horrible forms,
What and who are ye? Never yet there came
Phantasms so foul through monster-teeming Hell
From the all-miscreative brain of Jove;
Whilst I behold such execrable shapes,
Methinks I grow like what I contemplate,   450
And laugh and stare in loathsome sympathy.
 First Fury. We are the ministers of pain, and fear,
And disappointment, and mistrust, and hate,
And clinging crime; and as lean dogs pursue
Through wood and lake some struck and sobbing fawn,
We track all things that weep, and bleed, and live,
When the great King betrays them to our will.
 Prometheus. Oh! many fearful natures in one name,
I know ye; and these lakes and echoes know
The darkness and the clangour of your wings.   460
But why more hideous than your loathèd selves
Gather ye up in legions from the deep?

Second Fury. We knew not that: Sisters, rejoice, rejoice!
Prometheus. Can aught exult in its deformity?
Second Fury. The beauty of delight makes lovers glad,
Gazing on one another: so are we.
As from the rose which the pale priestess kneels
To gather for her festal crown of flowers
The aëreal crimson falls, flushing her cheek,
So from our victim's destined agony   470
The shade which is our form invests us round,
Else we are shapeless as our mother Night.
   Prometheus. I laugh your power, and his who sent you here,
To lowest scorn. Pour forth the cup of pain.
   First Fury. Thou thinkest we will rend thee bone from bone,
And nerve from nerve, working like fire within?
   Prometheus. Pain is my element, as hate is thine;
Ye rend me now: I care not.
   Second Fury.   Dost imagine
We will but laugh into thy lidless eyes?
   Prometheus. I weigh not what ye do, but what ye suffer,   480
Being evil. Cruel was the power which called
You, or aught else so wretched, into light.
   Third Fury. Thou think'st we will live through thee, one
                    by one,
Like animal life, and though we can obscure not
The soul which burns within, that we will dwell
Beside it, like a vain loud multitude
Vexing the self-content of wisest men:
That we will be dread thought beneath thy brain,
And foul desire round thine astonished heart,
And blood within thy labyrinthine veins   490
Crawling like agony?
   Prometheus.   Why, we are thus now;
Yet am I king over myself, and rule
The torturing and conflicting throngs within,
As Jove rules you when Hell grows mutinous.

Chorus of Furies.

From the ends of the earth, from the ends of the earth,
   Where the night has its grave and the morning its birth,
               Come, come, come!
Oh, ye who shake hills with the scream of your mirth,

When cities sink howling in ruin; and ye
Who with wingless footsteps trample the sea,   500
And close upon Shipwreck and Famine's track,
Sit chattering with joy on the foodless wreck;
          Come, come, come!
   Leave the bed, low, cold, and red,
   Strewed beneath a nation dead;
   Leave the hatred, as in ashes
     Fire is left for future burning:
   It will burst in bloodier flashes
     When ye stir it, soon returning:
   Leave the self-contempt implanted   510
   In young spirits, sense-enchanted,
     Misery's yet unkindled fuel:
   Leave Hell's secrets half unchanted
     To the maniac dreamer; cruel
More than ye can be with hate
     Is he with fear.
        Come, come, come!
We are steaming up from Hell's wide gate
And we burthen the blast of the atmosphere,
But vainly we toil till ye come here.   520

Ione. Sister, I hear the thunder of new wings.
Panthea. These solid mountains quiver with the sound
Even as the tremulous air: their shadows make
The space within my plumes more black than night.

First Fury.

   Your call was as a wingèd car
   Driven on whirlwinds fast and far;
   It rapped us from red gulfs of war.

Second Fury.

From wide cities, famine-wasted;

Third Fury.

Groans half heard, and blood untasted;

Fourth Fury.

Kingly conclaves stern and cold,   530
Where blood with gold is bought and sold;

Fifth Fury.

From the furnace, white and hot,
In which—

A Fury.

Speak not: whisper not:
I know all that ye would tell,
But to speak might break the spell
Which must bend the Invincible,
    The stern of thought;
He yet defies the deepest power of Hell.

A Fury.

Tear the veil!

Another Fury.

It is torn.

Chorus.

        The pale stars of the morn
Shine on a misery, dire to be borne.   540
Dost thou faint, mighty Titan? We laugh thee to scorn.
Dost thou boast the clear knowledge thou waken'dst for man?
Then was kindled within him a thirst which outran
Those perishing waters; a thirst of fierce fever,
Hope, love, doubt, desire, which consume him for ever.
    One came forth of gentle worth
    Smiling on the sanguine earth;
    His words outlived him, like swift poison
      Withering up truth, peace, and pity.
    Look! where round the wide horizon   550
      Many a million-peopled city
    Vomits smoke in the bright air.

Hark that outcry of despair!
'Tis his mild and gentle ghost
   Wailing for the faith he kindled:
Look again, the flames almost
   To a glow-worm's lamp have dwindled:
The survivors round the embers
   Gather in dread.

               Joy, joy, joy!   560
Past ages crowd on thee, but each one remembers,
And the future is dark, and the present is spread
Like a pillow of thorns for thy slumberless head.

Semichorus I.

Drops of bloody agony flow
From his white and quivering brow.
Grant a little respite now:
See a disenchanted nation
Springs like day from desolation;
To Truth its state is dedicate,
And Freedom leads it forth, her mate;   570
A legioned band of linkèd brothers
Whom Love calls children—

Semichorus II.

                  'Tis another's:
See how kindred murder kin:
'Tis the vintage-time for death and sin:
Blood, like new wine, bubbles within:
   Till Despair smothers
The struggling world, which slaves and tyrants win.
            [*All the* Furies *vanish, except one.*

  Ione. Hark, sister! what a low yet dreadful groan
Quite unsuppressed is tearing up the heart
Of the good Titan, as storms tear the deep,   580
And beasts hear the sea moan in inland caves.
Darest thou observe how the fiends torture him?
  Panthea. Alas! I looked forth twice, but will no more.
  Ione. What didst thou see?
  Panthea.   A woful sight: a youth
With patient looks nailed to a crucifix.

Ione. What next?
Panthea.   The heaven around, the earth below
Was peopled with thick shapes of human death,
All horrible, and wrought by human hands,
And some appeared the work of human hearts.
For men were slowly killed by frowns and smiles: 590
And other sights too foul to speak and live
Were wandering by. Let us not tempt worse fear
By looking forth: those groans are grief enough.
Fury. Behold an emblem: those who do endure
Deep wrongs for man, and scorn, and chains, but heap
Thousandfold torment on themselves and him.
Prometheus. Remit the anguish of that lighted stare;
Close those wan lips; let that thorn-wounded brow
Stream not with blood; it mingles with thy tears!
Fix, fix those tortured orbs in peace and death,   600
So thy sick throes shake not that crucifix,
So those pale fingers play not with thy gore.
O, horrible! Thy name I will not speak,
It hath become a curse. I see, I see
The wise, the mild, the lofty, and the just,
Whom thy slaves hate for being like to thee,
Some hunted by foul lies from their heart's home,
An early-chosen, late-lamented home;
As hooded ounces cling to the driven hind;
Some linked to corpses in unwholesome cells: 610
Some—Hear I not the multitude laugh loud?—
Impaled in lingering fire: and mighty realms
Float by my feet, like sea-uprooted isles,
Whose sons are kneaded down in common blood
By the red light of their own burning homes.
Fury. Blood thou canst see, and fire; and canst hear groans;
Worse things, unheard, unseen, remain behind.
Prometheus. Worse?
Fury.   In each human heart terror survives
The ravin it has gorged: the loftiest fear
All that they would disdain to think were true: 620
Hypocrisy and custom make their minds
The fanes of many a worship, now outworn.
They dare not devise good for man's estate,
And yet they know not that they do not dare.

The good want power, but to weep barren tears.
The powerful goodness want: worse need for them.
The wise want love; and those who love want wisdom;
And all best things are thus confused to ill.
Many are strong and rich, and would be just,
But live among their suffering fellow-men   630
As if none felt: they know not what they do.
   Prometheus. Thy words are like a cloud of wingèd snakes;
And yet I pity those they torture not.
    Fury. Thou pitiest them? I speak no more!   *[Vanishes.*
    Prometheus.   Ah woe!
Ah woe! Alas! pain, pain ever, for ever!
I close my tearless eyes, but see more clear
Thy works within my woe-illumèd mind,
Thou subtle tyrant! Peace is in the grave.
The grave hides all things beautiful and good:
I am a God and cannot find it there,   640
Nor would I seek it: for, though dread revenge,
This is defeat, fierce king, not victory.
The sights with which thou torturest gird my soul
With new endurance, till the hour arrives
When they shall be no types of things which are.
   Panthea. Alas! what sawest thou more?
   Prometheus.   There are two woes:
To speak, and to behold; thou spare me one.
Names are there, Nature's sacred watchwords, they
Were borne aloft in bright emblazonry;
The nations thronged around, and cried aloud,   650
As with one voice, Truth, Liberty, and Love!
Suddenly fierce confusion fell from heaven
Among them: there was strife, deceit, and fear:
Tyrants rushed in, and did divide the spoil.
This was the shadow of the truth I saw.
   The Earth. I felt thy torture, son, with such mixed joy
As pain and virtue give. To cheer thy state
I bid ascend those subtle and fair spirits,
Whose homes are the dim caves of human thought,
And who inhabit, as birds wing the wind,   660
Its world-surrounding aether: they behold
Beyond that twilight realm, as in a glass,
The future: may they speak comfort to thee!

Panthea. Look, sister, where a troop of spirits gather,
Like flocks of clouds in spring's delightful weather,
Thronging in the blue air!
Ione.   And see! more come,
Like fountain-vapours when the winds are dumb,
That climb up the ravine in scattered lines.
And, hark! is it the music of the pines?
Is it the lake? Is it the waterfall?   670
Panthea. 'Tis something sadder, sweeter far than all.

Chorus of Spirits.

From unremembered ages we
Gentle guides and guardians be
Of heaven-oppressed mortality;
And we breathe, and sicken not,
The atmosphere of human thought:
Be it dim, and dank, and gray,
Like a storm-extinguished day,
Travelled o'er by dying gleams;
     Be it bright as all between   680
Cloudless skies and windless streams,
     Silent, liquid, and serene;
As the birds within the wind,
     As the fish within the wave,
As the thoughts of man's own mind
     Float through all above the grave;
We make there our liquid lair,
Voyaging cloudlike and unpent
Through the boundless element:
Thence we bear the prophecy   690
Which begins and ends in thee!

Ione. More yet come, one by one: the air around them
Looks radiant as the air around a star.

First Spirit.

On a battle-trumpet's blast
I fled hither, fast, fast, fast,
'Mid the darkness upward cast.

From the dust of creeds outworn,
From the tyrant's banner torn,
Gathering 'round me, onward borne,
There was mingled many a cry—   700
Freedom! Hope! Death! Victory!
Till they faded through the sky;
And one sound, above, around,
One sound beneath, around, above,
Was moving; 'twas the soul of Love;
'Twas the hope, the prophecy,
Which begins and ends in thee.

Second Spirit.

A rainbow's arch stood on the sea,
Which rocked beneath, immovably;
And the triumphant storm did flee,   710
Like a conqueror, swift and proud,
Between, with many a captive cloud,
A shapeless, dark and rapid crowd,
Each by lightning riven in half:
I heard the thunder hoarsely laugh:
Mighty fleets were strewn like chaff
And spread beneath a hell of death
O'er the white waters. I alit
On a great ship lightning-split,
And speeded hither on the sigh   720
Of one who gave an enemy
His plank, then plunged aside to die.

Third Spirit.

I sate beside a sage's bed,
And the lamp was burning red
Near the book where he had fed,
When a Dream with plumes of flame,
To his pillow hovering came,
And I knew it was the same
Which had kindled long ago
Pity, eloquence, and woe;   730
And the world awhile below

Wore the shade its lustre made.
It has borne me here as fleet
As Desire's lightning feet:
I must ride it back ere morrow,
Or the sage will wake in sorrow.

Fourth Spirit.

On a poet's lips I slept
Dreaming like a love-adept
In the sound his breathing kept;
Nor seeks nor finds he mortal blisses,   740
But feeds on the aëreal kisses
Of shapes that haunt thought's wildernesses.
He will watch from dawn to gloom
The lake-reflected sun illume
The yellow bees in the ivy-bloom,
Nor heed nor see, what things they be;
But from these create he can
Forms more real than living man,
Nurslings of immortality!
One of these awakened me,   750
And I sped to succour thee.

Ione.

Behold'st thou not two shapes from the east and west
Come, as two doves to one belovèd nest,
Twin nurslings of the all-sustaining air
On swift still wings glide down the atmosphere?
And, hark! their sweet, sad voices! 'tis despair
Mingled with love and then dissolved in sound.
  Panthea. Canst thou speak, sister? all my words are drowned.
  Ione. Their beauty gives me voice. See how they float
On their sustaining wings of skiey grain   760
Orange and azure deepening into gold:
Their soft smiles light the air like a star's fire.

Chorus of Spirits.

Hast thou beheld the form of Love?

Fifth Spirit.

As over wide dominions
I sped, like some swift cloud that wings the wide air's wilder-
nesses,
That planet-crested shape swept by on lightning-braided pin-
ions,
Scattering the liquid joy of life from his ambrosial tresses:
His footsteps paved the world with light; but as I passed 'twas
fading,
And hollow Ruin yawned behind: great sages bound in mad-
ness,
And headless patriots, and pale youths who perished, unup-
braiding,
Gleamed in the night. I wandered o'er, till thou, O King of
sadness, 770
Turned by thy smile the worst I saw to recollected gladness.

Sixth Spirit.

Ah, sister! Desolation is a delicate thing:
It walks not on the earth, it floats not on the air,
But treads with lulling footstep, and fans with silent wing
The tender hopes which in their hearts the best and gentlest
bear;
Who, soothed to false repose by the fanning plumes above
And the music-stirring motion of its soft and busy feet,
Dream visions of aëreal joy, and call the monster, Love,
And wake, and find the shadow Pain, as he whom now we
greet.

Chorus.

Though Ruin now Love's shadow be, 780
Following him, destroyingly,
On Death's white and wingèd steed,
Which the fleetest cannot flee,
Trampling down both flower and weed,
Man and beast, and foul and fair,
Like a tempest through the air;
Thou shalt quell this horseman grim,
Woundless though in heart or limb.

Prometheus. Spirits! how know ye this shall be?

Chorus.

In the atmosphere we breathe,   790
As buds grow red when the snow-storms flee,
    From Spring gathering up beneath,
Whose mild winds shake the elder brake,
And the wandering herdsmen know
That the white-thorn soon will blow:
Wisdom, Justice, Love, and Peace,
When they struggle to increase,
    Are to us as soft winds be
    To shepherd boys, the prophecy
    Which begins and ends in thee.   800

Ione. Where are the Spirits fled?
    Panthea.   Only a sense
Remains of them, like the omnipotence
Of music, when the inspired voice and lute
Languish, ere yet the responses are mute,
Which through the deep and labyrinthine soul,
Like echoes through long caverns, wind and roll.
    Prometheus. How fair these airborn shapes! and yet I feel
Most vain all hope but love; and thou art far,
Asia! who, when my being overflowed,
Wert like a golden chalice to bright wine   810
Which else had sunk into the thirsty dust.
All things are still: alas! how heavily
This quiet morning weighs upon my heart;
Though I should dream I could even sleep with grief
If slumber were denied not. I would fain
Be what it is my destiny to be,
The saviour and the strength of suffering man,
Or sink into the original gulf of things:
There is no agony, and no solace left;
Earth can console, Heaven can torment no more.   820
    Panthea. Hast thou forgotten one who watches thee
The cold dark night, and never sleeps but when
The shadow of thy spirit falls on her?
    Prometheus. I said all hope was vain but love: thou lovest.
    Panthea. Deeply in truth; but the eastern star looks white,

And Asia waits in that far Indian vale,
The scene of her sad exile; rugged once
And desolate and frozen, like this ravine;
But now invested with fair flowers and herbs,
And haunted by sweet airs and sounds, which flow   830
Among the woods and waters, from the aether
Of her transforming presence, which would fade
If it were mingled not with thine. Farewell!

END OF THE FIRST ACT.

ACT II

SCENE I—*Morning. A lovely Vale in the Indian Caucasus.* ASIA
   alone.

   Asia. From all the blasts of heaven thou hast descended:
Yes, like a spirit, like a thought, which makes
Unwonted tears throng to the horny eyes,
And beatings haunt the desolated heart,
Which should have learnt repose: thou hast descended
Cradled in tempests; thou dost wake, O Spring!
O child of many winds! As suddenly
Thou comest as the memory of a dream,
Which now is sad because it hath been sweet;
Like genius, or like joy which riseth up   10
As from the earth, clothing with golden clouds
The desert of our life.
This is the season, this the day, the hour;
At sunrise thou shouldst come, sweet sister mine,
Too long desired, too long delaying, come!
How like death-worms the wingless moments crawl!
The point of one white star is quivering still
Deep in the orange light of widening morn
Beyond the purple mountains: through a chasm
Of wind-divided mist the darker lake   20
Reflects it: now it wanes: it gleams again
As the waves fade, and as the burning threads
Of woven cloud unravel in pale air:
'Tis lost! and through yon peaks of cloudlike snow

The roseate sunlight quivers: hear I not
The Æolian music of her sea-green plumes
Winnowing the crimson dawn?   [PANTHEA *enters*
            I feel, I see
Those eyes which burn through smiles that fade in tears,
Like stars half quenched in mists of silver dew.
Belovèd and most beautiful, who wearest   30
The shadow of that soul by which I live,
How late thou art! the spherèd sun had climbed
The sea; my heart was sick with hope, before
The printless air felt thy belated plumes.
   Panthea. Pardon, great Sister! but my wings were faint
With the delight of a remembered dream,
As are the noontide plumes of summer winds
Satiate with sweet flowers. I was wont to sleep
Peacefully, and awake refreshed and calm
Before the sacred Titan's fall, and thy   40
Unhappy love, had made, through use and pity,
Both love and woe familiar to my heart
As they had grown to thine: erewhile I slept
Under the glaucous caverns of old Ocean
Within dim bowers of green and purple moss,
Our young Ione's soft and milky arms
Locked then, as now, behind my dark, moist hair,
While my shut eyes and cheek were pressed within
The folded depth of her life-breathing bosom:
But not as now, since I am made the wind   50
Which fails beneath the music that I bear
Of thy most wordless converse; since dissolved
Into the sense with which love talks, my rest
Was troubled and yet sweet; my waking hours
Too full of care and pain.
   Asia.   Lift up thine eyes,
And let me read thy dream.
   Panthea.   As I have said
With our sea-sister at his feet I slept.
The mountain mists, condensing at our voice
Under the moon, had spread their snowy flakes,
From the keen ice shielding our linkèd sleep.   ·   60
Then two dreams came. One, I remember not.
But in the other his pale wound-worn limbs
Fell from Prometheus, and azure night

Grew radiant with the glory of that form
Which lives unchanged within, and his voice fell
Like music which makes giddy the dim brain,
Faint with intoxication of keen joy:
'Sister of her whose footsteps pave the world
With loveliness—more fair than aught but her,
Whose shadow thou art—lift thine eyes on me.'   **70**
I lifted them: the overpowering light
Of that immortal shape was shadowed o'er
By love; which, from his soft and flowing limbs,
And passion-parted lips, and keen, faint eyes,
Steamed forth like vaporous fire; an atmosphere
Which wrapped me in its all-dissolving power,
As the warm aether of the morning sun
Wraps ere it drinks some cloud of wandering dew.
I saw not, heard not, moved not, only felt
His presence flow and mingle through my blood   **80**
Till it became his life, and his grew mine,
And I was thus absorbed, until it passed,
And like the vapours when the sun sinks down,
Gathering again in drops upon the pines,
And tremulous as they, in the deep night
My being was condensed; and as the rays
Of thought were slowly gathered, I could hear
His voice, whose accents lingered ere they died
Like footsteps of weak melody: thy name
Among the many sounds alone I heard   **90**
Of what might be articulate; though still
I listened through the night when sound was none.
Ione wakened then, and said to me:
'Canst thou divine what troubles me to-night?
I always knew what I desired before,
Nor ever found delight to wish in vain.
But now I cannot tell thee what I seek;
I know not; something sweet, since it is sweet
Even to desire; it is thy sport, false sister;
Thou hast discovered some enchantment old,   **100**
Whose spells have stolen my spirit as I slept
And mingled it with thine: for when just now
We kissed, I felt within thy parted lips
The sweet air that sustained me, and the warmth
Of the life-blood, for loss of which I faint,

Quivered between our intertwining arms.'
I answered not, for the Eastern star grew pale,
But fled to thee.

    Asia.   Thou speakest, but thy words
Are as the air: I feel them not: Oh, lift
Thine eyes, that I may read his written soul!   110
    Panthea. I lift them though they droop beneath the load
Of that they would express: what canst thou see
But thine own fairest shadow imaged there?
    Asia. Thine eyes are like the deep, blue, boundless heaven
Contracted to two circles underneath
Their long, fine lashes; dark, far, measureless,
Orb within orb, and line through line inwoven.
    Panthea. Why lookest thou as if a spirit passed?
    Asia. There is a change: beyond their inmost depth
I see a shade, a shape: 'tis He, arrayed   120
In the soft light of his own smiles, which spread
Like radiance from the cloud-surrounded moon.
Prometheus, it is thine! depart not yet!
Say not those smiles that we shall meet again
Within that bright pavilion which their beams
Shall build o'er the waste world? The dream is told.
What shape is that between us? Its rude hair
Roughens the wind that lifts it, its regard
Is wild and quick, yet 'tis a thing of air,
For through its gray robe gleams the golden dew   130
Whose stars the noon has quenched not.
    Dream.   Follow! Follow!
    Panthea. It is mine other dream.
    Asia.   It disappears.
    Panthea. It passes now into my mind. Methought
As we sate here, the flower-infolding buds
Burst on yon lightning-blasted almond-tree,
When swift from the white Scythian wilderness
A wind swept forth wrinkling the Earth with frost:
I looked, and all the blossoms were blown down;
But on each leaf was stamped, as the blue bells
Of Hyacinth tell Apollo's written grief,   140
O, FOLLOW, FOLLOW!
    Asia.   As you speak, your words
Fill, pause by pause, my own forgotten sleep
With shapes. Methought among these lawns together

We wandered, underneath the young gray dawn,
And multitudes of dense white fleecy clouds
Were wandering in thick flocks along the mountains
Shepherded by the slow, unwilling wind;
And the white dew on the new-bladed grass,
Just piercing the dark earth, hung silently;
And there was more which I remember not: 150
But on the shadows of the morning clouds,
Athwart the purple mountain slope, was written
FOLLOW, O, FOLLOW! as they vanished by;
And on each herb, from which Heaven's dew had fallen,
The like was stamped, as with a withering fire;
A wind arose among the pines; it shook
The clinging music from their boughs, and then
Low, sweet, faint sounds, like the farewell of ghosts,
Were heard: O, FOLLOW, FOLLOW, FOLLOW ME!
And then I said: 'Panthea, look on me.'   160
But in the depth of those belovèd eyes
Still I saw, FOLLOW, FOLLOW!
   Echo.   Follow, follow!
   Panthea. The crags, this clear spring morning, mock
      our voices
As they were spirit-tongued.
   Asia.   It is some being
Around the crags. What fine clear sounds! O, list!

        Echoes (unseen).
        Echoes we: listen!
         We cannot stay:
        As dew-stars glisten
         Then fade away—
          Child of Ocean!   170

   Asia. Hark! Spirits speak. The liquid responses
Of their aëreal tongues yet sound.
   Panthea.   I hear.

        Echoes.
      O, follow, follow,
        As our voice recedeth
      Through the caverns hollow,
        Where the forest spreadeth;

(*More distant.*)
O, follow, follow!
Through the caverns hollow,
As the song floats thou pursue,
Where the wild bee never flew,   180
Through the noontide darkness deep,
By the odour-breathing sleep
Of faint night flowers, and the waves
At the fountain-lighted caves,
While our music, wild and sweet,
Mocks thy gently falling feet,
Child of Ocean!

Asia. Shall we pursue the sound? It grows more faint
And distant.
  Panthea.   List! the strain floats nearer now.

Echoes.

In the world unknown   190
  Sleeps a voice unspoken;
By thy step alone
  Can its rest be broken;
  Child of Ocean!

Asia. How the notes sink upon the ebbing wind!

Echoes.

O, follow, follow!
  Through the caverns hollow,
As the song floats thou pursue,
By the woodland noontide dew;
By the forest, lakes, and fountains,   200
Through the many-folded mountains;
To the rents, and gulfs, and chasms,
Where the Earth reposed from spasms,
On the day when He and thou
Parted, to commingle now;
  Child of Ocean!

Asia. Come, sweet Panthea, link thy hand in mine,
And follow, ere the voices fade away.

SCENE II—*A forest, intermingled with Rocks and Caverns.* ASIA *and* PANTHEA *pass into it. Two young Fauns are sitting on a Rock listening.*

Semichorus I. of Spirits.

The path through which that lovely twain
   Have passed, by cedar, pine, and yew,
   And each dark tree that ever grew,
   Is curtained out from Heaven's wide blue;
Nor sun, nor moon, nor wind, nor rain,
     Can pierce its interwoven bowers,
  Nor aught, save where some cloud of dew,
Drifted along the earth-creeping breeze,
Between the trunks of the hoar trees,
    Hangs each a pearl in the pale flowers   **10**
  Of the green laurel, blown anew;
And bends, and then fades silently,
One frail and fair anemone:
Or when some star of many a one
That climbs and wanders through steep night,
Has found the cleft through which alone
Beams fall from high those depths upon
Ere it is borne away, away,
By the swift Heavens that cannot stay,
It scatters drops of golden light,   **20**
Like lines of rain that ne'er unite:
And the gloom divine is all around,
And underneath is the mossy ground.

Semichorus II.

There the voluptuous nightingales,
  Are awake through all the broad noonday.
When one with bliss or sadness fails,
    And through the windless ivy-boughs,
  Sick with sweet love, droops dying away
On its mate's music-panting bosom;
Another from the swinging blossom,   **30**
    Watching to catch the languid close
  Of the last strain, then lifts on high
  The wings of the weak melody,

'Till some new strain of feeling bear
   The song, and all the woods are mute;
When there is heard through the dim air
The rush of wings, and rising there
   Like many a lake-surrounded flute,
Sounds overflow the listener's brain
So sweet, that joy is almost pain.   40

Semichorus I.

There those enchanted eddies play
   Of echoes, music-tongued, which draw,
   By Demogorgon's mighty law,
   With melting rapture, or sweet awe,
All spirits on that secret way;
   As inland boats are driven to Ocean
Down streams made strong with mountain-thaw:
     And first there comes a gentle sound
     To those in talk or slumber bound,
     And wakes the destined soft emotion,—   50
Attracts, impels them; those who saw
   Say from the breathing earth behind
   There steams a plume-uplifting wind
Which drives them on their path, while they
   Believe their own swift wings and feet
The sweet desires within obey:
And so they float upon their way,
   Until, still sweet, but loud and strong,
   The storm of sound is driven along,
     Sucked up and hurrying: as they fleet   60
     Behind, its gathering billows meet
   And to the fatal mountain bear
   Like clouds amid the yielding air.

First Faun. Canst thou imagine where those spirits live
Which make such delicate music in the woods?
We haunt within the least frequented caves
And closest coverts, and we know these wilds,
Yet never meet them, though we hear them oft:
Where may they hide themselves?
   Second Faun.   'Tis hard to tell:
I have heard those more skilled in spirits say,   70

The bubbles, which the enchantment of the sun
Sucks from the pale faint water-flowers that pave
The oozy bottom of clear lakes and pools,
Are the pavilions where such dwell and float
Under the green and golden atmosphere
Which noontide kindles through the woven leaves;
And when these burst, and the thin fiery air,
The which they breathed within those lucent domes,
Ascends to flow like meteors through the night,
They ride on them, and rein their headlong speed, 80
And bow their burning crests, and glide in fire
Under the waters of the earth again.
   First Faun. If such live thus, have others other lives,
Under pink blossoms or within the bells
Of meadow flowers, or folded violets deep,
Or on their dying odours, when they die,
Or in the sunlight of the spherèd dew?
   Second Faun. Ay, many more which we may well divine.
But, should we stay to speak, noontide would come,
And thwart Silenus find his goats undrawn, 90
And grudge to sing those wise and lovely songs
Of Fate, and Chance, and God, and Chaos old,
And Love, and the chained Titan's woful doom,
And how he shall be loosed, and make the earth
One brotherhood: delightful strains which cheer
Our solitary twilights, and which charm
To silence the unenvying nightingales.

Scene III—A Pinnacle of Rock among Mountains.
Asia and Panthea.

   Panthea. Hither the sound has borne us—to the realm
Of Demogorgon, and the mighty portal,
Like a volcano's meteor-breathing chasm,
Whence the oracular vapour is hurled up
Which lonely men drink wandering in their youth,
And call truth, virtue, love, genius, or joy,
That maddening wine of life, whose dregs they drain
To deep intoxication; and uplift,
Like Mænads who cry loud, Evoe! Evoe!
The voice which is contagion to the world. 10
   Asia. Fit throne for such a Power! Magnificent!

How glorious art thou, Earth! And if thou be
The shadow of some spirit lovelier still,
Though evil stain its work, and it should be
Like its creation, weak yet beautiful,
I could fall down and worship that and thee.
Even now my heart adoreth: Wonderful!
Look, sister, ere the vapour dim thy brain:
Beneath is a wide plain of billowy mist,
As a lake, paving in the morning sky,   20
With azure waves which burst in silver light,
Some Indian vale. Behold it, rolling on
Under the curdling winds, and islanding
The peak whereon we stand, midway, around,
Encinctured by the dark and blooming forests,
Dim twilight-lawns, and stream-illuméd caves,
And wind-enchanted shapes of wandering mist;
And far on high the keen sky-cleaving mountains
From icy spires of sun-like radiance fling
The dawn, as lifted Ocean's dazzling spray,   30
From some Atlantic islet scattered up,
Spangles the wind with lamp-like water-drops.
The vale is girdled with their walls, a howl
Of cataracts from their thaw-cloven ravines
Satiates the listening wind, continuous, vast,
Awful as silence. Hark! the rushing snow!
The sun-awakened avalanche! whose mass,
Thrice sifted by the storm, had gathered there
Flake after flake, in heaven-defying minds
As thought by thought is piled, till some great truth   40
Is loosened, and the nations echo round,
Shaken to their roots, as do the mountains now.
    Panthea. Look how the gusty sea of mist is breaking
In crimson foam, even at our feet! it rises
As Ocean at the enchantment of the moon
Round foodless men wrecked on some oozy isle.
    Asia. The fragments of the clouds are scattered up;
The wind that lifts them disentwines my hair;
Its billows now sweep o'er mine eyes; my brain
Grows dizzy; see'st thou shapes within the mist?   50
    Panthea. A countenance with beckoning smiles: there burns
An azure fire within its golden locks!
Another and another: hark! they speak!

Song of Spirits.

To the deep, to the deep,
　　　　Down, down!
Through the shade of sleep,
Through the cloudy strife
Of Death and of Life;
Through the veil and the bar
Of things which seem and are   60
Even to the steps of the remotest throne,
　　　　Down, down!

While the sound whirls around,
　　　　Down, down!
As the fawn draws the hound,
As the lightning the vapour,
As a weak moth the taper;
Death, despair; love, sorrow;
Time both; to-day, to-morrow;
As steel obeys the spirit of the stone,   70
　　　　Down, down!

Through the gray, void abysm,
　　　　Down, down!
Where the air is no prism,
And the moon and stars are not,
And the cavern-crags wear not
The radiance of Heaven,
Nor the gloom to Earth given,
Where there is One pervading, One alone,
　　　　Down, down!   80

In the depth of the deep,
　　　　Down, down!
Like veiled lightning asleep,
Like the spark nursed in embers,
The last look Love remembers,
Like a diamond, which shines
On the dark wealth of mines,
A spell is treasured but for thee alone.
　　　　Down, down!

We have bound thee, we guide thee;
       Down, down!
With the bright form beside thee;
Resist not the weakness,
Such strength is in meekness
That the Eternal, the Immortal,
Must unloose through life's portal
The snake-like Doom coiled underneath his throne
       By that alone.

SCENE IV—*The Cave of Demogorgon.* ASIA *and* PANTHEA.

Panthea. What veilèd form sits on that ebon throne?
Asia. The veil has fallen.
Panthea.   I see a mighty darkness
Filling the seat of power, and rays of gloom
Dart round, as light from the meridian sun.
Ungazed upon and shapeless; neither limb,
Nor form, nor outline; yet we feel it is
A living Spirit.
    Demogorgon. Ask what thou wouldst know.
Asia. What canst thou tell?
Demogorgon.   All things thou dar'st demand.
Asia. Who made the living world?
Demogorgon.   God.
Asia.   Who made all
That it contains? thought, passion, reason, will,   10
Imagination?
    Demogorgon. God: Almighty God.
Asia. Who made that sense which, when the winds of Spring
In rarest visitation, or the voice
Of one belovèd heard in youth alone,
Fills the faint eyes with falling tears which dim
The radiant looks of unbewailing flowers,
And leaves this peopled earth a solitude
When it returns no more?
    Demogorgon.   Merciful God.
Asia. And who made terror, madness, crime, remorse,
Which from the links of the great chain of things,   20
To every thought within the mind of man
Sway and drag heavily, and each one reels

Under the load towards the pit of death;
Abandoned hope, and love that turns to hate;
And self-contempt, bitterer to drink than blood;
Pain, whose unheeded and familiar speech
Is howling, and keen shrieks, day after day;
And Hell, or the sharp fear of Hell?
  Demogorgon.   He reigns.
  Asia. Utter his name: a world pining in pain
Asks but his name: curses shall drag him down.   30
  Demogorgon. He reigns.
  Asia.   I feel, I know it: who?
  Demogorgon.   He reigns.
  Asia. Who reigns? There was the Heaven and Earth at first,
And Light and Love; then Saturn, from whose throne
Time fell, an envious shadow: such the state
Of the earth's primal spirits beneath his sway,
As the calm joy of flowers and living leaves
Before the wind or sun has withered them
And semivital worms; but he refused
The birthright of their being, knowledge, power,
The skill which wields the elements, the thought   40
Which pierces this dim universe like light,
Self-empire, and the majesty of love;
For thirst of which they fainted. Then Prometheus
Gave wisdom, which is strength, to Jupiter,
And with this law alone, 'Let man be free,'
Clothed him with the dominion of wide Heaven.
To know nor faith, nor love, nor law; to be
Omnipotent but friendless is to reign;
And Jove now reigned; for on the race of man
First famine, and then toil, and then disease,   50
Strife, wounds, and ghastly death unseen before,
Fell; and the unseasonable seasons drove
With alternating shafts of frost and fire,
Their shelterless, pale tribes to mountain caves:
And in their desert hearts fierce wants he sent,
And mad disquietude, and shadows idle
Of unreal good, which levied mutual war,
So ruining the lair wherein they raged.
Prometheus saw, and waked the legioned hopes
Which sleep within folded Elysian flowers,   60

Nepenthe, Moly, Amaranth, fadeless blooms,
That they might hide with thin and rainbow wings
The shape of Death; and Love he sent to bind
The disunited tendrils of that vine
Which bears the wine of life, the human heart;
And he tamed fire which, like some beast of prey,
Most terrible, but lovely, played beneath
The frown of man; and tortured to his will
Iron and gold, the slaves and signs of power,
And gems and poisons, and all subtlest forms   70
Hidden beneath the mountains and the waves.
He gave man speech, and speech created thought,
Which is the measure of the universe;
And Science struck the thrones of earth and heaven,
Which shook, but fell not; and the harmonious mind
Poured itself forth in all-prophetic song;
And music lifted up the listening spirit
Until it walked, exempt from mortal care,
Godlike, o'er the clear billows of sweet sound;
And human hands first mimicked and then mocked,   80
With moulded limbs more lovely than its own,
The human form, till marble grew divine;
And mothers, gazing, drank the love men see
Reflected in their race, behold, and perish.
He told the hidden power of herbs and springs,
And Disease drank and slept. Death grew like sleep.
He taught the implicated orbits woven
Of the wide-wandering stars; and how the sun
Changes his lair, and by what secret spell
The pale moon is transformed, when her broad eye   90
Gazes not on the interlunar sea:
He taught to rule, as life directs the limbs,
The tempest-wingèd chariots of the Ocean,
And the Celt knew the Indian. Cities then
Were built, and through their snow-like columns flowed
The warm winds, and the azure aether shone,
And the blue sea and shadowy hills were seen.
Such, the alleviations of his state,
Prometheus gave to man, for which he hangs
Withering in destined pain: but who rains down   100
Evil, the immedicable plague, which, while

Man looks on his creation like a God
And sees that it is glorious, drives him on,
The wreck of his own will, the scorn of earth,
The outcast, the abandoned, the alone?
Not Jove: while yet his frown shook Heaven, ay, when
His adversary from adamantine chains
Cursed him, he trembled like a slave. Declare
Who is his master? Is he too a slave?

   Demogorgon. All spirits are enslaved which serve things evil:
Thou knowest if Jupiter be such or no.   111

   Asia. Whom calledst thou God?

   Demogorgon.   I spoke but as ye speak,
For Jove is the supreme of living things.

   Asia. Who is the master of the slave?

   Demogorgon.   If the abysm
Could vomit forth its secrets. . . . But a voice
Is wanting, the deep truth is imageless;
For what would it avail to bid thee gaze
On the revolving world? What to bid speak
Fate, Time, Occasion, Chance, and Change? To these
All things are subject but eternal Love.   120

   Asia. So much I asked before, and my heart gave
The response thou hast given; and of such truths
Each to itself must be the oracle.
One more demand; and do thou answer me
As mine own soul would answer, did it know
That which I ask. Prometheus shall arise
Henceforth the sun of this rejoicing world:
When shall the destined hour arrive?

   Demogorgon.   Behold!

   Asia. The rocks are cloven, and through the purple night
I see cars drawn by rainbow-wingèd steeds   130
Which trample the dim winds: in each there stands
A wild-eyed charioteer urging their flight.
Some look behind, as fiends pursued them there,
And yet I see no shapes but the keen stars:
Others, with burning eyes, lean forth, and drink
With eager lips the wind of their own speed,
As if the thing they loved fled on before,
And now, even now, they clasped it. Their bright locks
Stream like a comet's flashing hair: they all

Sweep onward.

 Demogorgon. These are the immortal Hours,   140
Of whom thou didst demand. One waits for thee.

 Asia. A spirit with a dreadful countenance
Checks its dark chariot by the craggy gulf.
Unlike thy brethren, ghastly charioteer,
Who art thou? Whither wouldst thou bear me? Speak!

 Spirit. I am the shadow of a destiny
More dread than is my aspect: ere yon planet
Has set, the darkness which ascends with me
Shall wrap in lasting night heaven's kingless throne.

 Asia. What meanest thou?

 Panthea.   That terrible shadow floats 150
Up from its throne, as may the lurid smoke
Of earthquake-ruined cities o'er the sea.
Lo! it ascends the car; the coursers fly
Terrified: watch its path among the stars
Blackening the night!

 Asia.   Thus I am answered: strange!

 Panthea. See, near the verge, another chariot stays;
An ivory shell inlaid with crimson fire,
Which comes and goes within its sculptured rim
Of delicate strange tracery; the young spirit
That guides it has the dove-like eyes of hope; 160
How its soft smiles attract the soul! as light
Lures wingèd insects through the lampless air.

Spirit.

  My coursers are fed with the lightning,
   They drink of the whirlwind's stream,
  And when the red morning is bright'ning
   They bathe in the fresh sunbeam;
   They have strength for their swiftness I deem,
  Then ascend with me, daughter of Ocean.

  I desire: and their speed makes night kindle;
   I fear: they outstrip the Typhoon; 170
  Ere the cloud piled on Atlas can dwindle
   We encircle the earth and the moon:
   We shall rest from long labours at noon:
  Then ascend with me, daughter of Ocean.

SCENE V—*The Car pauses within a Cloud on the top of a snowy Mountain.* ASIA, PANTHEA, *and the* SPIRIT OF THE HOUR.

Spirit.

On the brink of the night and the morning
    My coursers are wont to respire;
But the Earth has just whispered a warning
    That their flight must be swifter than fire:
    They shall drink the hot speed of desire!

Asia. Thou breathest on their nostrils, but my breath
Would give them swifter speed.
    Spirit.   Alas! it could not.
    Panthea. Oh Spirit! pause, and tell whence is the light
Which fills this cloud? the sun is yet unrisen.
    Spirit. The sun will rise not until noon. Apollo   10
Is held in heaven by wonder; and the light
Which fills this vapour, as the aëreal hue
Of fountain-gazing roses fills the water,
Flows from thy mighty sister.
    Panthea.   Yes, I feel—
    Asia. What is it with thee, sister? Thou art pale.
    Panthea. How thou art changed! I dare not look on thee;
I feel but see thee not. I scarce endure
The radiance of thy beauty. Some good change
Is working in the elements, which suffer
Thy presence thus unveiled. The Nereids tell   20
That on the day when the clear hyaline
Was cloven at thine uprise, and thou didst stand
Within a veinèd shell, which floated on
Over the calm floor of the crystal sea,
Among the Ægean isles, and by the shores
Which bear thy name; love, like the atmosphere
Of the sun's fire filling the living world,
Burst from thee, and illumined earth and heaven
And the deep ocean and the sunless caves
And all that dwells within them; till grief cast   30
Eclipse upon the soul from which it came:
Such art thou now; nor is it I alone,
Thy sister, thy companion, thine own chosen one,

But the whole world which seeks thy sympathy.
Hearest thou not sounds i' the air which speak the love
Of all articulate beings? Feelest thou not
The inanimate winds enamoured of thee? List!   [*Music.*

   Asia. Thy words are sweeter than aught else but his
Whose echoes they are: yet all love is sweet,
Given or returned. Common as light is love,   40
And its familiar voice wearies not ever.
Like the wide heaven, the all-sustaining air,
It makes the reptile equal to the God:
They who inspire it most are fortunate,
As I am now; but those who feel it most
Are happier still, after long sufferings,
As I shall soon become.
   Panthea.   List! Spirits speak.

       Voices in the Air, singing.

   Life of Life! thy lips enkindle
     With their love the breath between them;
   And thy smiles before they dwindle   50
     Make the cold air fire; then screen them
   In those looks, where whoso gazes
   Faints, entangled in their mazes.

   Child of Light! thy limbs are burning
     Through the vest which seems to hide them;
   As the radiant lines of morning
     Through the clouds ere they divide them;
   And this atmosphere divinest
   Shrouds thee wheresoe'er thou shinest.

   Fair are others; none beholds thee,   60
     But thy voice sounds low and tender
   Like the fairest, for it folds thee
     From the sight, that liquid splendour,
   And all feel, yet see thee never,
   As I feel now, lost for ever!

   Lamp of Earth! where'er thou movest
     Its dim shapes are clad with brightness,
   And the souls of whom thou lovest

Walk upon the winds with lightness,
Till they fail, as I am failing,   70
Dizzy, lost, yet unbewailing!

Asia.

My soul is an enchanted boat,
  Which, like a sleeping swan, doth float
Upon the silver waves of thy sweet singing;
  And thine doth like an angel sit
  Beside a helm conducting it,
Whilst all the winds with melody are ringing.
  It seems to float ever, for ever,
  Upon that many-winding river,
  Between mountains, woods, abysses,   80
  A paradise of wildernesses!
Till, like one in slumber bound,
Borne to the ocean, I float down, around,
Into a sea profound, of ever-spreading sound:

  Meanwhile thy spirit lifts its pinions
  In music's most serene dominions;
Catching the winds that fan that happy heaven.
  And we sail on, away, afar,
  Without a course, without a star,
But, by the instinct of sweet music driven;   90
  Till through Elysian garden islets
  By thee, most beautiful of pilots,
  Where never mortal pinnace glided,
  The boat of my desire is guided:
Realms where the air we breathe is love,
Which in the winds and on the waves doth move,
Harmonizing this earth with what we feel above.

  We have passed Age's icy caves,
  And Manhood's dark and tossing waves,
And Youth's smooth ocean, smiling to betray: 100
  Beyond the glassy gulfs we flee
  Of shadow-peopled Infancy,
Through Death and Birth, to a diviner day;
  A paradise of vaulted bowers,
  Lit by downward-gazing flowers,

 And watery paths that wind between
  Wildernesses calm and green,
 Peopled by shapes too bright to see,
 And rest, having beheld; somewhat like thee;
 Which walk upon the sea, and chant melodiously!   110

END OF THE SECOND ACT.

ACT III

SCENE I—*Heaven.* JUPITER *on his Throne;* THETIS *and the other*
      Deities assembled.

 Jupiter. Ye congregated powers of heaven, who share
The glory and the strength of him ye serve,
Rejoice! henceforth I am omnipotent.
All else had been subdued to me; alone
The soul of man, like unextinguished fire,
Yet burns towards heaven with fierce reproach, and doubt,
And lamentation, and reluctant prayer,
Hurling up insurrection, which might make
Our antique empire insecure, though built
On eldest faith, and hell's coeval, fear;   10
And though my curses through the pendulous air,
Like snow on herbless peaks, fall flake by flake,
And cling to it; though under my wrath's night
It climbs the crags of life, step after step,
Which wound it, as ice wounds unsandalled feet,
It yet remains supreme o'er misery,
Aspiring, unrepressed, yet soon to fall:
Even now have I begotten a strange wonder,
That fatal child, the terror of the earth,
Who waits but till the destined hour arrive,   20
Bearing from Demogorgon's vacant throne
The dreadful might of ever-living limbs
Which clothed that awful spirit unbeheld,
To redescend, and trample out the spark.

Pour forth heaven's wine, Idæan Ganymede,
And let it fill the Dædal cups like fire,
And from the flower-inwoven soil divine

Ye all-triumphant harmonies arise,
As dew from earth under the twilight stars:
Drink! be the nectar circling through your veins 30
The soul of joy, ye ever-living Gods,
Till exultation burst in one wide voice
Like music from Elysian winds.
                          And thou
Ascend beside me, veilèd in the light
Of the desire which makes thee one with me,
Thetis, bright image of eternity!
When thou didst cry, 'Insufferable might!
God! Spare me! I sustain not the quick flames,
The penetrating presence; all my being,
Like him whom the Numidian seps did thaw 40
Into a dew with poison, is dissolved,
Sinking through its foundations:' even then
Two mighty spirits, mingling, made a third
Mightier than either, which, unbodied now,
Between us floats, felt, although unbeheld,
Waiting the incarnation, which ascends
(Hear ye the thunder of the fiery wheels
Griding the winds?) from Demogorgon's throne.
Victory! victory! Feel'st thou not, O world,
The earthquake of his chariot thundering up 50
Olympus?

    [*The Car of the* HOUR *arrives.* DEMOGORGON *descends,
        and moves towards the Throne of* JUPITER.

      Awful shape, what art thou? Speak!
  Demogorgon. Eternity. Demand no direr name.
Descend, and follow me down the abyss.
I am thy child, as thou wert Saturn's child;
Mightier than thee: and we must dwell together
Henceforth in darkness. Lift thy lightnings not.
The tyranny of heaven none may retain,
Or reassume, or hold, succeeding thee:
Yet if thou wilt, as 'tis the destiny
Of trodden worms to writhe till they are dead, 60
Put forth thy might.
  Jupiter.   Detested prodigy!
Even thus beneath the deep Titanian prisons

I trample thee! thou lingerest?

                       Mercy! mercy!
No pity, no release, no respite! Oh,
That thou wouldst make mine enemy my judge,
Even where he hangs, seared by my long revenge,
On Caucasus! he would not doom me thus.
Gentle, and just, and dreadless, is he not
The monarch of the world? What then art thou?
No refuge! no appeal!

                    Sink with me then,   70
We two will sink on the wide waves of ruin,
Even as a vulture and a snake outspent
Drop, twisted in inextricable fight,
Into a shoreless sea. Let hell unlock
Its mounded oceans of tempestuous fire,
And whelm on them into the bottomless void
This desolated world, and thee, and me,
The conqueror and the conquered, and the wreck
Of that for which they combated.

                         Ai! Ai!

The elements obey me not. I sink   80
Dizzily down, ever, for ever, down.
And, like a cloud, mine enemy above
Darkens my fall with victory! Ai, Ai!

Scene II—*The Mouth of a great River in the Island Atlantis.*
Ocean *is discovered reclining near the Shore;* Apollo *stands beside him.*

   Ocean. He fell, thou sayest, beneath his conqueror's frown?
   Apollo. Ay, when the strife was ended which made dim
The orb I rule, and shook the solid stars,
The terrors of his eye illumined heaven
With sanguine light, through the thick ragged skirts
Of the victorious darkness, as he fell:
Like the last glare of day's red agony,
Which, from a rent among the fiery clouds,
Burns far along the tempest-wrinkled deep.
   Ocean. He sunk to the abyss? To the dark void?   10
   Apollo. An eagle so caught in some bursting cloud
On Caucasus, his thunder-baffled wings

Entangled in the whirlwind, and his eyes
Which gazed on the undazzling sun, now blinded
By the white lightning, while the ponderous hail
Beats on his struggling form, which sinks at length
Prone, and the aëreal ice clings over it.

   Ocean. Henceforth the fields of heaven-reflecting sea
Which are my realm, will heave, unstained with blood,
Beneath the uplifting winds, like plains of corn   **20**
Swayed by the summer air; my streams will flow
Round many-peopled continents, and round
Fortunate isles; and from their glassy thrones
Blue Proteus and his humid nymphs shall mark
The shadow of fair ships, as mortals see
The floating bark of the light-laden moon
With that white star, its sightless pilot's crest,
Borne down the rapid sunset's ebbing sea;
Tracking their path no more by blood and groans,
And desolation, and the mingled voice   **30**
Of slavery and command; but by the light
Of wave-reflected flowers, and floating odours,
And music soft, and mild, free, gentle voices,
That sweetest music, such as spirits love.

   Apollo. And I shall gaze not on the deeds which make
My mind obscure with sorrow, as eclipse
Darkens the sphere I guide; but list, I hear
The small, clear, silver lute of the young Spirit
That sits i' the morning star.

   Ocean.   Thou must away;
Thy steeds will pause at even, till when farewell: **40**
The loud deep calls me home even now to feed it
With azure calm out of the emerald urns
Which stand for ever full beside my throne.
Behold the Nereids under the green sea,
Their wavering limbs borne on the wind-like stream,
Their white arms lifted o'er their streaming hair
With garlands pied and starry sea-flower crowns,
Hastening to grace their mighty sister's joy.

                          [*A sound of waves is heard.*
It is the unpastured sea hungering for calm.
Peace, Monster; I come now. Farewell.

   Apollo.   Farewell.   **50**

SCENE III —*Caucasus*. PROMETHEUS, HERCULES, IONE, *the* EARTH,
SPIRITS, ASIA, *and* PANTHEA, *borne in the Car with the* SPIRIT
OF THE HOUR. HERCULES *unbinds* PROMETHEUS, *who descends*.

Hercules. Most glorious among Spirits, thus doth strength
To wisdom, courage, and long-suffering love,
And thee, who art the form they animate,
Minister like a slave.
    Prometheus.   Thy gentle words
Are sweeter even than freedom long desired
And long delayed.
               Asia, thou light of life,
Shadow of beauty unbeheld: and ye,
Fair sister nymphs, who made long years of pain
Sweet to remember, through your love and care:
Henceforth we will not part. There is a cave,   10
All overgrown with trailing odorous plants,
Which curtain out the day with leaves and flowers,
And paved with veinèd emerald, and a fountain
Leaps in the midst with an awakening sound.
From its curved roof the mountain's frozen tears
Like snow, or silver, or long diamond spires,
Hang downward, raining forth a doubtful light:
And there is heard the ever-moving air,
Whispering without from tree to tree, and birds,
And bees; and all around are mossy seats,   20
And the rough walls are clothed with long soft grass;
A simple dwelling, which shall be our own:
Where we will sit and talk of time and change,
As the world ebbs and flows, ourselves unchanged.
What can hide man from mutability?
And if ye sigh, then I will smile; and thou,
Ione, shalt chant fragments of sea-music,
Until I weep, when ye shall smile away
The tears she brought, which yet were sweet to shed.
We will entangle buds and flowers and beams   30
Which twinkle on the fountain's brim, and make
Strange combinations out of common things,
Like human babes in their brief innocence;
And we will search, with looks and words of love,
For hidden thoughts, each lovelier than the last,

Our unexhausted spirits; and like lutes
Touched by the skill of the enamoured wind,
Weave harmonies divine, yet ever new,
From difference sweet where discord cannot be;
And hither come, sped on the charmèd winds,   40
Which meet from all the points of heaven, as bees
From every flower aëreal Enna feeds,
At their known island-homes in Himera,
The echoes of the human world, which tell
Of the low voice of love, almost unheard,
And dove-eyed pity's murmured pain, and music,
Itself the echo of the heart, and all
That tempers or improves man's life, now free;
And lovely apparitions,—dim at first,
Then radiant, as the mind, arising bright   50
From the embrace of beauty (whence the forms
Of which these are the phantoms) casts on them
The gathered rays which are reality—
Shall visit us, the progeny immortal
Of Painting, Sculpture, and rapt Poesy,
And arts, though unimagined, yet to be.
The wandering voices and the shadows these
Of all that man becomes, the mediators
Of that best worship love, by him and us
Given and returned; swift shapes and sounds, which grow   60
More fair and soft as man grows wise and kind,
And, veil by veil, evil and error fall:
Such virtue has the cave and place around.

[*Turning to the* SPIRIT OF THE HOUR.

For thee, fair Spirit, one toil remains. Ione,
Give her that curvèd shell, which Proteus old
Made Asia's nuptial boon, breathing within it
A voice to be accomplished, and which thou
Didst hide in grass under the hollow rock.

Ione. Thou most desired Hour, more loved and lovely
Than all thy sisters, this is the mystic shell;   70
See the pale azure fading into silver
Lining it with a soft yet glowing light:
Looks it not like lulled music sleeping there?

Spirit. It seems in truth the fairest shell of Ocean:
Its sound must be at once both sweet and strange.

Prometheus. Go, borne over the cities of mankind

On whirlwind-footed coursers: once again
Outspeed the sun around the orbèd world;
And as thy chariot cleaves the kindling air,
Thou breathe into the many-folded shell,   80
Loosening its mighty music; it shall be
As thunder mingled with clear echoes: then
Return; and thou shalt dwell beside our cave.

And thou, O, Mother Earth!—
   The Earth.   I hear, I feel;
Thy lips are on me, and their touch runs down
Even to the adamantine central gloom
Along these marble nerves; 'tis life, 'tis joy,
And through my withered, old, and icy frame
The warmth of an immortal youth shoots down
Circling. Henceforth the many children fair   90
Folded in my sustaining arms; all plants,
And creeping forms, and insects rainbow-winged,
And birds, and beasts, and fish, and human shapes,
Which drew disease and pain from my wan bosom,
Draining the poison of despair, shall take
And interchange sweet nutriment; to me
Shall they become like sister-antelopes
By one fair dam, snow-white and swift as wind,
Nursed among lilies near a brimming stream.
The dew-mists of my sunless sleep shall float   100
Under the stars like balm: night-folded flowers
Shall suck unwithering hues in their repose:
And men and beasts in happy dreams shall gather
Strength for the coming day, and all its joy:
And death shall be the last embrace of her
Who takes the life she gave, even as a mother
Folding her child, says, 'Leave me not again.'
   Asia. Oh, mother! wherefore speak the name of death?
Cease they to love, and move, and breathe, and speak,
Who die?
   The Earth. It would avail not to reply: 110
Thou art immortal, and this tongue is known
But to the uncommunicating dead.
Death is the veil which those who live call life:
They sleep, and it is lifted: and meanwhile
In mild variety the seasons mild

With rainbow-skirted showers, and odorous winds,
And long blue meteors cleansing the dull night,
And the life-kindling shafts of the keen sun's
All-piercing bow, and the dew-mingled rain
Of the calm moonbeams, a soft influence mild,   120
Shall clothe the forests and the fields, ay, even
The crag-built deserts of the barren deep,
With ever-living leaves, and fruits, and flowers.
And thou! There is a cavern where my spirit
Was panted forth in anguish whilst thy pain
Made my heart mad, and those who did inhale it
Became mad too, and built a temple there,
And spoke, and were oracular, and lured
The erring nations round to mutual war,
And faithless faith, such as Jove kept with thee;   130
Which breath now rises, as amongst tall weeds
A violet's exhalation, and it fills
With a serener light and crimson air
Intense, yet soft, the rocks and woods around;
It feeds the quick growth of the serpent vine,
And the dark linkèd ivy tangling wild,
And budding, blown, or odour-faded blooms
Which star the winds with points of coloured light,
As they rain through them, and bright golden globes
Of fruit, suspended in their own green heaven,   140
And through their veinèd leaves and amber stems
The flowers whose purple and translucid bowls
Stand ever mantling with aëreal dew,
The drink of spirits: and it circles round,
Like the soft waving wings of noonday dreams,
Inspiring calm and happy thoughts, like mine,
Now thou art thus restored. This cave is thine.
Arise! Appear!
                    [A SPIRIT *rises in the likeness of a winged child.*
                 This is my torch-bearer;
Who let his lamp out in old time with gazing
On eyes from which he kindled it anew   150
With love, which is as fire, sweet daughter mine,
For such is that within thine own. Run, wayward,
And guide this company beyond the peak
Of Bacchic Nysa, Mænad-haunted mountain,
And beyond Indus and its tribute rivers,

Trampling the torrent streams and glassy lakes
With feet unwet, unwearied, undelaying,
And up the green ravine, across the vale,
Beside the windless and crystalline pool,
Where ever lies, on unerasing waves,   160
The image of a temple, built above,
Distinct with column, arch, and architrave,
And palm-like capital, and over-wrought,
And populous with most living imagery,
Praxitelean shapes, whose marble smiles
Fill the hushed air with everlasting love.
It is deserted now, but once it bore
Thy name, Prometheus; there the emulous youths
Bore to thy honour through the divine gloom
The lamp which was thine emblem; even as those   170
Who bear the untransmitted torch of hope
Into the grave, across the night of life,
As thou hast borne it most triumphantly
To this far goal of Time. Depart, farewell.
Beside that temple is the destined cave.

SCENE IV—*A Forest. In the Background a Cave.* PROMETHEUS,
    ASIA, PANTHEA, IONE, *and the* SPIRIT OF THE EARTH.

  Ione. Sister, it is not earthly: how it glides
Under the leaves! how on its head there burns
A light, like a green star, whose emerald beams
Are twined with its fair hair! how, as it moves,
The splendour drops in flakes upon the grass!
Knowest thou it?
  Panthea.   It is the delicate spirit
That guides the earth through heaven. From afar
The populous constellations call that light
The loveliest of the planets; and sometimes
It floats along the spray of the salt sea,   10
Or makes its chariot of a foggy cloud,
Or walks through fields or cities while men sleep,
Or o'er the mountain tops, or down the rivers,
Or through the green waste wilderness, as now,
Wondering at all it sees. Before Jove reigned
It loved our sister Asia, and it came
Each leisure hour to drink the liquid light

Out of her eyes, for which it said it thirsted
As one bit by a dipsas, and with her
It made its childish confidence, and told her   20
All it had known or seen, for it saw much,
Yet idly reasoned what it saw; and called her—
For whence it sprung it knew not, nor do I—
Mother, dear mother.

    The Spirit of the Earth (*running to Asia*). Mother, dearest
        mother;
May I then talk with thee as I was wont?
May I then hide my eyes in thy soft arms,
After thy looks have made them tired of joy?
May I then play beside thee the long noons,
When work is none in the bright silent air?

    Asia. I love thee, gentlest being, and henceforth   30
Can cherish thee unenvied: speak, I pray:
Thy simple talk once solaced, now delights.

    Spirit of the Earth. Mother, I am grown wiser, though a child
Cannot be wise like thee, within this day;
And happier too; happier and wiser both.
Thou knowest that toads, and snakes, and loathly worms,
And venomous and malicious beasts, and boughs
That bore ill berries in the woods, were ever
An hindrance to my walks o'er the green world:
And that, among the haunts of humankind,   40
Hard-featured men, or with proud, angry looks,
Or cold, staid gait, or false and hollow smiles,
Or the dull sneer of self-loved ignorance,
Or other such foul masks, with which ill thoughts
Hide that fair being whom we spirits call man;
And women too, ugliest of all things evil,
(Though fair, even in a world where thou art fair,
When good and kind, free and sincere like thee),
When false or frowning made me sick at heart
To pass them, though they slept, and I unseen.   50
Well, my path lately lay through a great city
Into the woody hills surrounding it:
A sentinel was sleeping at the gate:
When there was heard a sound, so loud, it shook
The towers amid the moonlight, yet more sweet
Than any voice but thine, sweetest of all;
A long, long sound, as it would never end:

And all the inhabitants leaped suddenly
Out of their rest, and gathered in the streets,
Looking in wonder up to Heaven, while yet   60
The music pealed along. I hid myself
Within a fountain in the public square,
Where I lay like the reflex of the moon
Seen in a wave under green leaves; and soon
Those ugly human shapes and visages
Of which I spoke as having wrought me pain,
Passed floating through the air, and fading still
Into the winds that scattered them; and those
From whom they passed seemed mild and lovely forms
After some foul disguise had fallen, and all   70
Were somewhat changed, and after brief surprise
And greetings of delighted wonder, all
Went to their sleep again: and when the dawn
Came, wouldst thou think that toads, and snakes, and efts,
Could e'er be beautiful? yet so they were,
And that with little change of shape or hue:
All things had put their evil nature off:
I cannot tell my joy, when o'er a lake
Upon a drooping bough with nightshade twined,
I saw two azure halcyons clinging downward   80
And thinning one bright bunch of amber berries,
With quick long beaks, and in the deep there lay
Those lovely forms imaged as in a sky;
So, with my thoughts full of these happy changes,
We meet again, the happiest change of all.
   Asia. And never will we part, till thy chaste sister
Who guides the frozen and inconstant moon
Will look on thy more warm and equal light
Till her heart thaw like flakes of April snow
And love thee.
   Spirit of the Earth. What! as Asia loves Prometheus?   90
   Asia. Peace, wanton, thou art yet not old enough.
Think ye by gazing on each other's eyes
To multiply your lovely selves, and fill
With spherèd fires the interlunar air?
   Spirit of the Earth. Nay, mother, while my sister trims her lamp
'Tis hard I should go darkling.
   Asia.   Listen; look!
                    [*The* SPIRIT OF THE HOUR *enters.*

Prometheus. We feel what thou hast heard and seen: yet speak.
Spirit of the Hour. Soon as the sound had ceased whose
    thunder filled
The abysses of the sky and the wide earth,
There was a change: the impalpable thin air   100
And the all-circling sunlight were transformed,
As if the sense of love dissolved in them
Had folded itself round the spherèd world.
My vision then grew clear, and I could see
Into the mysteries of the universe:
Dizzy as with delight I floated down,
Winnowing the lightsome air with languid plumes,
My coursers sought their birthplace in the sun,
Where they henceforth will live exempt from toil,
Pasturing flowers of vegetable fire;   110
And where my moonlike car will stand within
A temple, gazed upon by Phidian forms
Of thee, and Asia, and the Earth, and me,
And you fair nymphs looking the love we feel,—
In memory of the tidings it has borne,—
Beneath a dome fretted with graven flowers,
Poised on twelve columns of resplendent stone,
And open to the bright and liquid sky.
Yoked to it by an amphisbaenic snake
The likeness of those wingèd steeds will mock   120
The flight from which they find repose. Alas,
Whither has wandered now my partial tongue
When all remains untold which ye would hear?
As I have said, I floated to the earth:
It was, as it is still, the pain of bliss
To move, to breathe, to be; I wandering went
Among the haunts and dwellings of mankind,
And first was disappointed not to see
Such mighty change as I had felt within
Expressed in outward things; but soon I looked,   130
And behold, thrones were kingless, and men walked
One with the other even as spirits do,
None fawned, none trampled; hate, disdain, or fear,
Self-love or self-contempt, on human brows
No more inscribed, as o'er the gate of hell,
'All hope abandon ye who enter here;'
None frowned, none trembled, none with eager fear

Gazed on another's eye of cold command,
Until the subject of a tyrant's will
Became, worse fate, the abject of his own,   140
Which spurred him, like an outspent horse, to death.
None wrought his lips in truth-entangling lines
Which smiled the lie his tongue disdained to speak;
None, with firm sneer, trod out in his own heart
The sparks of love and hope till there remained
Those bitter ashes, a soul self-consumed,
And the wretch crept a vampire among men,
Infecting all with his own hideous ill;
None talked that common, false, cold, hollow talk
Which makes the heart deny the *yes* it breathes,   150
Yet question that unmeant hypocrisy
With such a self-mistrust as has no name.
And women, too, frank, beautiful, and kind
As the free heaven which rains fresh light and dew
On the wide earth, past; gentle radiant forms,
From custom's evil taint exempt and pure;
Speaking the wisdom once they could not think,
Looking emotions once they feared to feel,
And changed to all which once they dared not be,
Yet being now, made earth like heaven; nor pride,   160
Nor jealousy, nor envy, nor ill shame,
The bitterest of those drops of treasured gall,
Spoilt the sweet taste of the nepenthe, love.

Thrones, altars, judgment-seats, and prisons; wherein,
And beside which, by wretched men were borne
Sceptres, tiaras, swords, and chains, and tomes
Of reasoned wrong, glozed on by ignorance,
Were like those monstrous and barbaric shapes,
The ghosts of a no-more-remembered fame,
Which, from their unworn obelisks, look forth   170
In triumph o'er the palaces and tombs
Of those who were their conquerors: mouldering round,
These imaged to the pride of kings and priests
A dark yet mighty faith, a power as wide
As is the world it wasted, and are now
But an astonishment; even so the tools
And emblems of its last captivity,

Amid the dwellings of the peopled earth,
Stand, not o'erthrown, but unregarded now.
And those foul shapes, abhorred by god and man,—   180
Which, under many a name and many a form
Strange, savage, ghastly, dark and execrable,
Were Jupiter, the tyrant of the world;
And which the nations, panic-stricken, served
With blood, and hearts broken by long hope, and love
Dragged to his altars soiled and garlandless,
And slain amid men's unreclaiming tears,
Flattering the thing they feared, which fear was hate,—
Frown, mouldering fast, o'er their abandoned shrines:
The painted veil, by those who were, called life,   190
Which mimicked, as with colours idly spread,
All men believed or hoped, is torn aside;
The loathsome mask has fallen, the man remains
Sceptreless, free, uncircumscribed, but man
Equal, unclassed, tribeless, and nationless,
Exempt from awe, worship, degree, the king
Over himself; just, gentle, wise: but man
Passionless?——no, yet free from guilt or pain,
Which were, for his will made or suffered them,
Nor yet exempt, though ruling them like slaves,   200
From chance, and death, and mutability,
The clogs of that which else might oversoar
The loftiest star of unascended heaven,
Pinnacled dim in the intense inane.

END OF THE THIRD ACT.

ACT IV

SCENE—*A Part of the Forest near the Cave of* PROMETHEUS. PAN-
THEA *and* IONE *are sleeping: they awaken gradually during the
first Song.*

Voice of unseen Spirits.

The pale stars are gone!
For the sun, their swift shepherd,

To their folds them compelling,
In the depths of the dawn,
Hastes, in meteor-eclipsing array, and they flee
Beyond his blue dwelling,
As fawns flee the leopard.
But where are ye?

A Train of dark Forms and Shadows passes by confusedly, singing.

Here, oh, here:
We bear the bier   10
Of the Father of many a cancelled year
Spectres we
Of the dead Hours be,
We bear Time to his tomb in eternity.

Strew, oh, strew
Hair, not yew!
Wet the dusty pall with tears, not dew!
Be the faded flowers
Of Death's bare bowers
Spread on the corpse of the King of Hours!   20

Haste, oh, haste!
As shades are chased,
Trembling, by day, from heaven's blue waste.
We melt away,
Like dissolving spray,
From the children of a diviner day,
With the lullaby
Of winds that die
On the bosom of their own harmony!

Ione.

What dark forms were they?   30

Panthea.

The past Hours weak and gray,
With the spoil which their toil
Raked together
From the conquest but One could foil.

Ione.

Have they passed?

Panthea.

They have passed;
They outspeeded the blast,
While 'tis said, they are fled:

Ione.

Whither, oh, whither?

Panthea.

To the dark, to the past, to the dead.

Voice of unseen Spirits.

Bright clouds float in heaven,   40
Dew-stars gleam on earth,
Waves assemble on ocean,
They are gathered and driven
By the storm of delight, by the panic of glee!
They shake with emotion,
They dance in their mirth.
    But where are ye?

The pine boughs are singing
Old songs with new gladness,
The billows and fountains   50
Fresh music are flinging,
Like the notes of a spirit from land and from sea;
The storms mock the mountains
With the thunder of gladness.
    But where are ye?

Ione. What charioteers are these?
Panthea.   Where are their chariots?

Semichorus of Hours.

The voice of the Spirits of Air and of Earth
  Have drawn back the figured curtain of sleep
Which covered our being and darkened our birth
  In the deep.

A Voice.

    In the deep?

Semichorus II.

        Oh, below the deep.   60

Semichorus I.

An hundred ages we had been kept
  Cradled in visions of hate and care,
And each one who waked as his brother slept,
  Found the truth—

Semichorus II.

    Worse than his visions were!

Semichorus I.

We have heard the lute of Hope in sleep;
  We have known the voice of Love in dreams;
We have felt the wand of Power, and leap—

Semichorus II.

  As the billows leap in the morning beams!

Chorus.

Weave the dance on the floor of the breeze,
  Pierce with song heaven's silent light,
Enchant the day that too swiftly flees,   70
  To check its flight ere the cave of Night.

Once the hungry Hours were hounds
   Which chased the day like a bleeding deer,
And it limped and stumbled with many wounds
   Through the nightly dells of the desert year.

But now, oh weave the mystic measure
   Of music, and dance, and shapes of light,
Let the Hours, and the spirits of might and pleasure,
   Like the clouds and sunbeams, unite.

A Voice.

                 Unite!   80

Panthea. See, where the Spirits of the human mind
Wrapped in sweet sounds, as in bright veils, approach.

Chorus of Spirits.

   We join the throng
   Of the dance and the song,
By the whirlwind of gladness borne along;
    As the flying-fish leap
    From the Indian deep,
And mix with the sea-birds, half asleep.

Chorus of Hours.

Whence come ye, so wild and so fleet,
For sandals of lightning are on your feet,   90
And your wings are soft and swift as thought,
And your eyes are as love which is veilèd not?

Chorus of Spirits.

   We come from the mind
   Of human kind
Which was late so dusk, and obscene, and blind,
    Now 'tis an ocean
    Of clear emotion,
A heaven of serene and mighty motion.

    From that deep abyss
    Of wonder and bliss,   100

Whose caverns are crystal palaces;
    From those skiey towers
    Where Thought's crowned powers
Sit watching your dance, ye happy Hours!

    From the dim recesses
    Of woven caresses,
Where lovers catch ye by your loose tresses;
    From the azure isles,
    Where sweet Wisdom smiles,
Delaying your ships with her siren wiles.   110

    From the temples high
    Of Man's ear and eye,
Roofed over Sculpture and Poesy;
    From the murmurings
    Of the unsealed springs
Where Science bedews her Dædal wings.

    Years after years,
    Through blood, and tears,
And a thick hell of hatreds, and hopes, and fears;
    We waded and flew,   120
    And the islets were few
Where the bud-blighted flowers of happiness grew.

    Our feet now, every palm,
    Are sandalled with calm,
And the dew of our wings is a rain of balm;
    And, beyond our eyes,
    The human love lies
Which makes all it gazes on Paradise.

Chorus of Spirits and Hours.

    Then weave the web of the mystic measure;
From the depths of the sky and the ends of the earth,   130
    Come, swift Spirits of might and of pleasure,
Fill the dance and the music of mirth,
    As the waves of a thousand streams rush by
    To an ocean of splendour and harmony!

Chorus of Spirits.

Our spoil is won,
Our task is done,
We are free to dive, or soar, or run;
Beyond and around,
Or within the bound
Which clips the world with darkness round.   140

We'll pass the eyes
Of the starry skies
Into the hoar deep to colonize;
Death, Chaos, and Night,
From the sound of our flight,
Shall flee, like mist from a tempest's might.

And Earth, Air, and Light,
And the Spirit of Might,
Which drives round the stars in their fiery flight;
And Love, Thought, and Breath,   150
The powers that quell Death,
Wherever we soar shall assemble beneath.

And our singing shall build
In the void's loose field
A world for the Spirit of Wisdom to wield;
We will take our plan
From the new world of man,
And our work shall be called the Promethean.

Chorus of Hours.

Break the dance, and scatter the song;
Let some depart, and some remain.   160

Semichorus I.

We, beyond heaven, are driven along:

Semichorus II.

Us the enchantments of earth retain:

Semichorus I.

Ceaseless, and rapid, and fierce, and free,
With the Spirits which build a new earth and sea,
And a heaven where yet heaven could never be.

Semichorus II.

Solemn, and slow, and serene, and bright,
Leading the Day and outspeeding the Night,
With the powers of a world of perfect light.

Semichorus I.

We whirl, singing loud, round the gathering sphere,
Till the trees, and the beasts, and the clouds appear   170
From its chaos made calm by love, not fear.

Semichorus II.

We encircle the ocean and mountains of earth,
And the happy forms of its death and birth
Change to the music of our sweet mirth.

Chorus of Hours and Spirits.

Break the dance, and scatter the song,
    Let some depart, and some remain,
Wherever we fly we lead along
In leashes, like starbeams, soft yet strong,
    The clouds that are heavy with love's sweet rain.

Panthea. Ha! they are gone!
Ione.   Yet feel you no delight   180
From the past sweetness?
    Panthea.   As the bare green hill
When some soft cloud vanishes into rain,
Laughs with a thousand drops of sunny water
To the unpavilioned sky!
    Ione.   Even whilst we speak
New notes arise. What is that awful sound?

Panthea. 'Tis the deep music of the rolling world
Kindling within the strings of the waved air
Æolian modulation.
    Ione.   Listen too,
How every pause is filled with under-notes,
Clear, silver, icy, keen, awakening tones,   190
Which pierce the sense, and live within the soul,
As the sharp stars pierce winter's crystal air
And gaze upon themselves within the sea.
    Panthea. But see where through two openings in the forest
Which hanging branches overcanopy,
And where two runnels of a rivulet,
Between the close moss violet-inwoven,
Have made their path of melody, like sisters
Who part with sighs that they may meet in smiles,
Turning their dear disunion to an isle   200
Of lovely grief, a wood of sweet sad thoughts;
Two visions of strange radiance float upon
The ocean-like enchantment of strong sound,
Which flows intenser, keener, deeper yet
Under the ground and through the windless air.
    Ione. I see a chariot like that thinnest boat,
In which the Mother of the Months is borne
By ebbing light into her western cave
When she upsprings from interlunar dreams;
O'er which is curved an orblike canopy   210
Of gentle darkness, and the hills and woods,
Distinctly seen through that dusk aëry veil,
Regard like shapes in an enchanter's glass;
Its wheels are solid clouds, azure and gold,
Such as the genii of the thunderstorm
Pile on the floor of the illumined sea
When the sun rushes under it; they roll
And move and grow as with an inward wind;
Within it sits a wingèd infant, white
Its countenance, like the whiteness of bright snow,   220
Its plumes are as feathers of sunny frost,
Its limbs gleam white, through the wind-flowing folds
Of its white robe, woof of ethereal pearl.
Its hair is white, the brightness of white light
Scattered in strings; yet its two eyes are heavens
Of liquid darkness, which the Deity

Within seems pouring, as a storm is poured
From jaggèd clouds, out of their arrowy lashes,
Tempering the cold and radiant air around,
With fire that is not brightness; in its hand   230
It sways a quivering moonbeam, from whose point
A guiding power directs the chariot's prow
Over its wheelèd clouds, which as they roll
Over the grass, and flowers, and waves, wake sounds,
Sweet as a singing rain of silver dew.

    Panthea. And from the other opening in the wood
Rushes, with loud and whirlwind harmony,
A sphere, which is as many thousand spheres,
Solid as crystal, yet through all its mass
Flow, as through empty space, music and light: 240
Ten thousand orbs involving and involved,
Purple and azure, white, and green, and golden,
Sphere within sphere; and every space between
Peopled with unimaginable shapes,
Such as ghosts dream dwell in the lampless deep,
Yet each inter-transpicuous, and they whirl
Over each other with a thousand motions,
Upon a thousand sightless axles spinning,
And with the force of self-destroying swiftness,
Intensely, slowly, solemnly roll on,   250
Kindling with mingled sounds, and many tones,
Intelligible words and music wild.
With mighty whirl the multitudinous orb
Grinds the bright brook into an azure mist
Of elemental subtlety, like light;
And the wild odour of the forest flowers,
The music of the living grass and air,
The emerald light of leaf-entangled beams
Round its intense yet self-conflicting speed,
Seem kneaded into one aëreal mass   260
Which drowns the sense. Within the orb itself,
Pillowed upon its alabaster arms,
Like to a child o'erwearied with sweet toil,
On its own folded wings, and wavy hair,
The Spirit of the Earth is laid asleep,
And you can see its little lips are moving,
Amid the changing light of their own smiles,
Like one who talks of what he loves in dream.

Ione. 'Tis only mocking the orb's harmony.
   Panthea. And from a star upon its forehead, shoot,   270
Like swords of azure fire, or golden spears
With tyrant-quelling myrtle overtwined,
Embleming heaven and earth united now,
Vast beams like spokes of some invisible wheel
Which whirl as the orb whirls, swifter than thought,
Filling the abyss with sun-like lightenings,
And perpendicular now, and now transverse,
Pierce the dark soil, and as they pierce and pass,
Make bare the secrets of the earth's deep heart;
Infinite mines of adamant and gold,   280
Valueless stones, and unimagined gems,
And caverns on crystalline columns poised
With vegetable silver overspread;
Wells of unfathomed fire, and water springs
Whence the great sea, even as a child is fed,
Whose vapours clothe earth's monarch mountain-tops
With kingly, ermine snow. The beams flash on
And make appear the melancholy ruins
Of cancelled cycles; anchors, beaks of ships;
Planks turned to marble; quivers, helms, and spears,   290
And gorgon-headed targes, and the wheels
Of scythèd chariots, and the emblazonry
Of trophies, standards, and armorial beasts,
Round which death laughed, sepulchred emblems
Of dead destruction, ruin within ruin!
The wrecks beside of many a city vast,
Whose population which the earth grew over
Was mortal, but not human; see, they lie,
Their monstrous works, and uncouth skeletons,
Their statues, homes and fanes; prodigious shapes   300
Huddled in gray annihilation, split,
Jammed in the hard, black deep; and over these,
The anatomies of unknown wingèd things,
And fishes which were isles of living scale,
And serpents, bony chains, twisted around
The iron crags, or within heaps of dust
To which the tortuous strength of their last pangs
Had crushed the iron crags; and over these
The jaggèd alligator, and the might
Of earth-convulsing behemoth, which once   310

Were monarch beasts, and on the slimy shores,
And weed-overgrown continents of earth,
Increased and multiplied like summer worms
On an abandoned corpse, till the blue globe
Wrapped deluge round it like a cloak, and they
Yelled, gasped, and were abolished; or some God
Whose throne was in a comet, passed and cried,
'Be not!' And like my words they were no more.

The Earth.

The joy, the triumph, the delight, the madness!
The boundless, overflowing, bursting gladness,   320
The vaporous exultation not to be confined!
Ha! ha! the animation of delight
Which wraps me, like an atmosphere of light,
And bears me as a cloud is borne by its own wind.

The Moon.

Brother mine, calm wanderer,
Happy globe of land and air,
Some Spirit is darted like a beam from thee,
Which penetrates my frozen frame,
And passes with the warmth of flame,
With love, and odour, and deep melody   330
Through me, through me!

The Earth.

Ha! ha! the caverns of my hollow mountains,
My cloven fire-crags, sound-exulting fountains
Laugh with a vast and inextinguishable laughter.
The oceans, and the deserts, and the abysses,
And the deep air's unmeasured wildernesses,
Answer from all their clouds and billows, echoing after.

They cry aloud as I do. Sceptred curse,
Who all our green and azure universe
Threatenedst to muffle round with black destruction, sending 340
A solid cloud to rain hot thunderstones,

And splinter and knead down my children's bones,
All I bring forth, to one void mass battering and blending,—

Until each crag-like tower, and storied column,
Palace, and obelisk, and temple solemn,
My imperial mountains crowned with cloud, and snow, and fire;
My sea-like forests, every blade and blossom
Which finds a grave or cradle in my bosom,
Were stamped by thy strong hate into a lifeless mire:

How art thou sunk, withdrawn, covered, drunk up   350
By thirsty nothing, as the brackish cup
Drained by a desert-troop, a little drop for all;
And from beneath, around, within, above,
Filling thy void annihilation, love
Burst in like light on caves cloven by the thunder-ball.

The Moon.

The snow upon my lifeless mountains
Is loosened into living fountains,
My solid oceans flow, and sing, and shine:
A spirit from my heart bursts forth,
It clothes with unexpected birth   360
My cold bare bosom: Oh! it must be thine
On mine, on mine!

Gazing on thee I feel, I know
Green stalks burst forth, and bright flowers grow,
And living shapes upon my bosom move:
Music is in the sea and air,
Wingèd clouds soar here and there,
Dark with the rain new buds are dreaming of:
'Tis love, all love!

The Earth.

It interpenetrates my granite mass,   370
Through tangled roots and trodden clay doth pass
Into the utmost leaves and delicatest flowers;
Upon the winds, among the clouds 'tis spread,

It wakes a life in the forgotten dead,
They breathe a spirit up from their obscurest bowers.

And like a storm bursting its cloudy prison
   With thunder, and with whirlwind, has arisen
Out of the lampless caves of unimagined being:
   With earthquake shock and swiftness making shiver
   Thought's stagnant chaos, unremoved for ever,   380
Till hate, and fear, and pain, light-vanquished shadows, fleeing,

   Leave Man, who was a many-sided mirror,
   Which could distort to many a shape of error,
This true fair world of things, a sea reflecting love;
   Which over all his kind, as the sun's heaven
   Gliding o'er ocean, smooth, serene, and even,
Darting from starry depths radiance and life, doth move:

   Leave Man, even as a leprous child is left,
   Who follows a sick beast to some warm cleft
Of rocks, through which the might of healing springs is poured;
   Then when it wanders home with rosy smile,   391
   Unconscious, and its mother fears awhile
It is a spirit, then, weeps on her child restored.

   Man, oh, not men! a chain of linkèd thought,
   Of love and might to be divided not,
Compelling the elements with adamantine stress;
   As the sun rules, even with a tyrant's gaze,
   The unquiet republic of the maze
Of planets, struggling fierce towards heaven's free wilderness.

   Man, one harmonious soul of many a soul,   400
   Whose nature is its own divine control,
Where all things flow to all, as rivers to the sea;
   Familiar acts are beautiful through love;
   Labour, and pain, and grief, in life's green grove
Sport like tame beasts, none knew how gentle they could be!

   His will, with all mean passions, bad delights,
   And selfish cares, its trembling satellites,
A spirit ill to guide, but mighty to obey,
   Is as a tempest-wingèd ship, whose helm

Love rules, through waves which dare not overwhelm,   410
Forcing life's wildest shores to own its sovereign sway.

All things confess his strength. Through the cold mass
  Of marble and of colour his dreams pass;
Bright threads whence mothers weave the robes their children
        wear;
  Language is a perpetual Orphic song,
  Which rules with Dædal harmony a throng
Of thoughts and forms, which else senseless and shapeless were.

The lightning is his slave; heaven's utmost deep
  Gives up her stars, and like a flock of sheep
They pass before his eye, are numbered, and roll on!   420
  The tempest is his steed, he strides the air;
  And the abyss shouts from her depth laid bare,
Heaven, hast thou secrets? Man unveils me; I have none.

The Moon.

  The shadow of white death has passed
  From my path in heaven at last,
A clinging shroud of solid frost and sleep;
  And through my newly-woven bowers,
  Wander happy paramours,
Less mighty, but as mild as those who keep
    Thy vales more deep.   430

The Earth.

As the dissolving warmth of dawn may fold
A half unfrozen dew-globe, green, and gold,
And crystalline, till it becomes a wingèd mist,
  And wanders up the vault of the blue day,
  Outlives the noon, and on the sun's last ray
Hangs o'er the sea, a fleece of fire and amethyst.

The Moon.

Thou art folded, thou art lying
In the light which is undying
Of thine own joy, and heaven's smile divine;

All suns and constellations shower   440
  On thee a light, a life, a power
Which doth array thy sphere; thou pourest thine
        On mine, on mine!

The Earth.

I spin beneath my pyramid of night,
  Which points into the heavens dreaming delight,
Murmuring victorious joy in my enchanted sleep;
  As a youth lulled in love-dreams faintly sighing,
  Under the shadow of his beauty lying,
Which round his rest a watch of light and warmth doth keep.

The Moon.

As in the soft and sweet eclipse,   450
  When soul meets soul on lovers' lips,
High hearts are calm, and brightest eyes are dull;
  So when thy shadow falls on me,
  Then am I mute and still, by thee
Covered; of thy love, Orb most beautiful,
        Full, oh, too full!

Thou art speeding round the sun
  Brightest world of many a one;
Green and azure sphere which shinest
With a light which is divinest   460
Among all the lamps of Heaven
To whom life and light is given;
I, thy crystal paramour
Borne beside thee by a power
Like the polar Paradise,
Magnet-like of lovers' eyes;
I, a most enamoured maiden
Whose weak brain is overladen
With the pleasure of her love,
Maniac-like around thee move   470
Gazing, an insatiate bride,
On thy form from every side
Like a Mænad, round the cup
Which Agave lifted up

In the weird Cadmæan forest.
Brother, wheresoe'er thou soarest
I must hurry, whirl and follow
Through the heavens wide and hollow,
Sheltered by the warm embrace
Of thy soul from hungry space,   480
Drinking from thy sense and sight
Beauty, majesty, and might,
As a lover or a chameleon
Grows like what it looks upon,
As a violet's gentle eye
Gazes on the azure sky
Until its hue grows like what it beholds,
As a gray and watery mist
Grows like solid amethyst
Athwart the western mountain it enfolds,   490
When the sunset sleeps
Upon its snow—

The Earth.

And the weak day weeps
That it should be so.
Oh, gentle Moon, the voice of thy delight
Falls on me like thy clear and tender light
Soothing the seaman, borne the summer night,
Through isles for ever calm;
Oh, gentle Moon, thy crystal accents pierce
The caverns of my pride's deep universe,   500
Charming the tiger joy, whose tramplings fierce
Made wounds which need thy balm.

Panthea. I rise as from a bath of sparkling water,
A bath of azure light, among dark rocks,
Out of the stream of sound.
Ione.   Ah me! sweet sister,
The stream of sound has ebbed away from us,
And you pretend to rise out of its wave,
Because your words fall like the clear, soft dew
Shaken from a bathing wood-nymph's limbs and hair.
Panthea. Peace! peace! A mighty Power, which is as
darkness,   510

Is rising out of Earth, and from the sky
Is showered like night, and from within the air
Bursts, like eclipse which had been gathered up
Into the pores of sunlight: the bright visions,
Wherein the singing spirits rode and shone,
Gleam like pale meteors through a watery night.
 Ione. There is a sense of words upon mine ear.
 Panthea. An universal sound like words: Oh, list!

Demogorgon.

Thou, Earth, calm empire of a happy soul,
 Sphere of divinest shapes and harmonies,   520
Beautiful orb! gathering as thou dost roll
 The love which paves thy path along the skies:

The Earth.

I hear: I am as a drop of dew that dies.

Demogorgon.

Thou, Moon, which gazest on the nightly Earth
 With wonder, as it gazes upon thee;
Whilst each to men, and beasts, and the swift birth
 Of birds, is beauty, love, calm, harmony:

The Moon.

I hear: I am a leaf shaken by thee!

Demogorgon.

Ye Kings of suns and stars, Dæmons and Gods,
 Aetherial Dominations, who possess   530
Elysian, windless, fortunate abodes
 Beyond Heaven's constellated wilderness:

A Voice from above.

Our great Republic hears, we are blest, and bless.

Demogorgon.

Ye happy Dead, whom beams of brightest verse
   Are clouds to hide, not colours to portray,
Whether your nature is that universe
   Which once ye saw and suffered—

A Voice from beneath.

                Or as they
Whom we have left, we change and pass away.

Demogorgon.

Ye elemental Genii, who have homes
   From man's high mind even to the central stone   540
Of sullen lead; from heaven's star-fretted domes
   To the dull weed some sea-worm battens on:

A confused Voice.

We hear: thy words waken Oblivion.

Demogorgon.

Spirits, whose homes are flesh: ye beasts and birds,
   Ye worms, and fish; ye living leaves and buds;
Lightning and wind; and ye untameable herds,
   Meteors and mists, which throng air's solitudes:—

A Voice.

Thy voice to us is wind among still woods.

Demogorgon.

Man, who wert once a despot and a slave;
   A dupe and a deceiver; a decay;   550
A traveller from the cradle to the grave
   Through the dim night of this immortal day:

All.

Speak: thy strong words may never pass away.

Demogorgon.

This is the day, which down the void abysm
At the Earth-born's spell yawns for Heaven's despotism,
   And Conquest is dragged captive through the deep:
Love, from its awful throne of patient power
In the wise heart, from the last giddy hour
   Of dread endurance, from the slippery, steep,
And narrow verge of crag-like agony, springs   560
And folds over the world its healing wings.

Gentleness, Virtue, Wisdom, and Endurance,
These are the seals of that most firm assurance
   Which bars the pit over Destruction's strength;
And if, with infirm hand, Eternity,
Mother of many acts and hours, should free
   The serpent that would clasp her with his length,
These are the spells by which to reassume
An empire o'er the disentangled doom.

To suffer woes which Hope thinks infinite;   570
To forgive wrongs darker than death or night;
   To defy Power, which seems omnipotent;
To love, and bear; to hope, till Hope creates
From its own wreck the thing it contemplates;
   Neither to change, nor falter, nor repent;
This, like thy glory, Titan, is to be
Good, great and joyous, beautiful and free;
This is alone Life, Joy, Empire, and Victory.

[1818–1819; publ. 1820]

THE CENCI[1]

A TRAGEDY IN FIVE ACTS

DEDICATION, TO LEIGH HUNT, Esq.

My dear Friend—I inscribe with your name, from a distant country, and after an absence whose months have seemed years, this the latest of my literary efforts.

Those writings which I have hitherto published, have been little else than visions which impersonate my own apprehensions of the beautiful and the just. I can also perceive in them the literary defects incidental to youth and impatience; they are dreams of what ought to be, or may be. The drama which I now present to you is a sad reality. I lay aside the presumptuous attitude of an instructor, and am content to paint, with such colours as my own heart furnishes, that which has been.

Had I known a person more highly endowed than yourself with all that it becomes a man to possess, I had solicited for this work the ornament of his name. One more gentle, honourable, innocent and brave; one of more exalted toleration for all who do and think evil, and yet himself more free from evil; one who knows better how to receive, and how to confer a benefit, though he must ever confer far more than he can receive; one of simpler, and, in the highest sense of the word, of purer life and manners I never knew: and I had already been fortunate in friendships when your name was added to the list.

In that patient and irreconcilable enmity with domestic and political tyranny and imposture which the tenor of your life has illustrated, and which, had I health and talents, should illustrate mine, let us, comforting each other in our task, live and die.

All happiness attend you! Your affectionate friend,

PERCY B. SHELLEY.

Rome, *May* 29, 1819.

---

[1] The Preface Shelley wrote for *The Cenci* appears on **page 446** of the present edition.

COUNT FRANCESCO CENCI   SAVELLA, *the Pope's Legate*
GIACOMO } *his Sons*   OLIMPIO } *Assassins*
BERNARDO }   MARZIO   }
CARDINAL CAMILLO   ANDREA, *Servant to Cenci*
ORSINO, *a Prelate*   Nobles, Judges, Guards
PRINCE COLONNA   Servants

LUCRETIA, *Wife of* CENCI, *and Step-mother of his children.*
BEATRICE, *his Daughter.*

The SCENE lies principally in Rome, but changes during the
Fourth Act to Petrella, a castle among the Apulian Apennines.

TIME. During the Pontificate of Clement VIII.

ACT I

SCENE I—*An Apartment in the Cenci Palace.*

Enter COUNT CENCI, *and* CARDINAL CAMILLO.

Camillo. That matter of the murder is hushed up
If you consent to yield his Holiness
Your fief that lies beyond the Pincian gate.—
It needed all my interest in the conclave
To bend him to this point: he said that you
Bought perilous impunity with your gold;
That crimes like yours if once or twice compounded
Enriched the Church, and respited from hell
An erring soul which might repent and live:—
But that the glory and the interest   10
Of the high throne he fills, little consist
With making it a daily mart of guilt
As manifold and hideous as the deeds
Which you scarce hide from men's revolted eyes.
  Cenci. The third of my possessions—let it go!
Ay, I once heard the nephew of the Pope
Had sent his architect to view the ground,
Meaning to build a villa on my vines

The next time I compounded with his uncle:
I little thought he should outwit me so!   20
Henceforth no witness—not the lamp—shall see
That which the vassal threatened to divulge
Whose throat is choked with dust for his reward.
The deed he saw could not have rated higher
Than his most worthless life:—it angers me!
Respited me from Hell!—So may the Devil
Respite their souls from Heaven. No doubt Pope Clement,
And his most charitable nephews, pray
That the Apostle Peter and the Saints
Will grant for their sake that I long enjoy   30
Strength, wealth, and pride, and lust, and length of days
Wherein to act the deeds which are the stewards
Of their revenue.—But much yet remains
To which they show no title.
    Camillo.   Oh, Count Cenci!
So much that thou mightst honourably live
And reconcile thyself with thine own heart
And with thy God, and with the offended world.
How hideously look deeds of lust and blood
Through those snow white and venerable hairs!—
Your children should be sitting round you now,   40
But that you fear to read upon their looks
The shame and misery you have written there.
Where is your wife? Where is your gentle daughter?
Methinks her sweet looks, which make all things else
Beauteous and glad, might kill the fiend within you.
Why is she barred from all society
But her own strange and uncomplaining wrongs?
Talk with me, Count,—you know I mean you well.
I stood beside your dark and fiery youth
Watching its bold and bad career, as men   50
Watch meteors, but it vanished not—I marked
Your desperate and remorseless manhood; now
Do I behold you in dishonoured age
Charged with a thousand unrepented crimes.
Yet I have ever hoped you would amend,
And in that hope have saved your life three times.
    Cenci. For which Aldobrandino owes you now
My fief beyond the Pincian.—Cardinal,
One thing, I pray you, recollect henceforth,

And so we shall converse with less restraint.   60
A man you knew spoke of my wife and daughter—
He was accustomed to frequent my house;
So the next day *his* wife and daughter came
And asked if I had seen him; and I smiled:
I think they never saw him any more.
   Camillo. Thou execrable man, beware!—
   Cenci.   Of thee?
Nay this is idle:—We should know each other.
As to my character for what men call crime
Seeing I please my senses as I list,
And vindicate that right with force or guile,   70
It is a public matter, and I care not
If I discuss it with you. I may speak
Alike to you and my own conscious heart—
For you give out that you have half reformed me,
Therefore strong vanity will keep you silent
If fear should not; both will, I do not doubt.
All men delight in sensual luxury,
All men enjoy revenge; and most exult
Over the tortures they can never feel—
Flattering their secret peace with other's pain.   80
But I delight in nothing else. I love
The sight of agony, and the sense of joy,
When this shall be another's, and that mine.
And I have no remorse and little fear,
Which are, I think, the checks of other men.
This mood has grown upon me, until now
Any design my captious fancy makes
The picture of its wish, and it forms none
But such as men like you would start to know,
Is as my natural food and rest debarred   90
Until it be accomplished.
   Camillo.   Art thou not
Most miserable?
   Cenci.   Why miserable?—
No.—I am what your theologians call
Hardened;—which they must be in impudence,
So to revile a man's peculiar taste.
True, I was happier than I am, while yet
Manhood remained to act the thing I thought;
While lust was sweeter than revenge; and now

Invention palls:—Ay, we must all grow old—
And but that there yet remains a deed to act 100
Whose horror might make sharp an appetite
Duller than mine—I'd do—I know not what.
When I was young I thought of nothing else
But pleasure; and I fed on honey sweets:
Men, by St. Thomas! cannot live like bees,
And I grew tired:—yet, till I killed a foe,
And heard his groans, and heard his children's groans,
Knew I not what delight was else on earth,
Which now delights me little. I the rather
Look on such pangs as terror ill conceals, 110
The dry fixed eyeball; the pale quivering lip,
Which tell me that the spirit weeps within
Tears bitterer than the bloody sweat of Christ.
I rarely kill the body, which preserves,
Like a strong prison, the soul within my power,
Wherein I feed it with the breath of fear
For hourly pain.
    Camillo.   Hell's most abandoned fiend
Did never, in the drunkenness of guilt,
Speak to his heart as now you speak to me;
I thank my God that I believe you not. 120

Enter ANDREA.

    Andrea. My Lord, a gentleman from Salamanca
Would speak with you.
    Cenci.   Bid him attend me in
The grand saloon. [*Exit* ANDREA.
    Camillo.   Farewell; and I will pray
Almighty God that thy false, impious words
Tempt not his spirit to abandon thee. [*Exit* CAMILLO.
    Cenci. The third of my possessions! I must use
Close husbandry, or gold, the old man's sword,
Falls from my withered hand. But yesterday
There came an order from the Pope to make
Fourfold provision for my cursèd sons; 130
Whom I had sent from Rome to Salamanca,
Hoping some accident might cut them off;
And meaning if I could to starve them there.
I pray thee, God, send some quick death upon them!

Bernardo and my wife could not be worse
If dead and damned:—then, as to Beatrice—
                    [*Looking around him suspiciously.*
I think they cannot hear me at that door;
What if they should? And yet I need not speak
Though the heart triumphs with itself in words.
O, thou most silent air, that shalt not hear   140
What now I think! Thou, pavement, which I tread
Towards her chamber,—let your echoes talk
Of my imperious step scorning surprise,
But not of my intent!—Andrea!

Enter ANDREA.

  Andrea.   My lord?
    Cenci. Bid Beatrice attend me in her chamber
This evening:—no, at midnight and alone.   [*Exeunt.*

SCENE II—*A Garden of the Cenci Palace. Enter* BEATRICE *and*
            ORSINO, *as in conversation.*

  Beatrice. Pervert not truth,
Orsino. You remember where we held
That conversation;—nay, we see the spot
Even from this cypress;—two long years are past
Since, on an April midnight, underneath
The moonlight ruins of mount Palatine,
I did confess to you my secret mind.
    Orsino. You said you loved me then.
    Beatrice.   You are a Priest,
Speak to me not of love.
    Orsino.   I may obtain
The dispensation of the Pope to marry.   10
Because I am a Priest do you believe
Your image, as the hunter some struck deer,
Follows me not whether I wake or sleep?
    Beatrice. As I have said, speak to me not of love.
Had you a dispensation I have not;
Nor will I leave this home of misery
Whilst my poor Bernard, and that gentle lady
To whom I owe life, and these virtuous thoughts,
Must suffer what I still have strength to share.

Alas, Orsino! All the love that once
I felt for you, is turned to bitter pain.
Ours was a youthful contract, which you first
Broke, by assuming vows no Pope will loose.
And thus I love you still, but holily,
Even as a sister or a spirit might;
And so I swear a cold fidelity.
And it is well perhaps we shall not marry.
You have a sly, equivocating vein
That suits me not.—Ah, wretched that I am!
Where shall I turn? Even now you look on me   30
As you were not my friend, and as if you
Discovered that I thought so, with false smiles
Making my true suspicion seem your wrong.
Ah, no! forgive me; sorrow makes me seem
Sterner than else my nature might have been;
I have a weight of melancholy thoughts,
And they forebode,—but what can they forebode
Worse than I now endure?
   Orsino.   All will be well.
Is the petition yet prepared? You know
My zeal for all you wish, sweet Beatrice;   40
Doubt not but I will use my utmost skill
So that the Pope attend to your complaint.
   Beatrice. Your zeal for all I wish;—Ah me, you are cold!
Your utmost skill . . . speak but one word . . . (*aside*) Alas!
Weak and deserted creature that I am,
Here I stand bickering with my only friend! [*To* ORSINO.
This night my father gives a sumptuous feast,
Orsino; he has heard some happy news
From Salamanca, from my brothers there,
And with this outward show of love he mocks   50
His inward hate. 'Tis bold hypocrisy,
For he would gladlier celebrate their deaths,
Which I have heard him pray for on his knees:
Great God! that such a father should be mine!
But there is mighty preparation made,
And all our kin, the Cenci, will be there,
And all the chief nobility of Rome.
And he has bidden me and my pale mother
Attire ourselves in festival array.
Poor lady! She expects some happy change   60

In his dark spirit from this act; I none.
At supper I will give you the petition:
Till when—farewell.
  Orsino. Farewell. (*Exit* BEATRICE.) I know the Pope
Will ne'er absolve me from my priestly vow
But by absolving me from the revenue
Of many a wealthy see; and, Beatrice,
I think to win thee at an easier rate.
Nor shall he read her eloquent petition:
He might bestow her on some poor relation
Of his sixth cousin, as he did her sister,   70
And I should be debarred from all access.
Then as to what she suffers from her father,
In all this there is much exaggeration:—
Old men are testy and will have their way;
A man may stab his enemy, or his vassal,
And live a free life as to wine or women,
And with a peevish temper may return
To a dull home, and rate his wife and children;
Daughters and wives call this foul tyranny.
I shall be well content if on my conscience   80
There rest no heavier sin than what they suffer
From the devices of my love—a net
From which she shall escape not. Yet I fear
Her subtle mind, her awe-inspiring gaze,
Whose beams anatomize me nerve by nerve
And lay me bare, and make me blush to see
My hidden thoughts.—Ah, no! A friendless girl
Who clings to me, as to her only hope:—
I were a fool, not less than if a panther
Were panic-stricken by the antelope's eye,   90
If she escape me.   [*Exit*

SCENE III—*A Magnificent Hall in the Cenci Palace. A Banquet.*
 Enter CENCI, LUCRETIA, BEATRICE, ORSINO, PRINCE COLONNA,
 CAMILLO, NOBLES.

  Cenci. Welcome, my friends and kinsmen; welcome ye,
Princes and Cardinals, pillars of the church,
Whose presence honours our festivity.
I have too long lived like an anchorite,

And in my absence from your merry meetings
An evil word is gone abroad of me;
But I do hope that you, my noble friends,
When you have shared the entertainment here,
And heard the pious cause for which 'tis given,
And we have pledged a health or two together,   10
Will think me flesh and blood as well as you;
Sinful indeed, for Adam made all so,
But tender-hearted, meek and pitiful.

    First Guest. In truth, my Lord, you seem too light of heart,
Too sprightly and companionable a man,
To act the deeds that rumour pins on you.
(*To his Companion.*) I never saw such blithe and open cheer
In any eye!

    Second Guest. Some most desired event,
In which we all demand a common joy,
Has brought us hither; let us hear it, Count.   20

    Cenci. It is indeed a most desired event.
If, when a parent from a parent's heart
Lifts from this earth to the great Father of all
A prayer, both when he lays him down to sleep,
And when he rises up from dreaming it;
One supplication, one desire, one hope,
That he would grant a wish for his two sons,
Even all that he demands in their regard—
And suddenly beyond his dearest hope
It is accomplished, he should then rejoice,   30
And call his friends and kinsmen to a feast,
And task their love to grace his merriment,—
Then honour me thus far—for I am he.

    Beatrice (*to* LUCRETIA). Great God! How horrible! Some
            dreadful ill
Must have befallen my brothers.

    Lucretia.   Fear not, Child,
He speaks too frankly.

    Beatrice.   Ah! my blood runs cold.
I fear that wicked laughter round his eye,
Which wrinkles up the skin even to the hair.

    Cenci. Here are the letters brought from Salamanca;
Beatrice, read them to your mother. God!   40
I thank thee! In one night didst thou perform,

By ways inscrutable, the thing I sought.
My disobedient and rebellious sons
Are dead!—Why, dead!—What means this change of cheer?
You hear me not, I tell you they are dead;
And they will need no food or raiment more:
The tapers that did light them the dark way
Are their last cost. The Pope, I think, will not
Expect I should maintain them in their coffins.
Rejoice with me—my heart is wondrous glad.   50
      [LUCRETIA *sinks, half fainting;* BEATRICE *supports her.*
  Beatrice. It is not true!—Dear lady, pray look up.
Had it been true, there is a God in Heaven,
He would not live to boast of such a boon.
Unnatural man, thou knowest that it is false.
  Cenci. Ay, as the word of God; whom here I call
To witness that I speak the sober truth;—
And whose most favouring Providence was shown
Even in the manner of their deaths. For Rocco
Was kneeling at the mass, with sixteen others,
When the church fell and crushed him to a mummy,   60
The rest escaped unhurt. Cristofano
Was stabbed in error by a jealous man,
Whilst she he loved was sleeping with his rival;
All in the self-same hour of the same night;
Which shows that Heaven has special care of me.
I beg those friends who love me, that they mark
The day a feast upon their calendars.
It was the twenty-seventh of December:
Ay, read the letters if you doubt my oath.
   [*The Assembly appears confused; several of the guests rise.*
  First Guest. Oh, horrible! I will depart—
  Second Guest.   And I.—
  Third Guest.   No, stay!   70
I do believe it is some jest; though faith!
'Tis mocking us somewhat too solemnly.
I think his son has married the Infanta,
Or found a mine of gold in El Dorado;
'Tis but to season some such news; stay, stay!
I see 'tis only raillery by his smile.
  Cenci. (*filling a bowl of wine, and lifting it up*). Oh, thou
    bright wine whose purple splendour leaps

And bubbles gaily in this golden bowl
Under the lamplight, as my spirits do,
To hear the death of my accursèd sons! 80
Could I believe thou wert their mingled blood,
Then would I taste thee like a sacrament,
And pledge with thee the mighty Devil in Hell,
Who, if a father's curses, as men say,
Climb with swift wings after their children's souls,
And drag them from the very throne of Heaven,
Now triumphs in my triumph!—But thou art
Superfluous; I have drunken deep of joy,
And I will taste no other wine to-night.
Here, Andrea! Bear the bowl around.
   A Guest (rising).   Thou wretch! 90
Will none among this noble company
Check the abandoned villain?
   Camillo.   For God's sake
Let me dismiss the guests! You are insane,
Some ill will come of this.
   Second Guest.   Seize, silence him!
   First Guest. I will!
   Third Guest.   And I!
   Cenci (addressing those who rise with a threatening gesture).
    Who moves? Who speaks?   *(turning to the Company)*
                        'tis nothing,
Enjoy yourselves.—Beware! For my revenge
Is as the sealed commission of a king
That kills, and none dare name the murderer.
   [*The Banquet is broken up; several of the Guests are departing.*
   Beatrice. I do entreat you, go not, noble guests;
What, although tyranny and impious hate 100
Stand sheltered by a father's hoary hair?
What, if 'tis he who clothed us in these limbs
Who tortures them, and triumphs? What, if we,
The desolate and the dead, were his own flesh,
His children and his wife, whom he is bound
To love and shelter? Shall we therefore find
No refuge in this merciless wide world?
O think what deep wrongs must have blotted out
First love, then reverence in a child's prone mind,
Till it thus vanquish shame and fear! O think! 110

I have borne much, and kissed the sacred hand
Which crushed us to the earth, and thought its stroke
Was perhaps some paternal chastisement!
Have excused much, doubted; and when no doubt
Remained, have sought by patience, love, and tears
To soften him, and when this could not be
I have knelt down through the long sleepless nights
And lifted up to God, the Father of all,
Passionate prayers: and when these were not heard
I have still borne,—until I meet you here,   120
Princes and kinsmen, at this hideous feast
Given at my brothers' deaths. Two yet remain,
His wife remains and I, whom if ye save not,
Ye may soon share such merriment again
As fathers make over their children's graves.
O Prince Colonna, thou art near kinsman,
Cardinal, thou art the Pope's chamberlain,
Camillo, thou art chief justiciary,
Take us away!

    Cenci. (*He has been conversing with* Camillo *during the first
           part of* Beatrice's *speech; he hears the conclusion, and
           now advances.*) I hope my good friends here
Will think of their own daughters—or perhaps   130
Of their own throats—before they lend an ear
To this wild girl.

    Beatrice (*not noticing the words of Cenci*). Dare no one look
           on me?
None answer? Can one tyrant overbear
The sense of many best and wisest men?
Or is it that I sue not in some form
Of scrupulous law, that ye deny my suit?
O God! that I were buried with my brothers!
And that the flowers of this departed spring
Were fading on my grave! And that my father
Were celebrating now one feast for all!   140

    Camillo. A bitter wish for one so young and gentle;
Can we do nothing?

    Colonna.   Nothing that I see.
Count Cenci were a dangerous enemy:
Yet I would second any one.

    A Cardinal.   And I.

Cenci. Retire to your chamber, insolent girl!
  Beatrice. Retire thou, impious man! Ay, hide thyself
Where never eye can look upon thee more!
Wouldst thou have honour and obedience
Who art a torturer? Father, never dream
Though thou mayst overbear this company,   150
But ill must come of ill.—Frown not on me!
Haste, hide thyself, lest with avenging looks
My brothers' ghosts should hunt thee from thy seat!
Cover thy face from every living eye,
And start if thou but hear a human step:
Seek out some dark and silent corner, there,
Bow thy white head before offended God,
And we will kneel around, and fervently
Pray that he pity both ourselves and thee.
  Cenci. My friends, I do lament this insane girl   160
Has spoilt the mirth of our festivity.
Good night, farewell; I will not make you longer
Spectators of our dull domestic quarrels.
Another time.—   [*Exeunt all but* CENCI *and* BEATRICE.
           My brain is swimming round;
Give me a bowl of wine!   [*To* BEATRICE.
           Thou painted viper!
Beast that thou art! Fair and yet terrible!
I know a charm shall make thee meek and tame,
Now get thee from my sight!   [*Exit* BEATRICE.
           Here, Andrea,
Fill up this goblet with Greek wine. I said
I would not drink this evening; but I must;   170
For, strange to say, I feel my spirits fail
With thinking what I have decreed to do.—
           [*Drinking the wine.*
Be thou the resolution of quick youth
Within my veins, and manhood's purpose stern,
And age's firm, cold, subtle villainy;
As if thou wert indeed my children's blood
Which I did thirst to drink! The charm works well;
It must be done; it shall be done, I swear!   [*Exit.*

END OF THE FIRST ACT.

ACT II

SCENE I—*An Apartment in the Cenci Palace. Enter* LUCRETIA *and*
BERNARDO.

Lucretia. Weep not, my gentle boy; he struck but me
Who have borne deeper wrongs. In truth, if he
Had killed me, he had done a kinder deed.
O God, Almighty, do Thou look upon us,
We have no other friend but only Thee!
Yet weep not; though I love you as my own,
I am not your true mother.
    Bernardo.   O more, more,
Than ever mother was to any child,
That have you been to me! Had he not been
My father, do you think that I should weep!   10
    Lucretia. Alas! Poor boy, what else couldst thou have done?

Enter BEATRICE.

Beatrice (*in a hurried voice*). Did he pass this way? Have you
        seen him, brother?
Ah, no! that is his step upon the stairs;
'Tis nearer now; his hand is on the door;
Mother, if I to thee have ever been
A duteous child, now save me! Thou, great God,
Whose image upon earth a father is,
Dost Thou indeed abandon me? He comes;
The door is opening now; I see his face;
He frowns on others, but he smiles on me,   20
Even as he did after the feast last night.

Enter a Servant.

Almighty God, how merciful Thou art!
'Tis but Orsino's servant.—Well, what news?
    Servant. My master bids me say, the Holy Father
Has sent back your petition thus unopened.   [*Giving a paper.*
And he demands at what hour 'twere secure
To visit you again?
    Lucretia.   At the Ave Mary.   [*Exit Servant.*
So, daughter, our last hope has failed; Ah me!

How pale you look; you tremble, and you stand
Wrapped in some fixed and fearful meditation,   30
As if one thought were over strong for you:
Your eyes have a chill glare; O, dearest child!
Are you gone mad? If not, pray speak to me.
    Beatrice. You see I am not mad: I speak to you.
    Lucretia. You talked of something that your father did
After that dreadful feast? Could it be worse
Than when he smiled, and cried, 'My sons are dead!'
And every one looked in his neighbour's face
To see if others were as white as he?
At the first word he spoke I felt the blood   40
Rush to my heart, and fell into a trance;
And when it passed I sat all weak and wild;
Whilst you alone stood up, and with strong words
Checked his unnatural pride; and I could see
The devil was rebuked that lives in him.
Until this hour thus have you ever stood
Between us and your father's moody wrath
Like a protecting presence: your firm mind
Has been our only refuge and defence:
What can have thus subdued it? What can now   50
Have given you that cold melancholy look,
Succeeding to your unaccustomed fear?
    Beatrice. What is it that you say? I was just thinking
'Twere better not to struggle any more.
Men, like my father, have been dark and bloody,
Yet never—Oh! Before worse comes of it
'Twere wise to die: it ends in that at last.
    Lucretia. Oh, talk not so, dear child! Tell me at once
What did your father do or say to you?
He stayed not after that accursèd feast   60
One moment in your chamber.—Speak to me.
    Bernardo. Oh, sister, sister, prithee, speak to us!
    Beatrice (*speaking very slowly with a forced calmness*). It was
        one word, Mother, one little word;
One look, one smile. (*Wildly.*) Oh! He has trampled me
Under his feet, and made the blood stream down
My pallid cheeks. And he has given us all
Ditch-water, and the fever-stricken flesh
Of buffaloes, and bade us eat or starve,
And we have eaten.—He has made me look

On my beloved Bernardo, when the rust   70
Of heavy chains has gangrened his sweet limbs,
And I have never yet despaired—but now!
What could I say?   [*Recovering herself.*
                        Ah, no! 'tis nothing new.
The sufferings we all share have made me wild:
He only struck and cursed me as he passed;
He said, he looked, he did,—nothing at all
Beyond his wont, yet it disordered me.
Alas! I am forgetful of my duty,
I should preserve my senses for your sake.

    Lucretia. Nay, Beatrice; have courage, my sweet girl,   80
If any one despairs it should be I
Who loved him once, and now must live with him
Till God in pity call for him or me.
For you may, like your sister, find some husband,
And smile, years hence, with children round your knees;
Whilst I, then dead, and all this hideous coil
Shall be remembered only as a dream.

    Beatrice. Talk not to me, dear lady, of a husband.
Did you not nurse me when my mother died?
Did you not shield me and that dearest boy?   90
And had we any other friend but you
In infancy, with gentle words and looks,
To win our father not to murder us?
And shall I now desert you? May the ghost
Of my dead Mother plead against my soul
If I abandon her who filled the place
She left, with more, even, than a mother's love!

    Bernardo. And I am of my sister's mind. Indeed
I would not leave you in this wretchedness,
Even though the Pope should make me free to live   100
In some blithe place, like others of my age,
With sports, and delicate food, and the fresh air.
Oh, never think that I will leave you, Mother!

    Lucretia. My dear, dear children!

       Enter CENCI, *suddenly.*

Cenci.   What, Beatrice here!
Come hither!   [*She shrinks back, and covers her face.*
    Nay, hide not your face, 'tis fair;

Look up! Why, yesternight you dared to look
With disobedient insolence upon me,
Bending a stern and an inquiring brow
On what I meant; whilst I then sought to hide
That which I came to tell you—but in vain.   110
   Beatrice (*wildly, staggering towards the door*). O that the
     earth would gape! Hide me, O God!
   Cenci. Then it was I whose inarticulate words
Fell from my lips, and who with tottering steps
Fled from your presence, as you now from mine.
Stay, I command you—from this day and hour
Never again, I think, with fearless eye,
And brow superior, and unaltered cheek,
And that lip made for tenderness or scorn,
Shalt thou strike dumb the meanest of mankind;
Me least of all. Now get thee to thy chamber!   120
Thou too, loathed image of thy cursèd mother, [*To* BERNARDO.
Thy milky, meek face makes me sick with hate!
                 [*Exeunt* BEATRICE *and* BERNARDO.
   (*Aside*.) So much has passed between us as must make
Me bold, her fearful.—'Tis an awful thing
To touch such mischief as I now conceive:
So men sit shivering on the dewy bank,
And try the chill stream with their feet; once in . . .
How the delighted spirit pants for joy!
   Lucretia (*advancing timidly towards him*). O husband! Pray
     forgive poor Beatrice.
She meant not any ill.
   Cenci.   Nor you perhaps?   130
Nor that young imp, whom you have taught by rote
Parricide with his alphabet? Nor Giacomo?
Nor those two most unnatural sons, who stirred
Enmity up against me with the Pope?
Whom in one night merciful God cut off:
Innocent lambs! They thought not any ill.
You were not here conspiring? You said nothing
Of how I might be dungeoned as a madman;
Or be condemned to death for some offence,
And you would be the witnesses?—This failing,   140
How just it were to hire assassins, or
Put sudden poison in my evening drink?
Or smother me when overcome by wine?

Seeing we had no other judge but God,
And He had sentenced me, and there were none
But you to be the executioners
Of His decree enregistered in Heaven?
Oh, no! You said not this?

   Lucretia.   So help me God,
I never thought the things you charge me with!

   Cenci. If you dare speak that wicked lie again   150
I'll kill you. What! It was not by your counsel
That Beatrice disturbed the feast last night?
You did not hope to stir some enemies
Against me, and escape, and laugh to scorn
What every nerve of you now trembles at?
You judged that men were bolder than they are;
Few dare to stand between their grave and me.

   Lucretia. Look not so dreadfully! By my salvation
I knew not aught that Beatrice designed;
Nor do I think she designed any thing   160
Until she heard you talk of her dead brothers.

   Cenci. Blaspheming liar! You are damned for this!
But I will take you where you may persuade
The stones you tread on to deliver you:
For men shall there be none but those who dare
All things—not question that which I command.
On Wednesday next I shall set out: you know
That savage rock, the Castle of Petrella:
'Tis safely walled, and moated round about:
Its dungeons underground, and its thick towers   170
Never told tales; though they have heard and seen
What might make dumb things speak.—Why do you linger?
Make speediest preparation for the journey!   [*Exit* Lucretia.
The all-beholding sun yet shines; I hear
A busy stir of men about the streets;
I see the bright sky through the window panes:
It is a garish, broad, and peering day;
Loud, light, suspicious, full of eyes and ears,
And every little corner, nook, and hole
Is penetrated with the insolent light.   180
Come darkness! Yet, what is the day to me?
And wherefore should I wish for night, who do
A deed which shall confound both night and day?
'Tis she shall grope through a bewildering mist

Of horror: if there be a sun in heaven
She shall not dare to look upon its beams
Nor feel its warmth. Let her then wish for night;
The act I think shall soon extinguish all
For me: I bear a darker deadlier gloom
Than the earth's shade, or interlunar air,   190
Or constellations quenched in murkiest cloud,
In which I walk secure and unbeheld
Towards my purpose.—Would that it were done!   [*Exit.*

SCENE II—*A Chamber in the Vatican. Enter* CAMILLO *and* GIA-
COMO, *in conversation.*

   Camillo. There is an obsolete and doubtful law
By which you might obtain a bare provision
Of food and clothing—
   Giacomo.   Nothing more? Alas!
Bare must be the provision which strict law
Awards, and agèd, sullen avarice pays.
Why did my father not apprentice me
To some mechanic trade? I should have then
Been trained in no highborn necessities
Which I could meet not by my daily toil.
The eldest son of a rich nobleman   10
Is heir to all his incapacities;
He has wide wants, and narrow powers. If you,
Cardinal Camillo, were reduced at once
From thrice-driven beds of down, and delicate food,
An hundred servants, and six palaces,
To that which nature doth indeed require?—
   Camillo. Nay, there is reason in your plea; 'twere hard.
   Giacomo. 'Tis hard for a firm man to bear: but I
Have a dear wife, a lady of high birth
Whose dowry in ill hour I lent my father   20
Without a bond or witness to the deed:
And children, who inherit her fine senses,
The fairest creatures in this breathing world;
And she and they reproach me not. Cardinal,
Do you not think the Pope would interpose
And stretch authority beyond the law?
   Camillo. Though your peculiar case is hard, I know

The Pope will not divert the course of law.
After that impious feast the other night
I spoke with him, and urged him then to check   30
Your father's cruel hand; he frowned and said,
'Children are disobedient, and they sting
Their fathers' hearts to madness and despair,
Requiting years of care with contumely.
I pity the Count Cenci from my heart;
His outraged love perhaps awakened hate,
And thus he is exasperated to ill.
In the great war between the old and young
I, who have white hairs and a tottering body,
Will keep at least blameless neutrality.'   40

Enter ORSINO.

You, my good Lord Orsino, heard those words.
   Orsino. What words?
   Giacomo.   Alas, repeat them not again!
There then is no redress for me, at least
None but that which I may achieve myself,
Since I am driven to the brink.—But, say,
My innocent sister and my only brother
Are dying underneath my father's eye.
The memorable torturers of this land,
Galeaz Visconti, Borgia, Ezzelin,
Never inflicted on the meanest slave   50
What these endure; shall they have no protection?
   Camillo. Why, if they would petition to the Pope
I see not how he could refuse it—yet
He holds it of most dangerous example
In aught to weaken the paternal power,
Being, as 'twere, the shadow of his own.
I pray you now excuse me. I have business
That will not bear delay.   [*Exit* CAMILLO.
   Giacomo.   But you, Orsino,
Have the petition: wherefore not present it?
   Orsino. I have presented it, and backed it with   60
My earnest prayers, and urgent interest;
It was returned unanswered. I doubt not
But that the strange and execrable deeds
Alleged in it—in truth they might well baffle

Any belief—have turned the Pope's displeasure
Upon the accusers from the criminal:
So I should guess from what Camillo said.
   Giacomo. My friend, that palace-walking devil Gold
Has whispered silence to his Holiness:
And we are left, as scorpions ringed with fire.   70
What should we do but strike ourselves to death?
For he who is our murderous persecutor
Is shielded by a father's holy name,
Or I would—   *[Stops abruptly.*
   Orsino.   What? Fear not to speak your thought.
Words are but holy as the deeds they cover:
A priest who has forsworn the God he serves;
A judge who makes Truth weep at his decree;
A friend who should weave counsel, as I now,
But as the mantle of some selfish guile;
A father who is all a tyrant seems,   80
Were the profaner for his sacred name.
   Giacomo. Ask me not what I think; the unwilling brain
Feigns often what it would not; and we trust
Imagination with such phantasies
As the tongue dares not fashion into words,
Which have no words, their horror makes them dim
To the mind's eye.—My heart denies itself
To think what you demand.
   Orsino.   But a friend's bosom
Is as the inmost cave of our own mind
Where we sit shut from the wide gaze of day,   90
And from the all-communicating air.
You look what I suspected—
   Giacomo.   Spare me now!
I am as one lost in a midnight wood,
Who dares not ask some harmless passenger
The path across the wilderness, lest he,
As my thoughts are, should be—a murderer.
I know you are my friend, and all I dare
Speak to my soul that will I trust with thee.
But now my heart is heavy, and would take
Lone counsel from a night of sleepless care.   100
Pardon me, that I say farewell—farewell!
I would that to my own suspected self
I could address a word so full of peace.

Orsino. Farewell!—Be your thoughts better or more bold.

                              [*Exit* GIACOMO.

I had disposed the Cardinal Camillo
To feed his hope with cold encouragement:
It fortunately serves my close designs
That 'tis a trick of this same family
To analyse their own and other minds.
Such self-anatomy shall teach the will   110
Dangerous secrets: for it tempts our powers,
Knowing what must be thought, and may be done,
Into the depth of darkest purposes:
So Cenci fell into the pit; even I,
Since Beatrice unveiled me to myself,
And made me shrink from what I cannot shun,
Show a poor figure to my own esteem,
To which I grow half reconciled. I'll do
As little mischief as I can; that thought
Shall fee the accuser conscience.

   (*After a pause.*)   Now what harm   120
If Cenci should be murdered?—Yet, if murdered,
Wherefore by me? And what if I could take
The profit, yet omit the sin and peril
In such an action? Of all earthly things
I fear a man whose blows outspeed his words;
And such is Cenci: and while Cenci lives
His daughter's dowry were a secret grave
If a priest wins her.—Oh, fair Beatrice!
Would that I loved thee not, or loving thee
Could but despise danger and gold and all   130
That frowns between my wish and its effect,
Or smiles beyond it! There is no escape . . .
Her bright form kneels beside me at the altar,
And follows me to the resort of men,
And fills my slumber with tumultuous dreams,
So when I wake my blood seems liquid fire;
And if I strike my damp and dizzy head
My hot palm scorches it: her very name,
But spoken by a stranger, makes my heart
Sicken and pant; and thus unprofitably   140
I clasp the phantom of unfelt delights
Till weak imagination half possesses
The self-created shadow. Yet much longer

Will I not nurse this life of feverous hours:
From the unravelled hopes of Giacomo
I must work out my own dear purposes.
I see, as from a tower, the end of all:
Her father dead; her brother bound to me
By a dark secret, surer than the grave;
Her mother scared and unexpostulating   150
From the dread manner of her wish achieved:
And she!—Once more take courage, my faint heart;
What dares a friendless maiden matched with thee?
I have such foresight as assures success:
Some unbeheld divinity doth ever,
When dread events are near, stir up men's minds
To black suggestions; and he prospers best,
Not who becomes the instrument of ill,
But who can flatter the dark spirit, that makes
Its empire and its prey of other hearts   160
Till it became his slave . . . as I will do.   [*Exit.*

END OF THE SECOND ACT.

ACT III

Scene I—*An Apartment in the Cenci Palace.* Lucretia, *to her
enter* Beatrice.

  Beatrice. (*She enters staggering, and speaks wildly.*) Reach
me that handkerchief!—My brain is hurt;
My eyes are full of blood; just wipe them for me . . .
I see but indistinctly . . .
  Lucretia.   My sweet child,
You have no wound; 'tis only a cold dew
That starts from your dear brow . . . Alas! Alas!
What has befallen?
  Beatrice.   How comes this hair undone?
Its wandering strings must be what blind me so,
And yet I tied it fast.—O, horrible!
The pavement sinks under my feet! The walls
Spin round! I see a woman weeping there,   1^
And standing calm and motionless, whilst I
Slide giddily as the world reels. . . . My God!
The beautiful blue heaven is flecked with blood!

The sunshine on the floor is black! The air
Is changed to vapours such as the dead breathe
In charnel pits! Pah! I am choked! There creeps
A clinging, black, contaminating mist
About me . . . 'tis substantial, heavy, thick,
I cannot pluck it from me, for it glues
My fingers and my limbs to one another,   20
And eats into my sinews, and dissolves
My flesh to a pollution, poisoning
The subtle, pure, and inmost spirit of life!
My God! I never knew what the mad felt
Before; for I am mad beyond all doubt!
(*More wildly.*) No, I am dead! These putrefying limbs
Shut round and sepulchre the panting soul
Which would burst forth into the wandering air!   (*A pause.*)
What hideous thought was that I had even now?
'Tis gone; and yet its burthen remains here   30
O'er these dull eyes . . . upon this weary heart!
O, world! O, life! O, day! O, misery!
   Lucretia. What ails thee, my poor child? She answers not:
Her spirit apprehends the sense of pain,
But not its cause; suffering has dried away
The source from which it sprung . . .
   Beatrice (*franticly*).   Like Parricide . . .
Misery has killed its father: yet its father
Never like mine . . . O, God! What thing am I?
   Lucretia. My dearest child, what has your father done?
   Beatrice (*doubtfully*). Who art thou, questioner? I have no
      father.   40
(*Aside.*) She is the madhouse nurse who tends on me,
It is a piteous office.   [*To* LUCRETIA, *in a slow subdued voice.*
               Do you know
I thought I was that wretched Beatrice
Men speak of, whom her father sometimes hales
From hall to hall by the entangled hair;
At others, pens up naked in damp cells
Where scaly reptiles crawl, and starves her there,
Till she will eat strange flesh. This woful story
So did I overact in my sick dreams,
That I imagined . . . no, it cannot be!   50
Horrible things have been in this wide world,
Prodigious mixtures, and confusions strange

Of good and ill; and worse have been conceived
Than ever there was found a heart to do.
But never fancy imaged such a deed
As . . .   [*Pauses, suddenly recollecting herself.*
          Who art thou? Swear to me, ere I die
With fearful expectation, that indeed
Thou art not what seemest . . . Mother!
    Lucretia.   Oh!
My sweet child, know you . . .
    Beatrice.   Yet speak it not:
For then if this be truth, that other too   60
Must be a truth, a firm enduring truth,
Linked with each lasting circumstance of life,
Never to change, never to pass away.
Why so it is. This is the Cenci Palace;
Thou art Lucretia; I am Beatrice.
I have talked some wild words, but will no more.
Mother, come near me: from this point of time,
I am . . .   [*Her voice dies away faintly.*
    Lucretia. Alas! What has befallen thee, child?
What has thy father done?
    Beatrice.   What have I done?
Am I not innocent? Is it my crime   70
That one with white hair, and imperious brow,
Who tortured me from my forgotten years,
As parents only dare, should call himself
My father, yet should be!—Oh, what am I?
What name, what place, what memory shall be mine?
What retrospects, outliving even despair?
    Lucretia. He is a violent tyrant, surely, child:
We know that death alone can make us free;
His death or ours. But what can he have done
Of deadlier outrage or worse injury?   80
Thou art unlike thyself; thine eyes shoot forth
A wandering and strange spirit. Speak to me,
Unlock those pallid hands whose fingers twine
With one another.
    Beatrice.   'Tis the restless life
Tortured within them. If I try to speak
I shall go mad. Ay, something must be done;
What, yet I know not . . . something which shall make
The thing that I have suffered but a shadow

In the dread lightning which avenges it;
Brief, rapid, irreversible, destroying   90
The consequence of what it cannot cure.
Some such thing is to be endured or done:
When I know what, I shall be still and calm,
And never anything will move me more.
But now!—O blood, which art my father's blood,
Circling through these contaminated veins,
If thou, poured forth on the polluted earth,
Could wash away the crime, and punishment
By which I suffer . . . no, that cannot be!
Many might doubt there were a God above   100
Who sees and permits evil, and so die:
That faith no agony shall obscure in me.
    Lucretia. It must indeed have been some bitter wrong;
Yet what, I dare not guess. Oh, my lost child,
Hide not in proud impenetrable grief
Thy sufferings from my fear.
    Beatrice.   I hide them not.
What are the words which you would have me speak?
I, who can feign no image in my mind
Of that which has transformed me: I, whose thought
Is like a ghost shrouded and folded up   110
In its own formless horror: of all words,
That minister to mortal intercourse,
Which wouldst thou hear? For there is none to tell
My misery: if another ever knew
Aught like to it, she died as I will die,
And left it, as I must, without a name.
Death! Death! Our law and our religion call thee
A punishment and a reward . . . Oh, which
Have I deserved?
    Lucretia.   The peace of innocence;
Till in your season you be called to heaven.   120
Whate'er you may have suffered, you have done
No evil. Death must be the punishment
Of crime, or the reward of trampling down
The thorns which God has strewed upon the path
Which leads to immortality.
    Beatrice.   Ay, death . . .
The punishment of crime. I pray thee, God,
Let me not be bewildered while I judge.

If I must live day after day, and keep
These limbs, the unworthy temple of Thy spirit,
As a foul den from which what Thou abhorrest   **130**
May mock Thee, unavenged . . . it shall not be!
Self-murder . . . no, that might be no escape,
For Thy decree yawns like a Hell between
Our will and it:—O! in this mortal world
There is no vindication and no law
Which can adjudge and execute the doom
Of that through which I suffer.

Enter ORSINO.

(*She approaches him solemnly.*) Welcome, Friend!
I have to tell you that, since last we met,
I have endured a wrong so great and strange,
That neither life nor death can give me rest.   **140**
Ask me not what it is, for there are deeds
Which have no form, sufferings which have no tongue.
  Orsino. And what is he who has thus injured you?
  Beatrice. The man they call my father: a dread name.
  Orsino. It cannot be . . .
  Beatrice.   What it can be, or not,
Forbear to think. It is, and it has been;
Advise me how it shall not be again.
I thought to die; but a religious awe
Restrains me, and the dread lest death itself
Might be no refuge from the consciousness   **150**
Of what is yet unexpiated. Oh, speak!
  Orsino. Accuse him of the deed, and let the law
Avenge thee.
  Beatrice.   Oh, ice-hearted counsellor!
If I could find a word that might make known
The crime of my destroyer; and that done,
My tongue should like a knife tear out the secret
Which cankers my heart's core; ay, lay all bare
So that my unpolluted fame should be
With vilest gossips a stale mouthèd story;
A mock, a byword, an astonishment:—   **160**
If this were done, which never shall be done,
Think of the offender's gold, his dreaded hate,
And the strange horror of the accuser's tale,

Baffling belief, and overpowering speech;
Scarce whispered, unimaginable, wrapped
In hideous hints . . . Oh, most assured redress!
    Orsino. You will endure it then?
    Beatrice.   Endure?—Orsino,
It seems your counsel is small profit.
                [*Turns from him, and speaks half to herself.*
                    Ay,
All must be suddenly resolved and done.
What is this undistinguishable mist   170
Of thoughts, which rise, like shadow after shadow,
Darkening each other?
    Orsino.   Should the offender live?
Triumph in his misdeed? and make, by use,
His crime, whate'er it is, dreadful no doubt,
Thine element; until thou mayst become
Utterly lost; subdued even to the hue
Of that which thou permittest?
    Beatrice (*to herself*).   Mighty death!
Thou double-visaged shadow? Only judge!
Rightfullest arbiter!   [*She retires absorbed in thought.*
    Lucretia.   If the lightning
Of God has e'er descended to avenge . . .   180
    Orsino. Blaspheme not! His high Providence commits
Its glory on this earth, and their own wrongs
Into the hands of men; if they neglect
To punish crime . . .
    Lucretia.   But if one, like this wretch,
Should mock, with gold, opinion, law, and power?
If there be no appeal to that which makes
The guiltiest tremble? If because our wrongs,
For that they are unnatural, strange, and monstrous,
Exceed all measure of belief? O God!
If, for the very reasons which should make   **190**
Redress most swift and sure, our injurer triumphs?
And we, the victims, bear worse punishment
Than that appointed for their torturer?
    Orsino.   Think not
But that there is redress where there is wrong,
So we be bold enough to seize it.
    Lucretia.   How?
If there were any way to make all sure,

I know not . . . but I think it might be good
To . . .

   Orsino. Why, his late outrage to Beatrice;
For it is such, as I but faintly guess,
As makes remorse dishonour, and leaves her   200
Only one duty, how she may avenge:
You, but one refuge from ills ill endured;
Me, but one counsel . . .

   Lucretia.   For we cannot hope
That aid, or retribution, or resource
Will arise thence, where every other one
Might find them with less need.   [BEATRICE *advances.*

   Orsino.   Then . . .

   Beatrice.   Peace, Orsino!
And, honoured Lady, while I speak, I pray,
That you put off, as garments overworn,
Forbearance and respect, remorse and fear,
And all the fit restraints of daily life,   210
Which have been borne from childhood, but which now
Would be a mockery to my holier plea.
As I have said, I have endured a wrong,
Which, though it be expressionless, is such
As asks atonement; both for what is past,
And lest I be reserved, day after day,
To load with crimes an overburthened soul,
And be . . . what ye can dream not. I have prayed
To God, and I have talked with my own heart,
And have unravelled my entangled will,   220
And have at length determined what is right.
Art thou my friend, Orsino? False or true?
Pledge thy salvation ere I speak.

   Orsino.   I swear
To dedicate my cunning, and my strength,
My silence, and whatever else is mine,
To thy commands.

   Lucretia.   You think we should devise
His death?

   Beatrice. And execute what is devised,
And suddenly. We must be brief and bold.

   Orsino. And yet most cautious.

   Lucretia.   For the jealous laws
Would punish us with death and infamy   230

For that which it became themselves to do.

    Beatrice. Be cautious as ye may, but prompt. Orsino,
What are the means?

    Orsino.   I know two dull, fierce outlaws,
Who think man's spirit as a worm's, and they
Would trample out, for any slight caprice,
The meanest or the noblest life. This mood
Is marketable here in Rome. They sell
What we now want.

    Lucretia.   To-morrow before dawn,
Cenci will take us to that lonely rock,
Petrella, in the Apulian Apennines.   240
If he arrive there . . .

    Beatrice.   He must not arrive.

    Orsino. Will it be dark before you reach the tower?

    Lucretia. The sun will scarce be set.

    Beatrice.   But I remember
Two miles on this side of the fort, the road
Crosses a deep ravine; 'tis rough and narrow,
And winds with short turns down the precipice;
And in its depth there is a mighty rock,
Which has, from unimaginable years,
Sustained itself with terror and with toil
Over a gulf, and with the agony   250
With which it clings seems slowly coming down,
Even as a wretched soul hour after hour,
Clings to the mass of life; yet clinging, leans;
And leaning, makes more dark the dread abyss
In which it fears to fall: beneath this crag
Huge as despair, as if in weariness,
The melancholy mountain yawns . . . below,
You hear but see not an impetuous torrent
Raging among the caverns, and a bridge
Crosses the chasm; and high above there grow,   260
With intersecting trunks, from crag to crag,
Cedars, and yews, and pines; whose tangled hair
Is matted in one solid roof of shade
By the dark ivy's twine. At noonday here
'Tis twilight, and at sunset blackest night.

    Orsino. Before you reach that bridge make some excuse
For spurring on your mules, or loitering
Until . . .

   Beatrice. What sound is that?
   Lucretia. Hark! No, it cannot be a servant's step;
It must be Cenci, unexpectedly   270
Returned . . . Make some excuse for being here.
   Beatrice. (*To* Orsino, *as she goes out.*) That step we hear
       approach must never pass
The bridge of which we spoke.
                  [*Exeunt* Lucretia *and* Beatrice.
   Orsino.   What shall I do?
Cenci must find me here, and I must bear
The imperious inquisition of his looks
As to what brought me hither: let me mask
Mine own in some inane and vacant smile.

     Enter Giacomo, *in a hurried manner.*

How! Have you ventured hither? Know you then
That Cenci is from home?
   Giacomo.   I sought him here;
And now must wait till he returns.
   Orsino.   Great God!   280
Weigh you the danger of this rashness?
   Giacomo.   Ay!
Does my destroyer know his danger? We
Are now no more, as once, parent and child,
But man to man; the oppressor to the oppressed;
The slanderer to the slandered; foe to foe:
He has cast Nature off, which was his shield,
And Nature casts him off, who is her shame;
And I spurn both. Is it a father's throat
Which I will shake, and say, I ask not gold;
I ask not happy years; nor memories   290
Of tranquil childhood; nor home-sheltered love;
Though all these hast thou torn from me, and more;
But only my fair fame; only one hoard
Of peace, which I thought hidden from thy hate,
Under the penury heaped on me by thee,
Or I will . . . God can understand and pardon,
Why should I speak with man?
   Orsino.   Be calm, dear friend.
   Giacomo. Well, I will calmly tell you what he did.
This old Francesco Cenci, as you know,

Borrowed the dowry of my wife from me,   300
And then denied the loan; and left me so
In poverty, the which I sought to mend
By holding a poor office in the state.
It had been promised to me, and already
I bought new clothing for my raggèd babes,
And my wife smiled; and my heart knew repose.
When Cenci's intercession, as I found,
Conferred this office on a wretch, whom thus
He paid for vilest service. I returned
With this ill news, and we sate sad together   310
Solacing our despondency with tears
Of such affection and unbroken faith
As temper life's worst bitterness; when he,
As he is wont, came to upbraid and curse,
Mocking our poverty, and telling us
Such was God's scourge for disobedient sons.
And then, that I might strike him dumb with shame,
I spoke of my wife's dowry; but he coined
A brief yet specious tale, how I had wasted
The sum in secret riot; and he saw   320
My wife was touched, and he went smiling forth.
And when I knew the impression he had made,
And felt my wife insult with silent scorn
My ardent truth, and look averse and cold,
I went forth too; but soon returned again;
Yet not so soon but that my wife had taught
My children her harsh thoughts, and they all cried,
'Give us clothes, father! Give us better food!
What you in one night squander were enough
For months!' I looked, and saw that home was hell.   330
And to that hell will I return no more
Until mine enemy has rendered up
Atonement, or, as he gave life to me
I will, reversing Nature's law . . .
     Orsino.   Trust me,
The compensation which thou seekest here
Will be denied.
     Giacomo.   Then . . . Are you not my friend?
Did you not hint at the alternative,
Upon the brink of which you see I stand,

The other day when we conversed together?
My wrongs were then less. That word parricide,   340
Although I am resolved, haunts me like fear.
  Orsino. It must be fear itself, for the bare word
Is hollow mockery. Mark, how wisest God
Draws to one point the threads of a just doom,
So sanctifying it: what you devise
Is, as it were, accomplished.
  Giacomo.   Is he dead?
  Orsino. His grave is ready. Know that since we met
Cenci has done an outrage to his daughter.
  Giacomo. What outrage?
  Orsino.   That she speaks not, but you may
Conceive such half conjectures as I do,   350
From her fixed paleness, and the lofty grief
Of her stern brow bent on the idle air,
And her severe unmodulated voice,
Drowning both tenderness and dread; and last
From this; that whilst her step-mother and I,
Bewildered in our horror, talked together
With obscure hints; both self-misunderstood
And darkly guessing, stumbling, in our talk,
Over the truth, and yet to its revenge,
She interrupted us, and with a look   360
Which told before she spoke it, he must die: . . .
  Giacomo. It is enough. My doubts are well appeased;
There is a higher reason for the act
Than mine; there is a holier judge than me,
A more unblamed avenger. Beatrice,
Who in the gentleness of thy sweet youth
Hast never trodden on a worm, or bruised
A living flower, but thou hast pitied it
With needless tears! Fair sister, thou in whom
Men wondered how such loveliness and wisdom   370
Did not destroy each other! Is there made
Ravage of thee? O, heart, I ask no more
Justification! Shall I wait, Orsino,
Till he return, and stab him at the door?
  Orsino. Not so; some accident might interpose
To rescue him from what is now most sure;
And you are unprovided where to fly,

How to excuse or to conceal. Nay, listen:
All is contrived; success is so assured
That . . .

Enter BEATRICE.

Beatrice. 'Tis my brother's voice! You know me not?   380
Giacomo. My sister, my lost sister!
Beatrice.   Lost indeed!
I see Orsino has talked with you, and
That you conjecture things too horrible
To speak, yet far less than the truth. Now, stay not,
He might return: yet kiss me; I shall know
That then thou hast consented to his death.
Farewell, farewell! Let piety to God,
Brotherly love, justice and clemency,
And all things that make tender hardest hearts
Make thine hard, brother. Answer not . . . farewell.   390
                              [*Exeunt severally.*

SCENE II—*A mean Apartment in* GIACOMO'S *House.* GIACOMO
                              alone.

Giacomo. 'Tis midnight, and Orsino comes not yet.
                    [*Thunder, and the sound of a storm.*
What! can the everlasting elements
Feel with a worm like man? If so, the shaft
Of mercy-wingèd lightning would not fall
On stones and trees. My wife and children sleep:
They are now living in unmeaning dreams:
But I must wake, still doubting if that deed
Be just which is most necessary. O,
Thou unreplenishing lamp! whose narrow fire
Is shaken by the wind, and on whose edge   10
Devouring darkness hovers! Thou small flame,
Which, as a dying pulse rises and falls,
Still flickerest up and down, how very soon,
Did I not feed thee, wouldst thou fail and be
As thou hadst never been! So wastes and sinks
Even now, perhaps, the life that kindled mine:
But that no power can fill with vital oil
That broken lamp of flesh. Ha! 'tis the blood
Which fed these veins that ebbs till all is cold:

It is the form that moulded mine that sinks   20
Into the white and yellow spasms of death:
It is the soul by which mine was arrayed
In God's immortal likeness which now stands
Naked before Heaven's judgment seat!   [*A bell strikes.*
                                                One! Two!

The hours crawl on; and when my hairs are white,
My son will then perhaps be waiting thus,
Tortured between just hate and vain remorse;
Chiding the tardy messenger of news
Like those which I expect. I almost wish
He be not dead, although my wrongs are great;   30
Yet . . . 'tis Orsino's step . . .

                    Enter ORSINO.

                         Speak!
    Orsino.   I am come
To say he has escaped.
    Giacomo.   Escaped!
    Orsino   And safe
Within Petrella. He passed by the spot
Appointed for the deed an hour too soon.
    Giacomo. Are we the fools of such contingencies?
And do we waste in blind misgivings thus
The hours when we should act? Then wind and thunder,
Which seemed to howl his knell, is the loud laughter
With which Heaven mocks our weakness! I henceforth
Will ne'er repent of aught designed or done   40
But my repentance.
    Orsino.   See, the lamp is out.
    Giacomo. If no remorse is ours when the dim air
Has drank this innocent flame, why should we quail
When Cenci's life, that light by which ill spirits
See the worst deeds they prompt, shall sink for ever?
No, I am hardened.
    Orsino.   Why, what need of this?
Who feared the pale intrusion of remorse
In a just deed? Although our first plan failed,
Doubt not but he will soon be laid to rest.
But light the lamp; let us not talk i' the dark.   50
    Giacomo (*lighting the lamp*). And yet once quenched I

        cannot thus relume
My father's life: do you not think his ghost
Might plead that argument with God?
    Orsino.   Once gone
You cannot now recall your sister's peace;
Your own extinguished years of youth and hope;
Nor your wife's bitter words; nor all the taunts
Which, from the prosperous, weak misfortune takes;
Nor your dead mother; nor . . .
    Giacomo.   O, speak no more!
I am resolved, although this very hand
Must quench the life that animated it.   60
    Orsino. There is no need of that. Listen: you know
Olimpio, the castellan of Petrella
In old Colonna's time; him whom your father
Degraded from his post? And Marzio,
That desperate wretch, whom he deprived last year
Of a reward of blood, well earned and due?
    Giacomo. I knew Olimpio; and they say he hated
Old Cenci so, that in his silent rage
His lips grew white only to see him pass.
Of Marzio I know nothing.
    Orsino.   Marzio's hate   70
Matches Olimpio's. I have sent these men,
But in your name, and as at your request,
To talk with Beatrice and Lucretia.
    Giacomo. Only to talk?
    Orsino.   The moments which even now
Pass onward to to-morrow's midnight hour
May memorize their flight with death: ere then
They must have talked, and may perhaps have done,
And made an end . . .
    Giacomo.   Listen! What sound is that?
    Orsino. The house-dog moans, and the beams crack: nought else.
    Giacomo. It is my wife complaining in her sleep: 80
I doubt not she is saying bitter things
Of me, and all my children round her dreaming
That I deny them sustenance.
    Orsino.   Whilst he
Who truly took it from them, and who fills
Their hungry rest with bitterness, now sleeps

Lapped in bad pleasures, and triumphantly
Mocks thee in visions of successful hate
Too like the truth of day.
    Giacomo.   If e'er he wakes
Again, I will not trust to hireling hands . . .
    Orsino. Why, that were well. I must be gone; good night.   90
When next we meet—may all be done!
    Giacomo.   And all
Forgotten: Oh, that I had never been!   [*Exeunt.*

END OF THE THIRD ACT.

ACT IV

Scene I—*An Apartment in the Castle of Petrella. Enter* Cenci.

    Cenci. She comes not; yet I left her even now
Vanquished and faint. She knows the penalty
Of her delay: yet what if threats are vain?
Am I not now within Petrella's moat?
Or fear I still the eyes and ears of Rome?
Might I not drag her by the golden hair?
Stamp on her? Keep her sleepless till her brain
Be overworn? Tame her with chains and famine?
Less would suffice. Yet so to leave undone
What I most seek! No, 'tis her stubborn will   10
Which by its own consent shall stoop as low
As that which drags it down.

Enter Lucretia.

                  Thou loathèd wretch!
Hide thee from my abhorrence: fly, begone!
Yet stay! Bid Beatrice come hither.
    Lucretia.   Oh,
Husband! I pray for thine own wretched sake
Heed what thou dost. A man who walks like thee
Through crimes, and through the danger of his crimes,
Each hour may stumble o'er a sudden grave.
And thou art old; thy hairs are hoary gray;

As thou wouldst save thyself from death and hell,   20
Pity thy daughter; give her to some friend
In marriage: so that she may tempt thee not
To hatred, or worse thoughts, if worse there be.
   Cenci. What! like her sister who has found a home
To mock my hate from with prosperity?
Strange ruin shall destroy both her and thee
And all that yet remain. My death may be
Rapid, her destiny outspeeds it. Go,
Bid her come hither, and before my mood
Be changed, lest I should drag her by the hair.   30
   Lucretia. She sent me to thee, husband. At thy presence
She fell, as thou dost know, into a trance;
And in that trance she heard a voice which said,
'Cenci must die! Let him confess himself!
Even now the accusing Angel waits to hear
If God, to punish his enormous crimes,
Harden his dying heart!'
   Cenci.   Why—such things are . . .
No doubt divine revealings may be made.
'Tis plain I have been favoured from above,
For when I cursed my sons they died.—Ay . . . so . . .   40
As to the right or wrong, that's talk . . . repentance . . .
Repentance is an easy moment's work
And more depends on God than me. Well . . . well . . .
I must give up the greater point, which was
To poison and corrupt her soul.
                 [*A pause; *Lucretia* approaches anxiously, and*
                     then shrinks back as he speaks.
                        One, two;
Ay . . . Rocco and Cristofano my curse
Strangled: and Giacomo, I think, will find
Life a worse Hell than that beyond the grave:
Beatrice shall, if there be skill in hate,
Die in despair, blaspheming: to Bernardo,   50
He is so innocent, I will bequeath
The memory of these deeds, and make his youth
The sepulchre of hope, where evil thoughts
Shall grow like weeds on a neglected tomb.
When all is done, out in the wide Campagna,
I will pile up my silver and my gold;
My costly robes, paintings and tapestries;

My parchments and all records of my wealth,
And make a bonfire in my joy, and leave
Of my possessions nothing but my name;   60
Which shall be an inheritance to strip
Its wearer bare as infamy. That done
My soul, which is a scourge, will I resign
Into the hands of him who wielded it;
Be it for its own punishment or theirs,
He will not ask it of me till the lash
Be, broken in its last and deepest wound;
Until its hate be all inflicted. Yet,
Lest death outspeed my purpose, let me make
Short work and sure . . .   [*Going.*
    Lucretia. (*Stops him.*) Oh, stay! It was a feint: 70
She had no vision, and she heard no voice.
I said it but to awe thee.
    Cenci.   That is well.
Vile palterer with the sacred truth of God,
Be thy soul choked with that blaspheming lie!
For Beatrice worse terrors are in store
To bend her to my will.
    Lucretia.   Oh! to what will?
What cruel sufferings more than she has known
Canst thou inflict?
    Cenci.   Andrea! Go call my daughter,
And if she comes not tell her that I come.
What sufferings? I will drag her, step by step,   80
Through infamies unheard of among men:
She shall stand shelterless in the broad noon
Of public scorn, for acts blazoned abroad,
One among which shall be . . . What? Canst thou guess?
She shall become (for what she most abhors
Shall have a fascination to entrap
Her loathing will) to her own conscious self
All she appears to others; and when dead,
As she shall die unshrived and unforgiven,
A rebel to her father and her God,   90
Her corpse shall be abandoned to the hounds;
Her name shall be the terror of the earth;
Her spirit shall approach the throne of God
Plague-spotted with my curses. I will make
Body and soul a monstrous lump of ruin.

Enter ANDREA.

Andrea. The Lady Beatrice . . .
   Cenci.   Speak, pale slave! What
Said she?
   Andrea. My Lord, 'twas what she looked; she said:
'Go tell my father that I see the gulf
Of Hell between us two, which he may pass,
I will not.'

                               [*Exit* ANDREA.
   Cenci.   Go thou quick, Lucretia,   100
Tell her to come; yet let her understand
Her coming is consent: and say, moreover,
That if she come not I will curse her.

                            [*Exit* LUCRETIA.
                          Ha!
With what but with a father's curse doth God
Panic-strike armèd victory, and make pale
Cities in their prosperity? The world's Father
Must grant a parent's prayer against his child,
Be he who asks even what men call me.
Will not the deaths of her rebellious brothers
Awe her before I speak? For I on them   110
Did imprecate quick ruin, and it came.

Enter LUCRETIA.

Well; what? Speak, wretch!
   Lucretia.   She said, 'I cannot come;
Go tell my father that I see a torrent
Of his own blood raging between us.'
   Cenci (*kneeling*).   God!
Hear me! If this most specious mass of flesh,
Which Thou hast made my daughter; this my blood,
This particle of my divided being;
Or rather, this my bane and my disease,
Whose sight infects and poisons me; this devil
Which sprung from me as from a hell, was meant   120
To aught good use; if her bright loveliness
Was kindled to illumine this dark world;
If nursed by Thy selectest dew of love
Such virtues blossom in her as should make

The peace of life, I pray Thee for my sake,
As Thou the common God and Father art
Of her, and me, and all; reverse that doom!
Earth, in the name of God, let her food be
Poison, until she be encrusted round
With leprous stains! Heaven, rain upon her head   130
The blistering drops of the Maremma's dew,
Till she be speckled like a toad; parch up
Those love-enkindled lips, warp those fine limbs
To loathèd lameness! All-beholding sun,
Strike in thine envy those life-darting eyes
With thine own blinding beams!

    Lucretia.   Peace! Peace!
For thine own sake unsay those dreadful words.
When high God grants He punishes such prayers.

    Cenci (leaping up, and throwing his right hand towards
        Heaven). He does His will, I mine! This in addition,
That if she have a child . . .

    Lucretia.   Horrible thought!   140

    Cenci. That if she ever have a child; and thou,
Quick Nature! I adjure thee by thy God,
That thou be fruitful in her, and increase
And multiply, fulfilling his command,
And my deep imprecation! May it be
A hideous likeness of herself, that as
From a distorting mirror, she may see
Her image mixed with what she most abhors,
Smiling upon her from her nursing breast.
And that the child may from its infancy   150
Grow, day by day, more wicked and deformed,
Turning her mother's love to misery:
And that both she and it may live until
It shall repay her care and pain with hate,
Or what may else be more unnatural.
So he may hunt her through the clamorous scoffs
Of the loud world to a dishonoured grave.
Shall I revoke this curse? Go, bid her come,
Before my words are chronicled in Heaven.

                      [*Exit* LUCRETIA.
                           160
I do not feel as if I were a man,
But like a fiend appointed to chastise
The offences of some unremembered world.

My blood is running up and down my veins;
A fearful pleasure makes it prick and tingle:
I feel a giddy sickness of strange awe;
My heart is beating with an expectation
Of horrid joy.

Enter LUCRETIA.

What? Speak!
Lucretia.   She bids thee curse;
And if thy curses, as they cannot do,
Could kill her soul . . .
   Cenci.   She would not come. 'Tis well,
I can do both: first take what I demand,   170
And then extort concession. To thy chamber!
Fly ere I spurn thee: and beware this night
That thou cross not my footsteps. It were safer
To come between the tiger and his prey.   [*Exit* LUCRETIA.
It must be late; mine eyes grow weary dim
With unaccustomed heaviness of sleep.
Conscience! Oh, thou most insolent of lies!
They say that sleep, that healing dew of Heaven,
Steeps not in balm the foldings of the brain
Which thinks thee an impostor. I will go   180
First to belie thee with an hour of rest,
Which will be deep and calm, I feel: and then . . .
O, multitudinous Hell, the fiends will shake
Thine arches with the laughter of their joy!
There shall be lamentation heard in Heaven
As o'er an angel fallen; and upon Earth
All good shall droop and sicken, and ill things
Shall with a spirit of unnatural life
Stir and be quickened . . . even as I am now.   [*Exit.*

SCENE II—*Before the Castle of Petrella. Enter* BEATRICE *and*
        LUCRETIA *above on the Ramparts.*

Beatrice. They come not yet.
Lucretia.   'Tis scarce midnight.
Beatrice.   How slow
Behind the course of thought, even sick with speed,
Lags leaden-footed time!
   Lucretia.   The minutes pass . . .

If he should wake before the deed is done?
   Beatrice. O, mother! He must never wake again.
What thou hast said persuades me that our act
Will but dislodge a spirit of deep hell
Out of a human form.
   Lucretia.   'Tis true he spoke
Of death and judgment with strange confidence
For one so wicked; as a man believing   10
In God, yet recking not of good or ill.
And yet to die without confession! . . .
   Beatrice.   Oh!
Believe that Heaven is merciful and just,
And will not add our dread necessity
To the amount of his offences.

       Enter OLIMPIO *and* MARZIO, *below.*

   Lucretia.   See,
They come.
   Beatrice.   All mortal things must hasten thus
To their dark end. Let us go down.
             [*Exeunt* LUCRETIA *and* BEATRICE *from above.*
   Olimpio. How feel you to this work?
   Marzio.   As one who thinks
A thousand crowns excellent market price
For an old murderer's life. Your cheeks are pale.   20
   Olimpio. It is the white reflection of your own,
Which you call pale.
   Marzio.   Is that their natural hue?
   Olimpio. Or 'tis my hate and the deferred desire
To wreak it, which extinguishes their blood.
   Marzio. You are inclined then to this business?
   Olimpio.   **Ay.**
If one should bribe me with a thousand crowns
To kill a serpent which had stung my child,
I could not be more willing.

       Enter BEATRICE *and* LUCRETIA *below.*

               Noble ladies!
   Beatrice. Are ye resolved?
   Olimpio.   Is he asleep?

Marzio.   Is all
Quiet?
    Lucretia. I mixed an opiate with his drink: 30
He sleeps so soundly . . .
    Beatrice.   That his death will be
But as a change of sin-chastising dreams,
A dark continuance of the Hell within him,
Which God extinguish! But ye are resolved?
Ye know it is a high and holy deed?
    Olimpio. We are resolved.
    Marzio.   As to the how this act
Be warranted, it rests with you.
    Beatrice.   Well, follow!
    Olimpio. Hush! Hark! What noise is that?
    Marzio.   Ha! some one comes!
    Beatrice. Ye conscience-stricken cravens, rock to rest
Your baby hearts. It is the iron gate,   40
Which ye left open, swinging to the wind,
That enters whistling as in scorn. Come, follow!
And be your steps like mine, light, quick and bold.   [*Exeunt.*

Scene III—*An Apartment in the Castle. Enter* Beatrice *and*
Lucretia.

    Lucretia. They are about it now.
    Beatrice.   Nay, it is done.
    Lucretia. I have not heard him groan.
    Beatrice.   He will not groan.
    Lucretia. What sound is that?
    Beatrice.   List! 'tis the tread of feet
About his bed.
    Lucretia.   My God!
If he be now a cold stiff corpse . . .
    Beatrice.   O, fear not
What may be done, but what is left undone:
The act seals all.

Enter Olimpio *and* Marzio.

Is it accomplished?
    Marzio.   What?
    Olimpio. Did you not call?
    Beatrice.   When?

Olimpio.   Now.
Beatrice.   I ask if all is over?
  Olimpio. We dare not kill an old and sleeping man;
His thin gray hair, his stern and reverend brow,   10
His veinèd hands crossed on his heaving breast,
And the calm innocent sleep in which he lay,
Quelled me. Indeed, indeed, I cannot do it.
  Marzio. But I was bolder; for I chid Olimpio,
And bade him bear his wrongs to his own grave
And leave me the reward. And now my knife
Touched the loose wrinkled throat, when the old man
Stirred in his sleep, and said, 'God! hear, O, hear,
A father's curse! What, art Thou not our Father?'
And then he laughed. I knew it was the ghost   20
Of my dead father speaking through his lips,
And could not kill him.
  Beatrice.   Miserable slaves!
Where, if ye dare not kill a sleeping man,
Found ye the boldness to return to me
With such a deed undone? Base palterers!
Cowards and traitors! Why, the very conscience
Which ye would sell for gold and for revenge
Is an equivocation: it sleeps over
A thousand daily acts disgracing men;
And when a deed where mercy insults Heaven . . .   30
Why do I talk?
                    [*Snatching a dagger from one of them and raising it.*
                          Hadst thou a tongue to say,
'She murdered her own father!'—I must do it!
But never dream ye shall outlive him long!
  Olimpio. Stop, for God's sake!
  Marzio.   I will go back and kill him.
  Olimpio. Give me the weapon, we must do thy will.
  Beatrice. Take it! Depart! Return!
                              [*Exeunt* OLIMPIO *and* MARZIO.
                              How pale thou art!
We do but that which 'twere a deadly crime
To leave undone.
  Lucretia.   Would it were done!
  Beatrice.   Even whilst
That doubt is passing through your mind, the world
Is conscious of a change. Darkness and Hell   40

Have swallowed up the vapour they sent forth
To blacken the sweet light of life. My breath
Comes, methinks, lighter, and the jellied blood
Runs freely through my veins. Hark!

Enter OLIMPIO and MARZIO.

He is . . .

Olimpio.   Dead!
Marzio. We strangled him that there might be no blood;
And then we threw his heavy corpse i' the garden
Under the balcony; 'twill seem it fell.
Beatrice (*giving them a bag of coin*). Here, take this gold, and
      hasten to your homes.
And, Marzio, because thou wast only awed
By that which made me tremble, wear thou this!   50
                    [*Clothes him in a rich mantle.*
It was the mantle which my grandfather
Wore in his high prosperity, and men
Envied his state: so may they envy thine.
Thou wert a weapon in the hand of God
To a just use. Live long and thrive! And, mark,
If thou hast crimes, repent: this deed is none.
                          [*A horn is sounded.*
Lucretia. Hark, 'tis the castle horn; my God! it sounds
Like the last trump.
Beatrice.   Some tedious guest is coming.
Lucretia. The drawbridge is let down; there is a tramp
Of horses in the court; fly, hide yourselves!   60
                    [*Exeunt* OLIMPIO *and* MARZIO.
Beatrice. Let us retire to counterfeit deep rest;
I scarcely need to counterfeit it now:
The spirit which doth reign within these limbs
Seems strangely undisturbed. I could even sleep
Fearless and calm: all ill is surely past.   [*Exeunt.*

SCENE IV—*Another Apartment in the Castle. Enter on one side
the Legate* SAVELLA, *introduced by a Servant, and on the
other* LUCRETIA *and* BERNARDO.

Savella. Lady, my duty to his Holiness
Be my excuse that thus unseasonably

I break upon your rest. I must speak with
Count Cenci; doth he sleep?
 Lucretia (*in a hurried and confused manner*). I think he
 sleeps;
Yet wake him not, I pray, spare me awhile,
He is a wicked and wrathful man;
Should he be roused out of his sleep to-night,
Which is, I know, a hell of angry dreams,
It were not well; indeed it were not well.
Wait till day break . . . (*aside*) O, I am deadly sick! 10
 Savella. I grieve thus to distress you, but the Count
Must answer charges of the gravest import,
And suddenly; such my commission is.
 Lucretia (*with increased agitation*). I dare not rouse him: I
  know none who dare . . .
'Twere perilous; . . . you might as safely waken
A serpent; or a corpse in which some fiend
Were laid to sleep.
 Savella.   Lady, my moments here
Are counted. I must rouse him from his sleep,
Since none else dare.
 Lucretia (*aside*). O, terror! O, despair!
(*To* BERNARDO.) Bernardo, conduct you the Lord Legate to 20
 Your father's chamber. [*Exeunt* SAVELLA *and* BERNARDO.

Enter BEATRICE.

 Beatrice.   'Tis a messenger
Come to arrest the culprit who now stands
Before the throne of unappealable God.
Both Earth and Heaven, consenting arbiters,
Acquit our deed.
 Lucretia. Oh, agony of fear!
Would that he yet might live! Even now I heard
The Legate's followers whisper as they passed
They had a warrant for his instant death.
All was prepared by unforbidden means
Which we must pay so dearly, having done. 30
Even now they search the tower, and find the body;
Now they suspect the truth; now they consult
Before they come to tax us with the fact;
O, horrible, 'tis all discovered!

Beatrice.   Mother,
What is done wisely, is done well. Be bold
As thou art just. 'Tis like a truant child
To fear that others know what thou hast done,
Even from thine own strong consciousness, and thus
Write on unsteady eyes and altered cheeks
All thou wouldst hide. Be faithful to thyself,   40
And fear no other witness but thy fear.
For if, as cannot be, some circumstance
Should rise in accusation, we can blind
Suspicion with such cheap astonishment,
Or overbear it with such guiltless pride,
As murderers cannot feign. The deed is done,
And what may follow now regards not me.
I am as universal as the light;
Free as the earth-surrounding air; as firm
As the world's centre. Consequence, to me,   50
Is as the wind which strikes the solid rock
But shakes it not.   [*A cry within and tumult.*
   Voices.   Murder! Murder! Murder!

Enter BERNARDO *and* SAVELLA.

Savella (*to his followers*). Go search the castle round; sound
      the alarm;
Look to the gates that none escape!
   Beatrice.   What now?
   Bernardo. I know not what to say . . . my father's dead.
   Beatrice. How; dead! he only sleeps; you mistake, brother.
His sleep is very calm, very like death;
'Tis wonderful how well a tyrant sleeps.
He is not dead?
   Bernardo.   Dead; murdered.
   Lucretia (*with extreme agitation*). Oh no, no,
He is not murdered though he may be dead;   60
I have alone the keys of those apartments.
   Savella. Ha! Is it so?
   Beatrice.   My Lord, I pray excuse us;
We will retire; my mother is not well:
She seems quite overcome with this strange horror.
                        [*Exeunt* LUCRETIA *and* BEATRICE.
   Savella. Can you suspect who may have murdered him?

Bernardo. I know not what to think.

Savella.   Can you name any
Who had an interest in his death?

Bernardo.   Alas!
I can name none who had not, and those most
Who most lament that such a deed is done;
My mother, and my sister, and myself.   70

Savella. 'Tis strange! There were clear marks of violence.
I found the old man's body in the moonlight
Hanging beneath the window of his chamber,
Among the branches of a pine: he could not
Have fallen there, for all his limbs lay heaped
And effortless; 'tis true there was no blood . . .
Favour me, Sir—it much imports your house
That all should be made clear—to tell the ladies
That I request their presence.

                                    [*Exit* BERNARDO.

Enter GUARDS *bringing in* MARZIO.

Guard.   We have one.

Officer. My Lord, we found this ruffian and another   80
Lurking among the rocks; there is no doubt
But that they are the murderers of Count Cenci:
Each had a bag of coin; this fellow wore
A gold-inwoven robe, which shining bright
Under the dark rocks to the glimmering moon
Betrayed them to our notice: the other fell
Desperately fighting.

Savella.   What does he confess?

Officer. He keeps firm silence; but these lines found on him
May speak.

Savella.   Their language is at least sincere.   [*Reads.*
    'To the Lady Beatrice.   90
'That the atonement of what my nature sickens to conjecture
*may soon arrive, I send thee, at thy brother's desire, those who
will speak and do more than I dare write . . .*
                        '*Thy devoted servant, Orsino.*'

Enter LUCRETIA, BEATRICE, *and* BERNARDO.

Knowest thou this writing, Lady?

Beatrice.   No.

Savella.   Nor thou?

Lucretia. (*Her conduct throughout the scene is marked by extreme agitation.*) Where was it found? What is it? It should be
Orsino's hand! It speaks of that strange horror
Which never yet found utterance, but which made
Between that hapless child and her dead father
A gulf of obscure hatred.

Savella.   Is it so?   100
Is it true, Lady, that thy father did
Such outrages as to awaken in thee
Unfilial hate?

Beatrice.   Not hate, 'twas more than hate:
This is most true, yet wherefore question me?

Savella. There is a deed demanding question done;
Thou hast a secret which will answer not.

Beatrice. What sayest? My Lord, your words are bold and rash.

Savella. I do arrest all present in the name
Of the Pope's Holiness. You must to Rome.

Lucretia. O, not to Rome! Indeed we are not guilty.   110

Beatrice. Guilty! Who dares talk of guilt? My Lord,
I am more innocent of parricide
Than is a child born fatherless . . . Dear mother,
Your gentleness and patience are no shield
For this keen-judging world, this two-edged lie,
Which seems, but is not. What! will human laws,
Rather will ye who are their ministers,
Bar all access to retribution first,
And then, when Heaven doth interpose to do
What ye neglect, arming familiar things   120
To the redress of an unwonted crime,
Make ye the victims who demanded it
Culprits? 'Tis ye are culprits! That poor wretch
Who stands so pale, and trembling, and amazed,
If it be true he murdered Cenci, was
A sword in the right hand of justest God.
Wherefore should I have wielded it? Unless
The crimes which mortal tongue dare never name
God therefore scruples to avenge.

Savella.   You own
That you desired his death?

Beatrice.   It would have been   130

A crime no less than his, if for one moment
That fierce desire had faded in my heart.
'Tis true I did believe, and hope, and pray,
Ay, I even knew . . . for God is wise and just,
That some strange sudden death hung over him.
'Tis true that this did happen, and most true
There was no other rest for me on earth,
No other hope in Heaven . . . now what of this?

   Savella. Strange thoughts beget strange deeds; and here are
Both: I judge thee not.

   Beatrice.   And yet, if you arrest me,   140
You are the judge and executioner
Of that which is the life of life: the breath
Of accusation kills an innocent name,
And leaves for lame acquittal the poor life
Which is a mask without it. 'Tis most false
That I am guilty of foul parricide;
Although I must rejoice, for justest cause,
That other hands have sent my father's soul
To ask the mercy he denied to me.
Now leave us free; stain not a noble house   150
With vague surmises of rejected crime;
Add to our sufferings and your own neglect
No heavier sum: let them have been enough:
Leave us the wreck we have.

   Savella.   I dare not, Lady.
I pray that you prepare yourselves for Rome:
There the Pope's further pleasure will be known.

   Lucretia. O, not to Rome! O, take us not to Rome!

   Beatrice. Why not to Rome, dear mother? There as here
Our innocence is as an armèd heel
To trample accusation. God is there   160
As here, and with His shadow ever clothes
The innocent, the injured and the weak;
And such are we. Cheer up, dear Lady, lean
On me; collect your wandering thoughts. My Lord,
As soon as you have taken some refreshment,
And had all such examinations made
Upon the spot, as may be necessary
To the full understanding of this matter,
We shall be ready. Mother, will you come?

   Lucretia. Ha! they will bind us to the rack, and wrest   170

Self-accusation from our agony!
Will Giacomo be there? Orsino? Marzio?
All present; all confronted; all demanding
Each from the other's countenance the thing
Which is in every heart! O, misery!

[*She faints, and is borne out.*

  Savella. She faints: an ill appearance this.
  Beatrice   My Lord,
She knows not yet the uses of the world.
She fears that power is as a beast which grasps
And loosens not: a snake whose look transmutes
All things to guilt which is its nutriment.   180
She cannot know how well the supine slaves
Of blind authority read the truth of things
When written on a brow of guilelessness:
She sees not yet triumphant Innocence
Stand at the judgement-seat of mortal man,
A judge and an accuser of the wrong
Which drags it there. Prepare yourself, my Lord;
Our suite will join yours in the court below.   [*Exeunt.*

END OF THE FOURTH ACT.

ACT V

SCENE I—*An Apartment in* ORSINO's *Palace. Enter* ORSINO *and*
GIACOMO.

  Giacomo. Do evil deeds thus quickly come to end?
O, that the vain remorse which must chastise
Crimes done, had but as loud a voice to warn
As its keen sting is mortal to avenge!
O, that the hour when present had cast off
The mantle of its mystery, and shown
The ghastly form with which it now returns
When its scared game is roused, cheering the hounds
Of conscience to their prey! Alas! Alas!
It was a wicked thought, a piteous deed,   10
To kill an old and hoary-headed father.
  Orsino. It has turned out unluckily, in truth.

Giacomo. To violate the sacred doors of sleep;
To cheat kind Nature of the placid death
Which she prepares for overwearied age;
To drag from Heaven an unrepentant soul
Which might have quenched in reconciling prayers
A life of burning crimes . . .
  Orsino.   You cannot say
I urged you to the deed.
  Giacomo.   O, had I never
Found in thy smooth and ready countenance   20
The mirror of my darkest thoughts; hadst thou
Never with hints and questions made me look
Upon the monster of my thought, until
It grew familiar to desire . . .
  Orsino.   'Tis thus
Men cast the blame of their unprosperous acts
Upon the abettors of their own resolve;
Or anything but their weak, guilty selves.
And yet, confess the truth, it is the peril
In which you stand that gives you this pale sickness
Of penitence; confess 'tis fear disguised   30
From its own shame that takes the mantle now
Of thin remorse. What if we yet were safe?
  Giacomo. How can that be? Already Beatrice,
Lucretia and the murderer are in prison.
I doubt not officers are, whilst we speak,
Sent to arrest us.
  Orsino.   I have all prepared
For instant flight. We can escape even now,
So we take fleet occasion by the hair.
  Giacomo. Rather expire in tortures, as I may.
What! will you cast by self-accusing flight   40
Assured conviction upon Beatrice?
She, who alone in this unnatural work,
Stands like God's angel ministered upon
By fiends; avenging such a nameless wrong
As turns black parricide to piety;
Whilst we for basest ends . . . I fear, Orsino,
While I consider all your words and looks,
Comparing them with your proposal now,
That you must be a villain. For what end

Could you engage in such a perilous crime,   50
Training me on with hints, and signs, and smiles,
Even to this gulf? Thou art no liar? No,
Thou art a lie! Traitor and murderer!
Coward and slave! But, no, defend thyself;   [*Drawing.*
Let the sword speak what the indignant tongue
Disdains to brand thee with.
   Orsino.   Put up your weapon.
Is it the desperation of your fear
Makes you thus rash and sudden with a friend,
Now ruined for your sake? If honest anger
Have moved you, know, that what I just proposed   60
Was but to try you. As for me, I think,
Thankless affection led me to this point,
From which, if my firm temper could repent,
I cannot now recede. Even whilst we speak
The ministers of justice wait below:
They grant me these brief moments. Now if you
Have any word of melancholy comfort
To speak to your pale wife, 'twere best to pass
Out at the postern, and avoid them so.
   Giacomo. O, generous friend! How canst thou pardon me?   70
Would that my life could purchase thine!
   Orsino.   That wish
Now comes a day too late. Haste; fare thee well!
Hear'st thou not steps along the corridor?

                              [*Exit* GIACOMO.

I'm sorry for it; but the guards are waiting
At his own gate, and such was my contrivance
That I might rid me both of him and them.
I thought to act a solemn comedy
Upon the painted scene of this new world,
And to attain my own peculiar ends
By some such plot of mingled good and ill   80
As others weave; but there arose a Power
Which grasped and snapped the threads of my device
And turned it to a net of ruin . . . Ha!   [*A shout is heard.*
Is that my name I hear proclaimed abroad?
But I will pass, wrapped in a vile disguise;
Rags on my back, and a false innocence
Upon my face, through the misdeeming crowd

Which judges by what seems. 'Tis easy then
For a new name and for a country new,
And a new life, fashioned on old desires,   90
To change the honours of abandoned Rome.
And these must be the masks of that within,
Which must remain unaltered . . . Oh, I fear
That what is past will never let me rest!
Why, when none else is conscious, but myself,
Of my misdeeds, should my own heart's contempt
Trouble me? Have I not the power to fly
My own reproaches? Shall I be the slave
Of . . . what? A word? which those of this false world
Employ against each other, not themselves;   100
As men wear daggers not for self-offence.
But if I am mistaken, where shall I
Find the disguise to hide me from myself,
As now I skulk from every other eye?   [*Exit.*

SCENE II—*A Hall of Justice.* CAMILLO, JUDGES, *&c., are discovered
seated;* MARZIO *is led in.*

   First Judge. Accused, do you persist in your denial?
I ask you, are you innocent, or guilty?
I demand who were the participators
In your offence? Speak truth and the whole truth.
   Marzio. My God! I did not kill him; I know nothing;
Olimpio sold the robe to me from which
You would infer my guilt.
   Second Judge.   Away with him!
   First Judge. Dare you, with lips yet white from the rack's kiss
Speak false? Is it so soft a questioner,
That you would bandy lover's talk with it   10
Till it wind out your life and soul? Away!
   Marzio. Spare me! O, spare! I will confess.
   First Judge.   Then speak.
   Marzio. I strangled him in his sleep.
   First Judge.   Who urged you to it?
   Marzio. His own son Giacomo, and the young prelate
Orsino sent me to Petrella; there
The ladies Beatrice and Lucretia
Tempted me with a thousand crowns, and I

And my companion forthwith murdered him.
Now let me die.
   First Judge.   This sounds as bad as truth. Guards, there,
Lead forth the prisoners!

      Enter LUCRETIA, BEATRICE, *and* GIACOMO, *guarded.*

                     Look upon this man;   20
When did you see him last?
   Beatrice.   We never saw him.
   Marzio. You know me too well, Lady Beatrice.
   Beatrice. I know thee! How? where? when?
   Marzio.   You know 'twas I
Whom you did urge with menaces and bribes
To kill your father. When the thing was done
You clothed me in a robe of woven gold
And bade me thrive: how I have thriven, you see.
You, my Lord Giacomo, Lady Lucretia,
You know that what I speak is true.
         [BEATRICE *advances towards him; he covers his*
              face, and shrinks back.
                     Oh, dart
The terrible resentment of those eyes   30
On the dead earth! Turn them away from me!
They wound: 'twas torture forced the truth. My Lords,
Having said this let me be led to death.
   Beatrice. Poor wretch, I pity thee: yet stay awhile.
   Camillo. Guards, lead him not away.
   Beatrice.   Cardinal Camillo,
You have a good repute for gentleness
And wisdom: can it be that you sit here
To countenance a wicked farce like this?
When some obscure and trembling slave is dragged
From sufferings which might shake the sternest heart   40
And bade to answer, not as he believes,
But as those may suspect or do desire
Whose questions thence suggest their own reply:
And that in peril of such hideous torments
As merciful God spares even the damned. Speak now
The thing you surely know, which is that you,
If your fine frame were stretched upon that wheel,

And you were told: 'Confess that you did poison
Your little nephew; that fair blue-eyed child
Who was the lodestar of your life:'—and though   50
All see, since his most swift and piteous death,
That day and night, and heaven and earth, and time,
And all the things hoped for or done therein
Are changed to you, through your exceeding grief,
Yet you would say, 'I confess anything:'
And beg from your tormentors, like that slave,
The refuge of dishonourable death.
I pray thee, Cardinal, that thou assert
My innocence.
    Camillo (much moved). What shall we think, my Lords?
Shame on these tears! I thought the heart was frozen   60
Which is their fountain. I would pledge my soul
That she is guiltless.
    Judge.   Yet she must be tortured.
    Camillo. I would as soon have tortured mine own nephew
(If he now lived he would be just her age;
His hair, too, was her colour, and his eyes
Like hers in shape, but blue and not so deep)
As that most perfect image of God's love
That ever came sorrowing upon the earth.
She is as pure as speechless infancy!
    Judge. Well, be her purity on your head, my Lord,   70
If you forbid the rack. His Holiness
Enjoined us to pursue this monstrous crime
By the severest forms of law; nay, even
To stretch a point against the criminals.
The prisoners stand accused of parricide
Upon such evidence as justifies
Torture.
    Beatrice. What evidence? This man's?
    Judge.   Even so.
    Beatrice (to MARZIO*).* Come near. And who art thou thus
           chosen forth
Out of the multitude of living men
To kill the innocent?
    Marzio.   I am Marzio,   80
Thy father's vassal.
    Beatrice.   Fix thine eyes on mine;

Answer to what I ask.   [*Turning to the* Judges.
                    I prithee mark
His countenance: unlike bold calumny
Which sometimes dares not speak the thing it looks,
He dares not look the thing he speaks, but bends
His gaze on the blind earth.
(*To* Marzio.)   What! wilt thou say
That I did murder my own father?
     Marzio.   Oh!
Spare me! My brain swims round . . . I cannot speak . . .
It was that horrid torture forced the truth.
Take me away! Let her not look on me!   90
I am a guilty miserable wretch;
I have said all I know; now, let me die!
     Beatrice. My Lords, if by my nature I had been
So stern, as to have planned the crime alleged,
Which your suspicions dictate to this slave,
And the rack makes him utter, do you think
I should have left this two-edged instrument
Of my misdeed; this man, this bloody knife
With my own name engraven on the heft,
Lying unsheathed amid a world of foes,   100
For my own death? That with such horrible need
For deepest silence, I should have neglected
So trivial a precaution, as the making
His tomb the keeper of a secret written
On a thief's memory? What is his poor life?
What are a thousand lives? A parricide
Had trampled them like dust; and, see, he lives!
(*Turning to* Marzio.) And thou . . .
     Marzio.   Oh, spare me! Speak to me no more!
That stern yet piteous look, those solemn tones,
Wound worse than torture.
     (*To the* Judges.)   I have told it all;   110
For pity's sake lead me away to death.
     Camillo. Guards, lead him nearer the Lady Beatrice,
He shrinks from her regard like autumn's leaf
From the keen breath of the serenest north.
     Beatrice. O thou who tremblest on the giddy verge
Of life and death, pause ere thou answerest me;
So mayst thou answer God with less dismay:

What evil have we done thee? I, alas!
Have lived but on this earth a few sad years,
And so my lot was ordered, that a father   120
First turned the moments of awakening life
To drops, each poisoning youth's sweet hope; and then
Stabbed with one blow my everlasting soul;
And my untainted fame; and even that peace
Which sleeps within the core of the heart's heart;
But the wound was not mortal; so my hate
Became the only worship I could lift
To our great father, who in pity and love,
Armed thee, as thou dost say, to cut him off;
And thus his wrong becomes my accusation;   130
And art thou the accuser? If thou hopest
Mercy in heaven, show justice upon earth:
Worse than a bloody hand is a hard heart.
If thou hast done murders, made thy life's path
Over the trampled laws of God and man,
Rush not before thy Judge, and say: 'My maker,
I have done this and more; for there was one
Who was most pure and innocent on earth;
And because she endured what never any
Guilty or innocent endured before: 140
Because her wrongs could not be told, not thought;
Because thy hand at length did rescue her;
I with my words killed her and all her kin.'
Think, I adjure you, what it is to slay
The reverence living in the minds of men
Towards our ancient house, and stainless fame!
Think what it is to strangle infant pity,
Cradled in the belief of guileless looks,
Till it become a crime to suffer. Think
What 'tis to blot with infamy and blood   150
All that which shows like innocence, and is,
Hear me, great God! I swear, most innocent,
So that the world lose all discrimination
Between the sly, fierce, wild regard of guilt,
And that which now compels thee to reply
To what I ask: Am I or am I not
A parricide?
    Marzio.   Thou art not!

Judge.   What is this?
Marzio. I here declare those whom I did accuse
Are innocent. 'Tis I alone am guilty.
  Judge. Drag him away to torments; let them be   160
Subtle and long drawn out, to tear the folds
Of the heart's inmost cell. Unbind him not
Till he confess.
  Marzio.   Torture me as ye will:
A keener pang has wrung a higher truth
From my last breath. She is most innocent!
Bloodhounds, not men, glut yourselves well with me;
I will not give you that fine piece of nature
To rend and ruin.

                    [*Exit* MARZIO, *guarded.*
  Camillo.   What say ye now, my Lords?
  Judge. Let tortures strain the truth till it be white
As snow thrice sifted by the frozen wind.   170
  Camillo. Yet stained with blood.
  Judge (*to* BEATRICE).   Know you this paper, Lady?
  Beatrice. Entrap me not with questions. Who stands here
As my accuser? Ha! wilt thou be he,
Who art my judge? Accuser, witness, judge,
What, all in one? Here is Orsino's name;
Where is Orsino? Let his eye meet mine.
What means this scrawl? Alas! ye know not what,
And therefore on the chance that it may be
Some evil, will ye kill us?

                    Enter an Officer.

  Officer.   Marzio's dead.
  Judge. What did he say?
  Officer.   Nothing. As soon as we   180
Had bound him on the wheel, he smiled on us,
As one who baffles a deep adversary;
And holding his breath, died.
  Judge.   There remains nothing
But to apply the question to those prisoners,
Who yet remain stubborn.
  Camillo.   I overrule
Further proceedings, and in the behalf

Of these most innocent and noble persons
Will use my interest with the Holy Father.
   Judge. Let the Pope's pleasure then be done. Meanwhile
Conduct these culprits each to separate cells;   190
And be the engines ready: for this night
If the Pope's resolution be as grave,
Pious, and just as once, I'll wring the truth
Out of those nerves and sinews, groan by groan.   [*Exeunt.*

SCENE III—*The Cell of a Prison.* BEATRICE *is discovered asleep on
a couch. Enter* BERNARDO.

   Bernardo. How gently slumber rests upon her face,
Like the last thoughts of some day sweetly spent
Closing in night and dreams, and so prolonged.
After such torments as she bore last night,
How light and soft her breathing comes. Ay me!
Methinks that I shall never sleep again.
But I must shake the heavenly dew of rest
From this sweet folded flower, thus . . . wake! awake!
What, sister, canst thou sleep?
   Beatrice (awaking).   I was just dreaming
That we were all in Paradise. Thou knowest   10
This cell seems like a kind of Paradise
After our father's presence.
   Bernardo.   Dear, dear sister.
Would that thy dream were not a dream! O God!
How shall I tell?
   Beatrice.   What wouldst thou tell, sweet brother?
   Bernardo. Look not so calm and happy, or even whilst
I stand considering what I have to say
My heart will break.
   Beatrice.   See now, thou mak'st me weep:
How very friendless thou wouldst be, dear child,
If I were dead. Say what thou hast to say.
   Bernardo. They have confessed; they could endure no more 20
The tortures . . .
   Beatrice.   Ha! What was there to confess?
They must have told some weak and wicked lie
To flatter their tormentors. Have they said
That they were guilty? O white innocence,

That thou shouldst wear the mask of guilt to hide
Thine awful and serenest countenance
From those who know thee not!

Enter JUDGE *with* LUCRETIA *and* GIACOMO, *guarded.*

         Ignoble hearts!
For some brief spasms of pain, which are at least
As mortal as the limbs through which they pass,
Are centuries of high splendour laid in dust?   30
And that eternal honour which should live
Sunlike, above the reek of mortal fame,
Changed to a mockery and a byword? What!
Will you give up these bodies to be dragged
At horses' heels, so that our hair should sweep
The footsteps of the vain and senseless crowd,
Who, that they may make our calamity
Their worship and their spectacle, will leave
The churches and the theatres as void
As their own hearts? Shall the light multitude   40
Fling, at their choice, curses or faded pity,
Sad funeral flowers to deck a living corpse,
Upon us as we pass to pass away,
And leave . . . what memory of our having been?
Infamy, blood, terror, despair? O thou,
Who wert a mother to the parentless,
Kill not thy child! Let not her wrongs kill thee!
Brother, lie down with me upon the rack,
And let us each be silent as a corpse;
It soon will be as soft as any grave.   50
'Tis but the falsehood it can wring from fear
Makes the rack cruel.
  Giacomo.   They will tear the truth
Even from thee at last, those cruel pains:
For pity's sake say thou art guilty now.
  Lucretia. Oh, speak the truth! Let us all quickly die;
And after death, God is our judge, not they;
He will have mercy on us.
  Bernardo.   If indeed
It can be true, say so, dear sister mine;
And then the Pope will surely pardon you,
And all be well.

Judge.   Confess, or I will warp   60
Your limbs with such keen tortures . . .
   Beatrice.   Tortures! Turn
The rack henceforth into a spinning-wheel!
Torture your dog, that he may tell when last
He lapped the blood his master shed . . . not me!
My pangs are of the mind, and of the heart,
And of the soul; ay, of the inmost soul,
Which weeps within tears as of burning gall
To see, in this ill world where none are true,
My kindred false to their deserted selves.
And with considering all the wretched life   70
Which I have lived, and its now wretched end,
And the small justice shown by Heaven and Earth
To me or mine; and what a tyrant thou art,
And what slaves these; and what a world we make,
The oppressor and the oppressed . . . such pangs compel
My answer. What is it thou wouldst with me?
   Judge. Art thou not guilty of thy father's death?
   Beatrice. Or wilt thou rather tax high-judging God
That He permitted such an act as that
Which I have suffered, and which He beheld;   80
Made it unutterable, and took from it
All refuge, all revenge, all consequence,
But that which thou hast called my father's death?
Which is or is not what men call a crime,
Which either I have done, or have not done;
Say what ye will. I shall deny no more.
If ye desire it thus, thus let it be,
And so an end of all. Now do your will;
No other pains shall force another word.
   Judge. She is convicted, but has not confessed.   90
Be it enough. Until their final sentence
Let none have converse with them. You, young Lord,
Linger not here!
   Beatrice.   Oh, tear him not away!
   Judge. Guards, do your duty.
   Bernardo (embracing BEATRICE*).* Oh! would ye divide
Body from soul?
   Officer.   That is the headsman's business.
            [*Exeunt all but* LUCRETIA, BEATRICE, *and* GIACOMO.
   Giacomo. Have I confessed? Is it all over now?

No hope! No refuge! O weak, wicked tongue
Which hast destroyed me, would that thou hadst been
Cut out and thrown to dogs first! To have killed
My father first, and then betrayed my sister;   100
Ay, thee! the one thing innocent and pure
In this black guilty world, to that which I
So well deserve! My wife! my little ones!
Destitute, helpless, and I . . . Father! God!
Canst Thou forgive even the unforgiving,
When their full hearts break thus, thus! . . .

          [Covers his face and weeps.
 Lucretia.   O my child!
To what a dreadful end are we all come!
Why did I yield? Why did I not sustain
Those torments? Oh, that I were all dissolved
Into these fast and unavailing tears,   110
Which flow and feel not!
 Beatrice.   What 'twas weak to do,
'Tis weaker to lament, once being done;
Take cheer! The God who knew my wrong, and made
Our speedy act the angel of His wrath,
Seems, and but seems, to have abandoned us.
Let us not think that we shall die for this.
Brother, sit near me; give me your firm hand,
You had a manly heart. Bear up! Bear up!
O dearest Lady, put your gentle head
Upon my lap, and try to sleep awhile: 120
Your eyes look pale, hollow and overworn,
With heaviness of watching and slow grief.
Come, I will sing you some low, sleepy tune,
Not cheerful, nor yet sad; some dull old thing,
Some outworn and unused monotony,
Such as our country gossips sing and spin,
Till they almost forget they live: lie down!
So, that will do. Have I forgot the words?
Faith! They are sadder than I thought they were.

SONG

  False friend, wilt thou smile or weep   130
  When my life is laid asleep?
  Little cares for a smile or a tear,

The clay-cold corpse upon the bier!
    Farewell! Heigho!
    What is this whispers low?
There is a snake in thy smile, my dear;
And bitter poison within thy tear.

Sweet sleep, were death like to thee,
Or if thou couldst mortal be,
I would close these eyes of pain;   140
When to wake? Never again.
    O World! Farewell!
    Listen to the passing bell!
It says, thou and I must part,
With a light and a heavy heart.   [*The scene closes.*

SCENE IV—*A Hall of the Prison. Enter* CAMILLO *and* BERNARDO.

  Camillo. The Pope is stern; not to be moved or bent.
He looked as calm and keen as is the engine
Which tortures and which kills, exempt itself
From aught that it inflicts; a marble form,
A rite, a law, a custom: not a man.
He frowned, as if to frown had been the trick
Of his machinery, on the advocates
Presenting the defences, which he tore
And threw behind, muttering with hoarse, harsh voice:
'Which among ye defended their old father   10
Killed in his sleep?' Then to another: 'Thou
Dost this in virtue of thy place; 'tis well.'
He turned to me then, looking deprecation,
And said these three words, coldly: 'They must die.'
  Bernardo. And yet you left him not?
  Camillo.   I urged him still;
Pleading, as I could guess, the devilish wrong
Which prompted your unnatural parent's death.
And he replied: 'Paolo Santa Croce
Murdered his mother yester evening,
And he is fled. Parricide grows so rife   20
That soon, for some just cause no doubt, the young
Will strangle us all, dozing in our chairs.
Authority, and power, and hoary hair
Are grown crimes capital. You are my nephew,

You come to ask their pardon; stay a moment;
Here is their sentence; never see me more
Till, to the letter, it be all fulfilled.'
   Bernardo. O God, not so! I did believe indeed
That all you said was but sad preparation
For happy news. Oh, there are words and looks   **30**
To bend the sternest purpose! Once I knew them,
Now I forget them at my dearest need.
What think you if I seek him out, and bathe
His feet and robe with hot and bitter tears?
Importune him with prayers, vexing his brain
With my perpetual cries, until in rage
He strike me with his pastoral cross, and trample
Upon my prostrate head, so that my blood
May stain the senseless dust on which he treads,
And remorse waken mercy? I will do it!   **40**
Oh, wait till I return!   [*Rushes out.*
   Camillo.   Alas! poor boy!
A wreck-devoted seaman thus might pray
To the deaf sea.

      Enter LUCRETIA, BEATRICE, *and* GIACOMO, *guarded.*

   Beatrice.   I hardly dare to fear
That thou bring'st other news than a just pardon.
   Camillo. May God in heaven be less inexorable
To the Pope's prayers, than he has been to mine.
Here is the sentence and the warrant.
   Beatrice (*wildly*).
My God! Can it be possible I have
To die so suddenly? So young to go
Under the obscure, cold, rotting, wormy ground!   **50**
To be nailed down into a narrow place;
To see no more sweet sunshine; hear no more
Blithe voice of living thing; muse not again
Upon familiar thoughts, sad, yet thus lost—
How fearful! to be nothing! Or to be . . .
What? Oh, where am I? Let me not go mad!
Sweet Heaven, forgive weak thoughts! If there should be
No God, no Heaven, no Earth in the void world!
The wide, gray, lampless, deep, unpeopled world!
If all things then should be . . . my father's spirit,   **60**

His eye, his voice, his touch surrounding me;
The atmosphere and breath of my dead life!
If sometimes, as a shape more like himself,
Even the form which tortured me on earth,
Masked in gray hairs and wrinkles, he should come
And wind me in his hellish arms, and fix
His eyes on mine, and drag me down, down, down!
For was he not alone omnipotent
On Earth, and ever present? Even though dead,
Does not his spirit live in all that breathe,   70
And work for me and mine still the same ruin,
Scorn, pain, despair? Who ever yet returned
To teach the laws of Death's untrodden realm?
Unjust perhaps as those which drive us now,
Oh, whither, whither?
    Lucretia.   Trust in God's sweet love,
The tender promises of Christ: ere night,
Think, we shall be in Paradise.
    Beatrice.   'Tis past!
Whatever comes my heart shall sink no more.
And yet, I know not why, your words strike chill:
How tedious, false and cold seem all things. I   80
Have met with much injustice in this world;
No difference has been made by God or man,
Or any power moulding my wretched lot,
'Twixt good or evil, as regarded me.
I am cut off from the only world I know,
From light, and life, and love, in youth's sweet prime.
You do well telling me to trust in God,
I hope I do trust in Him. In whom else
Can any trust? And yet my heart is cold.
        [*During the latter speeches* Giacomo *has retired convers-
            ing with* Camillo, *who now goes out;* Giacomo *ad-
            vances.*
    Giacomo. Know you not, Mother . . . Sister, know you not? 90
Bernardo even now is gone to implore
The Pope to grant our pardon.
    Lucretia.   Child, perhaps
It will be granted. We may all then live
To make these woes a tale for distant years:
Oh, what a thought! It gushes to my heart
Like the warm blood.

Beatrice.   Yet both will soon be cold.
Oh, trample out that thought! Worse than despair,
Worse than the bitterness of death, is hope:
It is the only ill which can find place
Upon the giddy, sharp and narrow hour   100
Tottering beneath us. Plead with the swift frost
That it should spare the eldest flower of spring:
Plead with awakening earthquake, o'er whose couch
Even now a city stands, strong, fair, and free;
Now stench and blackness yawn, like death. Oh, plead
With famine, or wind-walking Pestilence,
Blind lightning, or the deaf sea, not with man!
Cruel, cold, formal man; righteous in words,
In deeds a Cain. No, Mother, we must die:
Since such is the reward of innocent lives;   110
Such the alleviation of worst wrongs.
And whilst our murderers live, and hard, cold men,
Smiling and slow, walk through a world of tears
To death as to life's sleep; 'twere just the grave
Were some strange joy for us. Come, obscure Death,
And wind me in thine all-embracing arms!
Like a fond mother hide me in thy bosom,
And rock me to the sleep from which none wake.
Live ye, who live, subject to one another
As we were once, who now . . .

BERNARDO *rushes in.*

Bernardo.   Oh, horrible!   120
That tears, that looks, that hope poured forth in prayer,
Even till the heart is vacant and despairs,
Should all be vain! The ministers of death
Are waiting round the doors. I thought I saw
Blood on the face of one . . . What if 'twere fancy?
Soon the heart's blood of all I love on earth
Will sprinkle him, and he will wipe it off
As if 'twere only rain. O life! O world!
Cover me! let me be no more! To see
That perfect mirror of pure innocence   130
Wherein I gazed, and grew happy and good,
Shivered to dust! To see thee, Beatrice,

Who made all lovely thou didst look upon . . .
Thee, light of life . . . dead, dark! while I say, sister,
To hear I have no sister; and thou, Mother,
Whose love was as a bond to all our loves . . .
Dead! The sweet bond broken!

Enter CAMILLO *and Guards.*

                        They come! Let me
Kiss those warm lips before their crimson leaves
Are blighted . . . white . . . cold. Say farewell, before
Death chokes that gentle voice! Oh, let me hear   140
You speak!
    Beatrice.   Farewell, my tender brother. Think
Of our sad fate with gentleness, as now:
And let mild, pitying thoughts lighten for thee
Thy sorrow's load. Err not in harsh despair,
But tears and patience. One thing more, my child:
For thine own sake be constant to the love
Thou bearest us; and to the faith that I,
Though wrapped in a strange cloud of crime and shame,
Lived ever holy and unstained. And though
Ill tongues shall wound me, and our common name   150
Be as a mark stamped on thine innocent brow
For men to point at as they pass, do thou
Forbear, and never think a thought unkind
Of those, who perhaps love thee in their graves.
So mayest thou die as I do; fear and pain
Being subdued. Farewell! Farewell! Farewell!
    Bernardo. I cannot say, farewell!
    Camillo.   Oh, Lady Beatrice!
    Beatrice. Give yourself no unnecessary pain,
My dear Lord Cardinal. Here, Mother, tie
My girdle for me, and bind up this hair   160
In any simple knot; ay, that does well.
And yours I see is coming down. How often
Have we done this for one another; now
We shall not do it any more. My Lord,
We are quite ready. Well, 'tis very well.

THE END.

[1819; publ. 1820]

THE MASQUE OF ANARCHY

WRITTEN ON THE OCCASION OF THE MASSACRE AT MANCHESTER

I

As I lay asleep in Italy
There came a voice from over the Sea,
And with great power it forth led me
To walk in the visions of Poesy.

II

I met Murder on the way—
He had a mask like Castlereagh—
Very smooth he looked, yet grim;
Seven blood-hounds followed him:

III

All were fat; and well they might
Be in admirable plight,
For one by one, and two by two,
He tossed them human hearts to chew
Which from his wide cloak he drew.

IV

Next came Fraud, and he had on,
Like Eldon, an ermined gown;
His big tears, for he wept well,
Turned to mill-stones as they fell.

V

And the little children, who
Round his feet played to and fro,

20

Thinking every tear a gem,
Had their brains knocked out by them.

VI

Clothed with the Bible, as with light,
And the shadows of the night,
Like Sidmouth, next, Hypocrisy
On a crocodile rode by.

VII

And many more destructions played
In this ghastly masquerade,
All disguised, even to the eyes,
Like Bishops, lawyers, peers, or spies.

VIII

Last came Anarchy: he rode
On a white horse, splashed with blood;
He was pale even to the lips,
Like Death in the Apocalypse.

30

IX

And he wore a kingly crown;
And in his grasp a sceptre shone;
On his brow this mark I saw—
'I AM GOD, AND KING, AND LAW!'

X

With a pace stately and fast,
Over English land he passed,
Trampling to a mire of blood
The adoring multitude.

40

XI

And a mighty troop around,
With their trampling shook the ground,

Waving each a bloody sword,
For the service of their Lord.

XII

And with glorious triumph, they
Rode through England proud and gay,
Drunk as with intoxication
Of the wine of desolation.

XIII

O'er fields and towns, from sea to sea,   50
Passed the Pageant swift and free,
Tearing up, and trampling down;
Till they came to London town.

XIV

And each dweller, panic-stricken,
Felt his heart with terror sicken
Hearing the tempestuous cry
Of the triumph of Anarchy.

XV

For with pomp to meet him came,
Clothed in arms like blood and flame,
The hired murderers, who did sing   60
'Thou art God, and Law, and King.

XVI

'We have waited, weak and lone
For thy coming, Mighty One!
Our purses are empty, our swords are cold,
Give us glory, and blood, and gold.'

XVII

Lawyers and priests, a motley crowd,
To the earth their pale brows bowed;

Like a bad prayer not over loud,
Whispering—'Thou art Law and God.'—

XVIII

Then all cried with one accord,   70
'Thou art King, and God, and Lord;
Anarchy, to thee we bow,
Be thy name made holy now!'

XIX

And Anarchy, the Skeleton,
Bowed and grinned to every one,
As well as if his education
Had cost ten millions to the nation.

XX

For he knew the Palaces
Of our Kings were rightly his;
His the sceptre, crown, and globe,   80
And the gold-inwoven robe.

XXI

So he sent his slaves before
To seize upon the Bank and Tower,
And was proceeding with intent
To meet his pensioned Parliament

XXII

When one fled past, a maniac maid,
And her name was Hope, she said:
But she looked more like Despair,
And she cried out in the air:

XXIII

'My father Time is weak and gray   90
With waiting for a better day;

See how idiot-like he stands,
Fumbling with his palsied hands!

XXIV

'He has had child after child,
And the dust of death is piled
Over every one but me—
Misery, oh, Misery!'

XXV

Then she lay down in the street,
Right before the horses' feet,
Expecting, with a patient eye,   100
Murder, Fraud, and Anarchy.

XXVI

When between her and her foes
A mist, a light, an image rose,
Small at first, and weak, and frail
Like the vapour of a vale:

XXVII

Till as clouds grow on the blast,
Like tower-crowned giants striding fast,
And glare with lightnings as they fly,
And speak in thunder to the sky,

XXVIII

It grew—a Shape arrayed in mail   110
Brighter than the viper's scale,
And upborne on wings whose grain
Was as the light of sunny rain.

XXIX

On its helm, seen far away,
A planet, like the Morning's, lay;

And those plumes its light rained through
Like a shower of crimson dew.

XXX

With step as soft as wind it passed
O'er the heads of men—so fast
That they knew the presence there, 120
And looked,—but all was empty air.

XXXI

As flowers beneath May's footstep waken,
As stars from Night's loose hair are shaken,
As waves arise when loud winds call,
Thoughts sprung where'er that step did fall.

XXXII

And the prostrate multitude
Looked—and ankle-deep in blood,
Hope, that maiden most serene,
Was walking with a quiet mien:

XXXIII

And Anarchy, the ghastly birth, 130
Lay dead earth upon the earth;
The Horse of Death tameless as wind
Fled, and with his hoofs did grind
To dust the murderers thronged behind.

XXXIV

A rushing light of clouds and splendour,
A sense awakening and yet tender
Was heard and felt—and at its close
These words of joy and fear arose

XXXV

As if their own indignant Earth
Which gave the sons of England birth 140

Had felt their blood upon her brow,
And shuddering with a mother's throe

XXXVI

Had turnèd every drop of blood
By which her face had been bedewed
To an accent unwithstood,—
As if her heart had cried aloud:

XXXVII

'Men of England, heirs of Glory,
Heroes of unwritten story,
Nurslings of one mighty Mother,
Hopes of her, and one another;   150

XXXVIII

'Rise like Lions after slumber
In unvanquishable number,
Shake your chains to earth like dew
Which in sleep had fallen on you—
Ye are many—they are few.

XXXIX

'What is Freedom?—ye can tell
That which slavery is, too well—
For its very name has grown
To an echo of your own.

XL

' 'Tis to work and have such pay   160
As just keeps life from day to day
In your limbs, as in a cell
For the tyrants' use to dwell,

XLI

'So that ye for them are made
Loom, and plough, and sword, and spade,

With or without your own will bent
To their defence and nourishment.

XLII

' 'Tis to see your children weak
With their mothers pine and peak,
When the winter winds are bleak,—   170
They are dying whilst I speak.

XLIII

' 'Tis to hunger for such diet
As the rich man in his riot
Casts to the fat dogs that lie
Surfeiting beneath his eye;

XLIV

' 'Tis to let the Ghost of Gold
Take from Toil a thousandfold
More than e'er its substance could
In the tyrannies of old.

XLV

'Paper coin—that forgery   180
Of the title-deeds, which ye
Hold to something of the worth
Of the inheritance of Earth.

XLVI

' 'Tis to be a slave in soul
And to hold no strong control
Over your own wills, but be
All that others make of ye.

XLVII

'And at length when ye complain
With a murmur weak and vain

'Tis to see the Tyrant's crew   190
Ride over your wives and you—
Blood is on the grass like dew.

XLVIII

'Then it is to feel revenge
Fiercely thirsting to exchange
Blood for blood—and wrong for wrong—
Do not thus when ye are strong.

XLIX

'Birds find rest, in narrow nest
When weary of their wingèd quest;
Beasts find fare, in woody lair
When storm and snow are in the air.   200

L

'Asses, swine, have litter spread
And with fitting food are fed;
All things have a home but one—
Thou, Oh, Englishman, hast none!

LI

'This is Slavery—savage men,
Or wild beasts within a den
Would endure not as ye do—
But such ills they never knew.

LII

'What art thou, Freedom? O! could slaves
Answer from their living graves   210
This demand—tyrants would flee
Like a dream's dim imagery.

LIII

'Thou art not, as impostors say,
A shadow soon to pass away,

A superstitition, and a name
Echoing from the cave of Fame.

LIV

'For the labourer thou art bread,
And a comely table spread
From his daily labour come
In a neat and happy home.   220

LV

'Thou art clothes, and fire, and food
For the trampled multitude—
No—in countries that are free
Such starvation cannot be
As in England now we see.

LVI

'To the rich thou art a check,
When his foot is on the neck
Of his victim, thou dost make
That he treads upon a snake.

LVII

'Thou art Justice—ne'er for gold   230
May thy righteous laws be sold
As laws are in England—thou
Shield'st alike the high and low.

LVIII

'Thou art Wisdom—Freemen never
Dream that God will damn for ever
All who think those things untrue
Of which Priests make such ado.

LIX

'Thou art Peace—never by thee
Would blood and treasure wasted be

As tyrants wasted them, when all   240
Leagued to quench thy flame in Gaul.

LX

'What if English toil and blood
Was poured forth, even as a flood?
It availed, Oh, Liberty,
To dim, but not extinguish thee.

LXI

'Thou art Love—the rich have kissed
Thy feet, and like him following Christ,
Give their substance to the free
And through the rough world follow thee,

LXII

'Or turn their wealth to arms, and make   250
War for thy belovèd sake
On wealth, and war, and fraud—whence they
Drew the power which is their prey.

LXIII

'Science, Poetry, and Thought
Are thy lamps; they make the lot
Of the dwellers in a cot
So serene, they curse it not.

LXIV

'Spirit, Patience, Gentleness,
All that can adorn and bless
Art thou—let deeds, not words, express   260
Thine exceeding loveliness.

LXV

'Let a great Assembly be
Of the fearless and the free

On some spot of English ground
Where the plains stretch wide around.

LXVI

'Let the blue sky overhead,
The green earth on which ye tread,
All that must eternal be
Witness the solemnity.

LXVII

'From the corners uttermost   270
Of the bounds of English coast;
From every hut, village, and town
Where those who live and suffer moan
For others' misery or their own,

LXVIII

'From the workhouse and the prison
Where pale as corpses newly risen,
Women, children, young and old
Groan for pain, and weep for cold—

LXIX

'From the haunts of daily life
Where is waged the daily strife   280
With common wants and common cares
Which sows the human heart with tares—

LXX

'Lastly from the palaces
Where the murmur of distress
Echoes, like the distant sound
Of a wind alive around

LXXI

'Those prison halls of wealth and fashion,
Where some few feel such compassion

For those who groan, and toil, and wail
As must make their brethren pale—   290

LXXII

'Ye who suffer woes untold,
Or to feel, or to behold
Your lost country bought and sold
With a price of blood and gold—

LXXIII

'Let a vast assembly be,
And with great solemnity
Declare with measured words that ye
Are, as God has made ye, free—

LXXIV

'Be your strong and simple words
Keen to wound as sharpened swords,   300
And wide as targes let them be,
With their shade to cover ye.

LXXV

'Let the tyrants pour around
With a quick and startling sound,
Like the loosening of a sea,
Troops of armed emblazonry.

LXXVI

'Let the charged artillery drive
Till the dead air seems alive
With the clash of clanging wheels,
And the tramp of horses' heels.   310

LXXVII

'Let the fixèd bayonet
Gleam with sharp desire to wet

Its bright point in English blood
Looking keen as one for food.

LXXVIII

'Let the horsemen's scimitars
Wheel and flash, like sphereless stars
Thirsting to eclipse their burning
In a sea of death and mourning.

LXXIX

'Stand ye calm and resolute,
Like a forest close and mute,   320
With folded arms and looks which are
Weapons of unvanquished war,

LXXX

'And let Panic, who outspeeds
The career of armèd steeds
Pass, a disregarded shade
Through your phalanx undismayed.

LXXXI

'Let the laws of your own land,
Good or ill, between ye stand
Hand to hand, and foot to foot,
Arbiters of the dispute,   330

LXXXII

'The old laws of England—they
Whose reverend heads with age are gray,
Children of a wiser day;
And whose solemn voice must be
Thine own echo—Liberty!

LXXXIII

'On those who first should violate
Such sacred heralds in their state

Rest the blood that must ensue,
And it will not rest on you.

LXXXIV

'And if then the tyrants dare   340
Let them ride among you there,
Slash, and stab, and maim, and hew,—
What they like, that let them do.

LXXXV

'With folded arms and steady eyes,
And little fear, and less surprise,
Look upon them as they slay
Till their rage has died away.

LXXXVI

'Then they will return with shame
And the blood thus shed will speak   350
To the place from which they came,
In hot blushes on their cheek.

LXXXVII

'Every woman in the land
Will point at them as they stand—
They will hardly dare to greet
Their acquaintance in the street.

LXXXVIII

'And the bold, true warriors
Who have hugged Danger in wars
Will turn to those who would be free,
Ashamed of such base company.

LXXXIX

'And that slaughter to the Nation   360
Shall steam up like inspiration,

Eloquent, oracular;
A volcano heard afar.

XC

'And these words shall then become
Like Oppression's thundered doom
Ringing through each heart and brain
Heard again—again—again—

XCI

'Rise like Lions after slumber
In unvanquishable number—
Shake your chains to earth like dew   370
Which in sleep had fallen on you—
Ye are many—they are few.'

[1819; publ. 1832]

THE WITCH OF ATLAS

TO MARY
(ON HER OBJECTING TO THE FOLLOWING POEM, UPON THE
SCORE OF ITS CONTAINING NO HUMAN INTEREST)

I

How, my dear Mary,—are you critic-bitten
    (For vipers kill, though dead) by some review,
That you condemn these verses I have written,
    Because they tell no story, false or true?
What, though no mice are caught by a young kitten,
    May it not leap and play as grown cats do,
Till its claws come? Prithee, for this one time,
Content thee with a visionary rhyme.

II

What hand would crush the silken-wingèd fly,
    The youngest of inconstant April's minions,   10
Because it cannot climb the purest sky,

Where the swan sings, amid the sun's dominions?
Not thine. Thou knowest 'tis its doom to die,
    When Day shall hide within her twilight pinions
The lucent eyes, and the eternal smile,
Serene as thine, which lent it life awhile.

III

To thy fair feet a wingèd Vision came,
    Whose date should have been longer than a day,
And o'er thy head did beat its wings for fame,
    And in thy sight its fading plumes display;   20
The watery bow burned in the evening flame,
    But the shower fell, the swift Sun went his way—
And that is dead.—O, let me not believe
That anything of mine is fit to live!

IV

Wordsworth informs us he was nineteen years
    Considering and retouching Peter Bell;
Watering his laurels with the killing tears
    Of slow, dull care, so that their roots to Hell
Might pierce, and their wide branches blot the spheres
    Of Heaven, with dewy leaves and flowers; this well   30
May be, for Heaven and Earth conspire to foil
The over-busy gardener's blundering toil.

V

My Witch indeed is not so sweet a creature
    As Ruth or Lucy, whom his graceful praise
Clothes for our grandsons—but she matches Peter,
    Though he took nineteen years, and she three days
In dressing. Light the vest of flowing metre
    She wears; he, proud as dandy with his stays,
Has hung upon his wiry limbs a dress
Like King Lear's 'looped and windowed raggedness.'   40

VI

If you strip Peter, you will see a fellow
    Scorched by Hell's hyperequatorial climate

Into a kind of a sulphureous yellow:
   A lean mark, hardly fit to fling a rhyme at;
In shape a Scaramouch, in hue Othello.
   If you unveil my Witch, no priest nor primate
Can shrive you of that sin,—if sin there be
In love, when it becomes idolatry.

THE WITCH OF ATLAS

I

BEFORE those cruel Twins, whom at one birth
   Incestuous Change bore to her father Time,
Error and Truth, had hunted from the Earth
   All those bright natures which adorned its prime,
And left us nothing to believe in, worth
   The pains of putting into learnèd rhyme,
A lady-witch there lived on Atlas' mountain
Within a cavern, by a secret fountain.

II

Her mother was one of the Atlantides:
   The all-beholding Sun had ne'er beholden   **10**
In his wide voyage o'er continents and seas
   So fair a creature, as she lay enfolden
In the warm shadow of her loveliness;—
   He kissed her with his beams, and made all golden
The chamber of gray rock in which she lay—
She, in that dream of joy, dissolved away.

III

'Tis said, she first was changed into a vapour,
   And then into a cloud, such clouds as flit,
Like splendour-wingèd moths about a taper,
   Round the red west when the sun dies in it: **20**
And then into a meteor, such as caper
   On hill-tops when the moon is in a fit:
Then, into one of those mysterious stars
Which hide themselves between the Earth and Mars.

IV

Ten times the Mother of the Months had bent
  Her bow beside the folding-star, and bidden
With that bright sign the billows to indent
  The sea-deserted sand—like children chidden,
At her command they ever came and went—
  Since in that cave a dewy splendour hidden   30
Took shape and motion: with the living form
Of this embodied Power, the cave grew warm.

V

A lovely lady garmented in light
  From her own beauty—deep her eyes, as are
Two openings of unfathomable night
  Seen through a Temple's cloven roof—her hair
Dark—the dim brain whirls dizzy with delight,
  Picturing her form; her soft smiles shone afar,
And her low voice was heard like love, and drew
All living things towards this wonder new.   40

VI

And first the spotted cameleopard came,
  And then the wise and fearless elephant;
Then the sly serpent, in the golden flame
  Of his own volumes intervolved;—all gaunt
And sanguine beasts her gentle looks made tame.
  They drank before her at her sacred fount;
And every beast of beating heart grew bold,
Such gentleness and power even to behold.

VII

The brinded lioness led forth her young,
  That she might teach them how they should forego   50
Their inborn thirst of death; the pard unstrung
  His sinews at her feet, and sought to know
With looks whose motions spoke without a tongue
  How he might be as gentle as the doe.

The magic circle of her voice and eyes
All savages natures did imparadise.

VIII

And old Silenus, shaking a green stick
    Of lilies, and the wood-gods in a crew
Came, blithe, as in the olive copses thick
    Cicadae are, drunk with the noonday dew: 60
And Dryope and Faunus followed quick,
    Teasing the God to sing them something new;
Till in this cave they found the lady lone,
Sitting upon a seat of emerald stone.

IX

And universal Pan, 'tis said, was there,
    And though none saw him,—through the adamant
Of the deep mountains, through the trackless air,
    And through those living spirits, like a want,
He passed out of his everlasting lair
    Where the quick heart of the great world doth pant,   70
And felt that wondrous lady all alone,—
And she felt him, upon her emerald throne.

X

And every nymph of stream and spreading tree,
    And every shepherdess of Ocean's flocks,
Who drives her white waves over the green sea,
    And Ocean with the brine on his gray locks,
And quaint Priapus with his company,
    All came, much wondering how the enwombèd rocks
Could have brought forth so beautiful a birth;—
Her love subdued their wonder and their mirth.   80

XI

The herdsmen and the mountain maidens came,
    And the rude kings of pastoral Garamant—
Their spirits shook within them, as a flame
    Stirred by the air under a cavern gaunt:
Pigmies, and Polyphemes, by many a name,

   Centaurs, and Satyrs, and such shapes as haunt
Wet clefts,—and lumps neither alive nor dead,
Dog-headed, bosom-eyed, and bird-footed.

XII

For she was beautiful—her beauty made
   The bright world dim, and everything beside   **90**
Seemed like the fleeting image of a shade:
   No thought of living spirit could abide,
Which to her looks had ever been betrayed,
   On any object in the world so wide,
On any hope within the circling skies,
But on her form, and in her inmost eyes.

XIII

Which when the lady knew, she took her spindle
   And twined three threads of fleecy mist, and three
Long lines of light, such as the dawn may kindle
   The clouds and waves and mountains with; and she   **100**
As many star-beams, ere their lamps could dwindle
   In the belated moon, wound skilfully;
And with these threads a subtle veil she wove—
A shadow for the splendour of her love.

XIV

The deep recesses of her odorous dwelling
   Were stored with magic treasures—sounds of air,
Which had the power all spirits of compelling,
   Folded in cells of crystal silence there;
Such as we hear in youth, and think the feeling
   Will never die—yet ere we are aware,   **110**
The feeling and the sound are fled and gone,
And the regret they leave remains alone.

XV

And there lay Visions swift, and sweet, and quaint,
   Each in its thin sheath, like a chrysalis,
Some eager to burst forth, some weak and faint
   With the soft burthen of intensest bliss.

It was its work to bear to many a saint
   Whose heart adores the shrine which holiest is,
Even Love's:—and others white, green, gray, and black,
And of all shapes—and each was at her beck.   120

XVI

And odours in a kind of aviary
   Of ever-blooming Eden-trees she kept,
Clipped in a floating net, a love-sick Fairy
   Had woven from dew-beams while the moon yet slept;
As bats at the wired window of a dairy,
   They beat their vans; and each was an adept,
When loosed and missioned, making wings of winds,
To stir sweet thoughts or sad, in destined minds.

XVII

And liquors clear and sweet, whose healthful might
   Could medicine the sick soul to happy sleep,   130
And change eternal death into a night
   Of glorious dreams—or if eyes needs must weep,
Could make their tears all wonder and delight,
   She in her crystal vials did closely keep:
If men could drink of those clear vials, 'tis said
The living were not envied of the dead.

XVIII

Her cave was stored with scrolls of strange device,
   The works of some Saturnian Archimage,
Which taught the expiations at whose price
   Men from the Gods might win that happy age   140
Too lightly lost, redeeming native vice;
   And which might quench the Earth-consuming rage
Of gold and blood—till men should live and move
Harmonious as the sacred stars above;

XIX

And how all things that seem untameable,
   Not to be checked and not to be confined,
Obey the spells of Wisdom's wizard skill;
   Time, earth, and fire—the ocean and the wind,

And all their shapes—and man's imperial will;
   And other scrolls whose writings did unbind   150
The inmost lore of Love—let the profane
Tremble to ask what secrets they contain.

XX

And wondrous works of substances unknown,
   To which the enchantment of her father's power
Had changed those ragged blocks of savage stone,
   Were heaped in the recesses of her bower;
Carved lamps and chalices, and vials which shone
   In their own golden beams—each like a flower,
Out of whose depth a fire-fly shakes his light
Under a cypress in a starless night.   160

XXI

At first she lived alone in this wild home,
   And her own thoughts were each a minister,
Clothing themselves, or with the ocean foam,
   Or with the wind, or with the speed of fire,
To work whatever purposes might come
   Into her mind; such power her mighty Sire
Had girt them with, whether to fly or run,
Through all the regions which he shines upon.

XXII

The Ocean-nymphs and Hamadryades,
   Oreads and Naiads, with long weedy locks,   **170**
Offered to do her bidding through the seas,
   Under the earth, and in the hollow rocks,
And far beneath the matted roots of trees,
   And in the gnarlèd heart of stubborn oaks,
So they might live for ever in the light
Of her sweet presence—each a satellite.

XXIII

'This may not be,' the wizard maid replied;
   'The fountains where the Naiades bedew
Their shining hair, at length are drained and dried;
   The solid oaks forget their strength, and strew   180

Their latest leaf upon the mountains wide;
  The boundless ocean like a drop of dew
Will be consumed—the stubborn centre must
Be scattered, like a cloud of summer dust.

XXIV

'And ye with them will perish, one by one;—
  If I must sigh to think that this shall be,
If I must weep when the surviving Sun
  Shall smile on your decay—oh, ask not me
To love you till your little race is run;
  I cannot die as ye must—over me   190
Your leaves shall glance—the streams in which ye dwell
Shall be my paths henceforth, and so—farewell!'—

XXV

She spoke and wept:—the dark and azure well
  Sparkled beneath the shower of her bright tears,
And every little circlet where they fell
  Flung to the cavern-roof inconstant spheres
And intertangled lines of light:—a knell
  Of sobbing voices came upon her ears
From those departing Forms, o'er the serene
Of the white streams and of the forest green.   200

XXVI

All day the wizard lady sate aloof,
  Spelling out scrolls of dread antiquity,
Under the cavern's fountain-lighted roof;
  Or broidering the pictured poesy
Of some high tale upon her growing woof,
  Which the sweet splendour of her smiles could dye
In hues outshining heaven—and ever she
Added some grace to the wrought poesy.

XXVII

While on her hearth lay blazing many a piece
  Of sandal wood, rare gums, and cinnamon;   210
Men scarcely know how beautiful fire is—
  Each flame of it is as a precious stone

Dissolved in ever-moving light, and this
    Belongs to each and all who gaze upon.
The Witch beheld it not, for in her hand
She held a woof that dimmed the burning brand.

XXVIII

This lady never slept, but lay in trance
    All night within the fountain—as in sleep.
Its emerald crags glowed in her beauty's glance;
    Through the green splendour of the water deep   220
She saw the constellations reel and dance
    Like fire-flies—and withal did ever keep
The tenour of her contemplations calm,
With open eyes, closed feet, and folded palm.

XXIX

And when the whirlwinds and the clouds descended
    From the white pinnacles of that cold hill,
She passed at dewfall to a space extended,
    Where in a lawn of flowering asphodel
Amid a wood of pines and cedars blended,
    There yawned an inextinguishable well   230
Of crimson fire—full even to the brim,
And overflowing all the margin trim.

XXX

Within the which she lay when the fierce war
    Of wintry winds shook that innocuous liquor
In many a mimic moon and bearded star
    O'er woods and lawns;—the serpent heard it flicker
In sleep, and dreaming still, he crept afar—
    And when the windless snow descended thicker
Than autumn leaves, she watched it as it came
Melt on the surface of the level flame.   240

XXXI

She had a boat, which some say Vulcan wrought
    For Venus, as the chariot of her star;
But it was found too feeble to be fraught
    With all the ardours in that sphere which are,

And so she sold it, and Apollo bought
   And gave it to this daughter: from a car
Changed to the fairest and the lightest boat
Which ever upon mortal stream did float.

XXXII

And others say, that, when but three hours old,
   The first-born Love out of his cradle lept,   250
And clove dun Chaos with his wings of gold,
   And like a horticultural adept,
Stole a strange seed, and wrapped it up in mould,
   And sowed it in his mother's star, and kept
Watering it all the summer with sweet dew,
And with his wings fanning it as it grew.

XXXIII

The plant grew strong and green, the snowy flower
   Fell, and the long and gourd-like fruit began
To turn the light and dew by inward power
   To its own substance; woven tracery ran   260
Of light firm texture, ribbed and branching, o'er
   The solid rind, like a leaf's veinèd fan—
Of which Love scooped this boat—and with soft motion
Piloted it round the circumfluous ocean.

XXXIV

This boat she moored upon her fount, and lit
   A living spirit within all its frame,
Breathing the soul of swiftness into it.
   Couched on the fountain like a panther tame,
One of the twain at Evan's feet that sit—
   Or as on Vesta's sceptre a swift flame—   270
Or on blind Homer's heart a wingèd thought,—
In joyous expectation lay the boat.

XXXV

Then by strange art she kneaded fire and snow
   Together, tempering the repugnant mass
With liquid love—all things together grow
   Through which the harmony of love can pass;

And a fair Shape out of her hands did flow—
   A living Image, which did far surpass
In beauty that bright shape of vital stone
Which drew the heart out of Pygmalion.   280

XXXVI

A sexless thing it was, and in its growth
   It seemed to have developed no defect
Of either sex, yet all the grace of both,—
   In gentleness and strength its limbs were decked;
The bosom lightly swelled with its full youth,
   The countenance was such as might select
Some artist that his skill should never die,
Imaging forth such perfect purity.

XXXVII

From its smooth shoulders hung two rapid wings,
   Fit to have borne it to the seventh sphere,   290
Tipped with the speed of liquid lightenings,
   Dyed in the ardours of the atmosphere:
She led her creature to the boiling springs
   Where the light boat was moored, and said: 'Sit here!'
And pointed to the prow, and took her seat
Beside the rudder, with opposing feet.

XXXVIII

And down the streams which clove those mountains vast,
   Around their inland islets, and amid
The panther-peopled forests, whose shade cast
   Darkness and odours, and a pleasure hid   300
In melancholy gloom, the pinnace passed;
   By many a star-surrounded pyramid
Of icy crag cleaving the purple sky,
And caverns yawning round unfathomably.

XXXIX

The silver noon into that winding dell,
   With slanted gleam athwart the forest tops,

Tempered like golden evening, feebly fell;
   A green and glowing light, like that which drops
From folded lilies in which glow-worms dwell,
   When Earth over her face Night's mantle wraps;   310
Between the severed mountains lay on high,
Over the stream, a narrow rift of sky.

XL

And ever as she went, the Image lay
   With folded wings and unawakened eyes;
And o'er its gentle countenance did play
   The busy dreams, as thick as summer flies,
Chasing the rapid smiles that would not stay,
   And drinking the warm tears, and the sweet sighs
Inhaling, which, with busy murmur vain,
They had aroused from that full heart and brain.   320

XLI

And ever down the prone vale, like a cloud
   Upon a stream of wind, the pinnace went:
Now lingering on the pools, in which abode
   The calm and darkness of the deep content
In which they paused; now o'er the shallow road
   Of white and dancing waters, all besprent
With sand and polished pebbles:—mortal boat
In such a shallow rapid could not float.

XLII

And down the earthquaking cataracts which shiver
   Their snow-like waters into golden air,   330
Or under chasms unfathomable ever
   Sepulchre them, till in their rage they tear
A subterranean portal for the river,
   It fled—the circling sunbows did upbear
Its fall down the hoar precipice of spray,
Lighting it far upon its lampless way.

XLIII

And when the wizard lady would ascend
   The labyrinths of some many-winding vale,

Which to the inmost mountain upward tend—
   She called 'Hermaphroditus!'—and the pale   340
And heavy hue which slumber could extend
   Over its lips and eyes, as on the gale
A rapid shadow from a slope of grass,
Into the darkness of the stream did pass.

XLIV

And it unfurled its heaven-coloured pinions,
   With stars of fire spotting the stream below;
And from above into the Sun's dominions
   Flinging a glory, like the golden glow
In which Spring clothes her emerald-wingèd minions,
   All interwoven with fine feathery snow   350
And moonlight splendour of intensest rime,
With which frost paints the pines in winter time.

XLV

And then it winnowed the Elysian air
   Which ever hung about that lady bright,
With its aethereal vans—and speeding there,
   Like a star up the torrent of the night,
Or a swift eagle in the morning glare
   Breasting the whirlwind with impetuous flight,
The pinnace, oared by those enchanted wings,
Clove the fierce streams towards their upper springs.   360

XLVI

The water flashed, like sunlight by the prow
   Of a noon-wandering meteor flung to Heaven;
The still air seemed as if its waves did flow
   In tempest down the mountains; loosely driven
The lady's radiant hair streamed to and fro:
   Beneath, the billows having vainly striven
Indignant and impetuous, roared to feel
The swift and steady motion of the keel.

XLVII

Or, when the weary moon was in the wane,
   Or in the noon of interlunar night,   370

The lady-witch in visions could not chain
    Her spirit; but sailed forth under the light
Of shooting stars, and bade extend amain
    Its storm-outspeeding wings, the Hermaphrodite;
She to the Austral waters took her way,
Beyond the fabulous Thamondocana,—

XLVIII

Where, like a meadow which no scythe has shaven,
    Which rain could never bend, or whirl-blast shake,
With the Antarctic constellations paven,
    Canopus and his crew, lay the Austral lake—   380
There she would build herself a windless haven
    Out of the clouds whose moving turrets make
The bastions of the storm, when through the sky
The spirits of the tempest thundered by:

XLIX

A haven beneath whose translucent floor
    The tremulous stars sparkled unfathomably,
And around which the solid vapours hoar,
    Based on the level waters, to the sky
Lifted their dreadful crags, and like a shore
    Of wintry mountains, inaccessibly   390
Hemmed in with rifts and precipices gray,
And hanging crags, many a cove and bay.

L

And whilst the outer lake beneath the lash
    Of the wind's scourge, foamed like a wounded thing,
And the incessant hail with stony clash
    Ploughed up the waters, and the flagging wing
Of the roused cormorant in the lightning flash
    Looked like the wreck of some wind-wandering
Fragment of inky thunder-smoke—this haven
Was as a gem to copy Heaven engraven,—   400

LI

On which that lady played her many pranks,
    Circling the image of a shooting star,

Even as a tiger on Hydaspes' banks
   Outspeeds the antelopes which speediest are,
In her light boat; and many quips and cranks
   She played upon the water, till the car
Of the late moon, like a sick matron wan,
To journey from the misty east began.

LII

And then she called out of the hollow turrets
   Of those high clouds, white, golden and vermilion,   410
The armies of her ministering spirits—
   In mighty legions, million after million,
They came, each troop emblazoning its merits
   On meteor flags; and many a proud pavilion
Of the intertexture of the atmosphere
They pitched upon the plain of the calm mere.

LIII

They framed the imperial tent of their great Queen
   Of woven exhalations, underlaid
With lambent lightning-fire, as may be seen
   A dome of thin and open ivory inlaid   420
With crimson silk—cressets from the serene
   Hung there, and on the water for her tread
A tapestry of fleece-like mist was strewn,
Dyed in the beams of the ascending moon.

LIV

And on a throne o'erlaid with starlight, caught
   Upon those wandering isles of aëry dew,
Which highest shoals of mountain shipwreck not,
   She sate, and heard all that had happened new
Between the earth and moon, since they had brought
   The last intelligence—and now she grew   430
Pale as that moon, lost in the watery night—
And now she wept, and now she laughed outright.

LV

These were tame pleasures; she would often climb
   The steepest ladder of the crudded rack

Up to some beakèd cape of cloud sublime,
    And like Arion on the dolphin's back
Ride singing through the shoreless air;—oft-time
    Following the serpent lightning's winding track,
She ran upon the platforms of the wind,
And laughed to hear the fire-balls roar behind.   440

LVI

And sometimes to those streams of upper air
    Which whirl the earth in its diurnal round,
She would ascend, and win the spirits there
    To let her join their chorus. Mortals found
That on those days the sky was calm and fair,
    And mystic snatches of harmonious sound
Wandered upon the earth where'er she passed,
And happy thoughts of hope, too sweet to last.

LVII

But her choice sport was, in the hours of sleep,
    To glide adown old Nilus, where he threads   450
Egypt and Aethiopia, from the steep
    Of utmost Axumè, until he spreads,
Like a calm flock of silver-fleecèd sheep,
    His waters on the plain: and crested heads
Of cities and proud temples gleam amid,
And many a vapour-belted pyramid.

LVIII

By Moeris and the Mareotid lakes,
    Strewn with faint blooms like bridal chamber floors,
Where naked boys bridling tame water-snakes,
    Or charioteering ghastly alligators,   460
Had left on the sweet waters mighty wakes
    Of those huge forms—within the brazen doors
Of the great Labyrinth slept both boy and beast,
Tired with the pomp of their Osirian feast.

LIX

And where within the surface of the river
    The shadows of the massy temples lie,

And never are erased—but tremble ever
   Like things which every cloud can doom to die,
Through lotus-paven canals, and wheresoever
   The works of man pierced that serenest sky   470
With tombs, and towers, and fanes, 'twas her delight
To wander in the shadow of the night.

LX

With motion like the spirit of that wind
   Whose soft step deepens slumber, her light feet
Passed through the peopled haunts of humankind,
   Scattering sweet visions from her presence sweet,
Through fane, and palace-court, and labyrinth mined
   With many a dark and subterranean street
Under the Nile, through chambers high and deep
She passed, observing mortals in their sleep.   480

LXI

A pleasure sweet doubtless it was to see
   Mortals subdued in all the shapes of sleep.
Here lay two sister twins in infancy;
   There, a lone youth who in his dreams did weep;
Within, two lovers linkèd innocently
   In their loose locks which over both did creep
Like ivy from one stem;—and there lay calm
Old age with snow-bright hair and folded palm.

LXII

But other troubled forms of sleep she saw,
   Not to be mirrored in a holy song—   490
Distortions foul of supernatural awe,
   And pale imaginings of visioned wrong;
And all the code of Custom's lawless law
   Written upon the brows of old and young:
'This,' said the wizard maiden, 'is the strife
Which stirs the liquid surface of man's life.'

LXIII

And little did the sight disturb her soul,—
   We, the weak mariners of that wide lake

Where'er its shores extend or billows roll,
   Our course unpiloted and starless make   500
O'er its wild surface to an unknown goal:—
   But she in the calm depths her way could take,
Where in bright bowers immortal forms abide
Beneath the weltering of the restless tide.

LXIV

And she saw princes couched under the glow
   Of sunlike gems; and round each temple-court
In dormitories ranged, row after row,
   She saw the priests asleep—all of one sort—
For all were educated to be so.—
   The peasants in their huts, and in the port   510
The sailors she saw cradled on the waves,
And the dead lulled within their dreamless graves.

LXV

And all the forms in which those spirits lay
   Were to her sight like the diaphanous
Veils, in which those sweet ladies oft array
   Their delicate limbs, who would conceal from us
Only their scorn of all concealment: they
   Move in the light of their own beauty thus.
But these and all now lay with sleep upon them,
And little thought a Witch was looking on them.   520

LXVI

She, all those human figures breathing there,
   Beheld as living spirits—to her eyes
The naked beauty of the soul lay bare,
   And often through a rude and worn disguise
She saw the inner form most bright and fair—
   And then she had a charm of strange device,
Which, murmured on mute lips with tender tone,
Could make that spirit mingle with her own.

LXVII

Alas! Aurora, what wouldst thou have given
   For such a charm when Tithon became gray?   530

Or how much, Venus, of thy silver heaven
   Wouldst thou have yielded, ere Proserpina
Had half (oh! why not all?) the debt forgiven
   Which dear Adonis had been doomed to pay,
To any witch who would have taught you it?
The Heliad doth not know its value yet.

LXVIII

'Tis said in after times her spirit free
   Knew what love was, and felt itself alone—
But holy Dian could not chaster be
   Before she stooped to kiss Endymion,   540
Than now this lady—like a sexless bee
   Tasting all blossoms, and confined to none,
Among those mortal forms, the wizard-maiden
Passed with an eye serene and heart unladen.

LXIX

To those she saw most beautiful, she gave
   Strange panacea in a crystal bowl:—
They drank in their deep sleep of that sweet wave,
   And lived thenceforward as if some control,
   Mightier than life, were in them; and the grave
   Of such, when death oppressed the weary soul,   550
Was as a green and overarching bower
Lit by the gems of many a starry flower.

LXX

For on the night when they were buried, she
   Restored the embalmers' ruining, and shook
The light out of the funeral lamps, to be
   A mimic day within that deathy nook;
And she unwound the woven imagery
   Of second childhood's swaddling bands, and took
The coffin, its last cradle, from its niche,
And threw it with contempt into a ditch.   560

LXXI

And there the body lay, age after age,
   Mute, breathing, beating, warm, and undecaying,

Like one asleep in a green hermitage,
   With gentle smiles about its eyelids playing,
And living in its dreams beyond the rage
   Of death or life; while they were still arraying
In liveries ever new, the rapid, blind
And fleeting generations of mankind.

LXXII

And she would write strange dreams upon the brain
   Of those who were less beautiful, and make   570
All harsh and crooked purposes more vain
   Than in the desert is the serpent's wake
Which the sand covers—all his evil gain
   The miser in such dreams would rise and shake
Into a beggar's lap;—the lying scribe
Would his own lies betray without a bribe.

LXXIII

The priests would write an explanation full,
   Translating hieroglyphics into Greek,
How the God Apis really was a bull,
   And nothing more; and bid the herald stick   580
The same against the temple doors, and pull
   The old cant down; they licensed all to speak
Whate'er they thought of hawks, and cats, and geese,
By pastoral letters to each diocese.

LXXIV

The king would dress an ape up in his crown,
   And robes, and seat him on his glorious seat,
And on the right hand of the sunlike throne
   Would place a gaudy mock-bird to repeat
The chatterings of the monkey.—Every one
   Of the prone courtiers crawled to kiss the feet   590
Of their great Emperor, when the morning came,
And kissed—alas, how many kiss the same!

LXXV

The soldiers dreamed that they were blacksmiths, and
   Walked out of quarters in somnambulism;

Round the red anvils you might see them stand
   Like Cyclopses in Vulcan's sooty abysm,
Beating their swords to ploughshares;—in a band
   The gaolers sent those of the liberal schism
Free through the streets of Memphis, much, I wis,
To the annoyance of king Amasis.   600

LXXVI

And timid lovers who had been so coy,
   They hardly knew whether they loved or not,
Would rise out of their rest, and take sweet joy,
   To the fulfilment of their inmost thought;
And when next day the maiden and the boy
   Met one another, both, like sinners caught,
Blushed at the thing which each believed was done
Only in fancy—till the tenth moon shone;

LXXVII

And then the Witch would let them take no ill:
   Of many thousand schemes which lovers find,   610
The Witch found one,—and so they took their fill
   Of happiness in marriage warm and kind.
Friends who, by practice of some envious skill,
   Were torn apart—a wide wound, mind from mind!—
She did unite again with visions clear
Of deep affection and of truth sincere.

LXXVIII

These were the pranks she played among the cities
   Of mortal men, and what she did to Sprites
And Gods, entangling them in her sweet ditties
   To do her will, and show their subtle sleights,   620
I will declare another time; for it is
   A tale more fit for the weird winter nights
Than for these garish summer days, when we
Scarcely believe much more than we can see.

                             [1820; publ. 1824]

OEDIPUS TYRANNUS

OR

SWELLFOOT THE TYRANT

A TRAGEDY IN TWO ACTS

TRANSLATED FROM THE ORIGINAL DORIC

'Choose Reform or Civil War,
When through thy streets, instead of hare with dogs,
A CONSORT-QUEEN shall hunt a KING with hogs,
Riding on the IONIAN MINOTAUR.'

ADVERTISEMENT

THIS Tragedy is one of a triad, or system of three Plays (an arrangement according to which the Greeks were accustomed to connect their dramatic representations), elucidating the wonderful and appalling fortunes of the SWELLFOOT dynasty. It was evidently written by some *learned Theban*, and, from its characteristic dulness, apparently before the duties on the importation of *Attic salt* had been repealed by the Boeotarchs. The tenderness with which he treats the PIGS proves him to have been a *sus Boeotiae*; possibly *Epicuri de grege porcus;* for, as the poet observes,

'A fellow feeling makes us wondrous kind.'

No liberty has been taken with the translation of this remarkable piece of antiquity, except the suppressing a seditious and blasphemous Chorus of the Pigs and Bulls at the last Act. The word Hoydipouse (or more properly Oedipus) has been rendered literally SWELLFOOT, without its having been conceived necessary to determine whether a swelling of the hind or the fore feet of the Swinish Monarch is particularly indicated.

Should the remaining portions of this Tragedy be found, entitled, *Swellfoot in Angaria,* and *Charité,* the Translator might be tempted to give them to the reading Public.

237

DRAMATIS PERSONÆ

TYRANT SWELLFOOT,
    King of Thebes.
IONA TAURINA, *his Queen.*
MAMMON, *Arch-Priest of Famine.*
PURGANAX ⎫
DAKRY   ⎬ *Wizards, Ministers of*
LAOCTONOS ⎭   SWELLFOOT.

The GADFLY.
The LEECH.
The MINOTAUR.
The RAT.
MOSES, *the Sow-gelder.*
SOLOMON, *the Porkman.*
ZEPHANIAH, *Pig-butcher.*

CHORUS *of the Swinish Multitude.*

GUARDS, ATTENDANTS, PRIESTS, *etc., etc.*

SCENE—THEBES

ACT I

SCENE I—*A magnificent Temple, built of thigh-bones and death's-heads, and tiled with scalps. Over the Altar the statue of Famine, veiled; a number of Boars, Sows, and Sucking-Pigs, crowned with thistle, shamrock, and oak, sitting on the steps, and clinging round the Altar of the Temple.*

Enter SWELLFOOT, *in his Royal robes, without perceiving the* PIGS.

Swellfoot. Thou supreme Goddess! by whose power divine
These graceful limbs are clothed in proud array
                    [*He contemplates himself with satisfaction.*
Of gold and purple, and this kingly paunch
Swells like a sail before a favouring breeze,
And these most sacred nether promontories
Lie satisfied with layers of fat; and these
Boeotian cheeks, like Egypt's pyramid,
(Nor with less toil were their foundations laid),[1]
Sustain the cone of my untroubled brain,
That point, the emblem of a pointless nothing!   10
Thou to whom Kings and laurelled Emperors,
Radical-butchers, Paper-money-millers,

[1] See Universal History for an account of the number of people who died, and the immense consumption of garlic by the wretched Egyptians, who made a sepulchre for the name as well as the bodies of their tyrants.—[SHELLEY'S NOTE.]

Bishops and Deacons, and the entire army
Of those fat martyrs to the persecution
Of stifling turtle-soup, and brandy-devils,
Offer their secret vows! Thou plenteous Ceres
Of their Eleusis, hail!

  The Swine. Eigh! eigh! eigh! eigh!
  Swellfoot.   Ha! what are ye,
Who, crowned with leaves devoted to the Furies,
Cling round this sacred shrine?

  Swine. Aigh! aigh! aigh!
  Swellfoot.   What! ye that are
The very beasts that, offered at her altar   20
With blood and groans, salt-cake, and fat, and inwards,
Ever propitiate her reluctant will
When taxes are withheld?

  Swine. Ugh! ugh! ugh!
  Swellfoot.   What! ye who grub
With filthy snouts my red potatoes up
In Allan's rushy bog? Who eat the oats
Up, from my cavalry in the Hebrides?
Who swill the hog-wash soup my cooks digest
From bones, and rags, and scraps of shoe-leather,
Which should be given to cleaner Pigs than you?

The Swine.—Semichorus I.

The same, alas! the same;   30
Though only now the name
  Of Pig remains to me.

Semichorus II.

If 'twere your kingly will
Us wretched Swine to kill,
  What should we yield to thee?

Swellfoot. Why, skin and bones, and some few hairs for mortar.

Chorus of Swine.

I have heard your Laureate sing,
That pity was a royal thing;

Under your mighty ancestors, we Pigs
Were bless'd as nightingales on myrtle sprigs,   40
Or grasshoppers that live on noonday dew,
And sung, old annals tell, as sweetly too;
But now our sties are fallen in, we catch
    The murrain and the mange, the scab and itch;
Sometimes your royal dogs tear down our thatch,
    And then we seek the shelter of a ditch;
Hog-wash or grains, or ruta-baga, none
Has yet been ours since your reign begun.

First Sow.

My Pigs, 'tis in vain to tug.

Second Sow.

I could almost eat my litter.   50

First Pig.

I suck, but no milk will come from the dug.

Second Pig.

Our skin and our bones would be bitter.

The Boars.

We fight for this rag of greasy rug,
    Though a trough of wash would be fitter.

Semichorus.

Happier Swine were they than we,
    Drowned in the Gadarean sea—
I wish that pity would drive out the devils,
Which in your royal bosom hold their revels,
And sink us in the waves of thy compassion!
Alas! the Pigs are an unhappy nation!   60
Now if your Majesty would have our bristles
    To bind your mortar with, or fill our colons

With rich blood, or make brawn out of our gristles,
    In policy—ask else your royal Solons—
You ought to give us hog-wash and clean straw,
And sties well thatched; besides it is the law!

Swellfoot. This is sedition, and rank blasphemy!
Ho! there, my guards!

Enter a GUARD.

Guard.   Your sacred Majesty.
    Swellfoot. Call in the Jews, Solomon the court porkman,
Moses the sow-gelder, and Zephaniah   70
The hog-butcher.
    Guard.   They are in waiting, Sire.

Enter SOLOMON, MOSES, and ZEPHANIAH.

Swellfoot. Out with your knife, old Moses, and spay those Sows
                    [The PIGS *run about in consternation.*
That load the earth with Pigs; cut close and deep.
Moral restraint I see has no effect,
Nor prostitution, nor our own example,
Starvation, typhus-fever, war, nor prison—
This was the art which the arch-priest of Famine
Hinted at in his charge to the Theban clergy—
Cut close and deep, good Moses.
    Moses.   Let your Majesty
Keep the Boars quiet, else——
    Swellfoot.   Zephaniah, cut   80
That fat Hog's throat, the brute seems overfed;
Seditious hunks! to whine for want of grains.
    Zephaniah. Your sacred Majesty, he has the dropsy;—
We shall find pints of hydatids in 's liver,
He has not half an inch of wholesome fat
Upon his carious ribs——
    Swellfoot.   'Tis all the same,
He'll serve instead of riot money, when
Our murmuring troops bivouac in Thebes' streets;
And January winds, after a day
Of butchering, will make them relish carrion.   90
Now, Solomon, I'll sell you in a lump

The whole kit of them.
   Solomon.   Why, your Majesty,
I could not give——
   Swellfoot.   Kill them out of the way,
That shall be price enough, and let me hear
Their everlasting grunts and whines no more!
                [*Exeunt, driving in the* SWINE.

Enter MAMMON, *the Arch-Priest; and* PURGANAX, *Chief of the Council of Wizards.*

   Purganax. The future looks as black as death, a cloud,
Dark as the frown of Hell, hangs over it—
The troops grow mutinous—the revenue fails—
There's something rotten in us—for the level
Of the State slopes, its very bases topple,   100
The boldest turn their backs upon themselves!
   Mammon. Why what's the matter, my dear fellow, now?
Do the troops mutiny?—decimate some regiments;
Does money fail?—come to my mint—coin paper,
Till gold be at a discount, and ashamed
To show his bilious face, go purge himself,
in emulation of her vestal whiteness.
   Purganax. Oh, would that this were all! The oracle!!
   Mammon. Why it was I who spoke that oracle,
And whether I was dead drunk or inspired,   110
I cannot well remember; nor, in truth,
The oracle itself!
   Purganax.   The words went thus:—
'Boeotia, choose reform or civil war!
When through the streets, instead of hare with dogs,
A Consort Queen shall hunt a King with Hogs,
Riding on the Ionian Minotaur.'
   Mammon. Now if the oracle had ne'er foretold
This sad alternative, it must arrive,
Or not, and so it must now that it has;
And whether I was urged by grace divine   120
Or Lesbian liquor to declare these words,
Which must, as all words must, be false or true,
It matters not: for the same Power made all,
Oracle, wine, and me and you—or none—
'Tis the same thing. If you knew as much

Of oracles as I do——
    Purganax.   You arch-priests
Believe in nothing; if you were to dream
Of a particular number in the Lottery,
You would not buy the ticket?
    Mammon.   Yet our tickets
Are seldom blanks. But what steps have you taken?   130
For prophecies, when once they get abroad,
Like liars who tell the truth to serve their ends,
Or hypocrites who, from assuming virtue,
Do the same actions that the virtuous do,
Contrive their own fulfilment. This Iona——
Well—you know what the chaste Pasiphae did,
Wife of that most religious King of Crete,
And still how popular the tale is here;
And these dull Swine of Thebes boast their descent
From the free Minotaur. You know they still   140
Call themselves Bulls, though thus degenerate,
And everything relating to a Bull
Is popular and respectable in Thebes.
Their arms are seven Bulls in a field gules;
They think their strength consists in eating beef,—
Now there were danger in the precedent
If Queen Iona——
    Purganax.   I have taken good care
That shall not be. I struck the crust o' the earth
With this enchanted rod, and Hell lay bare!
And from a cavern full of ugly shapes   150
I chose a LEECH, a GADFLY, and a RAT.
The Gadfly was the same which Juno sent
To agitate Io,[1] and which Ezekiel [2] mentions
That the Lord whistled for out of the mountains
Of utmost Aethiopia, to torment
Mesopotamian Babylon. The beast
Has a loud trumpet like the scarabee,
His crookèd tail is barbed with many stings,
Each able to make a thousand wounds, and each
Immedicable; from his convex eyes   160

----

[1] The *Prometheus Bound* of Aeschylus.—[SHELLEY'S NOTE.]
[2] And the Lord whistled for the gadfly out of Aethiopia, and for the
bee of Egypt, etc.—EZEKIEL.—[SHELLEY'S NOTE.]

He sees fair things in many hideous shapes,
And trumpets all his falsehood to the world.
Like other beetles he is fed on dung—
He has eleven feet with which he crawls,
Trailing a blistering slime, and this foul beast
Has tracked Iona from the Theban limits,
From isle to isle, from city unto city,
Urging her flight from the far Chersonese
To fabulous Solyma, and the Aetnean Isle,
Ortygia, Melite, and Calypso's Rock,   **170**
And the swart tribes of Garamant and Fez,
Aeolia and Elysium, and thy shores,
Parthenope, which now, alas! are free!
And through the fortunate Saturnian land,
Into the darkness of the West.

  Mammon.   But if
This Gadfly should drive Iona hither?

  Purganax. Gods, what an *if!* but there is my gray RAT:
So thin with want, he can crawl in and out
Of any narrow chink and filthy hole,
And he shall creep into her dressing-room,   **180**
And——

  Mammon. My dear friend, where are your wits? as if
She does not always toast a piece of cheese
And bait the trap? and rats, when lean enough
To crawl through *such* chinks——

  Purganax.   But my LEECH—a leech
Fit to suck blood, with lubricous round rings,
Capaciously expatiative, which make
His little body like a red balloon,
As full of blood as that of hydrogen,
Sucked from men's hearts; insatiably he sucks
And clings and pulls—a horse-leech, whose deep maw   **190**
The plethoric King Swellfoot could not fill,
And who, till full, will cling for ever.

  Mammon.   This
For Queen Iona would suffice, and less;
But 'tis the Swinish multitude I fear,
And in that fear I have——

  Purganax.   Done what?

  Mammon.   Disinherited
My eldest son Chrysaor, because he

Attended public meetings, and would always
Stand prating there of commerce, public faith,
Economy, and unadulterate coin,
And other topics, ultra-radical;   200
And have entailed my estate, called the Fool's Paradise,
And funds in fairy-money, bonds, and bills,
Upon my accomplished daughter Banknotina,
And married her to the gallows.[1]

  Purganax.   A good match!
  Mammon. A high connexion, Purganax. The bridegroom
Is of a very ancient family,
Of Hounslow Heath, Tyburn, and the New Drop,
And has great influence in both Houses;—oh!
He makes the fondest husband; nay, *too* fond,—
New-married people should not kiss in public;   210
But the poor souls love one another so!
And then my little grandchildren, the gibbets,
Promising children as you ever saw,—
The young playing at hanging, the elder learning
How to hold radicals. They are well taught too,
For every gibbet says its catechism
And reads a select chapter in the Bible
Before it goes to play.

                  [*A most tremendous humming is heard.*

  Purganax.   Ha! what do I hear?

Enter the GADFLY.

  Mammon. Your Gadfly, as it seems, is tired of gadding.

Gadfly.

        Hum! hum! hum!   220
From the lakes of the Alps, and the cold gray scalps
     Of the mountains, I come!
        Hum! hum! hum!
From Morocco and Fez, and the high palaces
     Of golden Byzantium;
From the temples divine of old Palestine,
     From Athens and Rome,

[1] 'If one should marry a gallows, and beget young gibbets, I never saw one so prone.'—CYMBELINE.—[SHELLEY'S NOTE.]

With a ha! and a hum!
I come! I come!

All inn-doors and windows   230
　　Were open to me:
I saw all that sin does,
　　Which lamps hardly see
That burn in the night by the curtained bed,—
The impudent lamps! for they blushed not red,
　　Dinging and singing,
　　From slumber I rung her,
Loud as the clank of an ironmonger;
　　　Hum! hum! hum!

Far, far, far!   240
With the trump of my lips, and the sting at my hips,
　　I drove her—afar!
Far, far, far!
From city to city, abandoned of pity,
　　A ship without needle or star;—
Homeless she passed, like a cloud on the blast,
　　Seeking peace, finding war;—
　　She is here in her car,
　　From afar, and afar;—
　　　Hum! hum!   250

I have stung her and wrung her,
　　The venom is working;—
And if you had hung her
　　With canting and quirking,
She could not be deader than she will be soon;—
I have driven her close to you, under the moon,
　　Night and day, hum! hum! ha!
I have hummed her and drummed her
From place to place, till at last I have dumbed her,
　　　Hum! hum! hum!   260

Enter the LEECH *and the* RAT.

Leech.

I will suck
Blood or muck!

The disease of the state is a plethory,
Who so fit to reduce it as I?

Rat.

I'll slily seize and
Let blood from her weasand,—
Creeping through crevice, and chink, and cranny,
With my snaky tail, and my sides so scranny.

Purganax.

Aroint ye! thou unprofitable worm!   [*To the* LEECH.
And thou, dull beetle, get thee back to hell!   270
                                                       [*To the* GADFLY.
To sting the ghosts of Babylonian kings,
And the ox-headed Io——

Swine (*within*).

Ugh, ugh, ugh!
Hail! Iona the divine,
We will be no longer Swine,
But Bulls with horns and dewlaps.

Rat.

                                        For,
You know, my lord, the Minotaur——

Purganax (*fiercely*).

Be silent! get to hell! or I will call
The cat out of the kitchen. Well, Lord Mammon,
This is a pretty business.   [*Exit the* RAT.

Mammon.

                    I will go
And spell some scheme to make it ugly then.—   [*Exit*.

Enter SWELLFOOT.

Swellfoot. She is returned! Taurina is in Thebes,   281
When Swellfoot wishes that she were in hell!

Oh, Hymen, clothed in yellow jealousy,
And waving o'er the couch of wedded kings
The torch of Discord with its fiery hair;
This is thy work, thou patron saint of queens!
Swellfoot is wived! though parted by the sea,
The very name of wife had conjugal rights;
Her cursèd image ate, drank, slept with me,
And in the arms of Adiposa oft   290
Her memory has received a husband's——

    [A *loud tumult, and cries of* 'Iona for ever!—No Swellfoot!'
                              Hark!

How the Swine cry Iona Taurina;
I suffer the real presence; Purganax,
Off with her head!
    Purganax.   But I must first impanel
A jury of the Pigs.
    Swellfoot.   Pack them then.
    Purganax. Or fattening some few in two separate sties,
And giving them clean straw, tying some bits
Of ribbon round their legs—giving their Sows
Some tawdry lace, and bits of lustre glass,
And their young Boars white and red rags, and tails   300
Of cows, and jay feathers, and sticking cauliflowers
Between the ears of the old ones; and when
They are persuaded, that by the inherent virtue
Of these things, they are all imperial Pigs,
Good Lord! they'd rip each other's bellies up,
Not to say, help us in destroying her.
    Swellfoot. This plan might be tried too;—where's General
Laoctonos?

                Enter LAOCTONOS *and* DAKRY.

        It is my royal pleasure
That you, Lord General, bring the head and body,
If separate it would please me better, hither   310
Of Queen Iona.
    Laoctonos.   That pleasure I well knew,
And made a charge with those battalions bold,
Called, from their dress and grin, the royal apes,
Upon the Swine, who in a hollow square
Enclosed her, and received the first attack

Like so many rhinoceroses, and then
Retreating in good order, with bare tusks
And wrinkled snouts presented to the foe,
Bore her in triumph to the public sty.
What is still worse, some Sows upon the ground   320
Have given the ape-guards apples, nuts, and gin,
And they all whisk their tails aloft, and cry,
'Long live Iona! down with Swellfoot!'
> *Purganax.*   Hark!
> *The Swine (without).* Long live Iona! down with Swellfoot!
> *Dakry.*   I

Went to the garret of the swineherd's tower,
Which overlooks the sty, and made a long
Harangue (all words) to the assembled Swine,
Of delicacy, mercy, judgement, law,
Morals, and precedents, and purity,
Adultery, destitution, and divorce,   330
Piety, faith, and state necessity,
And how I loved the Queen!—and then I wept
With the pathos of my own eloquence,
And every tear turned to a mill-stone, which
Brained many a gaping Pig, and there was made
A slough of blood and brains upon the place,
Greased with the pounded bacon; round and round
The mill-stones rolled, ploughing the pavement up,
And hurling Sucking-Pigs into the air,
With dust and stones.——

Enter MAMMON.

> *Mammon.*   I wonder that gray wizards   340
Like you should be so beardless in their schemes;
It had been but a point of policy
To keep Iona and the Swine apart.
Divide and rule! but ye have made a junction
Between two parties who will govern you
But for my art.—Behold this BAG! it is
The poison BAG of that Green Spider huge,
On which our spies skulked in ovation through
The streets of Thebes, when they were paved with dead:
A bane so much the deadlier fills it now   350
As calumny is worse than death,—for here

The Gadfly's venom, fifty times distilled,
Is mingled with the vomit of the Leech,
In due proportion, and black ratsbane, which
That very Rat, who, like the Pontic tyrant,
Nurtures himself on poison, dare not touch;—
All is sealed up with the broad seal of Fraud,
Who is the Devil's Lord High Chancellor,
And over it the Primate of all Hell
Murmured this pious baptism:—'Be thou called   360
The GREEN BAG; and this power and grace be thine:
That thy contents, on whomsoever poured,
Turn innocence to guilt, and gentlest looks
To savage, foul, and fierce deformity.
Let all baptized by thy infernal dew
Be called adulterer, drunkard, liar, wretch!
No name left out which orthodoxy loves,
Court Journal or legitimate Review!—
Be they called tyrant, beast, fool, glutton, lover
Of other wives and husbands than their own—   370
The heaviest sin on this side of the Alps!
Wither they to a ghastly caricature
Of what was human!—let not man or beast
Behold their face with unaverted eyes!
Or hear their names with ears that tingle not
With blood of indignation, rage, and shame!'—
This is a perilous liquor;—good my Lords.—
          [SWELLFOOT *approaches to touch the* GREEN BAG.
Beware! for God's sake, beware!—if you should break
The seal, and touch the fatal liquor——
    Purganax.   There,
Give it to me. I have been used to handle   380
All sorts of poisons. His dread Majesty
Only desires to see the colour of it.
    Mammon. Now, with a little common sense, my Lords,
Only undoing all that has been done
(Yet so as it may seem we but confirm it),
Our victory is assured. We must entice
Her Majesty from the sty, and make the Pigs
Believe that the contents of the GREEN BAG
Are the true test of guilt or innocence.
And that, if she be guilty, 'twill transform her   390
To manifest deformity like guilt.

If innocent, she will become transfigured
Into an angel, such as they say she is;
And they will see her flying through the air,
So bright that she will dim the noonday sun;
Showering down blessings in the shape of comfits.
This, trust a priest, is just the sort of thing
Swine will believe. I'll wager you will see them
Climbing upon the thatch of their low sties,
With pieces of smoked glass, to watch her sail   400
Among the clouds, and some will hold the flaps
Of one another's ears between their teeth,
To catch the coming hail of comfits in.
You, Purganax, who have the gift o' the gab,
Make them a solemn speech to this effect:
I go to put in readiness the feast
Kept to the honour of our goddess Famine,
Where, for more glory, let the ceremony
Take place of the uglification of the Queen.
   Dakry (*to* SWELLFOOT). I, as the keeper of your
        sacred conscience,   410
Humbly remind your Majesty that the care
Of your high office, as Man-milliner
To red Bellona, should not be deferred.
   Purganax. All part, in happier plight to meet again. [*Exeunt.*

END OF THE FIRST ACT.

ACT II

SCENE I—*The Public Sty. The* BOARS *in full Assembly.*

Enter PURGANAX.

   Purganax. Grant me your patience, Gentlemen and Boars,
Ye, by whose patience under public burthens
The glorious constitution of these sties
Subsists, and shall subsist. The Lean-Pig rates
Grow with the growing populace of Swine,
The taxes, that true source of Piggishness
(How can I find a more appropriate term
To include religion, morals, peace, and plenty,

And all that fit Boeotia as a nation
To teach the other nations how to live?),   10
Increase with Piggishness itself; and still
Does the revenue, that great spring of all
The patronage, and pensions, and by-payments,
Which free-born Pigs regard with jealous eyes,
Diminish, till at length, by glorious steps,
All the land's produce will be merged in taxes,
And the revenue will amount to—nothing!
The failure of a foreign market for
Sausages, bristles, and blood-puddings,
And such home manufactures, is but partial;   20
And, that the population of the Pigs,
Instead of hog-wash, has been fed on straw
And water, is a fact which is—you know—
That is—it is a state-necessity—
Temporary, of course. Those impious Pigs,
Who, by frequent squeaks, have dared impugn
The settled Swellfoot system, or to make
Irreverent mockery of the genuflexions
Inculcated by the arch-priest, have been whipped
Into a loyal and an orthodox whine.   30
Things being in this happy state, the Queen
Iona——
        [*A loud cry from the* PIGS. 'She is innocent! most innocent!'
    Purganax. That is the very thing that I was saying,
Gentlemen Swine; the Queen Iona being
Most innocent, no doubt, returns to Thebes,
And the lean Sows and Boars collect about her,
Wishing to make her think that WE believe
(I mean those more substantial Pigs, who swill
Rich hog-wash, while the others mouth damp straw)
That she is guilty; thus, the Lean-Pig faction   40
Seeks to obtain that hog-wash, which has been
Your immemorial right, and which I will
Maintain you in to the last drop of——
    A Boar (interrupting him).   What
Does any one accuse her of?
    Purganax.   Why, no one
Makes *any* positive accusation;—but
There were hints dropped, and so the privy wizards
Conceived that it became them to advise

His Majesty to investigate their truth;—
Not for his own sake; he could be content
To let his wife play any pranks she pleased,   50
If, by that suffrance, *he* could please the Pigs;
But then he fears the morals of the Swine,
The Sows especially, and what effect
It might produce upon the purity and
Religion of the rising generation
Of Sucking-Pigs, if it could be suspected
That Queen Iona——   [*A pause.*
   First Boar.   Well, go on; we long
To hear what she can possibly have done.
   Purganax. Why, it is hinted, that a certain Bull—
Thus much is *known:*—the milk-white Bulls that feed   60
Beside Clitumnus and the crystal lakes
Of the Cisalpine mountains, in fresh dews
Of lotus-grass and blossoming asphodel
Sleeking their silken hair, and with sweet breath
Loading the morning winds until they faint
With living fragrance, are so beautiful!—
Well, *I* say nothing;—but Europa rode
On such a one from Asia into Crete,
And the enamoured sea grew calm beneath
His gliding beauty. And Pasiphaë   70
Iona's grandmother,——but *she* is innocent!
And that both you and I, and all assert.
   First Boar. Most innocent!
   Purganax.   Behold this BAG; a bag——
   Second Boar. Oh! no GREEN BAGS!! Jealousy's eyes are green,
Scorpions are green, and water-snakes, and efts,
And verdigris, and——
   Purganax.   Honourable Swine,
In Piggish souls can prepossessions reign?
Allow me to remind you, grass is green—
All flesh is grass;—no bacon but is flesh—
Ye are but bacon. This divining BAG   80
(Which is not green, but only bacon colour)
Is filled with liquor, which if sprinkled o'er
A woman guilty of——we all know what—
Makes her so hideous, till she finds one blind
She never can commit the like again.
If innocent, she will turn into an angel,

And rain down blessings in the shape of comfits
As she flies up to heaven. Now, my proposal
Is to convert her sacred Majesty
Into an angel (as I am sure we shall do),   90
By pouring on her head this mystic water.   [*Showing the Bag.*
I know that she is innocent; I wish
Only to prove her so to all the world.

    First Boar. Excellent, just, and noble Purganax.

    Second Boar. How glorious it will be to see her Majesty
Flying above our heads, her petticoats
Streaming like—like—like—

    Third Boar.   Anything.

    Purganax.   Oh no!
But like a standard of an admiral's ship,
Or like the banner of a conquering host,
Or like a cloud dyed in the dying day,   100
Unravelled on the blast from a white mountain;
Or like a meteor, or a war-steed's mane,
Or waterfall from a dizzy precipice
Scattered upon the wind.

    First Boar.   Or a cow's tail.

    Second Boar. Or *anything*, as the learned Boar observed.

    Purganax. Gentlemen Boars, I move a resolution,
That her most sacred Majesty should be
Invited to attend the feast of Famine,
And to receive upon her chaste white body
Dews of Apotheosis from this BAG.   110

    [*A great confusion is heard of the* Pigs out of Doors, *which
communicates itself to those within. During the first Strophe,
the doors of the Sty are staved in, and a number of exceedingly lean* Pigs *and* Sows *and* Boars *rush in.*

Semichorus I.

No! Yes!

Semichorus II.

Yes! No!

Semichorus I.

A law!

Semichorus II.

A flaw!

Semichorus I.

Porkers, we shall lose our wash,
  Or must share it with the Lean-Pigs!

First Boar.

Order! order! be not rash!
  Was there ever such a scene, Pigs!

An old Sow (rushing in).

I never saw so fine a dash
  Since I first began to wean Pigs.   120

Second Boar (solemnly).

The Queen will be an angel time enough.
  I vote, in form of an amendment, that
Purganax rub a little of that stuff
  Upon his face.

Purganax (his heart is seen to beat through his waistcoat).

Gods! What would ye be at?

Semichorus I.

Purganax has plainly shown a
  Cloven foot and jackdaw feather.

Semichorus II.

I vote Swellfoot and Iona
  Try the magic test together;

Whenever royal spouses bicker,
Both should try the magic liquor.   130

An old Boar (aside).

A miserable state is that of Pigs,
For if their drivers would tear caps and wigs,
The Swine must bite each other's ear therefore.

An old Sow (aside).

A wretched lot Jove has assigned to Swine,
Squabbling makes Pig-herds hungry, and they **dine**
On bacon, and whip Sucking-Pigs the more.

Chorus.

Hog-wash has been ta'en away:
    If the Bull-Queen is divested,
We shall be in every way
    Hunted, stripped, exposed, molested;   140
Let us do whate'er we may,
    That she shall not be arrested.
Queen, we entrench you with walls of brawn,
    And palisades of tusks, sharp as a bayonet:
Place your most sacred person here. We pawn
    Our lives that none a finger dare to lay on it.
        Those who wrong you, wrong us;
        Those who hate you, hate us;
        Those who sting you, sting us;
        Those who bait you, bait us;   150
The *oracle* is now about to be
Fulfilled by circumvolving destiny;
Which says: 'Thebes, choose *reform* or *civil war*,
    When through your streets, instead of hare with dogs,
    A Consort Queen shall hunt a King with Hogs,
Riding upon the IONIAN MINOTAUR.'

Enter Iona Taurina.

Iona Taurina (*coming forward*). Gentlemen Swine and gentle
    Lady-Pigs,
The tender heart of every Boar acquits
Their QUEEN, of any act incongruous
With native Piggishness, and she, reposing   160
With confidence upon the grunting nation,
Has thrown herself, her cause, her life, her all,
Her innocence, into their Hoggish arms;
Nor has the expectation been deceived
Of finding shelter there. Yet know, great Boars,
(For such whoever lives among you finds you,
And so do I), the innocent are proud!
I have accepted your protection only
In compliment of your kind love and care,
Not for necessity. The innocent   170
Are safest there where trials and dangers wait;
Innocent Queens o'er white-hot ploughshares tread
Unsinged, and ladies, Erin's laureate sings it,[1]
Decked with rare gems, and beauty rarer still,
Walked from Killarney to the Giant's Causeway,
Through rebels, smugglers, troops of yeomanry,
White-boys and Orange-boys, and constables,
Tithe-proctors, and excise people, uninjured!
Thus I!——
Lord PURGANAX, I do commit myself   180
Into your custody, and am prepared
To stand the test, whatever it may be!
   Purganax. This magnanimity in your sacred Majesty
Must please the Pigs. You cannot fail of being
A heavenly angel. Smoke your bits of glass,
Ye loyal Swine, or her transfiguration
Will blind your wondering eyes.
   An old Boar (*aside*).   Take care, my Lord,
They do not smoke you first.
   Purganax.   At the approaching feast
Of Famine, let the expiation be.
   Swine. Content! content!
   Iona Taurina (*aside*).   I, most content of all,   190
Know that my foes even thus prepare their fall! [*Exeunt omnes.*

[1] 'Rich and rare were the gems she wore.' See Moore's *Irish Melodies.*
—[SHELLEY'S NOTE.]

SCENE II—*The interior of the Temple of Famine. The statue of the Goddess, a skeleton clothed in parti-coloured rags, seated upon a heap of skulls and loaves intermingled. A number of exceedingly fat Priests in black garments arrayed on each side, with marrow-bones and cleavers in their hands.* [SOLOMON, *the Court Porkman.*] *A flourish of trumpets.*

Enter MAMMON *as arch-priest,* SWELLFOOT, DAKRY, PURGANAX, LAOCTONOS, *followed by* IONA TAURINA *guarded. On the other side enter the* SWINE.

Chorus of PRIESTS, *accompanied by the* COURT PORKMAN *on marrow-bones and cleavers.*

> GODDESS bare, and gaunt, and pale,
> Empress of the world, all hail!
> What though Cretans old called thee
> City-crested Cybele?
>   We call thee FAMINE!
> Goddess of fasts and feasts, starving and cramming!
> Through thee, for emperors, kings, and priests and lords,
> Who rule by viziers, sceptres, bank-notes, words,
> The earth pours forth its plenteous fruits,
> Corn, wool, linen, flesh, and roots—   10
> Those who consume these fruits through thee grow fat,
>   Those who produce these fruits through thee grow lean,
> Whatever change takes place, oh, stick to that!
>   And let things be as they have ever been;
>   At least while we remain thy priests,
>   And proclaim thy fasts and feasts.
> Through thee the sacred SWELLFOOT dynasty
> Is based upon a rock amid that sea
> Whose waves are Swine—so let it ever be!

[SWELLFOOT, *etc., seat themselves at a table magnificently covered at the upper end of the Temple. Attendants pass over the stage with hog-wash in pails. A number of* PIGS, *exceedingly lean, follow them licking up the wash.*

Mammon. I fear your sacred Majesty has lost   20
The appetite which you were used to have.

Allow me now to recommend this dish—
A simple kickshaw by your Persian cook,
Such as is served at the great King's second table.
The price and pains which its ingredients cost
Might have maintained some dozen families
A winter or two—not more—so plain a dish
Could scarcely disagree.—
   Swellfoot.   After the trial,
And these fastidious Pigs are gone, perhaps
I may recover my lost appetite,—   30
I feel the gout flying about my stomach—
Give me a glass of Maraschino punch.
   Purganax (filling his glass, and standing up). The glorious
      Constitution of the Pigs!
   All. A toast! a toast! stand up, and three times three!
   Dakry. No heel-taps—darken daylights!—
   Laoctonos.   Claret, somehow,
Puts me in mind of blood, and blood of claret!
   Swellfoot. Laoctonos is fishing for a compliment,
But 'tis his due. Yes, you have drunk more wine,
And shed more blood, than any man in Thebes.
                       [*To* PURGANAX.
For God's sake stop the grunting of those Pigs!   40
   Purganax. We dare not, Sire, 'tis Famine's privilege.

        Chorus of Swine.

  Hail to thee, hail to thee, Famine!
    Thy throne is on blood, and thy robe is of rags;
  Thou devil which livest on damning;
    Saint of new churches, and cant, and GREEN BAGS,
  Till in pity and terror thou risest,
  Confounding the schemes of the wisest;
  When thou liftest thy skeleton form,
    When the loaves and the skulls roll about,
  We will greet thee—the voice of a storm   50
    Would be lost in our terrible shout!

  Then hail to thee, hail to thee, Famine!
    Hail to thee, Empress of Earth!
  When thou risest, dividing possessions;

When thou risest, uprooting oppressions,
    In the pride of thy ghastly mirth;
Over palaces, temples, and graves,
We will rush as thy minister-slaves,
Trampling behind in thy train,
Till all be made level again!   60

    Mammon. I hear a crackling of the giant bones
Of the dread image, and in the black pits
Which once were eyes, I see two livid flames.
These prodigies are oracular, and show
The presence of the unseen Deity.
Mighty events are hastening to their doom!
    Swellfoot. I only hear the lean and mutinous Swine
Grunting about the temple.
    Dakry.   In a crisis
Of such exceeding delicacy, I think
We ought to put her Majesty, the QUEEN,   70
Upon her trial without delay.
    Mammon.   THE BAG
Is here.
    Purganax. I have rehearsed the entire scene
With an ox-bladder and some ditchwater,
On Lady P——; it cannot fail. (*Taking up the Bag.*) Your
        Majesty   [*To* SWELLFOOT.
In such a filthy business had better
Stand on one side, lest it should sprinkle you.
A spot or two on me would do no harm,
Nay, it might hide the blood, which the sad Genius
Of the Green Isle has fixed, as by a spell,
Upon my brow—which would stain all its seas,   80
But which those seas could never wash away!
    Iona Taurina. My Lord, I am ready—nay, I am impatient
To undergo the test.

[*A graceful figure in a semi-transparent veil passes unnoticed
    through the Temple; the word* LIBERTY *is seen through
    the veil, as if it were written in fire upon its forehead. Its
    words are almost drowned in the furious grunting of the*
    PIGS, *and the business of the trial. She kneels on the steps*

*of the Altar, and speaks in tones at first faint and low, but
which ever become louder and louder.*

Mighty Empress! Death's white wife!
Ghastly mother-in-law of Life!
By the God who made thee such,
By the magic of thy touch,
By the starving and the cramming
Of fasts and feasts! by thy dread self, O Famine!
I charge thee! when thou wake the multitude,   90
Thou lead them not upon the paths of blood.
The earth did never mean her foison
For those who crown life's cup with poison
Of fanatic rage and meaningless revenge—
  But for those radiant spirits, who are still
The standard-bearers in the van of Change.
  Be they th' appointed stewards, to fill
The lap of Pain, and Toil, and Age!—
Remit, O Queen! thy accustomed rage!
Be what thou art not! In voice faint and low   100
FREEDOM calls *Famine,*—her eternal foe,
To brief alliance, hollow truce.—Rise now!

[*Whilst the Veiled Figure has been chanting this strophe,* MAM-
MON, DAKRY, LAOCTONOS, *and* SWELLFOOT *have surrounded*
IONA TAURINA, *who, with her hands folded on her breast,
and her eyes lifted to Heaven, stands, as with saint-like
resignation, to await the issue of the business, in perfect
confidence of her innocence.*

[PURGANAX, *after unsealing the* GREEN BAG, *is gravely about to
pour the liquor upon her head, when suddenly the whole expression of her figure and countenance changes; she snatches
it from his hand with a loud laugh of triumph, and empties it
over* SWELLFOOT *and his whole Court, who are instantly
changed into a number of filthy and ugly animals, and rush
out of the Temple. The image of* FAMINE *then arises with a
tremendous sound, the* PIGS *begin scrambling for the loaves,
and are tripped up by the skulls; all those who* EAT *the
loaves are turned into* BULLS, *and arrange themselves quietly
behind the altar. The image of* FAMINE *sinks through a
chasm in the earth, and a* MINOTAUR *rises.*

Minotaur. I am the Ionian Minotaur, the mightiest
Of all Europa's taurine progeny—
I am the old traditional Man-Bull;
And from my ancestors having been Ionian,
I am called Ion, which, by interpretation,
Is JOHN; in plain Theban, that is to say,
My name's JOHN BULL; I am a famous hunter,
And can leap any gate in all Boeotia,   110
Even the palings of the royal park,
Or double ditch about the new enclosures;
And if your Majesty will deign to mount me,
At least till you have hunted down your game,
I will not throw you.
    Iona Taurina. (*During this speech she has been putting on*
        boots and spurs, and a hunting-cap, buckishly cocked on one
        side, and tucking up her hair, she leaps nimbly on his back.)
        Hoa! hoa! tallyho! tallyho! ho! ho!
Come, let us hunt these ugly badgers down,
These stinking foxes, these devouring otters,
These hares, these wolves, these anything but men.
Hey, for a whipper-in! my loyal Pigs,
Now let your noses be as keen as beagles',   120
Your steps as swift as greyhounds', and your cries
More dulcet and symphonious than the bells
Of village-towers, on sunshine holiday;
Wake all the dewy woods with jangling music.
Give them no law (are they not beasts of blood?)
But such as they gave you. Tallyho! ho!
Through forest, furze, and bog, and den, and desert,
Pursue the ugly beasts! tallyho! ho!

Full Chorus of IONA *and the* SWINE.

        Tallyho! tallyho!
    Through rain, hail, and snow,   130
    Through brake, gorse, and briar,
    Through fen, flood, and mire,
        We go! we go!

        Tallyho! tallyho!
    Through pond, ditch, and slough,
    Wind them, and find them,

Like the Devil behind them,
Tallyho! tallyho!

[*Exeunt, in full cry;* IONA *driving on the* SWINE, *with the empty*
GREEN BAG.

THE END.

[1820; publ. 1820]

THE SENSITIVE PLANT

PART FIRST

A SENSITIVE PLANT in a garden grew,
And the young winds fed it with silver dew,
And it opened its fan-like leaves to the light,
And closed them beneath the kisses of Night.

And the Spring arose on the garden fair,
Like the Spirit of Love felt everywhere;
And each flower and herb on Earth's dark breast
Rose from the dreams of its wintry rest.

But none ever trembled and panted with bliss
In the garden, the field, or the wilderness,   10
Like a doe in the noontide with love's sweet want,
As the companionless Sensitive Plant.

The snowdrop, and then the violet,
Arose from the ground with warm rain wet,
And their breath was mixed with fresh odour, sent
From the turf, like the voice and the instrument.

Then the pied wind-flowers and the tulip tall,
And narcissi, the fairest among them all,
Who gaze on their eyes in the stream's recess,
Till they die of their own dear loveliness;   20

And the Naiad-like lily of the vale,
Whom youth makes so fair and passion so pale

That the light of its tremulous bells is seen
Through their pavilions of tender green;

And the hyacinth purple, and white, and blue,
Which flung from its bells a sweet peal anew
Of music so delicate, soft, and intense,
It was felt like an odour within the sense;

And the rose like a nymph to the bath addressed,
Which unveiled the depth of her glowing breast,   30
Till, fold after fold, to the fainting air
The soul of her beauty and love lay bare:

And the wand-like lily, which lifted up,
As a Maenad its moonlight-coloured cup,
Till the fiery star, which is its eye,
Gazed through clear dew on the tender sky;

And the jessamine faint, and the sweet tuberose,
The sweetest flower for scent that blows;
And all rare blossoms from every clime
Grew in that garden in perfect prime.   40

And on the stream whose inconstant bosom
Was pranked, under boughs of embowering blossom,
With golden and green light, slanting through
Their heaven of many a tangled hue,

Broad water-lilies lay tremulously,
And starry river-buds glimmered by,
And around them the soft stream did glide and dance
With a motion of sweet sound and radiance.

And the sinuous paths of lawn and of moss,
Which led through the garden along and across,   50
Some open at once to the sun and the breeze,
Some lost among bowers of blossoming trees,

Were all paved with daisies and delicate bells
As fair as the fabulous asphodels,
And flow'rets which, drooping as day drooped too,

Fell into pavilions, white, purple, and blue,
To roof the glow-worm from the evening dew.

And from this undefilèd Paradise
The flowers (as an infant's awakening eyes
Smile on its mother, whose singing sweet 60
Can first lull, and at last must awaken it),

When Heaven's blithe winds had unfolded them,
As mine-lamps enkindle a hidden gem,
Shone smiling to Heaven, and every one
Shared joy in the light of the gentle sun;

For each one was interpenetrated
With the light and the odour its neighbour shed,
Like young lovers whom youth and love make dear
Wrapped and filled by their mutual atmosphere.

But the Sensitive Plant which could give small fruit 70
Of the love which it felt from the leaf to the root,
Received more than all, it loved more than ever,
Where none wanted but it, could belong to the giver,—

For the Sensitive Plant has no bright flower;
Radiance and odour are not its dower;
It loves, even like Love, its deep heart is full,
It desires what it has not, the Beautiful!

The light winds which from unsustaining wings
Shed the music of many murmurings;
The beams which dart from many a star 80
Of the flowers whose hues they bear afar;

The plumèd insects swift and free,
Like golden boats on a sunny sea,
Laden with light and odour, which pass
Over the gleam of the living grass;

The unseen clouds of the dew, which lie
Like fire in the flowers till the sun rides high,
Then wander like spirits among the spheres,
Each cloud faint with the fragrance it bears;

The quivering vapours of dim noontide,   90
Which like a sea o'er the warm earth glide,
In which every sound, and odour, and beam,
Move, as reeds in a single stream;

Each and all like ministering angels were
For the Sensitive Plant sweet joy to bear,
Whilst the lagging hours of the day went by
Like windless clouds o'er a tender sky.

And when evening descended from Heaven above,
And the Earth was all rest, and the air was all love,
And delight, though less bright, was far more deep,   100
And the day's veil fell from the world of sleep,

And the beasts, and the birds, and the insects were drowned
In an ocean of dreams without a sound;
Whose waves never mark, though they ever impress
The light sand which paves it, consciousness;

(Only overhead the sweet nightingale
Ever sang more sweet as the day might fail,
And snatches of its Elysian chant
Were mixed with the dreams of the Sensitive Plant);—

The Sensitive Plant was the earliest   110
Upgathered into the bosom of rest;
A sweet child weary of its delight,
The feeblest and yet the favourite,
Cradled within the embrace of Night.

Part Second

There was a Power in this sweet place,
An Eve in this Eden; a ruling Grace
Which to the flowers, did they waken or dream,
Was as God is to the starry scheme.

A Lady, the wonder of her kind,
Whose form was upborne by a lovely mind
Which, dilating, had moulded her mien and motion
Like a sea-flower unfolded beneath the ocean,

Tended the garden from morn to even:
And the meteors of that sublunar Heaven,   10
Like the lamps of the air when Night walks forth,
Laughed round her footsteps up from the Earth!

She had no companion of mortal race,
But her tremulous breath and her flushing face
Told, whilst the morn kissed the sleep from her eyes,
That her dreams were less slumber than Paradise:

As if some bright Spirit for her sweet sake
Had deserted Heaven while the stars were awake,
As if yet around her he lingering were,
Though the veil of daylight concealed him from her.   20

Her step seemed to pity the grass it pressed;
You might hear by the heaving of her breast,
That the coming and going of the wind
Brought pleasure there and left passion behind.

And wherever her aëry footstep trod,
Her trailing hair from the grassy sod
Erased its light vestige, with shadowy sweep,
Like a sunny storm o'er the dark green deep.

I doubt not the flowers of that garden sweet
Rejoiced in the sound of her gentle feet;   30
I doubt not they felt the spirit that came
From her glowing fingers through all their frame.

She sprinkled bright water from the stream
On those that were faint with the sunny beam;
And out of the cups of the heavy flowers
She emptied the rain of the thunder-showers.

She lifted their heads with her tender hands,
And sustained them with rods and osier-bands;
If the flowers had been her own infants, she
Could never have nursed them more tenderly.   40

And all killing insects and gnawing worms,
And things of obscene and unlovely forms,

She bore, in a basket of Indian woof,
Into the rough woods far aloof,—

In a basket, of grasses and wild-flowers full,
The freshest her gentle hands could pull
For the poor banished insects, whose intent,
Although they did ill, was innocent.

But the bee and the beamlike ephemeris
Whose path is the lightning's, and soft moths that kiss   **50**
The sweet lips of the flowers, and harm not, did she
Make her attendant angels be.

And many an antenatal tomb,
Where butterflies dream of the life to come,
She left clinging round the smooth and dark
Edge of the odorous cedar bark.

This fairest creature from earliest Spring
Thus moved through the garden ministering
All the sweet season of Summertide,
And ere the first leaf looked brown—she died!   **60**

Part Third

Three days the flowers of the garden fair,
Like stars when the moon is awakened, were,
Or the waves of Baiae, ere luminous
She floats up through the smoke of Vesuvius.

And on the fourth, the Sensitive Plant
Felt the sound of the funeral chant,
And the steps of the bearers, heavy and slow,
And the sobs of the mourners, deep and low;

The weary sound and the heavy breath,
And the silent motions of passing death,   **10**
And the smell, cold, oppressive, and dank,
Sent through the pores of the coffin-plank;

The dark grass, and the flowers among the grass,
Were bright with tears as the crowd did pass;

From their sighs the wind caught a mournful tone,
And sate in the pines, and gave groan for groan.

The garden, once fair, became cold and foul,
Like the corpse of her who had been its soul,
Which at first was lovely as if in sleep,
Then slowly changed, till it grew a heap 20
To make men tremble who never weep.

Swift Summer into the Autumn flowed,
And frost in the mist of the morning rode,
Though the noonday sun looked clear and bright.
Mocking the spoil of the secret night.

The rose-leaves, like flakes of crimson snow,
Paved the turf and the moss below.
The lilies were drooping, and white, and wan,
Like the head and the skin of a dying man.

And Indian plants, of scent and hue 30
The sweetest that ever were fed on dew,
Leaf by leaf, day after day,
Were massed into the common clay.

And the leaves, brown, yellow, and gray, and red,
And white with the whiteness of what is dead,
Like troops of ghosts on the dry wind passed;
Their whistling noise made the birds aghast.

And the gusty winds waked the wingèd seeds,
Out of their birthplace of ugly weeds,
Till they clung round many a sweet flower's stem, 40
Which rotted into the earth with them.

The water-blooms under the rivulet
Fell from the stalks on which they were set;
And the eddies drove them here and there,
As the winds did those of the upper air.

Then the rain came down, and the broken stalks
Were bent and tangled across the walks;

And the leafless network of parasite bowers
Massed into ruin; and all sweet flowers.

Between the time of the wind and the snow   50
All loathliest weeds began to grow,
Whose coarse leaves were splashed with many a speck,
Like the water-snake's belly and the toad's back.

And thistles, and nettles, and darnels rank,
And the dock, and henbane, and hemlock dank,
Stretched out its long and hollow shank,
And stifled the air till the dead wind stank.

And plants, at whose names the verse feels loath,
Filled the place with a monstrous undergrowth,
Prickly, and pulpous, and blistering, and blue,   60
Livid, and starred with a lurid dew.

And agarics, and fungi, with mildew and mould
Started like mist from the wet ground cold;
Pale, fleshy, as if the decaying dead
With a spirit of growth had been animated!

Spawn, weeds, and filth, a leprous scum,
Made the running rivulet thick and dumb,
And at its outlet flags huge as stakes
Dammed it up with roots knotted like water-snakes.

And hour by hour, when the air was still,   70
The vapours arose which have strength to kill,
At morn they were seen, at noon they were felt,
At night they were darkness no star could melt.

And unctuous meteors from spray to spray
Crept and flitted in broad noonday
Unseen; every branch on which they alit
By a venomous blight was burned and bit.

The Sensitive Plant, like one forbid,
Wept, and the tears within each lid

Of its folded leaves, which together grew, 80
Were changed to a blight of frozen glue.

For the leaves soon fell, and the branches soon
By the heavy axe of the blast were hewn;
The sap shrank to the root through every pore
As blood to a heart that will beat no more.

For Winter came: the wind was his whip:
One choppy finger was on his lip:
He had torn the cataracts from the hills
And they clanked at his girdle like manacles;

His breath was a chain which without a sound 90
The earth, and the air, and the water bound;
He came, fiercely driven, in his chariot-throne
By the tenfold blasts of the Arctic zone.

Then the weeds which were forms of living death
Fled from the frost to the earth beneath.
Their decay and sudden flight from frost
Was but like the vanishing of a ghost!

And under the roots of the Sensitive Plant
The moles and the dormice died for want:
The birds dropped stiff from the frozen air 100
And were caught in the branches naked and bare.

First there came down a thawing rain
And its dull drops froze on the boughs again;
Then there steamed up a freezing dew
Which to the drops of the thaw-rain grew;

And a northern whirlwind, wandering about
Like a wolf that had smelt a dead child out,
Shook the boughs thus laden, and heavy, and stiff,
And snapped them off with his rigid griff.

When Winter had gone and Spring came back 110
The Sensitive Plant was a leafless wreck;
But the mandrakes, and toadstools, and docks, and darnels,
Rose like the dead from their ruined charnels.

CONCLUSION

Whether the Sensitive Plant, or that
Which within its boughs like a Spirit sat,
Ere its outward form had known decay,
Now felt this change, I cannot say.

Whether that Lady's gentle mind,
No longer with the form combined
Which scattered love, as stars do light,   **120**
Found sadness, where it left delight,

I dare not guess; but in this life
Of error, ignorance, and strife,
Where nothing is, but all things seem,
And we the shadows of the dream,

It is a modest creed, and yet
Pleasant if one considers it,
To own that death itself must be,
Like all the rest, a mockery.

That garden sweet, that lady fair,   **130**
And all sweet shapes and odours there,
In truth have never passed away:
'Tis we, 'tis ours, are changed; not they.

For love, and beauty, and delight,
There is no death nor change: their might
Exceeds our organs, which endure
No light, being themselves obscure.

[1820; publ. 1820]

EPIPSYCHIDION

VERSES ADDRESSED TO THE NOBLE AND UNFORTUNATE LADY, EMILIA V——,

NOW IMPRISONED IN THE CONVENT OF ——

L' anima amante si slancia fuori del creato, e si crea nell' infinito un Mondo tutto per essa, diverso assai da questo oscuro e pauroso baratro. HER OWN WORDS.

ADVERTISEMENT

THE WRITER of the following lines died at Florence, as he was preparing for a voyage to one of the wildest of the Sporades, which he had bought, and where he had fitted up the ruins of an old building, and where it was his hope to have realised a scheme of life, suited perhaps to that happier and better world of which he is now an inhabitant, but hardly practicable in this. His life was singular; less on account of the romantic vicissitudes which diversified it, than the ideal tinge which it received from his own character and feelings. The present Poem, like the *Vita Nuova* of Dante, is sufficiently intelligible to a certain class of readers without a matter-of-fact history of the circumstances to which it relates; and to a certain other class it must ever remain incomprehensible, from a defect of a common organ of perception for the ideas of which it treats. Not but that *gran vergogna sarebbe a colui, che rimasse cosa sotto veste di figura, o di colore rettorico: e domandato non sapesse denudare le sue parole da cotal veste, in guisa che avessero verace intendimento.*

The present poem appears to have been intended by the Writer as the dedication to some longer one. The stanza on the opposite [p. 274] page is almost a literal translation from Dante's famous Canzone

Voi, ch' intendendo, il terzo ciel movete, etc.

The presumptuous application of the concluding lines to his own composition will raise a smile at the expense of my unfortunate friend: be it a smile not of contempt, but pity.   S.

273

My Song, I fear that thou wilt find but few
Who fitly shall conceive thy reasoning,
Of such hard matter dost thou entertain;
Whence, if by misadventure, chance should bring
Thee to base company (as chance may do),
Quite unaware of what thou dost contain,
I prithee, comfort thy sweet self again,
My last delight! tell them that they are dull,
And bid them own that thou art beautiful.

EPIPSYCHIDION

Sweet Spirit! Sister of that orphan one,
Whose empire is the name thou weepest on,
In my heart's temple I suspend to thee
These votive wreaths of withered memory.

Poor captive bird! who, from thy narrow cage,
Pourest such music, that it might assuage
The ruggèd hearts of those who prisoned thee,
Were they not deaf to all sweet melody;
This song shall be thy rose: its petals pale
Are dead, indeed, my adored Nightingale!   10
But soft and fragant is the faded blossom,
And it has no thorn left to wound thy bosom.

High, spirit-wingèd Heart! who dost for ever
Beat thine unfeeling bars with vain endeavour,
Till those bright plumes of thought, in which arrayed
It over-soared this low and worldly shade,
Lie shattered; and thy panting, wounded breast
Stains with dear blood its unmaternal nest!
I weep vain tears: blood would less bitter be,
Yet poured forth gladlier, could it profit thee.   20

Seraph of Heaven! too gentle to be human,
Veiling beneath that radiant form of Woman
All that is insupportable in thee
Of light, and love, and immortality!
Sweet Benediction in the eternal Curse!
Veilèd Glory of this lampless Universe!

Thou Moon beyond the clouds! Thou living Form
Among the Dead! Thou Star above the Storm!
Thou Wonder, and thou Beauty, and thou Terror!
Thou Harmony of Nature's art! Thou Mirror 30
In whom, as in the splendour of the Sun,
All shapes look glorious which thou gazest on!
Ay, even the dim words which obscure thee now
Flash, lightning-like, with unaccustomed glow;
I pray thee that thou blot from this sad song
All of its much mortality and wrong,
With those clear drops, which start like sacred dew
From the twin lights thy sweet soul darkens through,
Weeping, till sorrow becomes ecstasy:
Then smile on it, so that it may not die. 40

I never thought before my death to see
Youth's vision thus made perfect. Emily,
I love thee; though the world by no thin name
Will hide that love from its unvalued shame.
Would we two had been twins of the same mother!
Or, that the name my heart lent to another
Could be a sister's bond for her and thee,
Blending two beams of one eternity!
Yet were one lawful and the other true,
These names, though dear, could paint not, as is due, 50
How beyond refuge I am thine. Ah me!
I am not thine: I am a part of *thee*.

Sweet Lamp! my moth-like Muse has burned its wings
Or, like a dying swan who soars and sings,
Young Love should teach Time, in his own gray style,
All that thou art. Art thou not void of guile,
A lovely soul formed to be blessed and bless?
A well of sealed and secret happiness,
Whose waters like blithe light and music are,
Vanquishing dissonance and gloom? A Star 60
Which moves not in the moving heavens, alone?
A Smile amid dark frowns? a gentle tone
Amid rude voices? a belovèd light?
A Solitude, a Refuge, a Delight?
A Lute, which those whom Love has taught to play

Make music on, to soothe the roughest day
And lull fond Grief asleep? a buried treasure?
A cradle of young thoughts of wingless pleasure?
A violet-shrouded grave of Woe?—I measure
The world of fancies, seeking one like thee,   70
And find—alas! mine own infirmity.

　　She met me, Stranger, upon life's rough way,
And lured me towards sweet Death; as Night by Day,
Winter by Spring, or Sorrow by swift Hope,
Led into light, life, peace. An antelope,
In the suspended impulse of its lightness,
Were less aethereally light: the brightness
Of her divinest presence trembles through
Her limbs, as underneath a cloud of dew
Embodied in the windless heaven of June   80
Amid the splendour-wingèd stars, the Moon
Burns, inextinguishably beautiful:
And from her lips, as from a hyacinth full
Of honey-dew, a liquid murmur drops,
Killing the sense with passion; sweet as stops
Of planetary music heard in trance.
In her mild lights the starry spirits dance,
The sunbeams of those wells which ever leap
Under the lightnings of the soul—too deep
For the brief fathom-line of thought or sense.   90
The glory of her being, issuing thence,
Stains the dead, blank, cold air with a warm shade
Of unentangled intermixture, made
By Love, of light and motion: one intense
Diffusion, one serene Omnipresence,
Whose flowing outlines mingle in their flowing,
Around her cheeks and utmost fingers glowing
With the unintermitted blood, which there
Quivers, (as in a fleece of snow-like air
The crimson pulse of living morning quiver,)   100
Continuously prolonged, and ending never,
Till they are lost, and in that Beauty furled
Which penetrates and clasps and fills the world;
Scarce visible from extreme loveliness.
Warm fragrance seems to fall from her light dress

And her loose hair; and where some heavy tress
The air of her own speed has disentwined,
The sweetness seems to satiate the faint wind;
And in the soul a wild odour is felt,
Beyond the sense, like fiery dews that melt   110
Into the bosom of a frozen bud.—
See where she stands! a mortal shape indued
With love and life and light and deity,
And motion which may change but cannot die;
An image of some bright Eternity;
A shadow of some golden dream; a Splendour
Leaving the third sphere pilotless; a tender
Reflection of the eternal Moon of Love
Under whose motions life's dull billows move;
A Metaphor of Spring and Youth and Morning;   120
A Vision like incarnate April, warning,
With smiles and tears, Frost the Anatomy
Into his summer grave.
                          Ah, woe is me!
What have I dared? where am I lifted? how
Shall I descend, and perish not? I know
That Love makes all things equal: I have heard
By mine own heart this joyous truth averred:
The spirit of the worm beneath the sod
In love and worship, blends itself with God.

Spouse! Sister! Angel! Pilot of the Fate   130
Whose course has been so starless! O too late
Belovèd! O too soon adored, by me!
For in the fields of Immortality
My spirit should at first have worshipped thine,
A divine presence in a place divine;
Or should have moved beside it on this earth,
A shadow of that substance, from its birth;
But not as now:—I love thee; yes, I feel
That on the fountain of my heart a seal
Is set, to keep its waters pure and bright   140
For thee, since those *tears* thou hast delight.
We—are we not formed, as notes of music are,
For one another, though dissimilar;
Such difference without discord, as can make

Those sweetest sounds, in which all spirits shake
As trembling leaves in a continuous air?

 Thy wisdom speaks in me, and bids me dare
Beacon the rocks on which high hearts are wrecked.
I never was attached to that great sect,
Whose doctrine is, that each one should select   **150**
Out of the crowd a mistress or a friend,
And all the rest, though fair and wise, commend
To cold oblivion, though it is in the code
Of modern morals, and the beaten road
Which those poor slaves with weary footsteps **tread,**
Who travel to their home among the dead
By the broad highway of the world, and so
With one chained friend, perhaps a jealous **foe,**
The dreariest and the longest journey go.

 True Love in this differs from gold and **clay,** **160**
That to divide is not to take away.
Love is like understanding, that grows **bright,**
Gazing on many truths; 'tis like thy light,
Imagination! which from earth and sky,
And from the depths of human fantasy,
As from a thousand prisms and mirrors, fills
The Universe with glorious beams, and kills
Error, the worm, with many a sun-like arrow
Of its reverberated lightning. Narrow
The heart that loves, the brain that contemplates, **170**
The life that wears, the spirit that creates
One object, and one form, and builds thereby
A sepulchre for its eternity.

 Mind from its object differs most in this:
Evil from good; misery from happiness;
The baser from the nobler; the impure
And frail, from what is clear and must endure.
If you divide suffering and dross, you may
Diminish till it is consumed away;
If you divide pleasure and love and thought, **180**
Each part exceeds the whole; and we know not
How much, while any yet remains unshared,
Of pleasure may be gained, of sorrow spared:

This truth is that deep well, whence sages draw
The unenvied light of hope; the eternal law
By which those live, to whom this world of life
Is as a garden ravaged, and whose strife
Tills for the promise of a later birth
The wilderness of this Elysian earth.

 There was a Being whom my spirit oft   190
Met on its visioned wanderings, far aloft,
In the clear golden prime of my youth's dawn,
Upon the fairy isles of sunny lawn,
Amid the enchanted mountains, and the caves
Of divine sleep, and on the air-like waves
Of wonder-level dream, whose tremulous floor
Paved her light steps;—on an imagined shore,
Under the gray beak of some promontory
She met me, robed in such exceeding glory,
That I beheld her not. In solitudes   200
Her voice came to me through the whispering woods,
And from the fountains, and the odours deep
Of flowers, which, like lips murmuring in their sleep
Of the sweet kisses which had lulled them there,
Breathed but of *her* to the enamoured air;
And from the breezes whether low or loud,
And from the rain of every passing cloud,
And from the singing of the summer-birds,
And from all sounds, all silence. In the words
Of antique verse and high romance,—in form,   210
Sound, colour—in whatever checks that Storm
Which with the shattered present chokes the past;
And in that best philosophy, whose taste
Makes this cold common hell, our life, a doom
As glorious as a fiery martyrdom;
Her Spirit was the harmony of truth.—

 Then, from the caverns of my dreamy youth
I sprang, as one sandalled with plumes of fire,
And towards the lodestar of my one desire,
I flitted, like a dizzy moth, whose flight   220
Is as a dead leaf's in the owlet light,
When it would seek in Hesper's setting sphere
A radiant death, a fiery sepulchre,

As if it were a lamp of earthly flame.—
But She, whom prayers or tears then could not tame,
Passed, like a God throned on a wingèd planet,
Whose burning plumes to tenfold swiftness fan it,
Into the dreary cone of our life's shade;
And as a man with mighty loss dismayed,
I would have followed, though the grave between   230
Yawned like a gulf whose spectres are unseen:
When a voice said:—'O thou of hearts the weakest,
The phantom is beside thee whom thou seekest.'
Then I—'Where?'—the world's echo answered 'where?'
And in that silence, and in my despair,
I questioned every tongueless wind that flew
Over my tower of mourning, if it knew
Whither 'twas fled, this soul out of my soul;
And murmured names and spells which have control
Over the sightless tyrants of our fate;   240
But neither prayer nor verse could dissipate
The night which closed on her; nor uncreate
That world within this Chaos, mine and me,
Of which she was the veiled Divinity,
The world I say of thoughts that worshipped her:
And therefore I went forth, with hope and fear
And every gentle passion sick to death,
Feeding my course with expectation's breath,
Into the wintry forest of our life;
And struggling through its error with vain strife,   250
And stumbling in my weakness and my haste,
And half bewildered by new forms, I passed,
Seeking among those untaught foresters
If I could find one form resembling hers,
In which she might have masked herself from me.
There,—One, whose voice was venomed melody
Sate by a well, under blue nightshade bowers;
The breath of her false mouth was like faint flowers,
Her touch was as electric poison,—flame
Out of her looks into my vitals came,   260
And from her living cheeks and bosom flew
A killing air, which pierced like honey-dew
Into the core of my green heart, and lay
Upon its leaves; until, as hair grown gray

O'er a young brow, they hid its unblown prime
With ruins of unseasonable time.

In many mortal forms I rashly sought
The shadow of that idol of my thought.
And some were fair—but beauty dies away:
Others were wise—but honeyed words betray: 270
And One was true—oh! why not true to me?
Then, as a hunted deer that could not flee,
I turned upon my thoughts, and stood at bay,
Wounded and weak and panting; the cold day
Trembled, for pity of my strife and pain.
When, like a noonday dawn, there shone again
Deliverance. One stood on my path who seemed
As like the glorious shape which I had dreamed
As is the Moon, whose changes ever run
Into themselves, to the eternal Sun;   280
The cold chaste Moon, the Queen of Heaven's bright isles,
Who makes all beautiful on which she smiles,
That wandering shrine of soft yet icy flame
Which ever is transformed, yet still the same,
And warms not but illumines. Young and fair
As the descended Spirit of that sphere,
She hid me, as the Moon may hide the night
From its own darkness, until all was bright
Between the Heaven and Earth of my calm mind,
And, as a cloud charioted by the wind,   290
She led me to a cave in that wild place,
And sate beside me, with her downward face
Illumining my slumbers, like the Moon
Waxing and waning o'er Endymion.
And I was laid asleep, spirit and limb,
And all my being became bright or dim
As the Moon's image in a summer sea,
According as she smiled or frowned on me;
And there I lay, within a chaste cold bed:
Alas, I then was nor alive nor dead:—   300
For at her silver voice came Death and Life,
Unmindful each of their accustomed strife,
Masked like twin babes, a sister and a brother,
The wandering hopes of one abandoned mother,

And through the cavern without wings they flew,
And cried 'Away, he is not of our crew.'
I wept, and though it be a dream, I weep.

What storms then shook the ocean of my sleep,
Blotting that Moon, whose pale and waning lips
Then shrank as in the sickness of eclipse;—   310
And how my soul was as a lampless sea,
And who was then its Tempest; and when She,
The Planet of that hour, was quenched, what frost
Crept o'er those waters, till from coast to coast
The moving billows of my being fell
Into a death of ice, immovable;—
And then—what earthquakes made it gape and split,
The white Moon smiling all the while on it,
These words conceal:—If not, each word would be
The key of staunchless tears. Weep not for me!   320

At length, into the obscure Forest came
The Vision I had sought through grief and shame.
Athwart that wintry wilderness of thorns
Flashed from her motion splendour like the Morn's,
And from her presence life was radiated
Through the gray earth and branches bare and dead;
So that her way was paved, and roofed above
With flowers as soft as thoughts of budding love;
And music from her respiration spread
Like light,—all other sounds were penetrated   330
By the small, still, sweet spirit of that sound,
So that the savage winds hung mute around;
And odours warm and fresh fell from her hair
Dissolving the dull cold in the frore air:
Soft as an Incarnation of the Sun,
When light is changed to love, this glorious One
Floated into the cavern where I lay,
And called my Spirit, and the dreaming clay
Was lifted by the thing that dreamed below
As smoke by fire, and in her beauty's glow   340
I stood, and felt the dawn of my long night
Was penetrating me with living light:
I knew it was the Vision veiled from me
So many years—that it was Emily.

Twin Spheres of light who rule this passive Earth,
This world of love, this *me;* and into birth
Awaken all its fruits and flowers, and dart
Magnetic might into its central heart;
And lift its billows and its mists, and guide
By everlasting laws, each wind and tide   350
To its fit cloud, and its appointed cave;
And lull its storms, each in the craggy grave
Which was its cradle, luring to faint bowers
The armies of the rainbow-wingèd showers;
And, as those married lights, which from the towers
Of Heaven look forth and fold the wandering globe
In liquid sleep and splendour, as a robe;
And all their many-mingled influence blend,
If equal, yet unlike, to one sweet end;—
So ye, bright regents, with alternate sway   360
Govern my sphere of being, night and day!
Thou, not disdaining even a borrowed might;
Thou, not eclipsing a remoter light;
And, through the shadow of the seasons three,
From Spring to Autumn's sere maturity,
Light it into the Winter of the tomb,
Where it may ripen to a brighter bloom.
Thou too, O Comet beautiful and fierce,
Who drew the heart of this frail Universe
Towards thine own; till, wrecked in that convulsion,   370
Alternating attraction and repulsion,
Thine went astray and that was rent in twain;
Oh, float into our azure heaven again!
Be there Love's folding-star at thy return;
The living Sun will feed thee from its urn
Of golden fire; the Moon will veil her horn
In thy last smiles; adoring Even and Morn
Will worship thee with incense of calm breath
And lights and shadows; as the star of Death
And Birth is worshipped by those sisters wild   380
Called Hope and Fear—upon the heart are piled
Their offerings,—of this sacrifice divine
A World shall be the altar.
                              Lady mine,
Scorn not these flowers of thought, the fading birth
Which from its heart of hearts that plant puts forth

Whose fruit, made perfect by thy sunny eyes,
Will be as of the trees of Paradise.

The day is come, and thou wilt fly with me.
To whatsoe'er of dull mortality
Is mine, remain a vestal sister still;   390
To the intense, the deep, the imperishable,
Not mine but me, henceforth be thou united
Even as a bride, delighting and delighted.
The hour is come:—the destined Star has risen
Which shall descend upon a vacant prison.
The walls are high, the gates are strong, thick set
The sentinels—but true Love never yet
Was thus constrained: it overleaps all fence:
Like lightning, with invisible violence
Piercing its continents; like Heaven's free breath,   400
Which he who grasps can hold not; liker Death,
Who rides upon a thought, and makes his way
Through temple, tower, and palace, and the array
Of arms: more strength has Love than he or they;
For it can burst his charnel, and make free
The limbs in chains, the heart in agony,
The soul in dust and chaos.
                            Emily,
A ship is floating in the harbour now,
A wind is hovering o'er the mountain's brow;
There is a path on the sea's azure floor,   410
No keel has ever ploughed that path before;
The halcyons brood around the foamless isles;
The treacherous Ocean has forsworn its wiles;
The merry mariners are bold and free:
Say, my heart's sister, wilt thou sail with me?
Our bark is as an albatross, whose nest
Is a far Eden of the purple East;
And we between her wings will sit, while Night,
And Day, and Storm, and Calm, pursue their flight,
Our ministers, along the boundless Sea,   420
Treading each other's heels, unheededly.
It is an isle under Ionian skies,
Beautiful as a wreck of Paradise,
And, for the harbours are not safe and good,
This land would have remained a solitude

But for some pastoral people native there,
Who from the Elysian, clear, and golden air
Draw the last spirit of the age of gold,
Simple and spirited; innocent and bold.
The blue Aegean girds this chosen home,   430
With ever-changing sound and light and foam,
Kissing the sifted sands, and caverns hoar;
And all the winds wandering along the shore
Undulate with the undulating tide:
There are thick woods where sylvan forms abide;
And many a fountain, rivulet, and pond,
As clear as elemental diamond,
Or serene morning air; and far beyond,
The mossy tracks made by the goats and deer
(Which the rough shepherd treads but once a year)   440
Pierce into glades, caverns, and bowers, and halls
Built round with ivy, which the waterfalls
Illumining, with sound that never fails
Accompany the noonday nightingales;
And all the place is peopled with sweet airs;
The light clear element which the isle wears
Is heavy with the scent of lemon-flowers,
Which floats like mist laden with unseen showers,
And falls upon the eyelids like faint sleep;
And from the moss violets and jonquils peep,   450
And dart their arrowy odour through the brain
Till you might faint with that delicious pain.
And every motion, odour, beam, and tone,
With that deep music is in unison:
Which is a soul within the soul—they seem
Like echoes of an antenatal dream.—
It is an isle 'twixt Heaven, Air, Earth, and Sea,
Cradled, and hung in clear tranquillity;
Bright as that wandering Eden Lucifer,
Washed by the soft blue Oceans of young air.   460
It is a favoured place. Famine or Blight,
Pestilence, War and Earthquake, never light
Upon its mountain-peaks; blind vultures, they
Sail onward far upon their fatal way:
The wingèd storms, chanting their thunder-psalm
To other lands, leave azure chasms of calm
Over this isle, or weep themselves in dew,

From which its fields and woods ever renew
Their green and golden immortality.
And from the sea there rise, and from the sky   470
There fall, clear exhalations, soft and bright,
Veil after veil, each hiding some delight,
Which Sun or Moon or zephyr draw aside,
Till the isle's beauty like a naked bride
Glowing at once with love and loveliness,
Blushes and trembles at its own excess:
Yet, like a buried lamp, a Soul no less
Burns in the heart of this delicious isle,
An atom of th' Eternal, whose own smile
Unfolds itself, and may be felt, not seen   480
O'er the gray rocks, blue waves, and forests green,
Filling their bare and void interstices.—
But the chief marvel of the wilderness
Is a lone dwelling, built by whom or how
None of the rustic island-people know:
'Tis not a tower of strength, though with its height
It overtops the woods; but, for delight,
Some wise and tender Ocean-King, ere crime
Had been invented, in the world's young prime,
Reared it, a wonder of that simple time,   490
An envy of the isles, a pleasure-house
Made sacred to his sister and his spouse.
It scarce seems now a wreck of human art,
But, as it were Titanic; in the heart
Of Earth having assumed its form, then grown
Out of the mountains, from the living stone,
Lifting itself in caverns light and high:
For all the antique and learnèd imagery
Has been erased, and in the place of it
The ivy and the wild-vine interknit   500
The volumes of their many-twining stems;
Parasite flowers illume with dewy gems
The lampless halls, and when they fade, the sky
Peeps through their winter-woof of tracery
With moonlight patches, or star atoms keen,
Or fragments of the day's intense serene;—
Working mosaic on their Parian floors.
And, day and night, aloof, from the high towers
And terraces, the Earth and Ocean seem

To sleep in one another's arms, and dream   510
Of waves, flowers, clouds, woods, rocks, and all that we
Read in their smiles, and call reality.

   This isle and house are mine, and I have vowed
Thee to be lady of the solitude.—
And I have fitted up some chambers there
Looking towards the golden Eastern air,
And level with the living winds, which flow
Like waves above the living waves below.—
I have sent books and music there, and all
Those instruments with which high Spirits call   520
The future from its cradle, and the past
Out of its grave, and make the present last
In thoughts and joys which sleep, but cannot die,
Folded within their own eternity.
Our simple life wants little, and true taste
Hires not the pale drudge Luxury, to waste
The scene it would adorn, and therefore still,
Nature with all her children haunts the hill.
The ring-dove, in the embowering ivy, yet
Keeps up her love-lament, and the owls flit   530
Round the evening tower, and the young stars glance
Between the quick bats in their twilight dance;
The spotted deer bask in the fresh moonlight
Before our gate, and the slow, silent night
Is measured by the pants of their calm sleep.
Be this our home in Life, and when years heap
Their withered hours, like leaves, on our decay,
Let us become the overhanging day,
The living soul of this Elysian isle,
Conscious, inseparable, one. Meanwhile   540
We two will rise, and sit, and walk together,
Under the roof of blue Ionian weather,
And wander in the meadows, or ascend
The mossy mountains, where the blue heavens bend
With lightest winds, to touch their paramour;
Or linger, where the pebble-paven shore,
Under the quick, faint kisses of the sea
Trembles and sparkles as with ecstasy,—
Possessing and possessed by all that is
Within that calm circumference of bliss,   550

And by each other, till to love and live
Be one:—or, at the noontide hour, arrive
Where some old cavern hoar seems yet to keep
The moonlight of the expired night asleep,
Through which the awakened day can never peep;
A veil for our seclusion, close as night's,
Where secure sleep may kill thine innocent lights;
Sleep, the fresh dew of languid love, the rain
Whose drops quench kisses till they burn again.
And we will talk, until thought's melody   560
Become too sweet for utterance, and it die
In words, to live again in looks, which dart
With thrilling tone into the voiceless heart,
Harmonizing silence without a sound.
Our breath shall intermix, our bosoms bound,
And our veins beat together; and our lips
With other eloquence than words, eclipse
The soul that burns between them, and the wells
Which boil under our being's inmost cells,
The fountains of our deepest life, shall be   570
Confused in Passion's golden purity,
As mountain-springs under the morning sun.
We shall become the same, we shall be one
Spirit within two frames, oh! wherefore two?
One passion in twin-hearts, which grows and grew,
Till like two meteors of expanding flame,
Those spheres instinct with it become the same,
Touch, mingle, are transfigured; ever still
Burning, yet ever inconsumable:
In one another's substance finding food,   580
Like flames too pure and light and unimbued
To nourish their bright lives with baser prey,
Which point to Heaven and cannot pass away:
One hope within two wills, one will beneath
Two overshadowing minds, one life, one death,
One Heaven, one Hell, one immortality,
And one annihilation. Woe is me!
The wingèd words on which my soul would pierce
Into the height of Love's rare Universe,
Are chains of lead around its flight of fire—   590
I pant, I sink, I tremble, I expire!

———————

Weak Verses, go, kneel at your Sovereign's feet,
And say:—'We are the masters of thy slave;
What wouldest thou with us and ours and thine?'
Then call your sisters from Oblivion's cave,
All singing loud: 'Love's very pain is sweet,
But its reward is in the world divine
Which, if not here, it builds beyond the grave.'
So shall ye live when I am there. Then haste
Over the hearts of men, until ye meet   600
Marina, Vanna, Primus, and the rest,
And bid them love each other and be blessed:
And leave the troop which errs, and which reproves,
And come and be my guest,—for I am Love's.

[1821; publ. 1821]

ADONAIS

AN ELEGY ON THE DEATH OF JOHN KEATS, AUTHOR OF ENDYMION, HYPERION, ETC.

'Αστὴρ πρὶν μὲν ἔλαμπες ἐνὶ ζωοῖσιν 'Εῷος.
νῦν δὲ θανὼν λάμπεις 'Εσπερος ἐν φθιμένοις.—PLATO.

PREFACE

Φάρμακον ἦλθε, Βίων, ποτὶ σὸν στόμα, φάρμακον εἶδες.
πῶς τευ τοῖς χείλεσσι ποτέδραμε, κοὐκ ἐγλυκάνθη;
τίς δὲ βροτὸς τοσσοῦτον ἀνάμερος, ἢ κεράσαι τοι,
ἢ δοῦναι λαλέοντι τὸ φάρμακον; ἔκφυγεν ᾠδάν.

—MOSCHUS, EPITAPH. BION.

IT is my intention to subjoin to the London edition of this poem a criticism upon the claims of its lamented object to be classed among the writers of the highest genius who have adorned our age. My known repugnance to the narrow principles of taste on which several of his earlier compositions were modelled prove at least that I am an impartial judge. I consider the fragment of *Hyperion* as second to nothing that was ever produced by a writer of the same years.

John Keats died at Rome of a consumption, in his twenty-fourth year, on the —— of —— 1821; and was buried in the romantic and lonely cemetery of the Protestants in that city, under the pyramid which is the tomb of Cestius, and the massy walls and towers, now mouldering and desolate, which formed the circuit of ancient Rome. The cemetery is an open space among the ruins, covered in winter with violets and daisies. It might make one in love with death, to think that one should be buried in so sweet a place.

The genius of the lamented person to whose memory I have dedicated these unworthy verses was not less delicate and fragile than it was beautiful; and where cankerworms abound, what wonder if its young flower was blighted in the bud? The savage criticism on his *Endymion*, which appeared in the *Quarterly Review*, produced the most violent effect on his susceptible mind; the agitation thus originated ended in the rupture of a blood-vessel in the lungs; a rapid consumption ensued, and the succeeding acknowledgements from more candid critics of the true greatness of his powers were ineffectual to heal the wound thus wantonly inflicted.

It may be well said that these wretched men know not what they do. They scatter their insults and their slanders without heed as to whether the poisoned shaft lights on a heart made callous by many blows or one like Keats's composed of more penetrable stuff. One of their associates is, to my knowledge, a most base and unprincipled calumniator. As to *Endymion*, was it a poem, whatever might be its defects, to be treated contemptuously by those who had celebrated, with various degrees of complacency and panegyric, *Paris*, and *Woman*, and a *Syrian Tale*, and Mrs. Lefanu, and Mr. Barrett, and Mr. Howard Payne, and a long list of the illustrious obscure? Are these the men who in their venal good nature presumed to draw a parallel between the Rev. Mr. Milman and Lord Byron? What gnat did they strain at here, after having swallowed all those camels? Against what woman taken in adultery dares the foremost of these literary prostitutes to cast his opprobrious stone? Miserable man! you, one of the meanest, have wantonly defaced one of the noblest specimens of the workmanship of God. Nor shall it be your excuse, that, murderer as you are, you have spoken daggers, but used none.

The circumstances of the closing scene of poor Keats's life were not made known to me until the *Elegy* was ready for the press. I am given to understand that the wound which his sensitive spirit

had received from the criticism of *Endymion* was exasperated by
the bitter sense of unrequited benefits; the poor fellow seems to
have been hooted from the stage of life, no less by those on whom
he had wasted the promise of his genius, than those on whom he
had lavished his fortune and his care. He was accompanied to
Rome, and attended in his last illness by Mr. Severn, a young
artist of the highest promise, who, I have been informed, 'almost
risked his own life, and sacrificed every prospect to unwearied at-
tendance upon his dying friend.' Had I known these circumstances before the completion of my poem, I should have been
tempted to add my feeble tribute of applause to the more solid
recompense which the virtuous man finds in the recollection of his
own motives. Mr. Severn can dispense with a reward from 'such
stuff as dreams are made of.' His conduct is a golden augury of
the success of his future career—may the unextinguished Spirit of
his illustrious friend animate the creations of his pencil, and plead
against Oblivion for his name!

I

I weep for Adonais—he is dead!
O, weep for Adonais! though our tears
Thaw not the frost which binds so dear a head!
And thou, sad Hour, selected from all years
To mourn our loss, rouse thy obscure compeers,
And teach them thine own sorrow, say: 'With me
Died Adonais; till the Future dares
Forget the Past, his fate and fame shall be
An echo and a light unto eternity!'

II

Where wert thou, mighty Mother, when he lay,   10
When thy Son lay, pierced by the shaft which flies
In darkness? where was lorn Urania
When Adonais died? With veilèd eyes,
'Mid listening Echoes, in her Paradise
She sate, while one, with soft enamoured breath,
Rekindled all the fading melodies,
With which, like flowers that mock the corse beneath,
He had adorned and hid the coming bulk of Death.

III

Oh, weep for Adonais—he is dead!
Wake, melancholy Mother, wake and weep!   20
Yet wherefore? Quench within their burning bed
Thy fiery tears, and let thy loud heart keep
Like his, a mute and uncomplaining sleep;
For he is gone, where all things wise and fair
Descend;—oh, dream not that the amorous Deep
Will yet restore him to the vital air;
Death feeds on his mute voice, and laughs at our despair.

IV

Most musical of mourners, weep again!
Lament anew, Urania!—He died,
Who was the Sire of an immortal strain,   30
Blind, old, and lonely, when his country's pride,
The priest, the slave, and the liberticide,
Trampled and mocked with many a loathèd rite
Of lust and blood; he went, unterrified,
Into the gulf of death; but his clear Sprite
Yet reigns o'er earth; the third among the sons of light.

V

Most musical of mourners, weep anew!
Not all to that bright station dared to climb;
And happier they their happiness who knew,
Whose tapers yet burn through that night of time   40
In which suns perished; others more sublime,
Struck by the envious wrath of man or god,
Have sunk, extinct in their refulgent prime;
And some yet live, treading the thorny road,
Which leads, through toil and hate, to Fame's serene abode.

VI

But now, thy youngest, dearest one, has perished—
The nursling of thy widowhood, who grew,
Like a pale flower by some sad maiden cherished,

And fed with true-love tears, instead of dew;
Most musical of mourners, weep anew!   50
Thy extreme hope, the loveliest and the last,
The bloom, whose petals nipped before they blew
Died on the promise of the fruit, is waste;
The broken lily lies—the storm is overpast.

VII

To that high Capital, where kingly Death
Keeps his pale court in beauty and decay,
He came; and bought, with price of purest breath,
A grave among the eternal.—Come away!
Haste, while the vault of blue Italian day
Is yet his fitting charnel-roof! while still   60
He lies, as if in dewy sleep he lay;
Awake him not! surely he takes his fill
Of deep and liquid rest, forgetful of all ill.

VIII

He will awake no more, oh, never more!—
Within the twilight chamber spreads apace
The shadow of white Death, and at the door
Invisible Corruption waits to trace
His extreme way to her dim dwelling-place;
The eternal Hunger sits, but pity and awe
Soothe her pale rage, nor dares she to deface   70
So fair a prey, till darkness, and the law
Of change, shall o'er his sleep the mortal curtain draw.

IX

Oh, weep for Adonais!—The quick Dreams,
The passion-wingèd Ministers of thought,
Who were his flocks, whom near the living streams
Of his young spirit he fed, and whom he taught
The love which was its music, wander not,—
Wander no more, from kindling brain to brain,
But droop there, whence they sprung; and mourn their lot
Round the cold heart, where, after their sweet pain,   80
They ne'er will gather strength, or find a home again.

X

And one with trembling hands clasps his cold head,
And fans him with her moonlight wings, and cries;
'Our love, our hope, our sorrow, is not dead;
See, on the silken fringe of his faint eyes,
Like dew upon a sleeping flower, there lies
A tear some Dream has loosened from his brain.'
Lost Angel of a ruined Paradise!
She knew not 'twas her own; as with no stain
She faded, like a cloud which had outwept its rain.   90

XI

One from a lucid urn of starry dew
Washed his light limbs as if embalming them;
Another clipped her profuse locks, and threw
The wreath upon him, like an anadem,
Which frozen tears instead of pearls begem;
Another in her wilful grief would break
Her bow and wingèd reeds, as if to stem
A greater loss with one which was more weak;
And dull the barbèd fire against his frozen cheek.

XII

Another Splendour on his mouth alit,   100
That mouth, whence it was wont to draw the breath
Which gave it strength to pierce the guarded wit,
And pass into the panting heart beneath
With lightning and with music: the damp death
Quenched its caress upon his icy lips;
And, as a dying meteor stains a wreath
Of moonlight vapour, which the cold night clips,
It flushed through his pale limbs, and passed to its eclipse.

XIII

And others came . . . Desires and Adorations,
Wingèd Persuasions and veiled Destinies,   110
Splendours, and Glooms, and glimmering Incarnations

Of hopes and fears, and twilight Phantasies;
And Sorrow with her family of Sighs,
And Pleasure, blind with tears, led by the gleam
Of her own dying smile instead of eyes,
Came in slow pomp;—the moving pomp might seem
Like pageantry of mist on an autumnal stream.

XIV

All he had loved, and moulded into thought,
From shape, and hue, and odour, and sweet sound,
Lamented Adonais. Morning sought   120
Her eastern watch-tower, and her hair unbound,
Wet with the tears which should adorn the ground,
Dimmed the aëreal eyes that kindle day;
Afar the melancholy thunder moaned,
Pale Ocean in unquiet slumber lay,
And the wild Winds flew round, sobbing in their dismay.

XV

Lost Echo sits amid the voiceless mountains,
And feeds her grief with his remembered lay,
And will no more reply to winds or fountains,
Or amorous birds perched on the young green spray,   130
Or herdsman's horn, or bell at closing day;
Since she can mimic not his lips, more dear
Than those for whose disdain she pined away
Into a shadow of all sounds:—a drear
Murmur, between their songs, is all the woodmen hear.

XVI

Grief made the young Spring wild, and she threw down
Her kindling buds, as if she Autumn were,
Or they dead leaves; since her delight is flown,
For whom should she have waked the sullen year?
To Phoebus was not Hyacinth so dear   140
Nor to himself Narcissus, as to both
Thou, Adonais: wan they stand and sere
Amid the faint companions of their youth,
With dew all turned to tears; odour, to sighing ruth.

XVII

Thy spirit's sister, the lorn nightingale
Mourns not her mate with such melodious pain;
Not so the eagle, who like thee could scale
Heaven, and could nourish in the sun's domain
Her mighty youth with mourning, doth complain,
Soaring and screaming round her empty nest,   150
As Albion wails for thee: the curse of Cain
Light on his head who pierced thy innocent breast,
And scared the angel soul that was its earthly guest!

XVIII

Ah, woe is me! Winter is come and gone,
But grief returns with the revolving year;
The airs and streams renew their joyous tone;
The ants, the bees, the swallows reappear;
Fresh leaves and flowers deck the dead Seasons' bier;
The amorous birds now pair in every brake,
And build their mossy homes in field and brere;   160
And the green lizard, and the golden snake,
Like unimprisoned flames, out of their trance awake.

XIX

Through wood and stream and field and hill and Ocean
A quickening life from the Earth's heart has burst
As it has ever done, with change and motion,
From the great morning of the world when first
God dawned on Chaos; in its stream immersed,
The lamps of Heaven flash with a softer light;
All baser things pant with life's sacred thirst;
Diffuse themselves; and spend in love's delight,   170
The beauty and the joy of their renewèd might.

XX

The leprous corpse, touched by this spirit tender,
Exhales itself in flowers of gentle breath;
Like incarnations of the stars, when splendour

Is changed to fragrance, they illumine death
And mock the merry worm that wakes beneath;
Nought we know, dies. Shall that alone which knows
Be as a sword consumed before the sheath
By sightless lightning?—the intense atom glows
A moment, then is quenched in a most cold repose.   180

XXI

Alas! that all we loved of him should be,
But for our grief, as if it had not been,
And grief itself be mortal! Woe is me!
Whence are we, and why are we? of what scene
The actors or spectators? Great and mean
Meet massed in death, who lends what life must borrow
As long as skies are blue, and fields are green,
Evening must usher night, night urge the morrow,
Month follow month with woe, and year wake year to sorrow

XXII

He will awake no more, oh, never more!   190
'Wake thou,' cried Misery, 'childless Mother, rise
Out of thy sleep, and slake, in thy heart's core,
A wound more fierce than his, with tears and sighs.'
And all the Dreams that watched Urania's eyes,
And all the Echoes whom their sister's song
Had held in holy silence, cried: 'Arise!'
Swift as a Thought by the snake Memory stung,
From her ambrosial rest the fading Splendour sprung.

XXIII

She rose like an autumnal Night, that springs
Out of the East, and follows wild and drear   200
The golden Day, which, on eternal wings,
Even as a ghost abandoning a bier,
Had left the Earth a corpse. Sorrow and fear
So struck, so roused, so rapped Urania;
So saddened round her like an atmosphere
Of stormy mist; so swept her on her way
Even to the mournful place where Adonais lay.

XXIV

Out of her secret Paradise she sped,
Through camps and cities rough with stone, and steel,
And human hearts, which to her aery tread   210
Yielding not, wounded the invisible
Palms of her tender feet where'er they fell:
And barbèd tongues, and thoughts more sharp than they,
Rent the soft Form they never could repel,
Whose sacred blood, like the young tears of May,
Paved with eternal flowers that undeserving way.

XXV

In the death-chamber for a moment Death,
Shamed by the presence of that living Might,
Blushed to annihilation, and the breath
Revisited those lips, and Life's pale light   220
Flashed through those limbs, so late her dear delight.
'Leave me not wild and drear and comfortless,
As silent lightning leaves the starless night!
Leave me not!' cried Urania: her distress
Roused Death: Death rose and smiled, and met her vain caress.

XXVI

'Stay yet awhile! speak to me once again;
Kiss me, so long but as a kiss may live;
And in my heartless breast and burning brain
That word, that kiss, shall all thoughts else survive,
With food of saddest memory kept alive,   230
Now thou art dead, as if it were a part
Of thee, my Adonais! I would give
All that I am to be as thou now art!
But I am chained to Time, and cannot thence depart!

XXVII

'O gentle child, beautiful as thou wert,
Why didst thou leave the trodden paths of men
Too soon, and with weak hands though mighty heart

Dare the unpastured dragon in his den?
Defenceless as thou wert, oh, where was then
Wisdom the mirrored shield, or scorn the spear?   240
Or hadst thou waited the full cycle, when
Thy spirit should have filled its crescent sphere,
The monsters of life's waste had fled from thee like deer.

XXVIII

'The herded wolves, bold only to pursue;
The obscene ravens, clamorous o'er the dead;
The vultures to the conqueror's banner true
Who feed where Desolation first has fed,
And whose wings rain contagion;—how they fled,
When, like Apollo, from his golden bow
The Pythian of the age one arrow sped   250
And smiled!—The spoilers tempt no second blow,
They fawn on the proud feet that spurn them lying low.

XXIX

'The sun comes forth, and many reptiles spawn;
He sets, and each ephemeral insect then
Is gathered into death without a dawn,
And the immortal stars awake again;
So is it in the world of living men:
A godlike mind soars forth, in its delight
Making earth bare and veiling heaven, and when
It sinks, the swarms that dimmed or shared its light   260
Leave to its kindred lamps the spirit's awful night.'

XXX

Thus ceased she: and the mountain shepherds came,
Their garlands sere, their magic mantles rent;
The Pilgrim of Eternity, whose fame
Over his living head like Heaven is bent,
An early but enduring monument,
Came, veiling all the lightnings of his song
In sorrow; from her wilds Ierne sent
The sweetest lyrist of her saddest wrong,
And Love taught Grief to fall like music from his tongue.   270

XXXI

Midst others of less note, came one frail Form,
A phantom among men; companionless
As the last cloud of an expiring storm
Whose thunder is its knell; he, as I guess,
Had gazed on Nature's naked loveliness,
Actaeon-like, and now he fled astray
With feeble steps o'er the world's wilderness,
And his own thoughts, along that rugged way,
Pursued, like raging hounds, their father and their prey.

XXXII

A pardlike Spirit beautiful and swift—   280
A Love in desolation masked;—a Power
Girt round with weakness;—it can scarce uplift
The weight of the superincumbent hour;
It is a dying lamp, a falling shower,
A breaking billow;—even whilst we speak
Is it not broken? On the withering flower
The killing sun smiles brightly: on a cheek
The life can burn in blood, even while the heart may break.

XXXIII

His head was bound with pansies overblown,
And faded violets, white, and pied, and blue;   290
And a light spear topped with a cypress cone,
Round whose rude shaft dark ivy-tresses grew
Yet dripping with the forest's noonday dew,
Vibrated, as the ever-beating heart
Shook the weak hand that grasped it; of that crew
He came the last, neglected and apart;
A herd-abandoned deer struck by the hunter's dart.

XXXIV

All stood aloof, and at his partial moan
Smiled through their tears; well knew that gentle band
Who in another's fate now wept his own,   300

As in the accents of an unknown land
He sung new sorrow; sad Urania scanned
The Stranger's mien, and murmured: 'Who art thou?'
He answered not, but with a sudden hand
Made bare his branded and ensanguined brow,
Which was like Cain's or Christ's—oh! that it should be so!

XXXV

What softer voice is hushed over the dead?
Athwart what brow is that dark mantle thrown?
What form leans sadly o'er the white death-bed,
In mockery of monumental stone,   310
The heavy heart heaving without a moan?
If it be He, who, gentlest of the wise,
Taught, soothed, loved, honoured the departed one,
Let me not vex, with inharmonious sighs,
The silence of that heart's accepted sacrifice.

XXXVI

Our Adonais has drunk poison—oh!
What deaf and viperous murderer could crown
Life's early cup with such a draught of woe?
The nameless worm would now itself disown:
It felt, yet could escape, the magic tone   320
Whose prelude held all envy, hate, and wrong,
But what was howling in one breast alone,
Silent with expectation of the song,
Whose master's hand is cold, whose silver lyre unstrung.

XXXVII

Live thou, whose infamy is not thy fame!
Live! fear no heavier chastisement from me,
Thou noteless blot on a remembered name!
But be thyself, and know thyself to be!
And ever at thy season be thou free
To spill the venom when thy fangs o'erflow;   330
Remorse and Self-contempt shall cling to thee;
Hot Shame shall burn upon thy secret brow,
And like a beaten hound tremble thou shalt—as now.

XXXVIII

Nor let us weep that our delight is fled
Far from these carrion kites that scream below;
He wakes or sleeps with the enduring dead;
Thou canst not soar where he is sitting now—
Dust to the dust! but the pure spirit shall flow
Back to the burning fountain whence it came,
A portion of the Eternal, which must glow   **340**
Through time and change, unquenchably the same,
Whilst thy cold embers choke the sordid hearth of shame.

XXXIX

Peace, peace! he is not dead, he doth not sleep—
He hath awakened from the dream of life—
'Tis we, who lost in stormy visions, keep
With phantoms an unprofitable strife,
And in mad trance, strike with our spirit's knife
Invulnerable nothings.—*We* decay
Like corpses in a charnel; fear and grief
Convulse us and consume us day by day,   **350**
And cold hopes swarm like worms within our living clay.

XL

He has outsoared the shadow of our night;
Envy and calumny and hate and pain,
And that unrest which men miscall delight,
Can touch him not and torture not again;
From the contagion of the world's slow stain
He is secure, and now can never mourn
A heart grown cold, a head grown gray in vain;
Nor, when the spirit's self has ceased to burn,
With sparkless ashes load an unlamented urn.   **360**

XLI

He lives, he wakes—'tis Death is dead, not he;
Mourn not for Adonais.—Thou young Dawn,
Turn all thy dew to splendour, for from thee

The spirit thou lamentest is not gone;
Ye caverns and ye forests, cease to moan!
Cease, ye faint flowers and fountains, and thou Air,
Which like a mourning veil thy scarf hadst thrown
O'er the abandoned Earth, now leave it bare
Even to the joyous stars which smile on its despair!

XLII

He is made one with Nature: there is heard   370
His voice in all her music, from the moan
Of thunder, to the song of night's sweet bird;
He is a presence to be felt and known
In darkness and in light, from herb and stone,
Spreading itself where'er that Power may move
Which has withdrawn his being to its own;
Which wields the world with never-wearied love,
Sustains it from beneath, and kindles it above.

XLIII

He is a portion of the loveliness
Which once he made more lovely: he doth bear   380
His part, while the one Spirit's plastic stress
Sweeps through the dull dense world, compelling there,
All new successions to the forms they wear;
Torturing th' unwilling dross that checks its flight
To its own likeness, as each mass may bear;
And bursting in its beauty and its might
From trees and beasts and men into the Heaven's light.

XLIV

The splendours of the firmament of time
May be eclipsed, but are extinguished not;
Like stars to their appointed height they climb,   390
And death is a low mist which cannot blot
The brightness it may veil. When lofty thought
Lifts a young heart above its mortal lair,
And love and life contend in it, for what
Shall be its earthly doom, the dead live there
And move like winds of light on dark and stormy air.

XLV

The inheritors of unfulfilled renown
Rose from their thrones, built beyond mortal thought,
Far in the Unapparent. Chatterton
Rose pale,—his solemn agony had not   400
Yet faded from him; Sidney, as he fought
And as he fell and as he lived and loved
Sublimely mild, a Spirit without spot,
Arose; and Lucan, by his death approved:
Oblivion as they rose shrank like a thing reproved.

XLVI

And many more, whose names on Earth are dark,
But whose transmitted effluence cannot die
So long as fire outlives the parent spark,
Rose, robed in dazzling immortality.
'Thou art become as one of us,' they cry,   410
'It was for thee yon kingless sphere has long
Swung blind in unascended majesty,
Silent alone amid an Heaven of Song.
Assume thy wingèd throne, thou Vesper of our throng!'

XLVII

Who mourns for Adonais? Oh, come forth,
Fond wretch! and know thyself and him aright.
Clasp with thy panting soul the pendulous Earth;
As from a centre, dart thy spirit's light
Beyond all worlds, until its spacious might
Satiate the void circumference: then shrink   420
Even to a point within our day and night;
And keep thy heart light lest it make thee sink
When hope has kindled hope, and lured thee to the brink.

XLVIII

Or go to Rome, which is the sepulchre,
Oh, not of him, but of our joy: 'tis nought
That ages, empires, and religions there

Lie buried in the ravage they have wrought;
For such as he can lend,—they borrow not
Glory from those who made the world their prey;
And he is gathered to the kings of thought   430
Who waged contention with their time's decay,
And of the past are all that cannot pass away.

XLIX

Go thou to Rome,—at once the Paradise,
The grave, the city, and the wilderness;
And where its wrecks like shattered mountains rise,
And flowering weeds, and fragrant copses dress
The bones of Desolation's nakedness
Pass, till the spirit of the spot shall lead
Thy footsteps to a slope of green access
Where, like an infant's smile, over the dead
A light of laughing flowers along the grass is spread;

L

And gray walls moulder round, on which dull Time
Feeds, like slow fire upon a hoary brand;
And one keen pyramid with wedge sublime,
Pavilioning the dust of him who planned
This refuge for his memory, doth stand
Like flame transformed to marble; and beneath,
A field is spread, on which a newer band
Have pitched in Heaven's smile their camp of death,
Welcoming him we lose with scarce extinguished breath.   450

LI

Here pause: these graves are all too young as yet
To have outgrown the sorrow which consigned
Its charge to each; and if the seal is set,
Here, on one fountain of a mourning mind,
Break it not thou! too surely shalt thou find
Thine own well full, if thou returnest home,
Of tears and gall. From the world's bitter wind
Seek shelter in the shadow of the tomb.
What Adonais is, why fear we to become?

LII

The One remains, the many change and pass; 460
Heaven's light forever shines, Earth's shadows fly;
Life, like a dome of many-coloured glass,
Stains the white radiance of Eternity,
Until Death tramples it to fragments.—Die,
If thou wouldst be with that which thou dost seek!
Follow where all is fled!—Rome's azure sky,
Flowers, ruins, statues, music, words, are weak
The glory they transfuse with fitting truth to speak.

LIII

Why linger, why turn back, why shrink, my Heart?
Thy hopes are gone before: from all things here 470
They have departed; thou shouldst now depart!
A light is passed from the revolving year,
And man, and woman; and what still is dear
Attracts to crush, repels to make thee wither.
The soft sky smiles,—the low wind whispers near:
'Tis Adonais calls! oh, hasten thither,
No more let Life divide what Death can join together.

LIV

That Light whose smile kindles the Universe,
That Beauty in which all things work and move,
That Benediction which the eclipsing Curse 480
Of birth can quench not, that sustaining Love
Which through the web of being blindly wove
By man and beast and earth and air and sea,
Burns bright or dim, as each are mirrors of
The fire for which all thirst; now beams on me,
Consuming the last clouds of cold mortality.

LV

The breath whose might I have invoked in song
Descends on me; my spirit's bark is driven,

Far from the shore, far from the trembling throng
Whose sails were never to the tempest given;   490
The massy earth and spherèd skies are riven!
I am borne darkly, fearfully, afar;
Whilst, burning through the inmost veil of Heaven,
The soul of Adonais, like a star,
Beacons from the abode where the Eternal are.

[1821; publ. 1821]

HELLAS[1]

A LYRICAL DRAMA

ΜΑΝΤΙΣ 'ΕΙΜ' 'ΕΣΘΛΩΝ 'ΑΓΩΝΩΝ.—Oedip. Colon.

TO HIS EXCELLENCY
PRINCE ALEXANDER MAVROCORDATO
LATE SECRETARY FOR FOREIGN AFFAIRS TO THE HOSPODAR OF
WALLACHIA

THE DRAMA OF HELLAS IS INSCRIBED AS AN
IMPERFECT TOKEN OF THE ADMIRATION,
SYMPATHY, AND FRIENDSHIP OF
THE AUTHOR

Pisa, *November* 1, 1821.

DRAMATIS PERSONAE

MAHMUD.   DAOOD.
HASSAN.   AHASUERUS, *a Jew.*
CHORUS *of Greek Captive Women.*
[*The Phantom of Mahomet II.*]
Messengers, Slaves, and Attendants.

[1] The Preface Shelley wrote for *Hellas* appears on page 451 of the
present edition.

SCENE, *Constantinople.*   TIME, *Sunset.*

SCENE—*A Terrace on the Seraglio.* MAHMUD *sleeping, an
Indian Slave sitting beside his Couch.*

Chorus of Greek Captive Women.

WE strew these opiate flowers
 On thy restless pillow,—
They were stripped from Orient bowers,
 By the Indian billow.
  Be thy sleep
  Calm and deep,
Like theirs who fell—not ours who weep!

Indian.

Away, unlovely dreams!
 Away, false shapes of sleep!
Be his, as Heaven seems,   **10**
 Clear, and bright, and deep!
Soft as love, and calm as death,
Sweet as a summer night without a breath.

Chorus.

Sleep, sleep! our song is laden
 With the soul of slumber;
It was sung by a Samian maiden,
 Whose lover was of the number
  Who now keep
  That calm sleep
Whence none may wake, where none shall weep.   **20**

Indian.

I touch thy temples pale!
 I breathe my soul on thee!
And could my prayers avail,
 All my joy should be
Dead, and I would live to weep,
So thou mightst win one hour of quiet sleep.

Chorus.

Breathe low, low
The spell of the mighty mistress now!
When Conscience lulls her sated snake,
And Tyrants sleep, let Freedom wake.   30
Breathe low—low
The words which, like secret fire, shall flow
Through the veins of the frozen earth—low, low!

Semichorus I.

Life may change, but it may fly not;
Hope may vanish, but can die not;
Truth be veiled, but still it burneth;
Love repulsed,—but it returneth!

Semichorus II.

Yet were life a charnel where
Hope lay coffined with Despair;
Yet were truth a sacred lie,   40
Love were lust—

Semichorus I.

If Liberty
Lent not life its soul of light,
Hope its iris of delight,
Truth its prophet's robe to wear,
Love its power to give and bear.

Chorus.

In the great morning of the world,
The Spirit of God with might unfurled
The flag of Freedom over Chaos,
And all its banded anarchs fled,
Like vultures frighted from Imaus,   50
Before an earthquake's tread.—
So from Time's tempestuous dawn
Freedom's splendour burst and shone:—

Thermopylae and Marathon
Caught, like mountains beacon-lighted,
    The springing Fire.—The wingèd glory
On Philippi half-alighted,
    Like an eagle on a promontory.
Its unwearied wings could fan
The quenchless ashes of Milan.   60
From age to age, from man to man,
    It lived; and lit from land to land
    Florence, Albion, Switzerland.

Then night fell; and, as from night,
Reassuming fiery flight,
From the West swift Freedom came,
    Against the course of Heaven and doom,
A second sun arrayed in flame,
    To burn, to kindle, to illume.
From far Atlantis its young beams   70
Chased the shadows and the dreams.
France, with all her sanguine steams,
    Hid, but quenched it not: again
    Through clouds its shafts of glory rain
    From utmost Germany to Spain.

As an eagle fed with morning
Scorns the embattled tempest's warning,
When she seeks her aerie hanging
    In the mountain-cedar's hair,
And her brood expect the clanging   80
    Of her wings through the wild air,
Sick with famine:—Freedom, so
To what of Greece remaineth now
Returns; her hoary ruins glow
Like Orient mountains lost in day;
    Beneath the safety of her wings
Her renovated nurslings prey,
    And in the naked lightenings
Of truth they purge their dazzled eyes.
Let Freedom leave—where'er she flies,   90
A Desert, or a Paradise:
    Let the beautiful and the brave
    Share her glory, or a grave.

Semichorus I.

With the gifts of gladness
   Greece did thy cradle strew;

Semichorus II.

With the tears of sadness
   Greece did thy shroud bedew!

Semichorus I.

With an orphan's affection
   She followed thy bier through Time;

Semichorus II.

And at thy resurrection   100
   Reappeareth, like thou, sublime!

Semichorus I.

If Heaven should resume thee,
   To Heaven shall her spirit ascend;

Semichorus II.

If Hell should entomb thee,
   To Hell shall her high hearts bend.

Semichorus I.

If Annihilation——

Semichorus II.

Dust let her glories be!
And a name and a nation
   Be forgotten, Freedom, with thee!

Indian.

His brow grows darker—breathe not—move not!   110
He starts—he shudders—ye that love not,
   With your panting loud and fast,
   Have awakened him at last.

 Mahmud (starting from his sleep). Man the Seraglio-guard!
  make fast the gate!
What! from a cannonade of three short hours?
'Tis false! that breach towards the Bosphorus
Cannot be practicable yet—who stirs?
Stand to the match; that when the foe prevails
One spark may mix in reconciling ruin
The conqueror and the conquered! Heave the tower   120
Into the gap—wrench off the roof!
 (*Enter* HASSAN.)   Ha! what!
The truth of day lightens upon my dream
And I am Mahmud still.
 Hassan.   Your Sublime Highness
Is strangely moved.
 Mahmud.   The times do cast strange shadows
On those who watch and who must rule their course,
Lest they, being first in peril as in glory,
Be whelmed in the fierce ebb:—and these are of them.
Thrice has a gloomy vision hunted me
As thus from sleep into the troubled day;
It shakes me as the tempest shakes the sea,   130
Leaving no figure upon memory's glass.
Would that——no matter. Thou didst say thou knewest
A Jew, whose spirit is a chronicle
Of strange and secret and forgotten things.
I bade thee summon him:—'tis said his tribe
Dream, and are wise interpreters of dreams.
 Hassan. The Jew of whom I spake is old,—so old
He seems to have outlived a world's decay;
The hoary mountains and the wrinkled ocean
Seem younger still than he;—his hair and beard   140
Are whiter than the tempest-sifted snow;
His cold pale limbs and pulseless arteries
Are like the fibres of a cloud instinct
With light, and to the soul that quickens them
Are as the atoms of the mountain-drift
To the winter wind:—but from his eye looks forth
A life of unconsumèd thought which pierces
The Present, and the Past, and the To-come.
Some say that this is he whom the great prophet
Jesus, the son of Joseph, for his mockery,   150
Mocked with the curse of immortality.

Some feign that he is Enoch: others dream
He was pre-adamite and has survived
Cycles of generation and of ruin.
The sage, in truth, by dreadful abstinence
And conquering penance of the mutinous flesh,
Deep contemplation, and unwearied study,
In years outstretched beyond the date of man,
May have attained to sovereignty and science
Over those strong and secret things and thoughts   160
Which others fear and know not.
    Mahmud.   I would talk
With this old Jew.
    Hassan.   Thy will is even now
Made known to him, where he dwells in a sea-cavern
'Mid the Demonesi, less accessible
Than thou or God! He who would question him
Must sail alone at sunset, where the stream
Of Ocean sleeps around those foamless isles,
When the young moon is westering as now,
And evening airs wander upon the wave;
And when the pines of that bee-pasturing isle,   170
Green Erebinthus, quench the fiery shadow
Of his gilt prow within the sapphire water,
Then must the lonely helmsman cry aloud
'Ahasuerus!' and the caverns round
Will answer 'Ahasuerus!' If his prayer
Be granted, a faint meteor will arise
Lighting him over Marmora, and a wind
Will rush out of the sighing pine-forest,
And with the wind a storm of harmony
Unutterably sweet, and pilot him   180
Through the soft twilight to the Bosphorus:
Thence at the hour and place and circumstance
Fit for the matter of their conference
The Jew appears. Few dare, and few who dare
Win the desired communion—but that shout
Bodes——
                                [*A shout within.*
    Mahmud. Evil, doubtless; like all human sounds.
Let me converse with spirits.
    Hassan.   That shout again.
    Mahmud. This Jew whom thou hast summoned—

Hassan.   Will be here—
Mahmud. When the omnipotent hour to which are yoked
He, I, and all things shall compel—enough!   190
Silence those mutineers—that drunken crew,
That crowd about the pilot in the storm.
Ay! strike the foremost shorter by a head!
They weary me, and I have need of rest.
Kings are like stars—they rise and set, they have
The worship of the world, but no repose.

                                        [*Exeunt severally.*

Chorus.

    Worlds on worlds are rolling ever
      From creation to decay,
    Like the bubbles on a river
      Sparkling, bursting, borne away.   200
        But they are still immortal
        Who, through birth's orient portal
    And death's dark chasm hurrying to and fro,
        Clothe their unceasing flight
        In the brief dust and light
    Gathered around their chariots as they go;
        New shapes they still may weave,
        New gods, new laws receive,
    Bright or dim are they as the robes they last
        On Death's bare ribs had cast.   210

    A power from the unknown God,
      A Promethean conqueror, came;
    Like a triumphal path he trod
      The thorns of death and shame.
        A mortal shape to him
        Was like the vapour dim
    Which the orient planet animates with light;
        Hell, Sin, and Slavery came,
        Like bloodhounds mild and tame,
    Nor preyed, until their Lord had taken flight;   220
        The moon of Mahomet
        Arose, and it shall set:
    While blazoned as on Heaven's immortal noon
      The cross leads generations on.

Swift as the radiant shapes of sleep
  From one whose dreams are Paradise
Fly, when the fond wretch wakes to weep,
  And Day peers forth with her blank eyes;
  So fleet, so faint, so fair,
  The Powers of earth and air   230
Fled from the folding-star of Bethlehem:
  Apollo, Pan, and Love,
  And even Olympian Jove
Grew weak, for killing Truth had glared on them;
  Our hills and seas and streams,
  Dispeopled of their dreams,
Their waters turned to blood, their dew to tears,
  Wailed for the golden years.

Enter Mahmud, Hassan, Daood, *and others.*

Mahmud. More gold? our ancestors bought gold with victory,
And shall I sell it for defeat?
  Daood.   The Janizars   240
Clamour for pay.
  Mahmud.   Go! bid them pay themselves
With Christian blood! Are there no Grecian virgins
Whose shrieks and spasms and tears they may enjoy?
No infidel children to impale on spears?
No hoary priests after that Patriarch
Who bent the curse against his country's heart,
Which clove his own at last? Go! bid them kill,
Blood is the seed of gold.
  Daood.   It has been sown,
And yet the harvest to the sicklemen
Is as a grain to each.
  Mahmud.   Then, take this signet,   250
Unlock the seventh chamber in which lie
The treasures of victorious Solyman,—
An empire's spoil stored for a day of ruin.
O spirit of my sires! is it not come?
The prey-birds and the wolves are gorged and sleep;
But these, who spread their feast on the red earth,
Hunger for gold, which fills not.—See them fed;
Then, lead them to the rivers of fresh death.   [*Exit* Daood
O miserable dawn, after a night

More glorious than the day which it usurped!   260
O faith in God! O power on earth! O word
Of the great prophet, whose o'ershadowing wings
Darkened the thrones and idols of the West,
Now bright!—For thy sake cursèd be the hour,
Even as a father by an evil child,
When the orient moon of Islam rolled in triumph
From Caucasus to White Ceraunia!
Ruin above, and anarchy below;
Terror without, and treachery within;
The Chalice of destruction full, and all   270
Thirsting to drink; and who among us dares
To dash it from his lips? and where is Hope?
   Hassan. The lamp of our dominion still rides high;
One God is God—Mahomet is His prophet.
Four hundred thousand Moslems, from the limits
Of utmost Asia, irresistibly
Throng, like full clouds at the Sirocco's cry;
But not like them to weep their strength in tears:
They bear destroying lightning, and their step
Wakes earthquake to consume and overwhelm,   280
And reign in ruin. Phrygian Olympus,
Tmolus, and Latmos, and Mycale, roughen
With horrent arms; and lofty ships even now,
Like vapours anchored to a mountain's edge,
Freighted with fire and whirlwind, wait at Scala
The convoy of the ever-veering wind.
Samos is drunk with blood;—the Greek has paid
Brief victory with swift loss and long despair.
The false Moldavian serfs fled fast and far,
When the fierce shout of 'Allah-illa-Allah!'   290
Rose like the war-cry of the northern wind
Which kills the sluggish clouds, and leaves a flock
Of wild swans struggling with the naked storm.
So were the lost Greeks on the Danube's day!
If night is mute, yet the returning sun
Kindles the voices of the morning birds;
Nor at thy bidding less exultingly
Than birds rejoicing in the golden day,
The Anarchies of Africa unleash
Their tempest-wingèd cities of the sea,   300
To speak in thunder to the rebel world.

Like sulphurous clouds, half-shattered by the storm,
They sweep the pale Aegean, while the Queen
Of Ocean, bound upon her island-throne,
Far in the West, sits mourning that her sons
Who frown on Freedom spare a smile for thee:
Russia still hovers, as an eagle might
Within a cloud, near which a kite and crane
Hang tangled in inextricable fight,
To stoop upon the victor;—for she fears   310
The name of Freedom, even as she hates thine.
But recreant Austria loves thee as the Grave
Loves Pestilence, and her slow dogs of war
Fleshed with the chase, come up from Italy,
And howl upon their limits; for they see
The panther, Freedom, fled to her old cover,
Amid seas and mountains, and a mightier brood
Crouch round. What Anarch wears a crown or mitre,
Or bears the sword, or grasps the key of gold,
Whose friends are not thy friends, whose foes thy foes?   320
Our arsenals and our armouries are full;
Our forts defy assault; ten thousand cannon
Lie ranged upon the beach, and hour by hour
Their earth-convulsing wheels affright the city;
The galloping of fiery steeds makes pale
The Christian merchant; and the yellow Jew
Hides his hoard deeper in the faithless earth.
Like clouds, and like the shadows of the clouds,
Over the hills of Anatolia,
Swift in wide troops the Tartar chivalry   330
Sweep;—the far flashing of their starry lances
Reverberates the dying light of day.
We have one God, one King, one Hope, one Law;
But many-headed Insurrection stands
Divided in itself, and soon must fall.
    Mahmud. Proud words, when deeds come short, are **seasonable:**
Look, Hassan, on yon crescent moon, emblazoned
Upon that shattered flag of fiery cloud
Which leads the rear of the departing day;
Wan emblem of an empire fading now!   340
See how it trembles in the blood-red air,
And like a mighty lamp whose oil is spent
Shrinks on the horizon's edge, while, from above,

One star with insolent and victorious light
Hovers above its fall, and with keen beams,
Like arrows through a fainting antelope,
Strikes its weak form to death.

    Hassan.   Even as that moon
Renews itself——

    Mahmud.   Shall we be not renewed!
Far other bark than ours were needed now
To stem the torrent of descending time: 350
The Spirit that lifts the slave before his lord
Stalks through the capitals of armèd kings,
And spreads his ensign in the wilderness:
Exults in chains; and, when the rebel falls,
Cries like the blood of Abel from the dust;
And the inheritors of the earth, like beasts
When earthquake is unleashed, with idiot fear
Cower in their kingly dens—as I do now.
What were Defeat when Victory must appal?
Or Danger, when Security looks pale?—   360
How said the messenger—who, from the fort
Islanded in the Danube, saw the battle
Of Bucharest?—that—

    Hassan.   Ibrahim's scimitar
Drew with its gleam swift victory from Heaven,
To burn before him in the night of battle—
A light and a destruction.

    Mahmud.   Ay! the day
Was ours: but how?——

    Hassan.   The light Wallachians,
The Arnaut, Servian, and Albanian allies
Fled from the glance of our artillery
Almost before the thunderstone alit.   370
One half the Grecian army made a bridge
Of safe and slow retreat, with Moslem dead;
The other—

    Mahmud. Speak—tremble not.—

    Hassan.   Islanded
By victor myriads, formed in hollow square
With rough and steadfast front, and thrice flung back
The deluge of our foaming cavalry;
Thrice their keen wedge of battle pierced our lines,
Our baffled army trembled like one man

Before a host, and gave them space; but soon,
From the surrounding hills, the batteries blazed,   380
Kneading them down with fire and iron rain:
Yet none approached; till, like a field of corn
Under the hook of the swart sickleman,
The band, intrenched in mounds of Turkish dead,
Grew weak and few.—Then said the Pacha, 'Slaves,
Render yourselves—they have abandoned you—
What hope of refuge, or retreat, or aid?
We grant your lives.' 'Grant that which is thine own!'
Cried one, and fell upon his sword and died!
Another—'God, and man, and hope abandon me;   390
But I to them, and to myself, remain
Constant:'—he bowed his head, and his heart burst.
A third exclaimed, 'There is a refuge, tyrant,
Where thou darest not pursue, and canst not harm
Shouldst thou pursue; there we shall meet again.'
Then held his breath, and, after a brief spasm,
The indignant spirit cast its mortal garment
Among the slain—dead earth upon the earth!
So these survivors, each by different ways,
Some strange, all sudden, none dishonourable,   400
Met in triumphant death; and when our army
Closed in, while yet wonder, and awe, and shame
Held back the base hyaenas of the battle
That feed upon the dead and fly the living,
One rose out of the chaos of the slain:
And if it were a corpse which some dread spirit
Of the old saviours of the land we rule
Had lifted in its anger, wandering by;—
Or if there burned within the dying man
Unquenchable disdain of death, and faith   410
Creating what it feigned;—I cannot tell—
But he cried, 'Phantoms of the free, we come!
Armies of the Eternal, ye who strike
To dust the citadels of sanguine kings,
And shake the souls throned on their stony hearts,
And thaw their frostwork diadems like dew;—
O ye who float around this clime, and weave
The garment of the glory which it wears,
Whose fame, though earth betray the dust it clasped,
Lies sepulchred in monumental thought;—   420

Progenitors of all that yet is great,
Ascribe to your bright senate, O accept
In your high ministrations, us, your sons—
Us first, and the more glorious yet to come!
And ye, weak conquerors! giants who look pale
When the crushed worm rebels beneath your tread,
The vultures and the dogs, your pensioners tame,
Are overgorged; but, like oppressors, still
They crave the relic of Destruction's feast.
The exhalations and the thirsty winds   **430**
Are sick with blood; the dew is foul with death;
Heaven's light is quenched in slaughter: thus, where'er
Upon your camps, cities, or towers, or fleets,
The obscene birds the reeking remnants cast
Of these dead limbs,—upon your streams and mountains,
Upon your fields, your gardens, and your housetops,
Where'er the winds shall creep, or the clouds fly,
Or the dews fall, or the angry sun look down
With poisoned light—Famine, and Pestilence,
And Panic, shall wage war upon our side!   **440**
Nature from all her boundaries is moved
Against ye: Time has found ye light as foam.
The Earth rebels; and Good and Evil stake
Their empire o'er the unborn world of men
On this one cast;—but ere the die be thrown,
The renovated genius of our race,
Proud umpire of the impious game, descends,
A seraph-wingèd Victory, bestriding
The tempest of the Omnipotence of God,
Which sweeps all things to their appointed doom,   **450**
And you to oblivion!'—More he would have said,
But—
    Mahmud. Died—as thou shouldst ere thy lips had painted
Their ruin in the hues of our success.
A rebel's crime, gilt with a rebel's tongue!
Your heart is Greek, Hassan.
    Hassan.   It may be so:
A spirit not my own wrenched me within,
And I have spoken words I fear and hate;
Yet would I die for—
    Mahmud.   Live! oh live! outlive
Me and this sinking empire. But the fleet—

Hassan. Alas——
   Mahmud.   The fleet which, like a flock of clouds   460
Chased by the wind, flies the insurgent banner!
Our wingèd castles from their merchant ships!
Our myriads before their weak pirate bands!
Our arms before their chains! our years of empire
Before their centuries of servile fear!
Death is awake! Repulse is on the waters!
They own no more the thunder-bearing banner
Of Mahmud; but, like hounds of a base breed,
Gorge from a stranger's hand, and rend their master.
   Hassan. Latmos, and Ampelos, and Phanae saw   470
The wreck——
   Mahmud.   The caves of the Icarian isles
Told each to the other in loud mockery,
And with the tongue as of a thousand echoes,
First of the sea-convulsing fight—and, then,—
Thou darest to speak—senseless are the mountains:
Interpret thou their voice!
   Hassan.   My presence bore
A part in that day's shame. The Grecian fleet
Bore down at daybreak from the North, and hung
As multitudinous on the ocean line,
As cranes upon the cloudless Thracian wind.   480
Our squadron, convoying ten thousand men,
Was stretching towards Nauplia when the battle
Was kindled.—
First through the hail of our artillery
The agile Hydriote barks with press of sail
Dashed:—ship to ship, cannon to cannon, man
To man were grappled in the embrace of war,
Inextricable but by death or victory.
The tempest of the raging fight convulsed
To its crystalline depths that stainless sea,   490
And shook Heaven's roof of golden morning clouds,
Poised on an hundred azure mountain-isles.
In the brief trances of the artillery
One cry from the destroyed and the destroyer
Rose, and a cloud of desolation wrapped
The unforeseen event, till the north wind
Sprung from the sea, lifting the heavy veil
Of battle-smoke—then victory—victory!

For, as we thought, three frigates from Algiers
Bore down from Naxos to our aid, but soon   500
The abhorrèd cross glimmered behind, before,
Among, around us; and that fatal sign
Dried with its beams the strength in Moslem hearts,
As the sun drinks the dew.—What more? We fled!—
Our noonday path over the sanguine foam
Was beaconed,—and the glare struck the sun pale,—
By our consuming transports; the fierce light
Made all the shadows of our sails blood-red,
And every countenance blank. Some ships lay feeding
The ravening fire, even to the water's level;   510
Some were blown up; some, settling heavily,
Sunk; and the shrieks of our companions died
Upon the wind, that bore us fast and far,
Even after they were dead. Nine thousand perished!
We met the vultures legioned in the air
Stemming the torrent of the tainted wind;
They, screaming from their cloudy mountain-peaks,
Stooped through the sulphurous battle-smoke and perched
Each on the weltering carcase that we loved,
Like its ill angel or its damnèd soul,   520
Riding upon the bosom of the sea.
We saw the dog-fish hastening to their feast.
Joy waked the voiceless people of the sea,
And ravening Famine left his ocean cave
To dwell with War, with us, and with Despair.
We met night three hours to the west of Patmos,
And with night, tempest——
    Mahmud.   Cease!

Enter a Messenger.

    Messenger.   Your Sublime Highness,
That Christian hound, the Muscovite Ambassador,
Has left the city.—If the rebel fleet
Had anchored in the port, had victory   530
Crowned the Greek legions in the Hippodrome,
Panic were tamer.—Obedience and Mutiny,
Like giants in contention planet-struck,
Stand gazing on each other.—There is peace
In Stamboul.—

   Mahmud.   Is the grave not calmer still?
Its ruins shall be mine.
   Hassan.   Fear not the Russian:
The tiger leagues not with the stag at bay
Against the hunter.—Cunning, base, and cruel,
He crouches, watching till the spoil be won,
And must be paid for his reserve in blood. 540
After the war is fought, yield the sleek Russian
That which thou canst not keep, his deserved portion
Of blood, which shall not flow through streets and fields,
Rivers and seas, like that which we may win,
But stagnate in the veins of Christian slaves!

Enter Second Messenger.

   Second Messenger. Nauplia, Tripolizza, Mothon, Athens,
Navarin, Artas, Monembasia,
Corinth, and Thebes are carried by assault,
And every Islamite who made his dogs
Fat with the flesh of Galilean slaves 550
Passed at the edge of the sword: the lust of blood,
Which made our warriors drunk, is quenched in death;
But like a fiery plague breaks out anew
In deeds which make the Christian cause look pale
In its own light. The garrison of Patras
Has store but for ten days, nor is there hope
But from the Briton: at once slave and tyrant,
His wishes still are weaker than his fears,
Or he would sell what faith may yet remain
From the oaths broke in Genoa and in Norway; 560
And if you buy him not, your treasury
Is empty even of promises—his own coin.
The freedman of a western poet-chief
Holds Attica with seven thousand rebels,
And has beat back the Pacha of Negropont:
The agèd Ali sits in Yanina
A crownless metaphor of empire:
His name, that shadow of his withered might,
Holds our besieging army like a spell
In prey to famine, pest, and mutiny; 570
He, bastioned in his citadel, looks forth
Joyless upon the sapphire lake that mirrors

The ruins of the city where he reigned
Childless and sceptreless. The Greek has reaped
The costly harvest his own blood matured,
Not the sower, Ali—who has bought a truce
From Ypsilanti with ten camel-loads
Of Indian gold.

Enter a Third Messenger.

Mahmud.   What more?
Third Messenger.   The Christian tribes
Of Lebanon and the Syrian wilderness
Are in revolt;—Damascus, Hems, Aleppo   580
Tremble;—the Arab menaces Medina,
The Aethiop has intrenched himself in Sennaar,
And keeps the Egyptian rebel well employed,
Who denies homage, claims investiture
As price of tardy aid. Persia demands
The cities on the Tigris, and the Georgians
Refuse their living tribute. Crete and Cyprus,
Like mountain-twins that from each other's veins
Catch the volcano-fire and earthquake-spasm,
Shake in the general fever. Through the city,   590
Like birds before a storm, the Santons shriek,
And prophesyings horrible and new
Are heard among the crowd: that sea of men
Sleeps on the wrecks it made, breathless and still.
A Dervise, learnèd in the Koran, preaches
That it is written how the sins of Islam
Must raise up a destroyer even now.
The Greeks expect a Saviour from the West,
Who shall not come, men say, in clouds and glory,
But in the omnipresence of that Spirit   600
In which all live and are. Ominous signs
Are blazoned broadly on the noonday sky:
One saw a red cross stamped upon the sun;
It has rained blood; and monstrous births declare
The secret wrath of Nature and her Lord.
The army encamped upon the Cydaris
Was roused last night by the alarm of battle,
And saw two hosts conflicting in the air,
The shadows doubtless of the unborn time

Cast on the mirror of the night. While yet   610
The fight hung balanced, there arose a storm
Which swept the phantoms from among the stars.
At the third watch the Spirit of the Plague
Was heard abroad flapping among the tents;
Those who relieved watch found the sentinels dead.
The last news from the camp is, that a thousand
Have sickened, and——

Enter a Fourth Messenger.

Mahmud.   And thou, pale ghost, dim shadow
Of some untimely rumour, speak!
 Fourth Messenger.   One comes
Fainting with toil, covered with foam and blood:
He stood, he says, on Chelonites'   620
Promontory, which o'erlooks the isles that groan
Under the Briton's frown, and all their waters
Then trembling in the splendour of the moon,
When as the wandering clouds unveiled or hid
Her boundless light, he saw two adverse fleets
Stalk through the night in the horizon's glimmer,
Mingling fierce thunders and sulphureous gleams,
And smoke which strangled every infant wind
That soothed the silver clouds through the deep air.
At length the battle slept, but the Sirocco   630
Awoke, and drove his flock of thunder-clouds
Over the sea-horizon, blotting out
All objects—save that in the faint moon-glimpse
He saw, or dreamed he saw, the Turkish admiral
And two the loftiest of our ships of war,
With the bright image of that Queen of Heaven,
Who hid, perhaps, her face for grief, reversed;
And the abhorrèd cross——

Enter an Attendant.

Attendant.   Your Sublime Highness,
The Jew, who——
 Mahmud.   Could not come more seasonably:
Bid him attend. I'll hear no more! too long   640
We gaze on danger through the mist of fear,

And multiply upon our shattered hopes
The images of ruin. Come what will!
To-morrow and to-morrow are as lamps
Set in our path to light us to the edge
Through rough and smooth, nor can we suffer aught
Which He inflicts not in whose hand we are.   [*Exeunt.*

Semichorus I.

Would I were the wingèd cloud
Of a tempest swift and loud!
　　　I would scorn   650
　　　The smile of morn
And the wave where the moonrise is born!
　　　I would leave
　　　The spirits of eve
A shroud for the corpse of the day to weave
From other threads than mine!
Bask in the deep blue noon divine.
　　　Who would? Not I.

Semichorus II.

Whither to fly?

Semichorus I.

Where the rocks that gird th' Aegean   660
Echo to the battle paean
　　　Of the free—
　　　I would flee
A tempestuous herald of victory!
　　　My golden rain
　　　For the Grecian slain
Should mingle in tears with the bloody main,
　　　And my solemn thunder-knell
　　　Should ring to the world the passing-bell
　　　Of Tyranny!   670

Semichorus II.

Ah king! wilt thou chain
The rack and the rain?

Wilt thou fetter the lightning and hurricane?
    The storms are free,
      But we—

Chorus.

O Slavery! thou frost of the world's prime,
  Killing its flowers and leaving its thorns bare!
Thy touch has stamped these limbs with crime,
  These brows thy branding garland bear,
    But the free heart, the impassive soul   680
      Scorn thy control!

Semichorus I.

Let there be light! said Liberty,
And like sunrise from the sea,
Athens arose!—Around her born,
Shone like mountains in the morn
Glorious states;—and are they now
Ashes, wrecks, oblivion?

Semichorus II.

          Go,
Where Thermae and Asopus swallowed
  Persia, as the sand does foam;
Deluge upon deluge followed,   690
  Discord, Macedon, and Rome:
And lastly thou!

Semichorus I.

      Temples and towers,
  Citadels and marts, and they
Who live and die there, have been ours,
  And may be thine, and must decay;
But Greece and her foundations are
Built below the tide of war,
Based on the crystàlline sea
Of thought and its eternity;
Her citizens, imperial spirits,   700

Rule the present from the past,
On all this world of men inherits
    Their seal is set.

Semichorus II.

                Hear ye the blast,
Whose Orphic thunder thrilling calls
From ruin her Titanian walls?
Whose spirit shakes the sapless bones
    Of Slavery? Argos, Corinth, Crete
Hear, and from their mountain thrones
    The daemons and the nymphs repeat
The harmony.

Semichorus I.

        I hear! I hear!   710

Semichorus II.

The world's eyeless charioteer,
    Destiny, is hurrying by!
What faith is crushed, what empire bleeds
Beneath her earthquake-footed steeds?
What eagle-wingèd victory sits
At her right hand? what shadow flits
    Before? what splendour rolls behind?
        Ruin and renovation cry
'Who but We?'

Semichorus I.

        I hear! I hear!
    The hiss as of a rushing wind,   720
The roar as of an ocean foaming,
The thunder as of earthquake coming
            I hear! I hear!
The crash as of an empire falling,
The shrieks as of a people calling
'Mercy! mercy!'—How they thrill!
Then a shout of 'kill! kill! kill!'
And then a small still voice, thus—

Semichorus II.

For
Revenge and Wrong bring forth their kind,
The foul cubs like their parents are,   730
Their den is in the guilty mind,
And Conscience feeds them with despair.

Semichorus I.

In sacred Athens, near the fane
Of Wisdom, Pity's altar stood:
Serve not the unknown God in vain,
But pay that broken shrine again,
Love for hate and tears for blood.

Enter Mahmud and Ahasuerus.

Mahmud. Thou art a man, thou sayest, even as we.
Ahasuerus. No more!
Mahmud.   But raised above thy fellow-men
By thought, as I by power.
Ahasuerus.   Thou sayest so.   740
Mahmud. Thou art an adept in the difficult lore
Of Greek and Frank philosophy; thou numberest
The flowers, and thou measurest the stars;
Thou severest element from element;
Thy spirit is present in the Past, and sees
The birth of this old world through all its cycles
Of desolation and of loveliness,
And when man was not, and how man became
The monarch and the slave of this low sphere,
And all its narrow circles—it is much—   750
I honour thee, and would be what thou art
Were I not what I am; but the unborn hour,
Cradled in fear and hope, conflicting storms,
Who shall unveil? Nor thou, nor I, nor any
Mighty or wise. I apprehended not
What thou hast taught me, but I now perceive
That thou art no interpreter of dreams;
Thou dost not own that art, device, or God,

Can make the Future present—let it come!
Moreover thou disdainest us and ours;   760
Thou art as God, whom thou contemplatest.
    Ahasuerus. Disdain thee?—not the worm beneath thy feet!
The Fathomless has care for meaner things
Than thou canst dream, and has made pride for those
Who would be what they may not, or would seem
That which they are not. Sultan! talk no more
Of thee and me, the Future and the Past;
But look on that which cannot change—the One,
The unborn and the undying. Earth and ocean,
Space, and the isles of life or light that gem   770
The sapphire floods of interstellar air,
This firmament pavilioned upon chaos,
With all its cressets of immortal fire,
Whose outwall, bastioned impregnably
Against the escape of boldest thoughts, repels them
As Calpe the Atlantic clouds—this Whole
Of suns, and worlds, and men, and beasts, and flowers,
With all the silent or tempestuous workings
By which they have been, are, or cease to be,
Is but a vision;—all that it inherits   780
Are motes of a sick eye, bubbles and dreams;
Thought is its cradle and its grave, nor less
The Future and the Past are idle shadows
Of thought's eternal flight—they have no being:
Nought is but that which feels itself to be.
    Mahmud. What meanest thou? Thy words stream like a tempest
Of dazzling mist within my brain—they shake
The earth on which I stand, and hang like night
On Heaven above me. What can they avail?
They cast on all things surest, brightest, best,   790
Doubt, insecurity, astonishment.
    Ahasuerus.   Mistake me not! All is contained in each.
Dodona's forest to an acorn's cup
Is that which has been, or will be, to that
Which is—the absent to the present. Thought
Alone, and its quick elements, Will, Passion,
Reason, Imagination, cannot die;
They are, what that which they regard appears,
The stuff whence mutability can weave
All that it hath dominion o'er, worlds, worms,   800

Empires, and superstitions. What has thought
To do with time, or place, or circumstance?
Wouldst thou behold the Future?—ask and have!
Knock and it shall be opened—look, and lo!
The coming age is shadowed on the Past
As on a glass.
   Mahmud.   Wild, wilder thoughts convulse
My spirit—Did not Mahomet the Second
Win Stamboul?
   Ahasuerus.   Thou wouldst ask that giant spirit
The written fortunes of thy house and faith.
Thou wouldst cite one out of the grave to tell   810
How what was born in blood must die.
   Mahmud.   Thy words
Have power on me! I see——
   Ahasuerus.   What hearest thou?
   Mahmud. A far whisper——
Terrible silence.
   Ahasuerus.   What succeeds?
   Mahmud.   The sound
As of the assault of an imperial city,
The hiss of inextinguishable fire,
The roar of giant cannon; the earthquaking
Fall of vast bastions and precipitous towers,
The shock of crags shot from strange enginery,
The clash of wheels, and clang of armèd hoofs,   820
And crash of brazen mail as of the wreck
Of adamantine mountains—the mad blast
Of trumpets, and the neigh of raging steeds,
The shrieks of women whose thrill jars the blood,
And one sweet laugh, most horrible to hear,
As of a joyous infant waked and playing
With its dead mother's breast, and now more loud
The mingled battle-cry,—ha! hear I not
'*'Εν τούτῳ νίκη!*' 'Allah-illa-Allah!'?
   Ahasuerus. The sulphurous mist is raised—thou seest—
   Mahmud.   A chasm,   830
As of two mountains, in the wall of Stamboul;
And in that ghastly breach the Islamites,
Like giants on the ruins of a world,
Stand in the light of sunrise. In the dust
Glimmers a kingless diadem, and one

Of regal port has cast himself beneath
The stream of war. Another proudly clad
In golden arms spurs a Tartarian barb
Into the gap, and with his iron mace
Directs the torrent of that tide of men,   840
And seems—he is—Mahomet!
   Ahasuerus.   What thou seest
Is but the ghost of thy forgotten dream.
A dream itself, yet less, perhaps, than that
Thou call'st reality. Thou mayest behold
How cities, on which Empire sleeps enthroned,
Bow their towered crests to mutability.
Poised by the flood, e'en on the height thou holdest,
Thou mayst now learn how the full tide of power
Ebbs to its depths.—Inheritor of glory,
Conceived in darkness, born in blood, and nourished   850
With tears and toil, thou seest the mortal throes
Of that whose birth was but the same. The Past
Now stands before thee like an Incarnation
Of the To-come; yet wouldst thou commune with
That portion of thyself which was ere thou
Didst start for this brief race whose crown is death,
Dissolve with that strong faith and fervent passion
Which called it from the uncreated deep,
Yon cloud of war, with its tempestuous phantoms
Of raging death; and draw with mighty will   860
The imperial shade hither.   [*Exit* AHASUERUS. *The
             Phantom of* MAHOMET THE SECOND *appears.*
  Mahmud.   Approach!
  Phantom.   I come
Thence whither thou must go! The grave is fitter
To take the living than give up the dead;
Yet has thy faith prevailed, and I am here.
The heavy fragments of the power which fell
When I arose, like shapeless crags and clouds,
Hang round my throne on the abyss, and voices
Of strange lament soothe my supreme repose,
Wailing for glory never to return.—
  A later Empire nods in its decay: 870
The autumn of a greener faith is come,
And wolfish change, like winter, howls to strip

The foliage in which Fame, the eagle, built
Her aerie, while Dominion whelped below.
The storm is in its branches, and the frost
Is on its leaves, and the blank deep expects
Oblivion on oblivion, spoil on spoil,
Ruin on ruin:—Thou art slow, my son;
The Anarchs of the world of darkness keep
A throne for thee, round which thine empire lies   880
Boundless and mute; and for thy subjects thou,
Like us, shalt rule the ghosts of murdered life,
The phantoms of the powers who rule thee now—
Mutinous passions, and conflicting fears,
And hopes that sate themselves on dust, and die!—
Stripped of their mortal strength, as thou of thine.
Islam must fall, but we will reign together
Over its ruins in the world of death:—
And if the trunk be dry, yet shall the seed
Unfold itself even in the shape of that   890
Which gathers birth in its decay. Woe! woe!
To the weak people tangled in the grasp
Of its last spasms.
   Mahmud.   Spirit, woe to all!
Woe to the wronged and the avenger! Woe
To the destroyer, woe to the destroyed!
Woe to the dupe, and woe to the deceiver!
Woe to the oppressed, and woe to the oppressor!
Woe both to those that suffer and inflict;
Those who are born and those who die! but say,
Imperial shadow of the thing I am,   900
When, how, by whom, Destruction must accomplish
Her consummation!
   Phantom.   Ask the cold pale Hour,
Rich in reversion of impending death,
When *he* shall fall upon whose ripe gray hairs
Sit Care, and Sorrow, and Infirmity—
The weight which Crime, whose wings are plumed with years,
Leaves in his flight from ravaged heart to heart
Over the heads of men, under which burthen
They bow themselves unto the grave: fond wretch!
He leans upon his crutch, and talks of years   910
To come, and how in hours of youth renewed

He will renew lost joys, and——
  Voice without.   Victory! Victory!
                [*The Phantom vanishes.*
 Mahmud. What sound of the importunate earth has broken
My mighty trance?
  Voice without.   Victory! Victory!
 Mahmud. Weak lightning before darkness! poor faint smile
Of dying Islam! Voice which art the response
Of hollow weakness! Do I wake and live?
Were there such things, or may the unquiet brain,
Vexed by the wise mad talk of the old Jew,
Have shaped itself these shadows of its fear?   920
It matters not!—for nought we see or dream,
Possess, or lose, or grasp at, can be worth
More than it gives or teaches. Come what may,
The Future must become the Past, and I
As they were to whom once this present hour,
This gloomy crag of time to which I cling,
Seemed an Elysian isle of peace and joy
Never to be attained.—I must rebuke
This drunkenness of triumph ere it die,
And dying, bring despair. Victory! poor slaves! 930
              [*Exit* MAHMUD.
 Voice without. Shout in the jubilee of death! The Greeks
Are as a brood of lions in the net
Round which the kingly hunters of the earth
Stand smiling. Anarchs, ye whose daily food
Are curses, groans, and gold, the fruit of death,
From Thule to the girdle of the world,
Come, feast! the board groans with the flesh of men;
The cup is foaming with a nation's blood,
Famine and Thirst await! eat, drink, and die!

Semichorus I.

 Victorious Wrong, with vulture scream,   940
  Salutes the rising sun, pursues the flying day!
   I saw her, ghastly as a tyrant's dream,
  Perch on the trembling pyramid of night,
  Beneath which earth and all her realms pavilioned lay
  In visions of the dawning undelight.

Who shall impede her flight?
Who rob her of her prey?

Voice without. Victory! Victory! Russia's famished eagles
Dare not to prey beneath the crescent's light.
Impale the remnant of the Greeks! despoil!   950
Violate! make their flesh cheaper than dust!

Semichorus II.

Thou voice which art
The herald of the ill in splendour hid!
Thou echo of the hollow heart
Of monarchy, bear me to thine abode
When desolation flashes o'er a world destroyed:
Oh, bear me to those isles of jaggèd cloud
Which float like mountains on the earthquake, mid
The momentary oceans of the lightning,
Or to some toppling promontory proud   960
Of solid tempest whose black pyramid,
Riven, overhangs the founts intensely bright'ning
Of those dawn-tinted deluges of fire
Before their waves expire,
When heaven and earth are light, and only light
In the thunder-night!

Voice without. Victory! Victory! Austria, Russia, England,
And that tame serpent, that poor shadow, France,
Cry peace, and that means death when monarchs speak.
Ho, there! bring torches, sharpen those red stakes,   970
These chains are light, fitter for slaves and poisoners
Than Greeks. Kill! plunder! burn! let none remain.

Semichorus I.

Alas! for Liberty!
If numbers, wealth, or unfulfilling years,
Or fate, can quell the free!
Alas! for Virtue, when
Torments, or contumely, or the sneers
Of erring judging men
Can break the heart where it abides.

Alas! if Love, whose smile makes this obscure world splendid,
    Can change with its false times and tides,   981
      Like hope and terror,—
        Alas for Love!
And Truth, who wanderest lone and unbefriended,
If thou canst veil thy lie-consuming mirror
    Before the dazzled eyes of Error,
    Alas for thee! Image of the Above.

Semichorus II.

  Repulse, with plumes from conquest torn,
Led the ten thousand from the limits of the morn
    Through many an hostile Anarchy!   990
At length they wept aloud, and cried, 'The Sea! the Sea!
    Through exile, persecution, and despair,
      Rome was, and young Atlantis shall become
      The wonder, or the terror, or the tomb
Of all whose step wakes Power lulled in her savage lair:
    But Greece was as a hermit-child,
      Whose fairest thoughts and limbs were built
    To woman's growth, by dreams so mild,
      She knew not pain or guilt;
And now, O Victory, blush! and Empire, tremble   1000
      When ye desert the free—
      If Greece must be
A wreck, yet shall its fragments reassemble,
And build themselves again impregnably
    In a diviner clime,
To Amphionic music on some Cape sublime,
Which frowns above the idle foam of Time.

Semichorus I.

Let the tyrants rule the desert they have made;
    Let the free possess the Paradise they claim;
Be the fortune of our fierce oppressors weighed   1010
    With our ruin, our resistance, and our name!

Semichorus II.

Our dead shall be the seed of their decay,
    Our survivors be the shadow of their pride,

Our adversity a dream to pass away—
  Their dishonour a remembrance to abide!

  Voice without. Victory! Victory! The bought Briton sends
The keys of ocean to the Islamite.—
Now shall the blazon of the cross be veiled,
And British skill directing Othman might,
Thunder-strike rebel victory. Oh, keep holy   1020
This jubilee of unrevengèd blood!
Kill! crush! despoil! Let not a Greek escape!

Semichorus I.

    Darkness has dawned in the East
        On the noon of time:
    The death-birds descend to their feast
        From the hungry clime.
    Let Freedom and Peace flee far
        To a sunnier strand,
    And follow Love's folding-star
        To the Evening land!   1030

Semichorus II.

    The young moon has fed
      Her exhausted horn
        With the sunset's fire:
    The weak day is dead,
      But the night is not born;
And, like loveliness panting with wild desire
  While it trembles with fear and delight,
  Hesperus flies from awakening night,
And pants in its beauty and speed with light
  Fast-flashing, soft, and bright.   1040
Thou beacon of love! thou lamp of the free!
    Guide us far, far away,
To climes where now veiled by the ardour of day
    Thou art hidden
    From waves on which weary Noon
    Faints in her summer swoon,
  Between kingless continents sinless as Eden,

Around mountains and islands inviolably
    Pranked on the sapphire sea.

Semichorus I.

Through the sunset of hope,   1050
    Like the shapes of a dream,
What Paradise islands of glory gleam!
    Beneath Heaven's cope,
    Their shadows more clear float by—
'The sound of their oceans, the light of their sky,
The music and fragrance their solitudes breathe
Burst, like morning on dream, or like Heaven on death,
    Through the walls of our prison;
And Greece, which was dead, is arisen!

Chorus.

The world's great age begins anew,   1060
    The golden years return,
The earth doth like a snake renew
    Her winter weeds outworn:
Heaven smiles, and faiths and empires gleam,
Like wrecks of a dissolving dream.

A brighter Hellas rears its mountains
    From waves serener far;
A new Peneus rolls his fountains
    Against the morning star.
Where fairer Tempes bloom, there sleep   1070
Young Cyclads on a sunnier deep.

A loftier Argo cleaves the main,
    Fraught with a later prize;
Another Orpheus sings again,
    And loves, and weeps, and dies.
A new Ulysses leaves once more
Calypso for his native shore.

Oh, write no more the tale of Troy,
    If earth Death's scroll must be!
Nor mix with Laian rage the joy   1080

Which dawns upon the free:
Although a subtler Sphinx renew
Riddles of death Thebes never knew.

Another Athens shall arise,
   And to remoter time
Bequeath, like sunset to the skies,
   The splendour of its prime;
And leave, if nought so bright may live,
All earth can take or Heaven can give.

Saturn and Love their long repose   1090
   Shall burst, more bright and good
Than all who fell, than One who rose,
   Than many unsubdued:
Not gold, not blood, their altar dowers,
But votive tears and symbol flowers.

Oh, cease! must hate and death return?
   Cease! must men kill and die?
Cease! drain not to its dregs the urn
   Of bitter prophecy.
The world is weary of the past,   1100
Oh, might it die or rest at last!

                  [1821; publ. 1822]

SHELLEY'S NOTES

(1) *The quenchless ashes of Milan* [line 60].

MILAN was the centre of the resistance of the Lombard league
against the Austrian tyrant. Frederic Barbarossa burnt the city to
the ground, but liberty lived in its ashes, and it rose like an exhalation from its ruin. See Sismondi's *Histoire des Républiques
Italiennes,* a book which has done much towards awakening the
Italians to an imitation of their great ancestors.

(2) *The Chorus* [lines 197–238].

The popular notions of Christianity are represented in this
chorus as true in their relation to the worship they superseded,

and that which in all probability they will supersede, without considering their merits in a relation more universal. The first stanza contrasts the immortality of the living and thinking beings which inhabit the planets, and to use a common and inadequate phrase, *clothe themselves in matter,* with the transience of the noblest manifestations of the external world.

The concluding verses indicate a progressive state of more or less exalted existence, according to the degree of perfection which every distinct intelligence may have attained. Let it not be supposed that I mean to dogmatise upon a subject, concerning which all men are equally ignorant, or that I think the Gordian knot of the origin of evil can be disentangled by that or any similar assertions. The received hypothesis of a Being resembling men in the moral attributes of His nature, having called us out of non-existence, and after inflicting on us the misery of the commission of error, should superadd that of the punishment and the privations consequent upon it, still would remain inexplicable and incredible. That there is a true solution of the riddle, and that in our present state that solution is unattainable by us, are propositions which may be regarded as equally certain: meanwhile, as it is the province of the poet to attach himself to those ideas which exalt and ennoble humanity, let him be permitted to have conjectured the condition of that futurity towards which we are all impelled by an inextinguishable thirst for immortality. Until better arguments can be produced than sophisms which disgrace the cause, this desire itself must remain the strongest and the only presumption that eternity is the inheritance of every thinking being.

(3) *No hoary priests after that Patriarch* [line 245].

The Greek Patriarch, after having been compelled to fulminate an anathema against the insurgents, was put to death by the Turks.

Fortunately the Greeks have been taught that they cannot buy security by degradation, and the Turks, though equally cruel, are less cunning than the smooth-faced tyrants of Europe. As to the anathema, his Holiness might as well have thrown his mitre at Mount Athos for any effect that it produced. The chiefs of the Greeks are almost all men of comprehension and enlightened views on religion and politics.

(4) *The freedman of a western poet-chief* [line 563].

A Greek who had been Lord Byron's servant commands the insurgents in Attica. This Greek, Lord Byron informs me, though a poet and an enthusiastic patriot, gave him rather the idea of a timid and unenterprising person. It appears that circumstances make men what they are, and that we all contain the germ of a degree of degradation or of greatness whose connection with our character is determined by events.

(5) *The Greeks expect a Saviour from the West* [line 598].

It is reported that this Messiah had arrived at a seaport near Lacedaemon in an American brig. The association of names and ideas is irresistibly ludicrous, but the prevalence of such a rumour strongly marks the state of popular enthusiasm in Greece.

(6) *The sound as of the assault of an imperial city*
[lines 814–15].

For the vision of Mahmud of the taking of Constantinople in 1453, see Gibbon's *Decline and Fall of the Roman Empire,* vol. xii, p. 223.

The manner of the invocation of the spirit of Mahomet the Second will be censured as oversubtle. I could easily have made the Jew a regular conjuror, and the Phantom an ordinary ghost. I have preferred to represent the Jew as disclaiming all pretension, or even belief, in supernatural agency, and as tempting Mahmud to that state of mind in which ideas may be supposed to assume the force of sensations through the confusion of thought with the objects of thought, and the excess of passion animating the creations of imagination.

It is a sort of natural magic, susceptible of being exercised in a degree by any one who should have made himself master of the secret associations of another's thoughts.

(7) *The Chorus* [lines 1060–1101].

The final chorus is indistinct and obscure, as the event of the living drama whose arrival it foretells. Prophecies of wars, and rumours of wars, etc.. may safely be made by poet or prophet in any age, but to anticipate however darkly a period of regeneration and happiness is a more hazardous exercise of the faculty which bards possess or feign. It will remind the reader 'magno *nec* proximus intervallo' of Isaiah and Virgil, whose ardent spirits overleaping the actual reign of evil which we endure and bewail, already saw the possible and perhaps approaching state of society in which the '*lion shall lie down with the lamb,*' and 'omnis feret omnia tellus.' Let these great names be my authority and my excuse.

(8) *Saturn and Love their long repose shall burst*
[line 1090].

Saturn and Love were among the deities of a real or imaginary state of innocence and happiness. *All* those *who fell,* or the Gods of Greece, Asia, and Egypt; the *One who rose,* or Jesus Christ, at whose appearance the idols of the Pagan World were amerced of their worship; and *the many unsubdued,* or the monstrous objects of the idolatry of China, India, the Antarctic islands, and the native tribes of America, certainly have reigned over the understandings of men in conjunction or in succession during periods in which all we know of evil has been in a state of portentous, and, until the revival of learning and the arts, perpetually increasing, activity. The Grecian gods seem indeed to have been personally more innocent, although it cannot be said, that as far as temperance and chastity are concerned, they gave so edifying an example as their successor. The sublime human character of Jesus Christ was deformed by an imputed identification with a Power, who tempted, betrayed, and punished the innocent beings who were called into existence by His sole will; and for the period of a thousand years, the spirit of this most just, wise, and benevolent of men has been propitiated with myriads of hecatombs of those who approached the nearest to His innocence and wisdom, sacrificed under every aggravation of atrocity and variety of torture. The horrors of the Mexican, the Peruvian, and the Indian superstitions are well known.

THE TRIUMPH OF LIFE

SWIFT as a spirit hastening to his task
Of glory and of good, the Sun sprang forth
Rejoicing in his splendour, and the mask

Of darkness fell from the awakened Earth—
The smokeless altars of the mountain snows
Flamed above crimson clouds, and at the birth

Of light, the Ocean's orison arose,
To which the birds tempered their matin lay.
All flowers in field or forest which unclose

Their trembling eyelids to the kiss of day,   10
Swinging their censers in the element,
With orient incense lit by the new ray

Burned slow and inconsumably, and sent
Their odorous sighs up to the smiling air;
And, in succession due, did continent,

Isle, ocean, and all things that in them wear
The form and character of mortal mould,
Rise as the Sun their father rose, to bear

Their portion of the toil, which he of old
Took as his own, and then imposed on them: 20
But I, whom thoughts which must remain untold

Had kept as wakeful as the stars that gem
The cone of night, now they were laid asleep
Stretched my faint limbs beneath the hoary stem

Which an old chestnut flung athwart the steep
Of a green Apennine: before me fled
The night; behind me rose the day; the deep

Was at my feet, and Heaven above my head,—
When a strange trance over my fancy grew
Which was not slumber, for the shade it spread   **30**

Was so transparent, that the scene came through
As clear as when a veil of light is drawn
O'er evening hills they glimmer; and I knew

That I had felt the freshness of that dawn
Bathe in the same cold dew my brow and hair,
And sate as thus upon that slope of lawn

Under the self-same bough, and heard as there
The birds, the fountains and the ocean hold
Sweet talk in music through the enamoured air,
And then a vision on my brain was rolled.

———————

As in that trance of wondrous thought I lay,
This was the tenour of my waking dream:—
Methought I sate beside a public way

Thick strewn with summer dust, and a great stream
Of people there was hurrying to and fro,
Numerous as gnats upon the evening gleam,

All hastening onward, yet none seemed to know
Whither he went, or whence he came, or why
He made one of the multitude, and so

Was borne amid the crowd, as through the sky   **50**
One of the million leaves of summer's bier;
Old age and youth, manhood and infancy,

Mixed in one mighty torrent did appear,
Some flying from the thing they feared, and some
Seeking the object of another's fear;

And others, as with steps towards the tomb,
Pored on the trodden worms that crawled beneath,
And others mournfully within the gloom

Of their own shadow walked, and called it death;
And some fled from it as it were a ghost, 60
Half fainting in the affliction of vain breath:

But more, with motions which each other crossed,
Pursued or shunned the shadows the clouds threw,
Or birds within the noonday aether lost,

Upon that path where flowers never grew,—
And, weary with vain toil and faint for thirst,
Heard not the fountains, whose melodious dew

Out of their mossy cells forever burst;
Nor felt the breeze which from the forest told
Of grassy paths and wood-lawns interspersed 70

With overarching elms and caverns cold,
And violet banks where sweet dreams brood, but they
Pursued their serious folly as of old.

And as I gazed, methought that in the way
The throng grew wilder, as the woods of June
When the south wind shakes the extinguished day,

And a cold glare, intenser than the noon,
But icy cold, obscured with blinding light
The sun, as he the stars. Like the young moon—

When on the sunlit limits of the night 80
Her white shell trembles amid crimson air,
And whilst the sleeping tempest gathers might—

Doth, as the herald of its coming, bear
The ghost of its dead mother, whose dim form
Bends in dark aether from her infant's chair,—

So came a chariot on the silent storm
Of its own rushing splendour, and a Shape
So sate within, as one whom years deform,

Beneath a dusky hood and double cape,
Crouching within the shadow of a tomb; 90
And o'er what seemed the head a cloud-like crape

Was bent, a dun and faint aethereal gloom
Tempering the light. Upon the chariot-beam
A Janus-visaged Shadow did assume

The guidance of that wonder-wingèd team;
The shapes which drew it in thick lightenings
Were lost:—I heard alone on the air's soft stream

The music of their ever-moving wings.
All the four faces of that Charioteer
Had their eyes banded; little profit brings   100

Speed in the van and blindness in the rear,
Nor then avail the beams that quench the sun,—
Or that with banded eyes could pierce the sphere

Of all that is, has been or will be done;
So ill was the car guided—but it passed
With solemn speed majestically on.

The crowd gave way, and I arose aghast,
Or seemed to rise, so mighty was the trance,
And saw, like clouds upon the thunder-blast,

The million with fierce song and maniac dance   110
Raging around—such seemed the jubilee
As when to greet some conqueror's advance

Imperial Rome poured forth her living sea
From senate-house, and forum, and theatre,
When   upon the free

Had bound a yoke, which soon they stooped to bear.
Nor wanted here the just similitude
Of a triumphal pageant, for where'er

The chariot rolled, a captive multitude
Was driven;—all those who had grown old in power   120
Or misery,—all who had their age subdued

By action or by suffering, and whose hour
Was drained to its last sand in weal or woe,
So that the trunk survived both fruit and flower;—

All those whose fame or infamy must grow
Till the great winter lay the form and name
Of this green earth with them for ever low;—

All but the sacred few who could not tame
Their spirits to the conqueror—but as soon
As they had touched the world with living flame,   130

Fled back like eagles to their native noon,
Or those who put aside the diadem
Of earthly thrones or gems . . .

Were there, of Athens or Jerusalem,
Were neither mid the mighty captives seen,
Nor mid the ribald crowd that followed them,

Nor those who went before fierce and obscene.
The wild dance maddens in the van, and those
Who lead it—fleet as shadows on the green,

Outspeed the chariot, and without repose   140
Mix with each other in tempestuous measure
To savage music, wilder as it grows,

They, tortured by their agonizing pleasure,
Convulsed and on the rapid whirlwinds spun
Of that fierce Spirit, whose unholy leisure

Was soothed by mischief since the world begun,
Throw back their heads and loose their streaming hair;
And in their dance round her who dims the sun,

Maidens and youths fling their wild arms in air
As their feet twinkle; they recede, and now   150
Bending within each other's atmosphere,

Kindle invisibly—and as they glow,
Like moths by light attracted and repelled,
Oft to their bright destruction come and go,

Till like two clouds into one vale impelled,
That shake the mountains when their lightnings mingle
And die in rain—the fiery band which held

Their natures, snaps—while the shock still may tingle;
One falls and then another in the path
Senseless—nor is the desolation single,   160

Yet ere I can say *where*—the chariot hath
Passed over them—nor other trace I find
But as of foam after the ocean's wrath

Is spent upon the desert shore;—behind,
Old men and women foully disarrayed,
Shake their gray hairs in the insulting wind,

And follow in the dance, with limbs decayed,
Seeking to reach the light which leaves them still
Farther behind and deeper in the shade.

But not the less with impotence of will   170
They wheel, though ghastly shadows interpose
Round them and round each other, and fulfil

Their work, and in the dust from whence they rose
Sink, and corruption veils them as they lie,
And past in these performs what   in those.

Struck to the heart by this sad pageantry,
Half to myself I said—'And what is this?
Whose shape is that within the car? And why—'

I would have added—'is all here amiss?—'
But a voice answered—'Life!'—I turned, and knew   180
(O Heaven, have mercy on such wretchedness!)

That what I thought was an old root which grew
To strange distortion out of the hill side,
Was indeed one of those deluded crew,

And that the grass, which methought hung so wide
And white, was but his thin discoloured hair,
And that the holes he vainly sought to hide,

Were or had been eyes:—'If thou canst, forbear
To join the dance, which I had well forborne!'
Said the grim Feature (of my thought aware).   190

'I will unfold that which to this deep scorn
Led me and my companions, and relate
The progress of the pageant since the morn;

'If thirst of knowledge shall not then abate,
Follow it thou even to the night, but I
Am weary.'—Then like one who with the weight

Of his own words is staggered, wearily
He paused; and ere he could resume, I cried:
'First, who art thou?'—'Before thy memory,

'I feared, loved, hated, suffered, did and died,   200
And if the spark with which Heaven lit my spirit
Had been with purer nutriment supplied,

'Corruption would not now thus much inherit
Of what was once Rousseau,—nor this disguise
Stain that which ought to have disdained to wear it;

'If I have been extinguished, yet there rise
A thousand beacons from the spark I bore'—
'And who are those chained to the car?'—'The wise,

'The great, the unforgotten,—they who wore
Mitres and helms and crowns, or wreaths of light,   210
Signs of thought's empire over thought—their lore

'Taught them not this, to know themselves; their might
Could not repress the mystery within,
And for the morn of truth they feigned, deep night

'Caught them ere evening.'—'Who is he with chin
Upon his breast, and hands crossed on his chain?'—
'The child of a fierce hour; he sought to win

'The world, and lost all that it did contain
Of greatness, in its hope destroyed; and more
Of fame and peace than virtue's self can gain   220

'Without the opportunity which bore
Him on its eagle pinions to the peak
From which a thousand climbers have before

'Fallen, as Napoleon fell.'—I felt my cheek
Alter, to see the shadow pass away,
Whose grasp had left the giant world so weak

That every pigmy kicked it as it lay;
And much I grieved to think how power and will
In opposition rule our mortal day,

And why God made irreconcilable   230
Good and the means of good; and for despair
I half disdained mine eyes' desire to fill

With the spent vision of the times that were
And scarce have ceased to be.—'Dost thou behold,'
Said my guide, 'those spoilers spoiled, Voltaire,

'Frederick, and Paul, Catherine, and Leopold,
And hoary anarchs, demagogues, and sage—
        names which the world thinks always old,

'For in the battle Life and they did wage,
She remained conqueror. I was overcome   240
By my own heart alone, which neither age,

'Nor tears, nor infamy, nor now the tomb
Could temper to its object.'—'Let them pass,'
I cried, 'the world and its mysterious doom

'Is not so much more glorious than it was,
That I desire to worship those who drew
New figures on its false and fragile glass

'As the old faded.'—'Figures ever new
Rise on the bubble, paint them as you may;
We have but thrown, as those before us threw,   250

'Our shadows on it as it passed away.
But mark how chained to the triumphal chair
The mighty phantoms of an elder day;

'All that is mortal of great Plato there
Expiates the joy and woe his master knew not;
The star that ruled his doom was far too fair.

'And life, where long that flower of Heaven grew not,
Conquered that heart by love, which gold, or pain,
Or age, or sloth, or slavery could subdue not.

'And near him walk the   twain,   260
The tutor and his pupil, whom Dominion
Followed as tame as vulture in a chain.

'The world was darkened beneath either pinion
Of him whom from the flock of conquerors
Fame singled out for her thunder-bearing minion;

'The other long outlived both woes and wars,
Throned in the thoughts of men, and still had kept
The jealous key of Truth's eternal doors,

'If Bacon's eagle spirit had not lept
Like lightning out of darkness—he compelled   270
The Proteus shape of Nature, as it slept

'To wake, and lead him to the caves that held
The treasure of the secrets of its reign.
See the great bards of elder time, who quelled

'The passions which they sung, as by their strain
May well be known: their living melody
Tempers its own contagion to the vein

'Of those who are infected with it—I
Have suffered what I wrote, or viler pain!
And so my words have seeds of misery—   280

'Even as the deeds of others, not as theirs.'
And then he pointed to a company,

'Midst whom I quickly recognized the heirs
Of Caesar's crime, from him to Constantine;
The anarch chiefs, whose force and murderous snares

Had founded many a sceptre-bearing line,
And spread the plague of gold and blood abroad:
And Gregory and John, and men divine,

Who rose like shadows between man and God;
Till that eclipse, still hanging over heaven,   290
Was worshipped by the world o'er which they strode,

For the true sun it quenched—'Their power was given
But to destroy,' replied the leader:—'I
Am one of those who have created, even

'If it be but a world of agony.'—
'Whence camest thou? and whither goest thou?
How did thy course begin?' I said, 'and why?

'Mine eyes are sick of this perpetual flow
Of people, and my heart sick of one sad thought—
Speak!'—'Whence I am, I partly seem to know,   300

'And how and by what paths I have been brought
To this dread pass, methinks even thou mayst guess;—
Why this should be, my mind can compass not;

'Whither the conqueror hurries me, still less;—
But follow thou, and from spectator turn
Actor or victim in this wretchedness,

'And what thou wouldst be taught I then may learn
From thee. Now listen:—In the April prime,
When all the forest-tips began to burn

'With kindling green, touched by the azure clime   310
Of the young season, I was laid asleep
Under a mountain, which from unknown time

'Had yawned into a cavern, high and deep;
And from it came a gentle rivulet,
Whose water, like clear air, in its calm sweep

'Bent the soft grass, and kept for ever wet
The stems of the sweet flowers, and filled the grove
With sounds, which whoso hears must needs forget

'All pleasure and all pain, all hate and love,
Which they had known before that hour of rest;   320
A sleeping mother then would dream not of

'Her only child who died upon the breast
At eventide—a king would mourn no more
The crown of which his brows were dispossessed

'When the sun lingered o'er his ocean floor
To gild his rival's new prosperity.
Thou wouldst forget thus vainly to deplore

'Ills, which if ills can find no cure from thee,
The thought of which no other sleep will quell,
Nor other music blot from memory,   330

'So sweet and deep is the oblivious spell;
And whether life had been before that sleep
The Heaven which I imagine, or a Hell

'Like this harsh world in which I wake to weep,
I know not. I arose, and for a space
The scene of woods and waters seemed to keep,

'Though it was now broad day, a gentle trace
Of light diviner than the common sun
Sheds on the common earth, and all the place

'Was filled with magic sounds woven into one   340
Oblivious melody, confusing sense
Amid the gliding waves and shadows dun;

'And, as I looked, the bright omnipresence
Of morning through the orient cavern flowed,
And the sun's image radiantly intense

'Burned on the waters of the well that glowed
Like gold, and threaded all the forest's maze
With winding paths of emerald fire; there stood

'Amid the sun, as he amid the blaze
Of his own glory, on the vibrating   350
Floor of the fountain, paved with flashing rays,

'A Shape all light, which with one hand did fling
Dew on the earth, as if she were the dawn,
And the invisible rain did ever sing

'A silver music on the mossy lawn;
And still before me on the dusky grass,
Iris her many-coloured scarf had drawn:

'In her right hand she bore a crystal glass,
Mantling with bright Nepenthe; the fierce splendour
Fell from her as she moved under the mass   360

'Of the deep cavern, and with palms so tender,
Their tread broke not the mirror of its billow,
Glided along the river, and did bend her

'Head under the dark boughs, till like a willow
Her fair hair swept the bosom of the stream
That whispered with delight to be its pillow.

'As one enamoured is upborne in dream
O'er lily-paven lakes, mid silver mist,
To wondrous music, so this shape might seem

'Partly to tread the waves with feet which kissed   370
The dancing foam; partly to glide along
The air which roughened the moist amethyst,

'Or the faint morning beams that fell among
The trees or the soft shadows of the trees;
And her feet, ever to the ceaseless song

'Of leaves, and winds, and waves, and birds, and bees,
And falling drops, moved in a measure new
Yet sweet, as on the summer evening breeze,

'Up from the lake a shape of golden dew
Between two rocks, athwart the rising moon,   380
Dances i' the wind, where never eagle flew;

'And still her feet, no less than the sweet tune
To which they moved, seemed as they moved to blot
The thoughts of him who gazed on them; and soon

'All that was, seemed as if it had been not;
And all the gazer's mind was strewn beneath
Her feet like embers; and she, thought by thought,

'Trampled its sparks into the dust of death;
As day upon the threshold of the east
Treads out the lamps of night, until the breath   390

'Of darkness re-illumine even the least
Of heaven's living eyes—like day she came,
Making the night a dream; and ere she ceased

'To move, as one between desire and shame
Suspended, I said—If, as it doth seem,
Thou comest from the realm without a name

'Into this valley of perpetual dream,
Show whence I came, and where I am, and why—
Pass not away upon the passing stream.

'Arise and quench thy thirst, was her reply.   400
And as a shut lily stricken by the wand
Of dewy morning's vital alchemy,

'I rose; and, bending at her sweet command,
Touched with faint lips the cup she raised,
And suddenly my brain became as sand

'Where the first wave had more than half erased
The track of deer on desert Labrador;
Whilst the wolf, from which they fled amazed,

'Leaves his stamp visibly upon the shore,
Until the second bursts;—so on my sight   410
Burst a new vision, never seen before,

'And the fair shape waned in the coming light,
As veil by veil the silent splendour drops
From Lucifer, amid the chrysolite

'Of sunrise, ere it tinge the mountain-tops;
And as the presence of that fairest planet,
Although unseen, is felt by one who hopes

'That his day's path may end as he began it,
In that star's smile, whose light is like the scent
Of a jonquil when evening breezes fan it,   420

'Or the soft note in which his dear lament
The Brescian[1] shepherd breathes, or the caress
That turned his weary slumber to content;

'So knew I in that light's severe excess
The presence of that Shape which on the stream
Moved, as I moved along the wilderness,

'More dimly than a day-appearing dream,
The ghost of a forgotten form of sleep;
A light of heaven, whose half-extinguished beam

'Through the sick day in which we wake to weep   430
Glimmers, for ever sought, for ever lost;
So did that shape its obscure tenour keep

'Beside my path, as silent as a ghost;
But the new Vision, and the cold bright car,
With solemn speed and stunning music, crossed

'The forest, and as if from some dread war
Triumphantly returning, the loud million
Fiercely extolled the fortune of her star.

'A moving arch of victory, the vermilion
And green and azure plumes of Iris had   440
Built high over her wind-wingèd pavilion,

'And underneath aethereal glory clad
The wilderness, and far before her flew
The tempest of the splendour, which forbade

'Shadow to fall from leaf and stone; the crew
Seemed in that light, like atomies to dance
Within a sunbeam;—some upon the new

'Embroidery of flowers, that did enhance
The grassy vesture of the desert, played,
Forgetful of the chariot's swift advance;   450

[1] The favourite song, *Stanco di pascolar le pecorelle*, is a Brescian national air.—[MRS. SHELLEY'S NOTE.]

'Others stood gazing, till within the shade
Of the great mountain its light left them dim;
Others outspeeded it; and others made

'Circles around it, like the clouds that swim
Round the high moon in a bright sea of air;
And more did follow, with exulting hymn,

'The chariot and the captives fettered there:—
But all like bubbles on an eddying flood
Fell into the same track at last, and were

'Borne onward.—I among the multitude   460
Was swept—me, sweetest flowers delayed not long;
Me, not the shadow nor the solitude;

'Me, not that falling stream's Lethean song;
Me, not the phantom of that early Form
Which moved upon its motion—but among

'The thickest billows of that living storm
I plunged, and bared my bosom to the clime
Of that cold light, whose airs too soon deform.

'Before the chariot had begun to climb
The opposing steep of that mysterious dell,   470
Behold a wonder worthy of the rhyme

'Of him who from the lowest depths of hell,
Through every paradise and through all glory,
Love led serene, and who returned to tell

'The words of hate and awe; the wondrous story
How all things are transfigured except Love;
For deaf as is a sea, which wrath makes hoary,

'The world can hear not the sweet notes that move
The sphere whose light is melody to lovers—
A wonder worthy of his rhyme.—The grove   480

'Grew dense with shadows to its inmost covers,
The earth was gray with phantoms, and the air
Was peopled with dim forms, as when there hovers

'A flock of vampire-bats before the glare
Of the tropic sun, bringing, ere evening,
Strange night upon some Indian isle;—thus were

'Phantoms diffused around; and some did fling
Shadows of shadows, yet unlike themselves,
Behind them; some like eaglets on the wing

'Were lost in the white day; others like elves   490
Danced in a thousand unimagined shapes
Upon the sunny streams and grassy shelves;

'And others sate chattering like restless apes
On vulgar hands, . . .
Some made a cradle of the ermined capes

'Of kingly mantles; some across the tiar
Of pontiffs sate like vultures; other played
Under the crown which girt with empire

'A baby's or an idiot's brow, and made
Their nests in it. The old anatomies   500
Sate hatching their bare broods under the shade

'Of daemon wings, and laughed from their dead eyes
To reassume the delegated power,
Arrayed in which those worms did monarchize,

'Who made this earth their charnel. Others more
Humble, like falcons, sate upon the fist
Of common men, and round their heads did soar;

'Or like small gnats and flies, as thick as mist
On evening marshes, thronged about the brow
Of lawyers, statesmen, priest and theorist;—   510

'And others, like discoloured flakes of snow
On fairest bosoms and the sunniest hair,
Fell, and were melted by the youthful glow

'Which they extinguished; and, like tears, they were
A veil to those from whose faint lids they rained
In drops of sorrow. I became aware

'Of whence those forms proceeded which thus stained
The track in which we moved. After brief space,
From every form the beauty slowly waned;

'From every firmest limb and fairest face   520
The strength and freshness fell like dust, and left
The action and the shape without the grace

'Of life. The marble brow of youth was cleft
With care; and in those eyes where once hope shone,
Desire, like a lioness bereft

'Of her last cub, glared ere it died; each one
Of that great crowd sent forth incessantly
These shadows, numerous as the dead leaves blown

'In autumn evening from a poplar tree.
Each like himself and like each other were   530
At first; but some distorted seemed to be

'Obscure clouds, moulded by the casual air;
And of this stuff the car's creative ray
Wrought all the busy phantoms that were there,

'As the sun shapes the clouds; thus on the way
Mask after mask fell from the countenance
And form of all; and long before the day

'Was old, the joy which waked like heaven's glance
The sleepers in the oblivious valley, died;
And some grew weary of the ghastly dance,   540

'And fell, as I have fallen, by the wayside;—
Those soonest from whose forms most shadows passed,
And least of strength and beauty did abide.

'Then, what is life? I cried.'—

[1822; publ. 1824]

Lyrical and Reflective Poems

TO ———

ΔΑΚΡΤΣΙ ΔΙΟΙΣΩ ΠΟΤΜΟΝ 'ΑΠΟΤΜΟΝ.

Oн! there are spirits of the air,
  And genii of the evening breeze,
And gentle ghosts, with eyes as fair
  As star-beams among twilight trees:—
Such lovely ministers to meet
Oft hast thou turned from men thy lonely feet.

With mountain winds, and babbling springs,
  And moonlight seas, that are the voice
Of these inexplicable things,
  Thou didst hold commune, and rejoice   10
When they did answer thee; but they
Cast, like a worthless boon, thy love away.

And thou hast sought in starry eyes
  Beams that were never meant for thine,
Another's wealth:—tame sacrifice
  To a fond faith! still dost thou pine?
Still dost thou hope that greeting hands,
Voice, looks, or lips, may answer thy demands?

Ah! wherefore didst thou build thine hope
  On the false earth's inconstancy?   20
Did thine own mind afford no scope
  Of love, or moving thoughts to thee?
That natural scenes or human smiles
Could steal the power to wind thee in their wiles?

Yes, all the faithless smiles are fled
  Whose falsehood left thee broken-hearted;
The glory of the moon is dead;
  Night's ghosts and dreams have now departed;
Thine own soul still is true to thee,
But changed to a foul fiend through misery.   30

This fiend, whose ghastly presence ever
   Beside thee like thy shadow hangs,
Dream not to chase;—the mad endeavour
   Would scourge thee to severer pangs.
Be as thou art. Thy settled fate,
Dark as it is, all change would aggravate.

[Publ. 1816]

MUTABILITY

We are as clouds that veil the midnight moon;
   How restlessly they speed, and gleam, and quiver,
Streaking the darkness radiantly!—yet soon
   Night closes round, and they are lost for ever:

Or like forgotten lyres, whose dissonant strings
   Give various response to each varying blast,
To whose frail frame no second motion brings
   One mood or modulation like the last.

We rest.—A dream has power to poison sleep;
   We rise.—One wandering thought pollutes the day;   **10**
We feel, conceive or reason, laugh or weep;
   Embrace fond woe, or cast our cares away:

It is the same!—For, be it joy or sorrow,
   The path of its departure still is free:
Man's yesterday may ne'er be like his morrow;
Nought may endure but Mutability.

[Publ. 1816]

A SUMMER EVENING CHURCHYARD

Lechlade, Gloucestershire

The wind has swept from the wide atmosphere
Each vapour that obscured the sunset's ray;

And pallid Evening twines its beaming hair
In duskier braids around the languid eyes of Day:
Silence and Twilight, unbeloved of men,
Creep hand in hand from yon obscurest glen.

They breathe their spells towards the departing day,
Encompassing the earth, air, stars, and sea;
Light, sound, and motion own the potent sway,
Responding to the charm with its own mystery.   10
The winds are still, or the dry church-tower grass
Knows not their gentle motions as they pass.

Thou too, aëreal Pile! whose pinnacles
Point from one shrine like pyramids of fire,
Obeyest in silence their sweet solemn spells,
Clothing in hues of heaven thy dim and distant spire,
Around whose lessening and invisible height
Gather among the stars the clouds of night.

The dead are sleeping in their sepulchres:
And, mouldering as they sleep, a thrilling sound,   20
Half sense, half thought, among the darkness stirs,
Breathed from their wormy beds all living things around,
And mingling with the still night and mute sky
Its awful hush is felt inaudibly.

Thus solemnized and softened, death is mild
And terrorless as this serenest night:
Here could I hope, like some inquiring child
Sporting on graves, that death did hide from human sight
Sweet secrets, or beside its breathless sleep
That loveliest dreams perpetual watch did keep.   30
                              [1815; publ. 1816]

TO WORDSWORTH

Poet of Nature, thou hast wept to know
That things depart which never may return:
Childhood and youth, friendship and love's first glow,

Have fled like sweet dreams, leaving thee to mourn.
These common woes I feel. One loss is mine
Which thou too feel'st, yet I alone deplore.
Thou wert as a lone star, whose light did shine
On some frail bark in winter's midnight roar:
Thou hast like to a rock-built refuge stood
Above the blind and battling multitude: 10
In honoured poverty thy voice did weave
Songs consecrate to truth and liberty,—
Deserting these, thou leavest me to grieve,
Thus having been, that thou shouldst cease to be.

[Publ. 1816]

FEELINGS OF A REPUBLICAN ON THE FALL OF BONAPARTE

I HATED thee, fallen tyrant! I did groan
To think that a most unambitious slave,
Like thou, shouldst dance and revel on the grave
Of Liberty. Thou mightst have built thy throne
Where it had stood even now: thou didst prefer
A frail and bloody pomp which Time has swept
In fragments towards Oblivion. Massacre,
For this I prayed, would on thy sleep have crept,
Treason and Slavery, Rapine, Fear, and Lust,
And stifled thee, their minister. I know   10
Too late, since thou and France are in the dust,
That Virtue owns a more eternal foe
Than Force or Fraud: old Custom, legal Crime,
And bloody Faith the foulest birth of Time.

[Publ. 1816]

HYMN TO INTELLECTUAL BEAUTY

I

THE awful shadow of some unseen Power
Floats though unseen among us,—visiting

This various world with as inconstant wing
As summer winds that creep from flower to flower,—
Like moonbeans that behind some piny mountain shower,
 It visits with inconstant glance
 Each human heart and countenance;
Like hues and harmonies of evening,—
 Like clouds in starlight widely spread,-
 Like memory of music fled,—
 Like aught that for its grace may be
Dear, and yet dearer for its mystery.

10

II

Spirit of BEAUTY, that dost consecrate
 With thine own hues all thou dost shine upon
 Of human thought or form,—where art thou gone?
Why dost thou pass away and leave our state,
This dim vast vale of tears, vacant and desolate?
 Ask why the sunlight not for ever
 Weaves rainbows o'er yon mountain-river,
Why aught should fail and fade that once is shown,
 Why fear and dream and death and birth
 Cast on the daylight of this earth
 Such gloom,—why man has such a scope
For love and hate, despondency and hope?

20

III

No voice from some sublimer world hath ever
 To sage or poet these responses given—
 Therefore the names of Demon, Ghost, and Heaven,
Remain the records of their vain endeavour,
Frail spells—whose uttered charm might not avail to sever,
 From all we hear and all we see,
 Doubt, chance and mutability.
Thy light alone—like mist o'er mountains driven,
 Or music by the night-wind sent
 Through strings of some still instrument,
 Or moonlight on a midnight stream,
Gives grace and truth to life's unquiet dream.

30

IV

Love, Hope, and Self-esteem, like clouds depart
  And come, for some uncertain moments lent.
  Man were immortal, and omnipotent,
Didst thou, unknown and awful as thou art,   40
Keep with thy glorious train firm state within his heart.
    Thou messenger of sympathies,
    That wax and wane in lovers' eyes—
Thou—that to human thought art nourishment,
    Like darkness to a dying flame!
    Depart not as thy shadow came,
    Depart not—lest the grave should be,
Like life and fear, a dark reality.

V

While yet a boy I sought for ghosts, and sped
  Through many a listening chamber, cave and ruin,   50
  And starlight wood, with fearful steps pursuing
Hopes of high talk with the departed dead.
I called on poisonous names with which our youth is fed;
    I was not heard—I saw them not—
    When musing deeply on the lot
Of life, at that sweet time when winds are wooing
    All vital things that wake to bring
    News of birds and blossoming,—
    Sudden, thy shadow fell on me;
I shrieked, and clasped my hands in ecstasy!   60

VI

I vowed that I would dedicate my powers
  To thee and thine—have I not kept the vow?
  With beating heart and streaming eyes, even now
I call the phantoms of a thousand hours
Each from his voiceless grave: they have in visioned bowers
    Of studious zeal or love's delight
    Outwatched with me the envious night—
They know that never joy illumed my brow

Unlinked with hope that thou wouldst free
This world from its dark slavery, 70
That thou—O awful LOVELINESS,
Wouldst give whate'er these words cannot express.

VII

The day becomes more solemn and serene
  When noon is past—there is a harmony
  In autumn, and a lustre in its sky,
Which through the summer is not heard or seen,
As if it could not be, as if it had not been!
    Thus let thy power, which like the truth
    Of nature on my passive youth
Descended, to my onward life supply 80
    Its calm—to one who worships thee,
    And every form containing thee,
    Whom, SPIRIT fair, thy spells did bind
To fear himself, and love all human kind.

[1816; publ. 1817]

MONT BLANC

LINES WRITTEN IN THE VALE OF CHAMOUNI

I

THE everlasting universe of things
Flows through the mind, and rolls its rapid waves,
Now dark—now glittering—now reflecting gloom—
Now lending splendour, where from secret springs
The source of human thought its tribute brings
Of waters,—with a sound but half its own,
Such as a feeble brook will oft assume
In the wild woods, among the mountains lone,
Where waterfalls around it leap for ever,

Where woods and winds contend, and a vast river   10
Over its rocks ceaselessly bursts and raves.

II

Thus thou, Ravine of Arve—dark, deep Ravine—
Thou many-coloured, many-voicèd vale,
Over whose pines, and crags, and caverns sail
Fast cloud-shadows and sunbeams: awful scene,
Where Power in likeness of the Arve comes down
From the ice-gulfs that gird his secret throne,
Bursting through these dark mountains like the flame
Of lightning through the tempest;—thou dost lie,
Thy giant brood of pines around thee clinging,   20
Children of elder time, in whose devotion
The chainless winds still come and ever came
To drink their odours, and their mighty swinging
To hear—an old and solemn harmony;
Thine earthly rainbows stretched across the sweep
Of the aethereal waterfall, whose veil
Robes some unsculptured image; the strange sleep
Which when the voices of the desert fail
Wraps all in its own deep eternity;—
Thy caverns echoing to the Arve's commotion,   30
A loud, lone sound no other sound can tame;
Thou art pervaded with that ceaseless motion,
Thou art the path of that unresting sound—
Dizzy Ravine! and when I gaze on thee
I seem as in a trance sublime and strange
To muse on my own separate fantasy,
My own, my human mind, which passively
Now renders and receives fast influencings,
Holding an unremitting interchange
With the clear universe of things around;   40
One legion of wild thoughts, whose wandering wings
Now float above thy darkness, and now rest
Where that or thou art no unbidden guest,
In the still cave of the witch Poesy,
Seeking among the shadows that pass by
Ghosts of all things that are, some shade of thee,
Some phantom, some faint image; till the breast
From which they fled recalls them; thou art there!

III

Some say that gleams of a remoter world
Visit the soul in sleep,—that death is slumber,   50
And that its shapes the busy thoughts outnumber
Of those who wake and live.—I look on high;
Has some unknown omnipotence unfurled
The veil of life and death? or do I lie
In dream, and does the mightier world of sleep
Spread far around and inaccessibly
Its circles? For the very spirit fails,
Driven like a homeless cloud from steep to steep
That vanishes among the viewless gales!
Far, far above, piercing the infinite sky,   60
Mont Blanc appears,—still, snowy, and serene—
Its subject mountains their unearthly forms
Pile around it, ice and rock; broad vales between
Of frozen floods, unfathomable deeps,
Blue as the overhanging heaven, that spread
And wind among the accumulated steeps;
A desert peopled by the storms alone,
Save when the eagle brings some hunter's bone,
And the wolf tracks her there—how hideously
Its shapes are heaped around! rude, bare, and high,   70
Ghastly, and scarred, and riven.—Is this the scene
Where the old Earthquake-daemon taught her young
Ruin? Were these their toys? or did a sea
Of fire envelop once this silent snow?
None can reply—all seems eternal now.
The wilderness has a mysterious tongue
Which teaches awful doubt, or faith so mild,
So solemn, so serene, that man may be,
But for such faith, with nature reconciled;
Thou hast a voice, great Mountain, to repeal   80
Large codes of fraud and woe; not understood
By all, but which the wise, and great, and good
Interpret, or make felt, or deeply feel.

IV

The fields, the lakes, the forests, and the streams,
Ocean, and all the living things that dwell

Within the daedal earth; lightning, and rain,
Earthquake, and fiery flood, and hurricane,
The torpor of the year when feeble dreams
Visit the hidden buds, or dreamless sleep
Holds every future leaf and flower;—the bound   90
With which from that detested trance they leap;
The works and ways of man, their death and birth,
And that of him and all that his may be;
All things that move and breathe with toil and sound
Are born and die; revolve, subside, and swell.
Power dwells apart in its tranquillity,
Remote, serene, and inaccessible:
And *this*, the naked countenance of earth,
On which I gaze, even these primaeval mountains
Teach the adverting mind. The glaciers creep   100
Like snakes that watch their prey, from their far fountains,
Slow rolling on; there, many a precipice,
Frost and the Sun in scorn of mortal power
Have piled: dome, pyramid, and pinnacle,
A city of death, distinct with many a tower
And wall impregnable of beaming ice.
Yet not a city, but a flood of ruin
Is there, that from the boundaries of the sky
Rolls its perpetual stream; vast pines are strewing
Its destined path, or in the mangled soil   110
Branchless and shattered stand; the rocks, drawn down
From yon remotest waste, have overthrown
The limits of the dead and living world,
Never to be reclaimed. The dwelling-place
Of insects, beasts, and birds, becomes its spoil;
Their food and their retreat for ever gone,
So much of life and joy is lost. The race
Of man flies far in dread; his work and dwelling
Vanish, like smoke before the tempest's stream,
And their place is not known. Below, vast caves   120
Shine in the rushing torrents' restless gleam,
Which from those secret chasms in tumult welling
Meet in the vale, and one majestic River,
The breath and blood of distant lands, for ever
Rolls its loud waters to the ocean-waves,
Breathes its swift vapours to the circling air.

v

Mont Blanc yet gleams on high:—the power is there,
The still and solemn power of many sights,
And many sounds, and much of life and death.
In the calm darkness of the moonless nights,   130
In the lone glare of day, the snows descend
Upon that Mountain; none beholds them there,
Nor when the flakes burn in the sinking sun,
Or the star-beams dart through them:—Winds contend
Silently there, and heap the snow with breath
Rapid and strong, but silently! Its home
The voiceless lightning in these solitudes
Keeps innocently, and like vapour broods
Over the snow. The secret Strength of things
Which governs thought, and to the infinite dome   140
Of Heaven is as a law, inhabits thee!
And what were thou, and earth, and stars, and sea,
If to the human mind's imaginings
Silence and solitude were vacancy?

[1816; publ. 1817]

TO CONSTANTIA, SINGING

I

THUS to be lost and thus to sink and die,
    Perchance were death indeed!—Constantia, turn!
In thy dark eyes a power like light doth lie,
    Even though the sounds which were thy voice, which burn
Between thy lips, are laid to sleep;
    Within thy breath, and on thy hair, like odour, it is yet,
And from thy touch like fire doth leap.
    Even while I write, my burning cheeks are wet,
    Alas, that the torn heart can bleed, but not forget!

II

A breathless awe, like the swift change   10
   Unseen, but felt in youthful slumbers,
Wild, sweet, but uncommunicably strange,
   Thou breathest now in fast ascending numbers.
The cope of heaven seems rent and cloven
   By the enchantment of thy strain,
And on my shoulders wings are woven,
   To follow its sublime career
Beyond the mighty moons that wane
   Upon the verge of Nature's utmost sphere,
   Till the world's shadowy walls are past and disappear.   20

III

Her voice is hovering o'er my soul—it lingers
   O'ershadowing it with soft and lulling wings,
The blood and life within those snowy fingers
   Teach witchcraft to the instrumental strings.
My brain is wild, my breath comes quick—
   The blood is listening in my frame,
And thronging shadows, fast and thick,
   Fall on my overflowing eyes;
My heart is quivering like a flame;
   As morning dew, that in the sunbeam dies,   30
   I am dissolved in these consuming ecstasies.

IV

I have no life, Constantia, now, but thee,
   Whilst, like the world-surrounding air, thy song
Flows on, and fills all things with melody.—
   Now is thy voice a tempest swift and strong,
On which, like one in trance upborne,
   Secure o'er rocks and waves I sweep,
Rejoicing like a cloud of morn.
   Now 'tis the breath of summer night,
Which when the starry waters sleep,   40
   Round western isles, with incense-blossoms bright
   Lingering, suspends my soul in its voluptuous flight.
                              [1817; publ. 1824]

OZYMANDIAS

I MET a traveller from an antique land
Who said: Two vast and trunkless legs of stone
Stand in the desert . . . Near them, on the sand,
Half sunk, a shattered visage lies, whose frown,
And wrinkled lip, and sneer of cold command,
Tell that its sculptor well those passions read
Which yet survive, stamped on these lifeless things,
The hand that mocked them, and the heart that fed:
And on the pedestal these words appear:
'My name is Ozymandias, king of kings: 10
Look on my works, ye Mighty, and despair!'
Nothing beside remains. Round the decay
Of that colossal wreck, boundless and bare
The lone and level sands stretch far away.

                                    [1817; publ. 1818]

TO THE NILE

MONTH after month the gathered rains descend
Drenching yon secret Aethiopian dells,
And from the desert's ice-girt pinnacles
Where Frost and Heat in strange embraces blend
On Atlas, fields of moist snow half depend.
Girt there with blasts and meteors Tempest dwells
By Nile's aëreal urn, with rapid spells
Urging those waters to their mighty end.
O'er Egypt's land of Memory floods are level
And they are thine, O Nile—and well thou knowest   10
That soul-sustaining airs and blasts of evil
And fruits and poisons spring where'er thou flowest.
Beware, O Man—for knowledge must to thee,
Like the great flood to Egypt, ever be.

                                    [1818; publ. 1876]

LINES WRITTEN AMONG THE EUGANEAN HILLS

OCTOBER, 1818

MANY a green isle needs must be
In the deep wide sea of Misery,
Or the mariner, worn and wan,
Never thus could voyage on—
Day and night, and night and day,
Drifting on his dreary way,
With the solid darkness black
Closing round his vessel's track;
Whilst above the sunless sky,
Big with clouds, hangs heavily,   10
And behind the tempest fleet
Hurries on with lightning feet,
Riving sail, and cord, and plank,
Till the ship has almost drank
Death from the o'er-brimming deep;
And sinks down, down, like that sleep
When the dreamer seems to be
Weltering through eternity;
And the dim low line before
Of a dark and distant shore   20
Still recedes, as ever still
Longing with divided will,
But no power to seek or shun,
He is ever drifted on
O'er the unreposing wave
To the haven of the grave.
What, if there no friends will greet;
What, if there no heart will meet
His with love's impatient beat;
Wander wheresoe'er he may.   30
Can he dream before that day
To find refuge from distress
In friendship's smile, in love's caress?
Then 'twill wreak him little woe
Whether such there be or no:
Senseless is the breast, and cold,
Which relenting love would fold;

Bloodless are the veins and chill
Which the pulse of pain did fill;
Every little living nerve   40
That from bitter words did swerve
Round the tortured lips and brow,
Are like sapless leaflets now
Frozen upon December's bough.

On the beach of a northern sea
Which tempests shake eternally,
As once the wretch there lay to sleep,
Lies a solitary heap,
One white skull and seven dry bones,
On the margin of the stones,   50
Where a few gray rushes stand,
Boundaries of the sea and land:
Nor is heard one voice of wail
But the sea-mews, as they sail
O'er the billows of the gale;
Or the whirlwind up and down
Howling, like a slaughtered town,
When a king in glory rides
Through the pomp of fratricides:
Those unburied bones around   60
There is many a mournful sound;
There is no lament for him,
Like a sunless vapour, dim,
Who once clothed with life and thought
What now moves nor murmurs not.

Ay, many flowering islands lie
In the waters of wide Agony:
To such a one this morn was led,
My bark by soft winds piloted:
'Mid the mountains Euganean   70
I stood listening to the paean
With which the legioned rooks did hail
The sun's uprise majestical;
Gathering round with wings all hoar,
Through the dewy mist they soar
Like gray shades, till the eastern heaven
Bursts, and then, as clouds of even,

Flecked with fire and azure, lie
In the unfathomable sky,
So their plumes of purple grain, 80
Starred with drops of golden rain,
Gleam above the sunlight woods,
As in silent multitudes
On the morning's fitful gale
Through the broken mist they sail,
And the vapours cloven and gleaming
Follow down the dark steep streaming,
'Till all is bright, and clear, and still,
Round the solitary hill.

Beneath is spread like a green sea 90
The waveless plain of Lombardy,
Bounded by the vaporous air,
Islanded by cities fair;
Underneath Day's azure eyes
Ocean's nursling, Venice lies,
A peopled labyrinth of walls,
Amphitrite's destined halls,
Which her hoary sire now paves
With his blue and beaming waves.
Lo! the sun upsprings behind, 100
Broad, red, radiant, half-reclined
On the level quivering line
Of the waters crystalline;
And before that chasm of light,
As within a furnace bright,
Column, tower, and dome, and spire,
Shine like obelisks of fire,
Pointing with inconstant motion
From the altar of dark ocean
To the sapphire-tinted skies; 110
As the flames of sacrifice
From the marble shrines did rise,
As to pierce the dome of gold
Where Apollo spoke of old.

Sun-girt City, thou hast been
Ocean's child, and then his queen;
Now is come a darker day,

And thou soon must be his prey,
If the power that raised thee here
Hallow so thy watery bier.   120
A less drear ruin then than now,
With thy conquest-branded brow
Stooping to the slave of slaves
From thy throne, among the waves
Wilt thou be, when the sea-mew
Flies, as once before it flew,
O'er thine isles depopulate,
And all is in its ancient state,
Save where many a palace gate
With green sea-flowers overgrown   130
Like a rock of Ocean's own,
Topples o'er the abandoned sea
As the tides change sullenly.
The fisher on his watery way,
Wandering at the close of day,
Will spread his sail and seize his oar
Till he pass the gloomy shore,
Lest thy dead should, from their sleep
Bursting o'er the starlight deep,
Lead a rapid masque of death   140
O'er the waters of his path.

Those who alone thy towers behold
Quivering through aëreal gold,
As I now behold them here,
Would imagine not they were
Sepulchres, where human forms,
Like pollution-nourished worms,
To the corpse of greatness cling,
Murdered, and now mouldering:
But if Freedom should awake   150
In her omnipotence, and shake
From the Celtic Anarch's hold
All the keys of dungeons cold,
Where a hundred cities lie
Chained like thee, ingloriously,
Thou and all thy sister band
Might adorn this sunny land,
Twining memories of old time

With new virtues more sublime;
If not, perish thou and they!—   160
Clouds which stain truth's rising day
By her sun consumed away—
Earth can spare ye: while like flowers,
In the waste of years and hours,
From your dust new nations spring
With more kindly blossoming.

Perish—let there only be
Floating o'er thy hearthless sea
As the garment of thy sky
Clothes the world immortally,   170
One remembrance, more sublime
Than the tattered pall of time,
Which scarce hides thy visage wan;—
That a tempest-cleaving Swan
Of the songs of Albion,
Driven from his ancestral streams
By the might of evil dreams,
Found a nest in thee; and Ocean
Welcomed him with such emotion
That its joy grew his, and sprung   180
From his lips like music flung
O'er a mighty thunder-fit,
Chastening terror:—what though yet
Poesy's unfailing River,
Which through Albion winds forever
Lashing with melodious wave
Many a sacred Poet's grave,
Mourn its latest nursling fled?
What though thou with all thy dead
Scarce can for this fame repay   190
Aught thine own? oh, rather say
Though thy sins and slaveries foul
Overcloud a sunlike soul?
As the ghost of Homer clings
Round Scamander's wasting springs;
As divinest Shakespeare's might
Fills Avon and the world with light
Like omniscient power which he
Imaged 'mid mortality;

As the love from Petrarch's urn,   200
Yet amid yon hills doth burn,
A quenchless lamp by which the heart
Sees things unearthly;—so thou art,
Mighty spirit—so shall be
The City that did refuge thee.

Lo, the sun floats up the sky
Like thought-wingèd Liberty,
Till the universal light
Seems to level plain and height;
From the sea a mist has spread,   210
And the beams of morn lie dead
On the towers of Venice now,
Like its glory long ago.
By the skirts of that gray cloud
Many-domèd Padua proud
Stands, a peopled solitude,
'Mid the harvest-shining plain,
Where the peasant heaps his grain
In the garner of his foe,
And the milk-white oxen slow   220
With the purple vintage strain,
Heaped upon the creaking wain,
That the brutal Celt may swill
Drunken sleep with savage will;
And the sickle to the sword
Lies unchanged, though many a lord,
Like a weed whose shade is poison,
Overgrows this region's foison,
Sheaves of whom are ripe to come
To destruction's harvest-home: 230
Men must reap the things they sow,
Force from force must ever flow,
Or worse; but 'tis a bitter woe
That love or reason cannot change
The despot's rage, the slave's revenge.
Padua, thou within whose walls
Those mute guests at festivals,
Son and Mother, Death and Sin,
Played at dice for Ezzelin,
Till Death cried, 'I win, I win!'   240

And Sin cursed to lose the wager,
But Death promised, to assuage her,
That he would petition for
Her to be made Vice-Emperor,
When the destined years were o'er,
Over all between the Po
And the eastern Alpine snow,
Under the mighty Austrian.
Sin smiled so as Sin only can,
And since that time, ay, long before,   250
Both have ruled from shore to shore,—
That incestuous pair, who follow
Tyrants as the sun the swallow,
As Repentance follows Crime,
And as changes follow Time.

In thine halls the lamp of learning,
Padua, now no more is burning;
Like a meteor, whose wild way
Is lost over the grave of day,
It gleams betrayed and to betray: 260
Once remotest nations came
To adore that sacred flame,
When it lit not many a hearth
On this cold and gloomy earth:
Now new fires from antique light
Spring beneath the wide world's might;
But their spark lies dead in thee,
Trampled out by Tyranny.
As the Norway woodman quells,
In the depth of piny dells,   270
One light flame among the brakes,
While the boundless forest shakes,
And its mighty trunks are torn
By the fire thus lowly born:
The spark beneath his feet is dead,
He starts to see the flames it fed
Howling through the darkened sky
With a myriad tongues victoriously,
And sinks down in fear: so thou,
O Tyranny, beholdest now   280
Light around thee, and thou hearest

The loud flames ascend, and fearest:
Grovel on the earth; ay, hide
In the dust thy purple pride!

Noon descends around me now:
'Tis the noon of autumn's glow,
When a soft and purple mist
Like a vaporous amethyst,
Or an air-dissolvèd star
Mingling light and fragrance, far   290
From the curved horizon's bound
To the point of Heaven's profound,
Fills the overflowing sky;
And the plains that silent lie
Underneath, the leaves unsodden
Where the infant Frost has trodden
With his morning-wingèd feet,
Whose bright print is gleaming yet;
And the red and golden vines,
Piercing with their trellised lines   300
The rough, dark-skirted wilderness;
The dun and bladed grass no less,
Pointing from this hoary tower
In the windless air; the flower
Glimmering at my feet; the line
Of the olive-sandalled Apennine
In the south dimly islanded;
And the Alps, whose snows are spread
High between the clouds and sun;
And of living things each one;   310
And my spirit which so long
Darkened this swift stream of song,—
Interpenetrated lie
By the glory of the sky:
Be it love, light, harmony,
Odour, or the soul of all
Which from Heaven like dew doth fall,
Or the mind which feeds this verse
Peopling the lone universe.

Noon descends, and after noon   320
Autumn's evening meets me soon,

Leading the infantine moon,
And that one star, which to her
Almost seems to minister
Half the crimson light she brings
From the sunset's radiant springs;
And the soft dreams of the morn
(Which like wingèd winds had borne
To that silent isle, which lies
Mid remembered agonies,   330
The frail bark of this lone being)
Pass, to other sufferers fleeing,
And its ancient pilot, Pain,
Sits beside the helm again.

Other flowering isles must be
In the sea of Life and Agony:
Other spirits float and flee
O'er that gulf: even now, perhaps,
On some rock the wild wave wraps,
With folded wings they waiting sit   340
For my bark, to pilot it
To some calm and blooming cove,
Where for me, and those I love,
May a windless bower be built,
Far from passion, pain, and guilt,
In a dell mid lawny hills,
Which the wild-sea murmur fills,
And soft sunshine, and the sound
Of old forests echoing round,
And the light and smell divine   350
Of all flowers that breathe and shine:
We may live so happy there,
That the Spirits of the Air,
Envying us, may even entice
To our healing Paradise
The polluting multitude;
But their rage would be subdued
By that clime divine and calm,
And the winds whose wings rain balm
On the uplifted soul, and leaves   360
Under which the bright sea heaves;

While each breathless interval
In their whisperings musical
The inspired soul supplies
With its own deep melodies,
And the love which heals all strife
Circling, like the breath of life,
All things in that sweet abode
With its own mild brotherhood:
They, not it, would change; and soon   370
Every sprite beneath the moon
Would repent its envy vain,
And the earth grow young again.

[1818; publ. 1819]

STANZAS

WRITTEN IN DEJECTION, NEAR NAPLES

I

THE sun is warm, the sky is clear,
    The waves are dancing fast and bright,
Blue isles and snowy mountains wear
    The purple noon's transparent might,
    The breath of the moist earth is light,
Around its unexpanded buds;
    Like many a voice of one delight,
The winds, the birds, the ocean floods,
The City's voice itself, is soft like Solitude's.

II

I see the Deep's untrampled floor   10
    With green and purple seaweeds strown;
I see the waves upon the shore,
    Like light dissolved in star-showers, thrown:
    I sit upon the sands alone,—

The lightning of the noontide ocean
  Is flashing round me, and a tone
Arises from its measured motion,
How sweet! did any heart now share in my emotion.

III

Alas! I have nor hope nor health,
  Nor peace within nor calm around,   20
Nor that content surpassing wealth
  The sage in meditation found,
  And walked with inward glory crowned—
Nor fame, nor power, nor love, nor leisure.
  Others I see whom these surround—
  Smiling they live, and call life pleasure;—
To me that cup has been dealt in another measure.

IV

Yet now despair itself is mild,
  Even as the winds and waters are;
I could lie down like a tired child,   30
  And weep away the life of care
  Which I have borne and yet must bear,
Till death like sleep might steal on me,
  And I might feel in the warm air
  My cheek grow cold, and hear the sea
Breathe o'er my dying brain its last monotony.

V

Some might lament that I were cold,
  As I, when this sweet day is gone,
Which my lost heart, too soon grown old,
  Insults with this untimely moan;   40
  They might lament—for I am one
Whom men love not,—and yet regret,
  Unlike this day, which, when the sun
  Shall on its stainless glory set,
Will linger, though enjoyed, like joy in memory yet.

                    [1818; publ. 1824]

SONNET

Lift not the painted veil which those who live
Call Life: though unreal shapes be pictured there,
And it but mimic all we would believe
With colours idly spread,—behind, lurk Fear
And Hope, twin Destinies; who ever weave
Their shadows, o'er the chasm, sightless and drear.
I knew one who had lifted it—he sought,
For his lost heart was tender, things to love,
But found them not, alas! nor was there aught
The world contains, the which he could approve. 10
Through the unheeding many he did move,
A splendour among shadows, a bright blot
Upon this gloomy scene, a Spirit that strove
For truth, and like the Preacher found it not.

[1818; publ. 1824]

SONNET: ENGLAND IN 1819

An old, mad, blind, despised, and dying king,—
Princes, the dregs of their dull race, who flow
Through public scorn,—mud from a muddy spring,—
Rulers who neither see, nor feel, nor know,
But leech-like to their fainting country cling,
Till they drop, blind in blood, without a blow,—
A people starved and stabbed in the untilled field,—
An army, which liberticide and prey
Makes as a two-edged sword to all who wield,—
Golden and sanguine laws which tempt and slay; 10
Religion Christless, Godless—a book sealed;
A Senate,—Time's worst statute unrepealed,—
Are graves, from which a glorious Phantom may
Burst, to illumine our tempestuous day.

[1819; publ. 1839]

A NEW NATIONAL ANTHEM

I

God prosper, speed, and save,
God raise from England's grave
    Her murdered Queen!
Pave with swift victory
The steps of Liberty,
Whom Britons own to be
    Immortal Queen.

II

See, she comes throned on high,
On swift Eternity!
    God save the Queen!   10
Millions on millions wait,
Firm, rapid, and elate,
On her majestic state!
    God save the Queen!

III

She is Thine own pure soul
Moulding the mighty whole,—
    God save the Queen!
She is Thine own deep love
Rained down from Heaven above,—
Wherever she rest or move,   20
    God save our Queen!

IV

'Wilder her enemies
In their own dark disguise,—
    God save our Queen!
All earthly things that dare
Her sacred name to bear,
Strip them, as kings are, bare;
    God save the Queen!

V

Be her eternal throne
Built in our hearts alone—   30
    God save the Queen!
Let the oppressor hold
Canopied seats of gold;
She sits enthroned of old
    O'er our hearts Queen.

VI

Lips touched by seraphim
Breathe out the choral hymn
    'God save the Queen!'
Sweet as if angels sang,
Loud as that trumpet's clang   40
Wakening the world's dead gang,—
    God save the Queen!

                  [1819; publ. 1839]

AN EXHORTATION

CHAMELEONS feed on light and air:
    Poets' food is love and fame:
If in this wide world of care
    Poets could but find the same
With as little toil as they,
    Would they ever change their hue
    As the light chameleons do,
Suiting it to every ray
    Twenty times a day?

Poets are on this cold earth,   10
    As chameleons might be,
Hidden from their early birth
    In a cave beneath the sea;
Where light is, chameleons change:

Where love is not, poets do:
Fame is love disguised: if few
Find either, never think it strange
    That poets range.

Yet dare not stain with wealth or power
    A poet's free and heavenly mind: . 20
If bright chameleons should devour
    Any food but beams and wind,
They would grow as earthly soon
    As their brother lizards are.
    Children of a sunnier star,
Spirits from beyond the moon,
    Oh, refuse the boon!

                     [1819; publ. 1820]

ODE TO THE WEST WIND[1]

I

O WILD West Wind, thou breath of Autumn's being,
Thou, from whose unseen presence the leaves dead
Are driven, like ghosts from an enchanter fleeing,

Yellow, and black, and pale, and hectic red,
Pestilence-stricken multitudes: O thou,
Who chariotest to their dark wintry bed

The wingèd seeds, where they lie cold and low,
Each like a corpse within its grave, until
Thine azure sister of the Spring shall blow

[1] This poem was conceived and chiefly written in a wood that skirts
the Arno, near Florence, and on a day when that tempestuous wind,
whose temperature is at once mild and animating, was collecting the
vapours which pour down the autumnal rains. They began, as I fore-
saw, at sunset with a violent tempest of hail and rain, attended by that
magnificent thunder and lightning peculiar to the Cisalpine regions.

The phenomenon alluded to at the conclusion of the third stanza is
well known to naturalists. The vegetation at the bottom of the sea, of
rivers, and of lakes, sympathizes with that of the land in the change
of seasons, and is consequently influenced by the winds which announce
it.—[SHELLEY'S NOTE.]

Her clarion o'er the dreaming earth, and fill   10
(Driving sweet buds like flocks to feed in air)
With living hues and odours plain and hill:

Wild Spirit, which art moving everywhere;
Destroyer and preserver; hear, oh, hear!

II

Thou on whose stream, mid the steep sky's commotion,
Loose clouds like earth's decaying leaves are shed,
Shook from the tangled boughs of Heaven and Ocean,

Angels of rain and lightning: there are spread
On the blue surface of thine aëry surge,
Like the bright hair uplifted from the head   20

Of some fierce Maenad, even from the dim verge
Of the horizon to the zenith's height,
The locks of the approaching storm. Thou dirge

Of the dying year, to which this closing night
Will be the dome of a vast sepulchre,
Vaulted with all thy congregated might

Of vapours, from whose solid atmosphere
Black rain, and fire, and hail will burst: oh, hear!

III

Thou who didst waken from his summer dreams
The blue Mediterranean, where he lay,   30
Lulled by the coil of his crystàlline streams,

Beside a pumice isle in Baiae's bay,
And saw in sleep old palaces and towers
Quivering within the wave's intenser day,

All overgrown with azure moss and flowers
So sweet, the sense faints picturing them! Thou
For whose path the Atlantic's level powers

Cleave themselves into chasms, while far below
The sea-blooms and the oozy woods which wear
The sapless foliage of the ocean, know   40

Thy voice, and suddenly grow gray with fear,
And tremble and despoil themselves: oh, hear!

IV

If I were a dead leaf thou mightest bear;
If I were a swift cloud to fly with thee;
A wave to pant beneath thy power, and share

The impulse of thy strength, only less free
Than thou, O uncontrollable! If even
I were as in my boyhood, and could be

The comrade of thy wanderings over Heaven,
As then, when to outstrip thy skiey speed   50
Scarce seemed a vision; I would ne'er have striven

As thus with thee in prayer in my sore need.
Oh, lift me as a wave, a leaf, a cloud!
I fall upon the thorns of life! I bleed!

A heavy weight of hours has chained and bowed
One too like thee: tameless, and swift, and proud.

V

Make me thy lyre, even as the forest is:
What if my leaves are falling like its own!
The tumult of thy mighty harmonies

Will take from both a deep, autumnal tone,   60
Sweet though in sadness. Be thou, Spirit fierce,
My spirit! Be thou me, impetuous one!

Drive my dead thoughts over the universe
Like withered leaves to quicken a new birth!
And, by the incantation of this verse,

Scatter, as from an unextinguished hearth
Ashes and sparks, my words among mankind!
Be through my lips to unawakened earth

The trumpet of a prophecy! O, Wind,
If Winter comes, can Spring be far behind?   70

[1819; publ. 1820]

ON THE MEDUSA OF LEONARDO DA VINCI IN THE FLORENTINE GALLERY

I

It lieth, gazing on the midnight sky,
    Upon the cloudy mountain-peak supine;
Below, far lands are seen tremblingly;
    Its horror and its beauty are divine.
Upon its lips and eyelids seems to lie
    Loveliness like a shadow, from which shine,
Fiery and lurid, struggling underneath,
The agonies of anguish and of death.

II

Yet it is less the horror than the grace
    Which turns the gazer's spirit into stone,   10
Whereon the lineaments of that dead face
    Are graven, till the characters be grown
Into itself, and thought no more can trace;
    'Tis the melodious hue of beauty thrown
Athwart the darkness and the glare of pain,
Which humanize and harmonize the strain.

III

And from its head as from one body grow,
    As   grass out of a watery rock,
Hairs which are vipers, and they curl and flow

And their long tangles in each other lock,   20
And with unending involutions show
   Their mailèd radiance, as it were to mock
The torture and the death within, and saw
The solid air with many a raggèd jaw.

IV

And, from a stone beside, a poisonous eft
   Peeps idly into those Gorgonian eyes;
Whilst in the air a ghastly bat, bereft
   Of sense, has flitted with a mad surprise
Out of the cave this hideous light had cleft,
   And he comes hastening like a moth that hies   30
After a taper; and the midnight sky
Flares, a light more dread than obscurity.

V

'Tis the tempestuous loveliness of terror;
   For from the serpents gleams a brazen glare
Kindled by that inextricable error,
   Which makes a thrilling vapour of the air
Become a   and ever-shifting mirror
   Of all the beauty and the terror there—
A woman's countenance, with serpent-locks,
Gazing in death on Heaven from those wet rocks.   40

                 [1819; publ. 1824]

THE CLOUD

I BRING fresh showers for the thirsting flowers,
   From the seas and the streams;
I bear light shade for the leaves when laid
   In their noonday dreams.
From my wings are shaken the dews that waken
   The sweet buds every one,
When rocked to rest on their mother's breast,
   As she dances about the sun.

I wield the flail of the lashing hail,
    And whiten the green plains under, 10
And then again I dissolve it in rain,
    And laugh as I pass in thunder.

I sift the snow on the mountains below,
    And their great pines groan aghast;
And all the night 'tis my pillow white,
    While I sleep in the arms of the blast.
Sublime on the towers of my skiey bowers,
    Lightning my pilot sits;
In a cavern under is fettered the thunder,
    It struggles and howls at fits; 20
Over earth and ocean, with gentle motion,
    This pilot is guiding me,
Lured by the love of the genii that move
    In the depths of the purple sea;
Over the rills, and the crags, and the hills,
    Over the lakes and the plains,
Wherever he dream, under mountain or stream,
    The Spirit he loves remains;
And I all the while bask in Heaven's blue smile,
    Whilst he is dissolving in rains. 30

The sanguine Sunrise, with his meteor eyes,
    And his burning plumes outspread,
Leaps on the back of my sailing rack,
    When the morning star shines dead;
As on the jag of a mountain crag,
    Which an earthquake rocks and swings,
An eagle alit one moment may sit
    In the light of its golden wings.
And when Sunset may breathe, from the lit sea beneath,
    Its ardours of rest and of love, 40
And the crimson pall of eve may fall
    From the depth of Heaven above,
With wings folded I rest, on mine aëry nest,
    As still as a brooding dove.

That orbèd maiden with white fire laden,
    Whom mortals call the Moon,

Glides glimmering o'er my fleece-like floor,
    By the midnight breezes strewn;
And wherever the beat of her unseen feet,
    Which only the angels hear,   50
May have broken the woof of my tent's thin roof,
    The stars peep behind her and peer;
And I laugh to see them whirl and flee,
    Like a swarm of golden bees,
When I widen the rent in my wind-built tent,
    Till the calm rivers, lakes, and seas,
Like strips of the sky fallen through me on high,
    Are each paved with the moon and these.

I bind the Sun's throne with a burning zone,
    And the Moon's with a girdle of pearl;   60
The volcanoes are dim, and the stars reel and swim,
    When the whirlwinds my banner unfurl.
From cape to cape, with a bridge-like shape,
    Over a torrent sea,
Sunbeam-proof, I hang like a roof,—
    The mountains its columns be.
The triumphal arch through which I march
    With hurricane, fire, and snow,
When the Powers of the air are chained to my chair,
    Is the million-coloured bow;   70
The sphere-fire above its soft colours wove,
    While the moist Earth was laughing below.

I am the daughter of Earth and Water,
    And the nursling of the Sky;
I pass through the pores of the ocean and shores;
    I change, but I cannot die.
For after the rain when with never a stain
    The pavilion of Heaven is bare,
And the winds and sunbeams with their convex gleams
    Build up the blue dome of air,   80
I silently laugh at my own cenotaph,
    And out of the caverns of rain,
Like a child from the womb, like a ghost from the tomb,
    I arise and unbuild it again.

                          [1820; publ. 1820]

TO A SKYLARK

HAIL to thee, blithe Spirit!
  Bird thou never wert,
That from Heaven, or near it,
  Pourest thy full heart
In profuse strains of unpremeditated art.

Higher still and higher
  From the earth thou springest
Like a cloud of fire;
  The blue deep thou wingest,
And singing still dost soar, and soaring ever singest.   10

In the golden lightning
  Of the sunken sun,
O'er which clouds are bright'ning,
  Thou dost float and run;
Like an unbodied joy whose race is just begun.

The pale purple even
  Melts around thy flight;
Like a star of Heaven,
  In the broad daylight
Thou art unseen, but yet I hear thy shrill delight,   20

Keen as are the arrows
  Of that silver sphere,
Whose intense lamp narrows
  In the white dawn clear
Until we hardly see—we feel that it is there.

All the earth and air
  With thy voice is loud,
As, when night is bare,
  From one lonely cloud
The moon rains out her beams, and Heaven is overflowed.   30

What thou art we know not;
  What is most like thee?

From rainbow clouds there flow not
    Drops so bright to see
As from thy presence showers a rain of melody.

Like a Poet hidden
    In the light of thought,
Singing hymns unbidden,
    Till the world is wrought
To sympathy with hopes and fears it heeded not: 40

Like a high-born maiden
    In a palace-tower,
Soothing her love-laden
    Soul in secret hour
With music sweet as love, which overflows her bower:

Like a glow-worm golden
    In a dell of dew,
Scattering unbeholden
    Its aëreal hue
Among the flowers and grass, which screen it from the view!   50

Like a rose embowered
    In its own green leaves,
By warm winds deflowered,
    Till the scent it gives
Makes faint with too much sweet those heavy-wingèd thieves:

Sound of vernal showers
    On the twinkling grass,
Rain-awakened flowers,
    All that ever was
Joyous, and clear, and fresh, thy music doth surpass: 60

Teach us, Sprite or Bird,
    What sweet thoughts are thine:
I have never heard
    Praise of love or wine
That panted forth a flood of rapture so divine.

Chorus Hymeneal,
    Or triumphal chant,

Matched with thine would be all
    But an empty vaunt,
A thing wherein we feel there is some hidden want.   70

What objects are the fountains
    Of thy happy strain?
What fields, or waves, or mountains?
    What shapes of sky or plain?
What love of thine own kind? what ignorance of pain?

With thy clear keen joyance
    Languor cannot be:
Shadow of annoyance
    Never came near thee:
Thou lovest—but ne'er knew love's sad satiety.   80

Waking or asleep,
    Thou of death must deem
Things more true and deep
    Than we mortals dream,
Or how could thy notes flow in such a crystal stream?

We look before and after,
    And pine for what is not:
Our sincerest laughter
    With some pain is fraught:
Our sweetest songs are those that tell of saddest thought.   90

Yet if we could scorn
    Hate, and pride, and fear;
If we were things born
    Not to shed a tear,
I know not how thy joy we ever should come near.

Better than all measures
    Of delightful sound,
Better than all treasures
    That in books are found,
Thy skill to poet were, thou scorner of the ground!   100

Teach me half the gladness
    That thy brain must know,

Such harmonious madness
　　From my lips would flow
The world should listen then—as I am listening now.

[1820; publ. 1820]

ODE TO LIBERTY

Yet, Freedom, yet, thy banner, torn but flying,
Streams like a thunder-storm against the wind.—BYRON.

I

A GLORIOUS people vibrated again
　　The lightning of the nations: Liberty
From heart to heart, from tower to tower, o'er Spain,
　　Scattering contagious fire into the sky,
Gleamed. My soul spurned the chains of its dismay,
　　　　And in the rapid plumes of song
　　　　Clothed itself, sublime and strong,
(As a young eagle soars the morning clouds among,)
　　Hovering in verse o'er its accustomed prey;
　　　Till from its station in the Heaven of fame　　10
　　The Spirit's whirlwind rapped it, and the ray
　　Of the remotest sphere of living flame
Which paves the void was from behind it flung,
　　As foam from a ship's swiftness, when there came
　　A voice out of the deep: I will record the same.

II

The Sun and the serenest Moon sprang forth:
　　The burning stars of the abyss were hurled
Into the depths of Heaven. The daedal earth,
　　That island in the ocean of the world,
Hung in its cloud of all-sustaining air:　　20
　　　　But this divinest universe
　　　　Was yet a chaos and a curse,
For thou wert not: but, power from worst producing worse,
　　The spirit of the beasts was kindled there,

And of the birds, and of the watery forms,
  And there was war among them, and despair
    Within them, raging without truce or terms:
The bosom of their violated nurse
  Groaned, for beasts warred on beasts, and worms on worms,
  And men on men; each heart was as a hell of storms.   30

III

Man, the imperial shape, then multiplied
  His generations under the pavilion
Of the Sun's throne: palace and pyramid,
  Temple and prison, to many a swarming million
Were, as to mountain-wolves their ragged caves.
    This human living multitude
    Was savage, cunning, blind, and rude,
For thou wert not; but o'er the populous solitude,
  Like one fierce cloud over a waste of waves,
    Hung Tyranny; beneath, sate deified   40
  The sister-pest, congregator of slaves;
    Into the shadow of her pinions wide
Anarchs and priests, who feed on gold and blood
  Till with the stain their inmost souls are dyed,
  Drove the astonished herds of men from every side.

IV

The nodding promontories, and blue isles,
  And cloud-like mountains, and dividuous waves
Of Greece, basked glorious in the open smiles
  Of favouring Heaven: from their enchanted caves
Prophetic echoes flung dim melody.   50
    On the unapprehensive wild
    The vine, the corn, the olive mild,
Grew savage yet, to human use unreconciled;
  And, like unfolded flowers beneath the sea,
    Like the man's thought dark in the infant's brain,
  Like aught that is which wraps what is to be,
    Art's deathless dreams lay veiled by many a vein
Of Parian stone; and, yet a speechless child,
  Verse murmured, and Philosophy did strain
  Her lidless eyes for thee; when o'er the Aegean main   60

V

Athens arose: a city such as vision
  Builds from the purple crags and silver towers
Of battlemented cloud, as in derision
  Of kingliest masonry: the ocean-floors
Pave it; the evening sky pavilions it;
        Its portals are inhabited
        By thunder-zonèd winds, each head
Within its cloudy wings with sun-fire garlanded,—
  A divine work! Athens, diviner yet,
    Gleamed with its crest of columns, on the will   70
  Of man, as on a mount of diamond, set;
    For thou wert, and thine all-creative skill
Peopled, with forms that mock the eternal dead
  In marble immortality, that hill
  Which was thine earliest throne and latest oracle.

VI

Within the surface of Time's fleeting river
  Its wrinkled image lies, as then it lay
Immovably unquiet, and for ever
  It trembles, but it cannot pass away!
The voices of thy bards and sages thunder   80
        With an earth-awakening blast
        Through the caverns of the past:
(Religion veils her eyes; Oppression shrinks aghast:)
  A wingèd sound of joy, and love, and wonder,
    Which soars where Expectation never flew,
  Rending the veil of space and time asunder!
    One ocean feeds the clouds, and streams, and dew;
One Sun illumines Heaven; one Spirit vast
  With life and love makes chaos ever new,
  As Athens doth the world with thy delight renew.   90

VII

Then Rome was, and from thy deep bosom fairest,
  Like a wolf-cub from a Cadmaean Maenad,[1]
    [1] See the *Bacchae* of Euripides.—[SHELLEY'S NOTE.]

She drew the milk of greatness, though thy dearest
    From that Elysian food was yet unweanèd;
And many a deed of terrible uprightness
        By thy sweet love was sanctified;
        And in thy smile, and by thy side,
Saintly Camillus lived, and firm Atilius died.
    But when tears stained thy robe of vestal whiteness,
      And gold profaned thy Capitolian throne,   100
    Thou didst desert, with spirit-wingèd lightness,
      The senate of the tyrants: they sunk prone
Slaves of one tyrant: Palatinus sighed
    Faint echoes of Ionian song; that tone
    Thou didst delay to hear, lamenting to disown.

VIII

From what Hyrcanian glen or frozen hill,
    Or piny promontory of the Arctic main,
Or utmost islet inaccessible,
    Didst thou lament the ruin of thy reign,
Teaching the woods and waves, and desert rocks,   110
        And every Naiad's ice-cold urn,
        To talk in echoes sad and stern
Of that sublimest lore which man had dared unlearn?
    For neither didst thou watch the wizard flocks
      Of the Scald's dreams, nor haunt the Druid's sleep.
    What if the tears rained through thy shattered locks
      Were quickly dried? for thou didst groan, not weep,
When from its sea of death, to kill and burn,
    The Galilean serpent forth did creep,
    And made thy world an undistinguishable heap.   120

IX

A thousand years the Earth cried, 'Where art thou?'
    And then the shadow of thy coming fell
On Saxon Alfred's olive-cinctured brow:
    And many a warrior-peopled citadel,
Like rocks which fire lifts out of the flat deep,
        Arose in sacred Italy,
        Frowning o'er the tempestuous sea
Of kings, and priests, and slaves, in tower-crowned majesty;
    That multitudinous anarchy did sweep

And burst around their walls, like idle foam, 130
  Whilst from the human spirit's deepest deep
    Strange melody with love and awe struck dumb
Dissonant arms; and Art, which cannot die,
  With divine wand traced on our earthly home
  Fit imagery to pave Heaven's everlasting dome.

X

Thou huntress swifter than the Moon! thou terror
  Of the world's wolves! thou bearer of the quiver,
Whose sunlike shafts pierce tempest-wingèd Error,
  As light may pierce the clouds when they dissever
In the calm regions of the orient day! 140
    Luther caught thy wakening glance;
    Like lightning, from his leaden lance
Reflected, it dissolved the visions of the trance
  In which, as in a tomb, the nations lay;
    And England's prophets hailed thee as their queen,
  In songs whose music cannot pass away,
    Though it must flow forever: not unseen
Before the spirit-sighted countenance
  Of Milton didst thou pass, from the sad scene
  Beyond whose night he saw, with a dejected mien. 150

XI

The eager hours and unreluctant years
  As on a dawn-illumined mountain stood,
Trampling to silence their loud hopes and fears,
  Darkening each other with their multitude,
And cried aloud, 'Liberty!' Indignation
    Answered Pity from her cave;
    Death grew pale within the grave,
And Desolation howled to the destroyer, Save!
  When like Heaven's Sun girt by the exhalation
    Of its own glorious light, thou didst arise, 160
  Chasing thy foes from nation unto nation
    Like shadows: as if day had cloven the skies
At dreaming midnight o'er the western wave,
  Men started, staggering with a glad surprise,
  Under the lightnings of thine unfamiliar eyes.

XII

Thou Heaven of earth! what spells could pall thee then
  In ominous eclipse? a thousand years
Bred from the slime of deep Oppression's den,
  Dyed all thy liquid light with blood and tears,
Till thy sweet stars could weep the stain away;   170
        How like Bacchanals of blood
        Round France, the ghastly vintage, stood
Destruction's sceptred slaves, and Folly's mitred brood!
    When one, like them, but mightier far than they,
      The Anarch of thine own bewildered powers,
    Rose: armies mingled in obscure array,
      Like clouds with clouds, darkening the sacred bowers
Of serene Heaven. He, by the past pursued,
    Rests with those dead, but unforgotten hours,
    Whose ghosts scare victor kings in their ancestral towers. 180

XIII

England yet sleeps: was she not called of old?
  Spain calls her now, as with its thrilling thunder
Vesuvius wakens Aetna, and the cold
  Snow-crags by its reply are cloven in sunder:
O'er the lit waves every Aeolian isle
        From Pithecusa to Pelorus
        Howls, and leaps, and glares in chorus:
They cry, 'Be dim; ye lamps of Heaven suspended o'er us!'
    Her chains are threads of gold, she need but smile
      And they dissolve; but Spain's were links of steel,   190
    Till bit to dust by virtue's keenest file.
      Twins of a single destiny! appeal
To the eternal years enthroned before us
    In the dim West; impress us from a seal,
    All ye have thought and done! Time cannot dare conceal.

XIV

Tomb of Arminius! render up thy dead
  Till, like a standard from a watch-tower's staff,
His soul may stream over the tyrant's head;
  Thy victory shall be his epitaph,

Wild Bacchanal of truth's mysterious wine,   200
    King-deluded Germany,
     His dead spirit lives in thee.
Why do we fear or hope? thou art already free!
  And thou, lost Paradise of this divine
    And glorious world! thou flowery wilderness!
Thou island of eternity! thou shrine
    Where Desolation, clothed with loveliness,
Worships the thing thou wert! O Italy,
  Gather thy blood into thy heart; repress
  The beasts who make their dens thy sacred palaces.   210

XV

Oh, that the free would stamp the impious name
  Of KING into the dust! or write it there,
So that this blot upon the page of fame
  Were as a serpent's path, which the light air
Erases, and the flat sands close behind!
    Ye the oracle have heard:
    Lift the victory-flashing sword,
And cut the snaky knots of this foul gordian word,
  Which, weak itself as stubble, yet can bind
    Into a mass, irrefragably firm,   220
  The axes and the rods which awe mankind;
    The sound has poison in it, 'tis the sperm
Of what makes life foul, cankerous, and abhorred;
  Disdain not thou, at thine appointed term,
  To set thine armèd heel on this reluctant worm.

XVI

Oh, that the wise from their bright minds would kindle
  Such lamps within the dome of this dim world,
That the pale name of PRIEST might shrink and dwindle
  Into the hell from which it first was hurled,
A scoff of impious pride from fiends impure;   230
    Till human thoughts might kneel alone,
    Each before the judgment-throne
Of its own aweless soul, or of the Power unknown!
  Oh, that the words which make the thoughts obscure
    From which they spring, as clouds of glimmering dew

From a white lake blot Heaven's blue portraiture,
    Were stripped of their thin masks and various hue
And frowns and smiles and splendours not their own,
    Till in the nakedness of false and true
    They stand before their Lord, each to receive its due!   240

XVII

He who taught man to vanquish whatsoever
    Can be between the cradle and the grave
Crowned him the King of Life. Oh, vain endeavour!
    If on his own high will, a willing slave,
He has enthroned the oppression and the oppressor.
        What if earth can clothe and feed
        Amplest millions at their need,
And power in thought be as the tree within the seed?
    Or what if Art, an ardent intercessor,
        Driving on fiery wings to Nature's throne,   250
    Checks the great mother stooping to caress her,
        And cries: 'Give me, thy child, dominion
Over all height and depth'? if Life can breed
    New wants, and wealth from those who toil and groan,
    Rend of thy gifts and hers a thousandfold for one!

XVIII

Come thou, but lead out of the inmost cave
    Of man's deep spirit, as the morning-star
Beckons the Sun from the Eoan wave,
    Wisdom. I hear the pennons of her car
Self-moving, like cloud charioted by flame;   260
        Comes she not, and come ye not,
        Rulers of eternal thought,
To judge, with solemn truth, life's ill-apportioned lot?
    Blind Love, and equal Justice, and the Fame
        Of what has been, the Hope of what will be?
O Liberty! if such could be thy name
    Wert thou disjoined from these, or they from thee:
If thine or theirs were treasures to be bought
    By blood or tears, have not the wise and free
    Wept tears, and blood like tears?—The solemn harmony   270

XIX

Paused, and the Spirit of that mighty singing
   To its abyss was suddenly withdrawn;
Then, as a wild swan, when sublimely winging
   Its path athwart the thunder-smoke of dawn,
Sinks headlong through the aëreal golden light
      On the heavy-sounding plain,
       When the bolt has pierced its brain;
As summer clouds dissolve, unburthened of their rain;
  As a far taper fades with fading night,
    As a brief insect dies with dying day,—   280
  My song, its pinions disarrayed of might,
    Drooped; o'er it closed the echoes far away
Of the great voice which did its flight sustain,
  As waves which lately paved his watery way
  Hiss round a drowner's head in their tempestuous play.
                [1820; publ. 1820]

LETTER TO MARIA GISBORNE

LEGHORN, July 1, 1820

THE spider spreads her webs, whether she be
In poet's tower, cellar, or barn, or tree;
The silk-worm in the dark green mulberry leaves
His winding sheet and cradle ever weaves;
So I, a thing whom moralists call worm,
Sit spinning still round this decaying form,
From the fine threads of rare and subtle thought—
No net of words in garish colours wrought
To catch the idle buzzers of the day—
But a soft cell, where when that fades away,   10
Memory may clothe in wings my living name
And feed it with the asphodels of fame,
Which in those hearts which must remember me
Grow, making love an immortality.

Whoever should behold me now, I wist,
Would think I were a mighty mechanist,
Bent with sublime Archimedean art
To breathe a soul into the iron heart
Of some machine portentous, or strange gin,
Which by the force of figured spells might win   20
Its way over the sea, and sport therein;
For round the walls are hung dread engines, such
As Vulcan never wrought for Jove to clutch
Ixion or the Titan:—or the quick
Wit of that man of God, St. Dominic,
To convince Atheist, Turk, or Heretic,
Or those in philanthropic council met,
Who thought to pay some interest for the debt
They owed to Jesus Christ for their salvation,
By giving a faint foretaste of damnation   30
To Shakespeare, Sidney, Spenser, and the rest
Who made our land an island of the blest.
When lamp-like Spain, who now relumes her fire
On Freedom's hearth, grew dim with Empire:—
With thumbscrews, wheels, with tooth and spike and jag,
Which fishers found under the utmost crag
Of Cornwall and the storm-encompassed isles,
Where to the sky the rude sea rarely smiles
Unless in treacherous wrath, as on the morn
When the exulting elements in scorn,   40
Satiated with destroyed destruction, lay
Sleeping in beauty on their mangled prey,
As panthers sleep;—and other strange and dread
Magical forms the brick floor overspread,—
Proteus transformed to metal did not make
More figures, or more strange; nor did he take
Such shapes of unintelligible brass,
Or heap himself in such a horrid mass
Of tin and iron not to be understood;
And forms of unimaginable wood,   50
To puzzle Tubal Cain and all his brood:
Great screws, and cones, and wheels, and groovèd blocks,
The elements of what will stand the shocks
Of wave and wind and time.—Upon the table
More knacks and quips there be than I am able
To catalogize in this verse of mine:—

A pretty bowl of wood—not full of wine,
But quicksilver; that dew which the gnomes drink
When at their subterranean toil they swink,
Pledging the demons of the earthquake, who   60
Reply to them in lava—cry halloo!
And call out to the cities o'er their head,—
Roofs, towers, and shrines, the dying and the dead,
Crash through the chinks of earth—and then all quaff
Another rouse, and hold their sides and laugh.
This quicksilver no gnome has drunk—within
The walnut bowl it lies, veinèd and thin,
In colour like the wake of light that stains
The Tuscan deep, when from the moist moon rains
The inmost shower of its white fire—the breeze   70
Is still—blue Heaven smiles over the pale seas,
And in this bowl of quicksilver—for I
Yield to the impulse of an infancy
Outlasting manhood—I have made to float
A rude idealism of a paper boat:—
A hollow screw with cogs—Henry will know
The thing I mean and laugh at me,—if so
He fears not I should do more mischief.—Next
Lie bills and calculations much perplexed,
With steam-boats, frigates, and machinery quaint   80
Traced over them in blue and yellow paint.
Then comes a range of mathematical
Instruments, for plans nautical and statical;
A heap of rosin, a queer broken glass
With ink in it;—a china cup that was
What it will never be again, I think,—
A thing from which sweet lips were wont to drink
The liquor doctors rail at—and which I
Will quaff in spite of them—and when we die
We'll toss up who died first of drinking tea,   90
And cry out,—'Heads or tails?' where'er we be.
Near that a dusty paint-box, some odd hooks,
A half-burnt match, an ivory block, three books,
Where conic sections, spherics, logarithms,
To great Laplace, from Saunderson and Sims,
Lie heaped in their harmonious disarray
Of figures,—disentangle them who may.
Baron de Tott's Memoirs beside them lie,

And some odd volumes of old chemistry.
Near those a most inexplicable thing,   100
With lead in the middle—I'm conjecturing
How to make Henry understand; but no—
I'll leave, as Spenser says, with many mo,
This secret in the pregnant womb of time,
Too vast a matter for so weak a rhyme.

And here like some weird Archimage sit I,
Plotting dark spells, and devilish enginery,
The self-impelling steam-wheels of the mind
Which pump up oaths from clergymen, and grind
The gentle spirit of our meek reviews   110
Into a powdery foam of salt abuse,
Ruffling the ocean of their self-content;—
I sit—and smile or sigh as is my bent,
But not for them—Libeccio rushes round
With an inconstant and an idle sound,
I heed him more than them—the thunder-smoke
Is gathering on the mountains, like a cloak
Folded athwart their shoulders broad and bare;
The ripe corn under the undulating air
Undulates like an ocean;—and the vines   120
Are trembling wide in all their trellised lines—
The murmur of the awakening sea doth fill
The empty pauses of the blast;—the hill
Looks hoary through the white electric rain,
And from the glens beyond, in sullen strain,
The interrupted thunder howls; above
One chasm of Heaven smiles, like the eye of Love
On the unquiet world;—while such things are,
How could one worth your friendship heed the war
Of worms? the shriek of the world's carrion jays,   130
Their censure, or their wonder, or their praise?

You are not here! the quaint witch Memory sees,
In vacant chairs, your absent images,
And points where once you sat, and now should be
But are not.—I demand if ever we
Shall meet as then we met;—and she replies,
Veiling in awe her second-sighted eyes;
'I know the past alone—but summon home

My sister Hope,—she speaks of all to come.'
But I, an old diviner, who knew well   140
Every false verse of that sweet oracle,
Turned to the sad enchantress once again,
And sought a respite from my gentle pain,
In citing every passage o'er and o'er
Of our communion—how on the sea-shore
We watched the ocean and the sky together,
Under the roof of blue Italian weather;
How I ran home through last year's thunder-storm,
And felt the transverse lightning linger warm
Upon my cheek—and how we often made   150
Feasts for each other, where good will outweighed
The frugal luxury of our country cheer,
As well it might, were it less firm and clear
Than ours must ever be;—and how we spun
A shroud of talk to hide us from the sun
Of this familiar life, which seems to be
But is not:—or is but quaint mockery
Of all we would believe, and sadly blame
The jarring and inexplicable frame
Of this wrong world:—and then anatomize   160
The purposes and thoughts of men whose eyes
Were closed in distant years;—or widely guess
The issue of the earth's great business,
When we shall be as we no longer are—
Like babbling gossips safe, who hear the war
Of winds, and sigh, but tremble not;—or how
You listened to some interrupted flow
Of visionary rhyme,—in joy and pain
Struck from the inmost fountains of my brain,
With little skill perhaps;—or how we sought   170
Those deepest wells of passion or of thought
Wrought by wise poets in the waste of years,
Staining their sacred waters with our tears;
Quenching a thirst ever to be renewed!
Or how I, wisest lady! then endued
The language of a land which now is free,
And, winged with thoughts of truth and majesty,
Flits round the tyrant's sceptre like a cloud,
And bursts the peopled prisons, and cries aloud,
'My name is Legion!'—that majestic tongue   180

Which Calderon over the desert flung
Of ages and of nations; and which found
An echo in our hearts, and with the sound
Startled oblivion;—thou wert then to me
As is a nurse—when inarticulately
A child would talk as its grown parents do.
If living winds the rapid clouds pursue,
If hawks chase doves through the aethereal way,
Huntsmen the innocent deer, and beasts their prey,
Why should not we rouse with the spirit's blast   190
Out of the forest of the pathless past
These recollected pleasures?
                  You are now
In London, that great sea, whose ebb and flow
At once is deaf and loud, and on the shore
Vomits its wrecks, and still howls on for more.
Yet in its depth what treasures! You will see
That which was Godwin,—greater none than he
Though fallen—and fallen on evil times—to stand
Among the spirits of our age and land,
Before the dread tribunal of *to come*   200
The foremost,—while Rebuke cowers pale and dumb.
You will see Coleridge—he who sits obscure
In the exceeding lustre and the pure
Intense irradiation of a mind,
Which, with its own internal lightning blind,
Flags wearily through darkness and despair—
A cloud-encircled meteor of the air,
A hooded eagle among blinking owls.—
You will see Hunt—one of those happy souls
Which are the salt of the earth, and without whom   210
This world would smell like what it is—a tomb;
Who is, what others seem; his room no doubt
Is still adorned with many a cast from Shout,
With graceful flowers tastefully placed about;
And coronals of bay from ribbons hung,
And brighter wreaths in neat disorder flung;
The gifts of the most learned among some dozens
Of female friends, sisters-in-law, and cousins.
And there is he with his eternal puns,
Which beat the dullest brain for smiles, like duns   220
Thundering for money at a poet's door;

Alas! it is no use to say, 'I'm poor!'
Or oft in graver mood, when he will look
Things wiser than were ever read in book,
Except in Shakespeare's wisest tenderness.—
You will see Hogg,—and I cannot express
His virtues,—though I know that they are great,
Because he locks, then barricades the gate
Within which they inhabit;—of his wit
And wisdom, you'll cry out when you are bit.   230
He is a pearl within an oyster shell,
One of the richest of the deep;—and there
Is English Peacock, with his mountain Fair,
Turned into a Flamingo;—that shy bird
That gleams i' the Indian air—have you not heard
When a man marries, dies, or turns Hindoo,
His best friends hear no more of him?—but you
Will see him, and will like him too, I hope,
With the milk-white Snowdonian Antelope
Matched with this cameleopard—his fine wit   240
Makes such a wound, the knife is lost in it;
A strain too learnèd for a shallow age,
Too wise for selfish bigots; let his page,
Which charms the chosen spirits of the time,
Fold itself up for the serener clime
Of years to come, and find its recompense
In that just expectation.—Wit and sense,
Virtue and human knowledge; all that might
Make this dull world a business of delight,
Are all combined in Horace Smith.—And these,   250
With some exceptions, which I need not tease
Your patience by descanting on,—are all
You and I know in London.
                              I recall
My thoughts, and bid you look upon the night.
As water does a sponge, so the moonlight
Fills the void, hollow, universal air—
What see you?—unpavilioned Heaven is fair,
Whether the moon, into her chamber gone,
Leaves midnight to the golden stars, or wan
Climbs with diminished beams the azure steep;   260
Or whether clouds sail o'er the inverse deep,
Piloted by the many-wandering blast,

And the rare stars rush through them dim and fast:—
All this is beautiful in every land.—
But what see you beside?—a shabby stand
Of Hackney coaches—a brick house or wall
Fencing some lonely court, white with the scrawl
Of our unhappy politics;—or worse—
A wretched woman reeling by, whose curse
Mixed with the watchman's, partner of her trade,   270
You must accept in place of serenade—
Or yellow-haired Pollonia murmuring
To Henry, some unutterable thing.
I see a chaos of green leaves and fruit
Built round dark caverns, even to the root
Of the living stems that feed them—in whose bowers
There sleep in their dark dew the folded flowers;
Beyond, the surface of the unsickled corn
Trembles not in the slumbering air, and borne
In circles quaint, and ever-changing dance,   280
Like wingèd stars the fire-flies flash and glance,
Pale in the open moonshine, but each one
Under the dark trees seems a little sun,
A meteor tamed; a fixed star gone astray
From the silver regions of the milky way;—
Afar the Contadino's song is heard,
Rude, but made sweet by distance—and a bird
Which cannot be the Nightingale, and yet
I know none else that sings so sweet as it
At this late hour;—and then all is still—   290
Now—Italy or London, which you will!

    Next winter you must pass with me; I'll have
My house by that time turned into a grave
Of dead despondence and low-thoughted care,
And all the dreams which our tormentors are;
Oh! that Hunt, Hogg, Peacock, and Smith were there,
With everything belonging to them fair!—
We will have books, Spanish, Italian, Greek;
And ask one week to make another week
As like his father, as I'm unlike mine,   300
Which is not his fault, as you may divine.
Though we eat little flesh and drink no wine,
Yet let's be merry: we'll have tea and toast;

Custards for supper, and an endless host
Of syllabubs and jellies and mince-pies,
And other such lady-like luxuries,—
Feasting on which we will philosophize!
And we'll have fires out of the Grand Duke's wood,
To thaw the six weeks' winter in our blood.
And then we'll talk;—what shall we talk about?   310
Oh! there are themes enough for many a bout
Of thought-entangled descant;—as to nerves—
With cones and parallelograms and curves
I've sworn to strangle them if once they dare
To bother me—when you are with me there.
And they shall never more sip laudanum,
From Helicon or Himeros[1];—well, come,
And in despite of God and of the devil,
We'll make our friendly philosophic revel
Outlast the leafless time; till buds and flowers   320
Warn the obscure inevitable hours,
Sweet meeting by sad parting to renew;—
'To-morrow to fresh woods and pastures new.'

[1820; publ. 1824]

ODE TO NAPLES[2]

EPODE I α

1 STOOD within the City disinterred;[3]
  And heard the autumnal leaves like light footfalls

[1] Ἴμερος, from which the river Himera was named, is, with some
slight shade of difference, a synonym of Love.—[SHELLEY's NOTE.]

[2] The Author has connected many recollections of his visit to Pompeii
and Baiae with the enthusiasm excited by the intelligence of the proclamation of a Constitutional Government at Naples. This has given a
tinge of picturesque and descriptive imagery to the introductory Epodes
which depicture these scenes, and some of the majestic feelings permanently connected with the scene of this animating event.—[SHELLEY's
NOTE.]

[3] Pompeii.—[SHELLEY s NOTE.]

Of spirits passing through the streets; and heard
   The Mountain's slumberous voice at intervals
     Thrill through those roofless halls;
The oracular thunder penetrating shook
   The listening soul in my suspended blood;
I felt that Earth out of her deep heart spoke—
   I felt, but heard not:—through white columns glowed
     The isle-sustaining ocean-flood,   10
A plane of light between two heavens of azure!
   Around me gleamed many a bright sepulchre
Of whose pure beauty, Time, as if his pleasure
Were to spare Death, had never made erasure;
   But every living lineament was clear
   As in the sculptor's thought; and there
The wreaths of stony myrtle, ivy, and pine,
   Like winter leaves o'ergrown by moulded snow,
   Seemed only not to move and grow
Because the crystal silence of the air   20
   Weighed on their life; even as the Power divine
   Which then lulled all things, brooded upon mine.

EPODE II α

   Then gentle winds arose
   With many a mingled close
Of wild Aeolian sound, and mountain-odours keen;
     And where the Baian ocean
     Welters with airlike motion,
Within, above, around its bowers of starry green,
   Moving the sea-flowers in those purple caves,
     Even as the ever stormless atmosphere   30
       Floats o'er the Elysian realm.
   It bore me, like an Angel, o'er the waves
    Of sunlight, whose swift pinnace of dewy air
     No storm can overwhelm.
     I sailed, where ever flows
     Under the calm Serene
     A spirit of deep emotion
     From the unknown graves
     Of the dead Kings of Melody.[1]

[1] Homer and Virgil.—[SHELLEY'S NOTE.]

Shadowy Aornos darkened o'er the helm   40
The horizontal aether; Heaven stripped bare
Its depth over Elysium, where the prow
Made the invisible water white as snow;
From that Typhaean mount, Inarime,
    There streamed a sunbright vapour, like the standard
        Of some aethereal host;
      Whilst from all the coast,
    Louder and louder, gathering round, there wandered
Over the oracular woods and divine sea
Prophesyings which grew articulate—   50
They seize me—I must speak them!—be they fate!

STROPHE I

Naples! thou Heart of men which ever pantest
    Naked, beneath the lidless eye of Heaven!
Elysian City, which to calm enchantest
    The mutinous air and sea! they round thee, even
    As sleep round Love, are driven!
Metropolis of a ruined Paradise
    Long lost, late won, and yet but half regained!
Bright Altar of the bloodless sacrifice,
    Which armèd Victory offers up unstained   60
    To Love, the flower-enchained!
Thou which wert once, and then didst cease to be,
Now art, and henceforth ever shalt be, free,
    If Hope, and Truth, and Justice can avail,
        Hail, hail, all hail!

STROPHE II

    Thou youngest giant birth
    Which from the groaning earth
Leap'st, clothed in armour of impenetrable scale!
    Last of the Intercessors!
    Who 'gainst the Crowned Transgressors   70
Pleadest before God's love! Arrayed in Wisdom's mail,
    Wave thy lightning lance in mirth
    Nor let thy high heart fail,
Though from their hundred gates the leagued Oppressors

With hurried legions move!
Hail, hail, all hail!

ANTISTROPHE I α

What though Cimmerian Anarchs dare blaspheme
    Freedom and thee? thy shield is as a mirror
To make their blind slaves see, and with fierce gleam
    To turn his hungry sword upon the wearer;   80
        A new Actaeon's error
Shall theirs have been—devoured by their own hounds!
    Be thou like the imperial Basilisk
Killing thy foe with unapparent wounds!
    Gaze on Oppression, till at that dread risk
    Aghast she pass from the Earth's disk:
Fear not, but gaze—for freemen mightier grow,
And slaves more feeble, gazing on their foe:—
    If Hope, and Truth, and Justice may avail,
        Thou shalt be great—All hail!   90

ANTISTROPHE II α

        From Freedom's form divine,
        From Nature's inmost shrine,
Strip every impious gawd, rend Error veil by veil;
        O'er Ruin desolate,
        O'er Falsehood's fallen state,
Sit thou sublime, unawed; be the Destroyer pale!
        And equal laws be thine,
        And wingèd words let sail,
Freighted with truth even from the throne of God:
        That wealth, surviving fate,   100
        Be thine.—All hail!

ANTISTROPHE I β

Didst thou not start to hear Spain's thrilling paean
    From land to land re-echoed solemnly,
Till silence became music? From the Aeaean[1]

---

[1] Aeaea, the island of Circe.—[SHELLEY'S NOTE.]

To the cold Alps, eternal Italy
    Starts to hear thine! The Sea
Which paves the desert streets of Venice laughs
  In light and music; widowed Genoa wan
By moonlight spells ancestral epitaphs,
    Murmuring, 'Where is Doria?' fair Milan,   110
      Within whose veins long ran
The viper's[1] palsying venom, lifts her heel
To bruise his head. The signal and the seal
  (If Hope and Truth and Justice can avail)
Art thou of all these hopes.—O hail!

ANTISTROPHE II β

Florence! beneath the sun,
    Of cities fairest one,
Blushes within her bower for Freedom's expectation:
    From eyes of quenchless hope
    Rome tears the priestly cope,   120
As ruling once by power, so now by admiration,—
    An athlete stripped to run
    From a remoter station
For the high prize lost on Philippi's shore:—
  As then Hope, Truth, and Justice did avail,
  So now may Fraud and Wrong! O hail!

EPODE I β

Hear ye the march as of the Earth-born Forms
  Arrayed against the ever-living Gods?
The crash and darkness of a thousand storms
    Bursting their inaccessible abodes   130
      Of crags and thunder-clouds?
See ye the banners blazoned to the day,
  Inwrought with emblems of barbaric pride?
Dissonant threats kill Silence far away,
    The serene Heaven which wraps our Eden wide
      With iron light is dyed;

[1] The viper was the armorial device of the Visconti, tyrants of Milan.
—[SHELLEY'S NOTE.]

The Anarchs of the North lead forth their legions
    Like Chaos o'er creation, uncreating;
An hundred tribes nourished on strange religions
And lawless slaveries,—down the aëreal regions   140
    Of the white Alps, desolating,
    Famished wolves that bide no waiting,
Blotting the glowing footsteps of old glory,
Trampling our columned cities into dust,
      Their dull and savage lust
    On Beauty's corse to sickness satiating—
They come! The fields they tread look black and hoary
With fire—from their red feet the streams run gory!

EPODE II β

    Great Spirit, deepest Love!
    Which rulest and dost move   150
All things which live and are, within the Italian shore;
    Who spreadest Heaven around it,
    Whose woods, rocks, waves, surround it;
Who sittest in thy star, o'er Ocean's western floor;
Spirit of beauty! at whose soft command
    The sunbeams and the showers distil its foison
    From the Earth's bosom chill;
Oh, bid those beams be each a blinding brand
    Of lightning! bid those showers be dews of poison!
      Bid the Earth's plenty kill!   160
      Bid thy bright Heaven above,
      Whilst light and darkness bound it,
      Be their tomb who planned
      To make it ours and thine!
    Or, with thine harmonizing ardours fill
And raise thy sons, as o'er the prone horizon
Thy lamp feeds every twilight wave with fire—
Be man's high hope and unextinct desire
The instrument to work thy will divine!
    Then clouds from sunbeams, antelopes from leopards,   170
      And frowns and fears from thee,
      Would not more swiftly flee
Than Celtic wolves from the Ausonian shepherds.—

Whatever, Spirit, from thy starry shrine
  Thou yieldest or withholdest, oh, let be
  This city of thy worship ever free!

                       [1820; publ. 1824]

DIRGE FOR THE YEAR

I

Orphan Hours, the Year is dead,
  Come and sigh, come and weep!
Merry Hours, smile instead,
  For the Year is but asleep.
See, it smiles as it is sleeping,
Mocking your untimely weeping.

II

As an earthquake rocks a corse
  In its coffin in the clay,
So White Winter, that rough nurse,
  Rocks the death-cold Year to-day;   10
Solemn Hours! wail aloud
For your mother in her shroud.

III

As the wild air stirs and sways
  The tree-swung cradle of a child,
So the breath of these rude days
  Rocks the Year:—be calm and mild,
Trembling Hours, she will arise
With new love within her eyes.

IV

January gray is here,
  Like a sexton by her grave;   **20**

February bears the bier,
　March with grief doth howl and rave,
And April weeps—but, O ye Hours!
Follow with May's fairest flowers.

[1821; publ. 1824]

SONG

I

RARELY, rarely, comest thou,
　Spirit of Delight!
Wherefore hast thou left me now
　Many a day and night?
Many a weary night and day
'Tis since thou art fled away.

II

How shall ever one like me
　Win thee back again?
With the joyous and the free
　Thou wilt scoff at pain.　　　　　　**10**
Spirit false! thou hast forgot
All but those who need thee not.

III

As a lizard with the shade
　Of a trembling leaf,
Thou with sorrow art dismayed;
　Even the sighs of grief
Reproach thee, that thou art not near,
And reproach thou wilt not hear.

IV

Let me set my mournful ditty
　To a merry measure;　　　　　　**20**

Thou wilt never come for pity,
　　Thou wilt come for pleasure;
Pity then will cut away
Those cruel wings, and thou wilt stay.

V

I love all that thou lovest,
　　Spirit of Delight!
The fresh Earth in new leaves dressed,
　　And the starry night;
Autumn evening, and the morn
When the golden mists are born.   30

VI

I love snow, and all the forms
　　Of the radiant frost;
I love waves, and winds, and storms,
　　Everything almost
Which is Nature's, and may be
Untainted by man's misery.

VII

I love tranquil solitude,
　　And such society
As is quiet, wise, and good;
　　Between thee and me   40
What difference? but thou dost possess
The things I seek, not love them less.

VIII

I love Love—though he has wings,
　　And like light can flee,
But above all other things,
　　Spirit, I love thee—
Thou art love and life! Oh, come,
Make once more my heart thy home.

                              [1821; publ. 1824]

TO NIGHT

I

SWIFTLY walk o'er the western wave,
      Spirit of Night!
Out of the misty eastern cave,
Where, all the long and lone daylight,
Thou wovest dreams of joy and fear,
Which make thee terrible and dear,—
      Swift be thy flight!

II

Wrap thy form in a mantle gray,
      Star-inwrought!
Blind with thine hair the eyes of Day;   **10**
Kiss her until she be wearied out,
Then wander o'er city, and sea, and land,
Touching all with thine opiate wand—
      Come, long-sought!

III

When I arose and saw the dawn,
      I sighed for thee;
When light rode high, and the dew was gone,
And noon lay heavy on flower and tree,
And the weary Day turned to his rest,
Lingering like an unloved guest,   **20**
      I sighed for thee.

IV

Thy brother Death came, and cried,
      Wouldst thou me?
Thy sweet child Sleep, the filmy-eyed,
Murmured like a noontide bee,
Shall I nestle near thy side?
Wouldst thou me?—And I replied,
      No, not thee!

V

Death will come when thou art dead,
    Soon, too soon—   30
Sleep will come when thou art fled;
Of neither would I ask the boon
I ask of thee, belovèd Night—
Swift be thine approaching flight,
    Come soon, soon!

           [1821; publ. 1824]

SONNET: POLITICAL GREATNESS

Nor happiness, nor majesty, nor fame,
Nor peace, nor strength, nor skill in arms or arts,
Shepherd those herds whom tyranny makes tame;
Verse echoes not one beating of their hearts,
History is but the shadow of their shame,
Art veils her glass, or from the pageant starts
As to oblivion their blind millions fleet,
Staining that Heaven with obscene imagery
Of their own likeness. What are numbers knit
By force or custom? Man who man would be,   10
Must rule the empire of himself; in it
Must be supreme, establishing his throne
On vanquished will, quelling the anarchy
Of hopes and fears, being himself alone.

           [1821; publ. 1824]

A LAMENT

I

O world! O life! O time!
On whose last steps I climb,
   Trembling at that where I had stood before;

When will return the glory of your prime?
　　No more—Oh, never more!

II

Out of the day and night
A joy has taken flight;
　　Fresh spring, and summer, and winter hoar,
Move my faint heart with grief, but with delight
　　No more—Oh, never more!

[1821; publ. 1824]

LINES: 'WHEN THE LAMP IS SHATTERED'

I

　　When the lamp is shattered
The light in the dust lies dead—
　　When the cloud is scattered
The rainbow's glory is shed.
　　When the lute is broken,
Sweet tones are remembered not;
　　When the lips have spoken,
Loved accents are soon forgot.

II

　　As music and splendour
Survive not the lamp and the lute,   10
　　The heart's echoes render
No song when the spirit is mute:—
　　No song but sad dirges,
Like the wind through a ruined cell,
　　Or the mournful surges
That ring the dead seaman's knell.

III

　　When hearts have once mingled
Love first leaves the well-built nest;

The weak one is singled
To endure what it once possessed.   20
  O Love! who bewailest
The frailty of all things here,
  Why choose you the frailest
For your cradle, your home, and your bier?

IV

  Its passions will rock thee
As the storms rock the ravens on high;
  Bright reason will mock thee,
Like the sun from a wintry sky.
  From thy nest every rafter
Will rot, and thine eagle home   30
  Leave thee naked to laughter,
When leaves fall and cold winds come.

                            [1822; publ. 1824]

WITH A GUITAR, TO JANE

ARIEL to Miranda:—Take
This slave of Music, for the sake
Of him who is the slave of thee,
And teach it all the harmony
In which thou canst, and only thou,
Make the delighted spirit glow,
Till joy denies itself again,
And, too intense, is turned to pain;
For by permission and command
Of thine own Prince Ferdinand,   10
Poor Ariel sends this silent token
Of more than ever can be spoken;
Your guardian spirit, Ariel, who,
From life to life, must still pursue
Your happiness;—for thus alone
Can Ariel ever find his own.
From Prospero's enchanted cell,
As the mighty verses tell,

To the throne of Naples, he
Lit you o'er the trackless sea, 20
Flitting on, your prow before,
Like a living meteor.
When you die, the silent Moon,
In her interlunar swoon,
Is not sadder in her cell
Than deserted Ariel.
When you live again on earth,
Like an unseen star of birth,
Ariel guides you o'er the sea
Of life from your nativity. 30
Many changes have been run
Since Ferdinand and you begun
Your course of love, and Ariel still
Has tracked your steps, and served your will;
Now, in humbler, happier lot,
This is all remembered not;
And now, alas! the poor sprite is
Imprisoned, for some fault of his,
In a body like a grave;—
From you he only dares to crave, 40
For his service and his sorrow,
A smile to-day, a song to-morrow.

The artist who this idol wrought,
To echo all harmonious thought,
Felled a tree, while on the steep
The woods were in their winter sleep,
Rocked in that repose divine
On the wind-swept Apennine;
And dreaming, some of Autumn past,
And some of Spring approaching fast, 50
And some of April buds and showers,
And some of songs in July bowers,
And all of love; and so this tree,—
O that such our death may be!—
Died in sleep, and felt no pain,
To live in happier form again:
From which, beneath Heaven's fairest star,
The artist wrought this loved Guitar,
And taught it justly to reply,
To all who question skilfully, 60

In language gentle as thine own;
Whispering in enamoured tone
Sweet oracles of woods and dells,
And summer winds in sylvan cells;
For it had learned all harmonies
Of the plains and of the skies,
Of the forests and the mountains,
And the many-voicèd fountains;
The clearest echoes of the hills,
The softest notes of falling rills,   70
The melodies of birds and bees,
The murmuring of summer seas,
And pattering rain, and breathing dew,
And airs of evening; and it knew
That seldom-heard mysterious sound,
Which, driven on its diurnal round,
As it floats through boundless day,
Our world enkindles on its way.—
All this it knows, but will not tell
To those who cannot question well   80
The Spirit that inhabits it;
It talks according to the wit
Of its companions; and no more
Is heard than has been felt before,
By those who tempt it to betray
These secrets of an elder day:
But, sweetly as its answers will
Flatter hands of perfect skill,
It keeps its highest, holiest tone
For our belovèd Jane alone.   90

[1822; publ. 1832]

A DIRGE

Rough wind, that moanest loud
      Grief too sad for song;
Wild wind, when sullen cloud
      Knells all the night long;
Sad storm, whose tears are vain,

Bare woods, whose branches strain,
Deep caves and dreary main,—
  Wail, for the world's wrong!

[1822; publ. 1824]

LINES WRITTEN IN THE BAY OF LERICI

SHE left me at the silent time
When the moon had ceased to climb
The azure path of Heaven's steep,
And like an albatross asleep,
Balanced on her wings of light,
Hovered in the purple night,
Ere she sought her ocean nest
In the chambers of the West.
She left me, and I stayed alone
Thinking over every tone   10
Which, though silent to the ear,
The enchanted heart could hear,
Like notes which die when born, but still
Haunt the echoes of the hill;
And feeling ever—oh, too much!—
The soft vibration of her touch,
As if her gentle hand, even now,
Lightly trembled on my brow;
And thus, although she absent were,
Memory gave me all of her   20
That even Fancy dares to claim:—
Her presence had made weak and tame
All passions, and I lived alone
In the time which is our own;
The past and future were forgot,
As they had been, and would be, not.
But soon, the guardian angel gone,
The daemon reassumed his throne
In my faint heart. I dare not speak
My thoughts, but thus disturbed and weak   30
I sat and saw the vessels glide
Over the ocean bright and wide,
Like spirit-wingèd chariots sent

O'er some serenest element
For ministrations strange and far;
As if to some Elysian star
Sailed for drink to medicine
Such sweet and bitter pain as mine.
And the wind that winged their flight
From the land came fresh and light,   40
And the scent of wingèd flowers,
And the coolness of the hours
Of dew, and sweet warmth left by day,
Were scattered o'er the twinkling day,
And the fisher with his lamp
And spear about the low rocks damp
Crept, and struck the fish which came
To worship the delusive flame.
Too happy they, whose pleasure sought
Extinguishes all sense and thought   50
Of the regret that pleasure leaves,
Destroying life alone, not peace!

[1822; publ. 1862]

Prefaces and Essays

THE REVOLT OF ISLAM

PREFACE

THE Poem which I now present to the world is an attempt from which I scarcely dare to expect success, and in which a writer of established fame might fail without disgrace. It is an experiment on the temper of the public mind, as to how far a thirst for a happier condition of moral and political society survives, among the enlightened and refined, the tempests which have shaken the age in which we live. I have sought to enlist the harmony of metrical language, the ethereal combinations of the fancy, the rapid and subtle transitions of human passion, all those elements which essentially compose a Poem, in the cause of a liberal and comprehensive morality; and in the view of kindling within the bosoms of my readers a virtuous enthusiasm for those doctrines of liberty and justice, that faith and hope in something good, which neither violence nor misrepresentation nor prejudice can ever totally extinguish among mankind.

For this purpose I have chosen a story of human passion in its most universal character, diversified with moving and romantic adventures, and appealing, in contempt of all artificial opinions or institutions, to the common sympathies of every human breast. I have made no attempt to recommend the motives which I would substitute for those at present governing mankind, by methodical and systematic argument. I would only awaken the feelings, so that the reader should see the beauty of true virtue, and be incited to those inquiries which have led to my moral and political creed, and that of some of the sublimest intellects in the world. The Poem therefore (with the exception of the first canto, which is purely introductory) is narrative, not didactic. It is a succession of pictures illustrating the growth and progress of individual mind aspiring after excellence, and devoted to the love of mankind; its influence in refining and making pure the most daring and uncommon impulses of the imagination, the understanding, and the senses; its impatience at 'all the oppressions which are done under the sun'; its tendency to awaken public hope, and to enlighten and improve mankind; the rapid effects of the application of that tendency;

the awakening of an immense nation from their slavery and degradation to a true sense of moral dignity and freedom; the bloodless dethronement of their oppressors, and the unveiling of the religious frauds by which they had been deluded into submission; the tranquillity of successful patriotism, and the universal toleration and benevolence of true philanthrophy; the treachery and barbarity of hired soldiers; vice not the object of punishment and hatred, but kindness and pity; the faithlessness of tyrants; the confederacy of the Rulers of the World, and the restoration of the expelled Dynasty by foreign arms; the massacre and extermination of the Patriots, and the victory of established power; the consequences of legitimate despotism, —civil war, famine, plague, superstition, and an utter extinction of the domestic affections; the judicial murder of the advocates of Liberty; the temporary triumph of oppression, that secure earnest of its final and inevitable fall; the transient nature of ignorance and error, and the eternity of genius and virtue. Such is the series of delineations of which the Poem consists. And, if the lofty passions with which it has been my scope to distinguish this story shall not excite in the reader a generous impulse, an ardent thirst for excellence, an interest profound and strong such as belongs to no meaner desires, let not the failure be imputed to a natural unfitness for human sympathy in these sublime and animating themes. It is the business of the Poet to communicate to others the pleasure and the enthusiasm arising out of those images and feelings in the vivid presence of which within his own mind consists at once his inspiration and his reward.

The panic which, like an epidemic transport, seized upon all classes of men during the excesses consequent upon the French Revolution, is gradually giving place to sanity. It has ceased to be believed that whole generations of mankind ought to consign themselves to a hopeless inheritance of ignorance and misery, because a nation of men who had been dupes and slaves for centuries were incapable of conducting themselves with the wisdom and tranquillity of freemen so soon as some of their fetters were partially loosened. That their conduct could not have been marked by any other characters than ferocity and thoughtlessness is the historical fact from which liberty derives all its recommendations, and falsehood the worst features of its deformity. There is a reflux in the tide of human things which bears the shipwrecked hopes of men into a secure haven after the storms are past. Methinks, those who now live have survived an age of despair.

The French Revolution may be considered as one of those manifestations of a general state of feeling among civilised mankind produced by a defect of correspondence between the knowledge existing in society and the improvement or gradual abolition of political institutions. The year 1788 may be assumed as the epoch of one of the most important crises produced by this feeling. The sympathies connected with that event extended to every bosom. The most generous and amiable natures were those which participated the most extensively in these sympathies. But such a degree of unmingled good was expected as it was impossible to realise. If the Revolution had been in every respect prosperous, then misrule and superstition would lose half their claims to our abhorrence, as fetters which the captive can unlock with the slightest motion of his fingers, and which do not eat with poisonous rust into the soul. The revulsion occasioned by the atrocities of the demagogues, and the re-establishment of successive tyrannies in France, was terrible, and felt in the remotest corner of the civilised world. Could they listen to the plea of reason who had groaned under the calamities of a social state according to the provisions of which one man riots in luxury whilst another famishes for want of bread? Can he who the day before was a trampled slave suddenly become liberal-minded, forbearing, and independent? This is the consequence of the habits of a state of society to be produced by resolute perseverance and indefatigable hope, and long-suffering and long-believing courage, and the systematic efforts of generations of men of intellect and virtue. Such is the lesson which experience teaches now. But, on the first reverses of hope in the progress of French liberty, the sanguine eagerness for good overleaped the solution of these questions, and for a time extinguished itself in the unexpectedness of their result. Thus, many of the most ardent and tender-hearted of the worshippers of public good have been morally ruined by what a partial glimpse of the events they deplored appeared to show as the melancholy desolation of all their cherished hopes. Hence gloom and misanthropy have become the characteristics of the age in which we live, the solace of a disappointment that unconsciously finds relief only in the wilful exaggeration of its own despair. This influence has tainted the literature of the age with the hopelessness of the minds from which it flows. Metaphysics,[1] and inquiries into moral and political science, have become little

[1] I ought to except Sir W. Drummond's *Academical Questions;* a volume of very acute and powerful metaphysical criticism.

else than vain attempts to revive exploded superstitions, or sophisms like those[1] of Mr. Malthus, calculated to lull the oppressors of mankind into a security of everlasting triumph. Our works of fiction and poetry have been overshadowed by the same infectious gloom. But mankind appear to me to be emerging from their trance. I am aware, methinks, of a slow, gradual, silent change. In that belief I have composed the following Poem.

I do not presume to enter into competition with our greatest contemporary Poets. Yet I am unwilling to tread in the footsteps of any who have preceded me. I have sought to avoid the imitation of any style of language or versification peculiar to the original minds of which it is the character; designing that, even if what I have produced be worthless, it should still be properly my own. Nor have I permitted any system relating to mere words to divert the attention of the reader, from whatever interest I may have succeeded in creating, to my own ingenuity in contriving to disgust them according to the rules of criticism. I have simply clothed my thoughts in what appeared to me the most obvious and appropriate language. A person familiar with nature, and with the most celebrated productions of the human mind, can scarcely err in following the instinct, with respect to selection of language, produced by that familiarity.

There is an education peculiarly fitted for a Poet, without which genius and sensibility can hardly fill the circle of their capacities. No education, indeed, can entitle to this appellation a dull and unobservant mind, or one, though neither dull nor unobservant, in which the channels of communication between thought and expression have been obstructed or closed. How far it is my fortune to belong to either of the latter classes I cannot know. I aspire to be something better. The circumstances of my accidental education have been favourable to this ambition. I have been familiar from boyhood with mountains and lakes and the sea, and the solitude of forests: Danger, which sports upon the brink of precipices, has been my playmate. I have trodden the glaciers of the Alps, and lived under the eye of Mont Blanc. I have been a wanderer among distant fields. I have sailed

---

[1] It is remarkable, as a symptom of the revival of public hope, that Mr. Malthus has assigned, in the later editions of his work, an indefinite dominion to moral restraint over the principle of population. This concession answers all the inferences from his doctrine unfavourable to human improvement, and reduces the *Essay on Population* to a commentary illustrative of the unanswerableness of *Political Justice*.

down mighty rivers, and seen the sun rise and set, and the stars come forth, whilst I have sailed night and day down a rapid stream among mountains. I have seen populous cities, and have watched the passions which rise and spread, and sink and change, amongst assembled multitudes of men. I have seen the theatre of the more visible ravages of tyranny and war; cities and villages reduced to scattered groups of black and roofless houses, and the naked inhabitants sitting famished upon their desolated thresholds. I have conversed with living men of genius. The poetry of ancient Greece and Rome, and modern Italy, and our own country, has been to me, like external nature, a passion and an enjoyment. Such are the sources from which the materials for the imagery of my Poem have been drawn. I have considered Poetry in its most comprehensive sense; and have read the Poets and the Historians and the Metaphysicians[1] whose writings have been accessible to me, and have looked upon the beautiful and majestic scenery of the earth, as common sources of those elements which it is the province of the Poet to embody and combine. Yet the experience and the feelings to which I refer do not in themselves constitute men Poets, but only prepares them to be the auditors of those who are. How far I shall be found to possess that more essential attribute of Poetry, the power of awakening in others sensations like those which animate my own bosom, is that which, to speak sincerely, I know not; and which, with an acquiescent and contented spirit, I expect to be taught by the effect which I shall produce upon those whom I now address.

I have avoided, as I have said before, the imitation of any contemporary style. But there must be a resemblance, which does not depend upon their own will, between all the writers of any particular age. They cannot escape from subjection to a common influence which arises out of an infinite combination of circumstances belonging to the times in which they live; though each is in a degree the author of the very influence by which his being is thus pervaded. Thus, the tragic poets of the age of Pericles; the Italian revivers of ancient learning; those mighty intellects of our own country that succeeded the Reformation, the translators of the Bible, Shakespeare, Spenser, the dramatists of

[1] In this sense there may be such a thing as perfectibility in works of fiction, notwithstanding the concession often made by the advocates of human improvement, that perfectibility is a term applicable only to science.

the reign of Elizabeth, and Lord Bacon[1]; the colder spirits of the interval that succeeded;—all resemble each other, and differ from every other in their several classes. In this view of things, Ford can no more be called the imitator of Shakespeare than Shakespeare the imitator of Ford. There were perhaps few other points of resemblance between these two men than that which the universal and inevitable influence of their age produced. And this is an influence which neither the meanest scribbler nor the sublimest genius of any era can escape; and which I have not attempted to escape.

I have adopted the stanza of Spenser (a measure inexpressibly beautiful), not because I consider it a finer model of poetical harmony than the blank verse of Shakespeare and Milton, but because in the latter there is no shelter for mediocrity; you must either succeed or fail. This perhaps an aspiring spirit should desire. But I was enticed also by the brilliancy and magnificence of sound which a mind that has been nourished upon musical thoughts can produce by a just and harmonious arrangement of the pauses of this measure. Yet there will be found some instances where I have completely failed in this attempt; and one, which I here request the reader to consider as an erratum, where there is left, most inadvertently, an alexandrine in the middle of a stanza.

But in this as in every other respect I have written fearlessly. It is the misfortune of this age that its Writers, too thoughtless of immortality, are exquisitely sensible to temporary praise or blame. They write with the fear of Reviews before their eyes. This system of criticism sprang up in that torpid interval when Poetry was not. Poetry, and the art which professes to regulate and limit its powers, cannot subsist together. Longinus could not have been the contemporary of Homer, nor Boileau of Horace. Yet this species of criticism never presumed to assert an understanding of its own: it has always, unlike true science, followed, not preceded, the opinion of mankind, and would even now bribe with worthless adulation some of our greatest Poets to impose gratuitous fetters on their own imaginations, and become unconscious accomplices in the daily murder of all genius either not so aspiring or not so fortunate as their own. I have sought therefore to write, as I believe that Homer, Shakespeare, and Milton, wrote, with an utter disregard of anonymous censure. I am certain that calumny and misrepresentation, though it may

[1] Milton stands alone in the age which he illumined.

move me to compassion, cannot disturb my peace. I shall understand the expressive silence of those sagacious enemies who dare not trust themselves to speak. I shall endeavour to extract, from the midst of insult and contempt and maledictions, those admonitions which may tend to correct whatever imperfections such censurers may discover in this my first serious appeal to the Public. If certain Critics were as clear-sighted as they are malignant, how great would be the benefit to be derived from their virulent writings! As it is, I fear I shall be malicious enough to be amused with their paltry tricks and lame invectives. Should the Public judge that my composition is worthless, I shall indeed bow before the tribunal from which Milton received his crown of immortality; and shall seek to gather, if I live, strength from that defeat, which may nerve me to some new enterprise of thought which may *not* be worthless. I cannot conceive that Lucretius, when he meditated that poem whose doctrines are yet the basis of our metaphysical knowledge, and whose eloquence has been the wonder of mankind, wrote in awe of such censure as the hired sophists of the impure and superstitious noblemen of Rome might affix to what he should produce. It was at the period when Greece was led captive, and Asia made tributary to the Republic, fast verging itself to slavery and ruin, that a multitude of Syrian captives, bigoted to the worship of their obscene Ashtaroth, and the unworthy successors of Socrates and Zeno, found there a precarious subsistence by administering, under the name of freedmen, to the vices and vanities of the great. These wretched men were skilled to plead, with a superficial but plausible set of sophisms, in favour of that contempt for virtue which is the portion of slaves, and that faith in portents, the most fatal substitute for benevolence in the imaginations of men, which, arising from the enslaved communities of the East, then first began to overwhelm the western nations in its stream. Were these the kind of men whose disapprobation the wise and lofty-minded Lucretius should have regarded with a salutary awe? The latest and perhaps the meanest of those who follow in his footsteps would disdain to hold life on such conditions.

The Poem now presented to the Public occupied little more than six months in the composition. That period has been devoted to the task with unremitting ardour and enthusiasm. I have exercised a watchful and earnest criticism on my work as it grew under my hands. I would willingly have sent it forth to the world with that perfection which long labour and revision is said to bestow. But I found that, if I should gain something in exactness by this method, I might lose much of the newness and energy of imagery and language as it flowed fresh from my mind. And, although the mere composition occupied no more than six months, the thoughts thus arranged were slowly gathered in as many years.

I trust that the reader will carefully distinguish between those opinions which have a dramatic propriety in reference to the characters which they are designed to elucidate, and such as are properly my own. The erroneous and degrading idea which men have conceived of a Supreme Being, for instance, is spoken against, but not the Supreme Being itself. The belief which some superstitious persons whom I have brought upon the stage entertain of the Deity, as injurious to the character of his benevolence, is widely different from my own. In recommending also a great and important change in the spirit which animates the social institutions of mankind, I have avoided all flattery to those violent and malignant passions of our nature which are ever on the watch to mingle with and to alloy the most beneficial innovations. There is no quarter given to Revenge, or Envy, or Prejudice. Love is celebrated everywhere as the sole law which should govern the moral world.

[1817; publ. 1818]

PROMETHEUS UNBOUND

PREFACE

THE GREEK tragic writers, in selecting as their subject any portion of their national history or mythology, employed in their treatment of it a certain arbitrary discretion. They by no means conceived themselves bound to adhere to the common interpretation or to imitate in story as in title their rivals and predecessors. Such a system would have amounted to a resignation of those claims to preference over their competitors which incited the composition. The Agamemnonian story was exhibited on the Athenian theatre with as many variations as dramas.

I have presumed to employ a similar licence. The *Prometheus*

Unbound of Æschylus supposed the reconciliation of Jupiter with his victim as the price of the disclosure of the danger threatened to his empire by the consummation of his marriage with Thetis. Thetis, according to this view of the subject, was given in marriage to Peleus, and Prometheus, by the permission of Jupiter, delivered from his captivity by Hercules. Had I framed my story on this model, I should have done no more than have attempted to restore the lost drama of Æschylus; an ambition which, if my preference to this mode of treating the subject had incited me to cherish, the recollection of the high comparison such an attempt would challenge might well abate. But, in truth, I was averse from a catastrophe so feeble as that of reconciling the Champion with the Oppressor of mankind. The moral interest of the fable, which is so powerfully sustained by the sufferings and endurance of Prometheus, would be annihilated if we could conceive of him as unsaying his high language and quailing before his successful and perfidious adversary. The only imaginary being resembling in any degree Prometheus, is Satan; and Prometheus is, in my judgement, a more poetical character than Satan, because, in addition to courage, and majesty, and firm and patient opposition to omnipotent force, he is susceptible of being described as exempt from the taints of ambition, envy, revenge, and a desire for personal aggrandisement, which, in the Hero of *Paradise Lost,* interfere with the interest. The character of Satan engenders in the mind a pernicious casuistry which leads us to weigh his faults with his wrongs, and to excuse the former because the latter exceed all measure. In the minds of those who consider that magnificent fiction with a religious feeling it engenders something worse. But Prometheus is, as it were, the type of the highest perfection of moral and intellectual nature, impelled by the purest and truest motives to the best and noblest ends.

This Poem was chiefly written upon the mountainous ruins of the Baths of Caracalla, among the flowery glades, and thickets of odoriferous blossoming trees, which are extended in ever winding labyrinths upon its immense platforms and dizzy arches suspended in the air. The bright blue sky of Rome, and the effect of the vigorous awakening spring in that divinest climate, and the new life with which it drenches the spirits even to intoxication, were the inspiration of this drama.

The imagery which I have employed will be found, in many instances, to have been drawn from the operations of the human mind, or from those external actions by which they are expressed.

This is unusual in modern poetry, although Dante and Shakespeare are full of instances of the same kind: Dante indeed more than any other poet, and with greater success. But the Greek poets, as writers to whom no resource of awakening the sympathy of their contemporaries was unknown, were in the habitual use of this power; and it is the study of their works (since a higher merit would probably be denied me) to which I am willing that my readers should impute this singularity.

One word is due in candour to the degree in which the study of contemporary writings may have tinged my composition, for such has been a topic of censure with regard to poems far more popular, and indeed more deservedly popular, than mine. It is impossible that any one who inhabits the same age with such writers as those who stand in the foremost ranks of our own, can conscientiously assure himself that his language and tone of thought may not have been modified by the study of the productions of those extraordinary intellects. It is true, that, not the spirit of their genius, but the forms in which it has manifested itself, are due less to the peculiarities of their own minds than to the peculiarity of the moral and intellectual condition of the minds among which they have been produced. Thus a number of writers possess the form, whilst they want the spirit of those whom, it is alleged, they imitate; because the former is the endowment of the age in which they live, and the latter must be the uncommunicated lightning of their own mind.

The peculiar style of intense and comprehensive imagery which distinguishes the modern literature of England, has not been, as a general power, the product of the imitation of any particular writer. The mass of capabilities remains at every period materially the same; the circumstances which awaken it to action perpetually change. If England were divided into forty republics, each equal in population and extent to Athens, there is no reason to suppose but that, under institutions not more perfect than those of Athens, each would produce philosophers and poets equal to those who (if we except Shakespeare) have never been surpassed. We owe the great writers of the golden age of our literature to that fervid awakening of the public mind which shook to dust the oldest and most oppressive form of the Christian religion. We owe Milton to the progress and development of the same spirit: the sacred Milton was, let it ever be remembered, a republican, and a bold inquirer into morals and religion. The great writers of our own age are, we have reason to suppose, the companions and forerunners of some unimagined change in our social condition or the opinions which cement it. The cloud of mind is discharging its collected lightning, and the equilibrium between institutions and opinions is now restoring, or is about to be restored.

As to imitation, poetry is a mimetic art. It creates, but it creates by combination and representation. Poetical abstractions are beautiful and new, not because the portions of which they are composed had no previous existence in the mind of man or in nature, but because the whole produced by their combination has some intelligible and beautiful analogy with those sources of emotion and thought, and with the contemporary condition of them: one great poet is a masterpiece of nature which another not only ought to study but must study. He might as wisely and as easily determine that his mind should no longer be the mirror of all that is lovely in the visible universe, as exclude from his contemplation the beautiful which exists in the writings of a great contemporary. The pretence of doing it would be a presumption in any but the greatest; the effect, even in him, would be strained, unnatural, and ineffectual. A poet is the combined product of such internal powers as modify the nature of others; and of such external influences as excite and sustain these powers; he is not one, but both. Every man's mind is, in this respect, modified by all the objects of nature and art; by every word and every suggestion which he ever admitted to act upon his consciousness; it is the mirror upon which all forms are reflected, and in which they compose one form. Poets, not otherwise than philosophers, painters, sculptors, and musicians, are, in one sense, the creators, and, in another, the creations, of their age. From this subjection the loftiest do not escape. There is a similarity between Homer and Hesiod, between Æschylus and Euripides, between Virgil and Horace, between Dante and Petrarch, between Shakespeare and Fletcher, between Dryden and Pope; each has a generic resemblance under which their specific distinctions are arranged. If this similarity be the result of imitation, I am willing to confess that I have imitated.

Let this opportunity be conceded to me of acknowledging that I have, what a Scotch philosopher characteristically terms, 'a passion for reforming the world': what passion incited him to write and publish his book, he omits to explain. For my part I had rather be damned with Plato and Lord Bacon, than go to Heaven with Paley and Malthus. But it is a mistake to suppose that I dedicate my poetical compositions solely to the direct enforcement of reform, or that I consider them in any degree as containing a reasoned system on the theory of human life. Didactic poetry is my abhorrence; nothing can be equally well expressed in prose that is not tedious and supererogatory in verse. My purpose has hitherto been simply to familiarise the highly refined imagination of the more select classes of poetical readers with beautiful idealisms of moral excellence; aware that until the mind can love, and admire, and trust, and hope, and endure, reasoned principles of moral conduct are seeds cast upon the highway of life which the unconscious passenger tramples into dust, although they would bear the harvest of his happiness. Should I live to accomplish what I purpose, that is, produce a systematical history of what appear to me to be the genuine elements of human society, let not the advocates of injustice and superstition flatter themselves that I should take Æschylus rather than Plato as my model.

The having spoken of myself with unaffected freedom will need little apology with the candid; and let the uncandid consider that they injure me less than their own hearts and minds by misrepresentation. Whatever talents a person may possess to amuse and instruct others, be they ever so inconsiderable, he is yet bound to exert them: if his attempt be ineffectual, let the punishment of an unaccomplished purpose have been sufficient; let none trouble themselves to heap the dust of oblivion upon his efforts; the pile they raise will betray his grave which might otherwise have been unknown.

[1818–1819; publ. 1820]

THE CENCI

PREFACE

A MANUSCRIPT was communicated to me during my travels in Italy, which was copied from the archives of the Cenci Palace at Rome, and contains a detailed account of the horrors which ended in the extinction of one of the noblest and richest families of that city during the Pontificate of Clement VIII, in the year 1599. The story is, that an old man having spent his life in debauchery and wickedness, conceived at length an implacable hatred towards his children; which showed itself towards one daughter under the form of an incestuous passion, aggravated by every circumstance of cruelty and violence. This daughter, after long and vain attempts to escape from what she considered a perpetual contamination both of body and mind, at length plotted with her mother-in-law and brother to murder their common tyrant. The young maiden, who was urged to this tremendous deed by an impulse which overpowered its horror, was evidently a most gentle and amiable being, a creature formed to adorn and be admired, and thus violently thwarted from her nature by the necessity of circumstance and opinion. The deed was quickly discovered, and, in spite of the most earnest prayers made to the Pope by the highest persons in Rome, the criminals were put to death. The old man had during his life repeatedly bought his pardon from the Pope for capital crimes of the most enormous and unspeakable kind, at the price of a hundred thousand crowns; the death therefore of his victims can scarcely be accounted for by the love of justice. The Pope, among other motives for severity, probably felt that whoever killed the Count Cenci deprived his treasury of a certain and copious source of revenue.[1] Such a story, if told so as to present to the reader all the feelings of those who once acted it, their hopes and fears, their confidences and misgivings, their various interests, passions, and opinions, acting upon and with each other, yet all conspiring to one tremendous end, would be as a light to make apparent some of the most dark and secret caverns of the human heart.

On my arrival at Rome I found that the story of the Cenci was a subject not to be mentioned in Italian society without awakening a deep and breathless interest; and that the feelings of the company never failed to incline to a romantic pity for the wrongs, and a passionate exculpation of the horrible deed to which they urged her, who has been mingled two centuries with the common dust. All ranks of people knew the outlines of this history, and participated in the overwhelming interest which it seems to have the magic of exciting in the human heart. I had a copy of Guido's picture of Beatrice which is preserved in the Colonna Palace, and my servant instantly recognized it as the portrait of *La Cenci*.

[1] The Papal Government formerly took the most extraordinary precautions against the publicity of facts which offer so tragical a demonstration of its own wickedness and weakness; so that the communication of the MS. had become, until very lately, a matter of some difficulty.

This national and universal interest which the story produces and has produced for two centuries and among all ranks of people in a great City, where the imagination is kept for ever active and awake, first suggested to me the conception of its fitness for a dramatic purpose. In fact it is a tragedy which has already received, from its capacity of awakening and sustaining the sympathy of men, approbation and success. Nothing remained as I imagined, but to clothe it to the apprehensions of my countrymen in such language and action as would bring it home to their hearts. The deepest and the sublimest tragic compositions, *King Lear* and the two plays in which the tale of Œdipus is told, were stories which already existed in tradition, as matters of popular belief and interest, before Shakespeare and Sophocles made them familiar to the sympathy of all succeeding generations of mankind.

This story of the Cenci is indeed eminently fearful and monstrous: anything like a dry exhibition of it on the stage would be insupportable. The person who would treat such a subject must increase the ideal, and diminish the actual horror of the events, so that the pleasure which arises from the poetry which exists in these tempestuous sufferings and crimes may mitigate the pain of the contemplation of the moral deformity from which they spring. There must also be nothing attempted to make the exhibition subservient to what is vulgarly termed a moral purpose. The highest moral purpose aimed at in the highest species of the drama, is the teaching the human heart, through its sympathies and antipathies, the knowledge of itself; in proportion to the possession of which knowledge, every human being is wise, just, sincere, tolerant and kind. If dogmas can do more, it is well: but a drama is no fit place for the enforcement of them. Undoubtedly, no person can be truly dishonoured by the act of another; and the fit return to make to the most enormous injuries is kindness and forbearance, and a resolution to convert the injurer from his dark passions by peace and love. Revenge, retaliation, atonement, are pernicious mistakes. If Beatrice had thought in this manner she would have been wiser and better; but she would never have been a tragic character: the few whom such an exhibition would have interested, could never have been sufficiently interested for a dramatic purpose, from the want of finding sympathy in their interest among the mass who surround them. It is in the restless and anatomizing casuistry with which men seek the justification of Beatrice, yet feel that she has done what needs justification; it is in the superstitious horror with which they contemplate alike her wrongs and their revenge, that the dramatic character of what she did and suffered consists.

I have endeavoured as nearly as possible to represent the characters as they probably were, and have sought to avoid the error of making them actuated by my own conceptions of right or wrong, false or true: thus under a thin veil converting names and actions of the sixteenth century into cold impersonations of my own mind. They are represented as Catholics, and as Catholics deeply tinged with religion. To a Protestant apprehension there will appear something unnatural in the earnest and perpetual sentiment of the relations between God and men which pervade the tragedy of the Cenci. It will especially be startled at the combination of an undoubting persuasion of the truth of the popular religion with a cool and determined perseverance in enormous guilt. But religion in Italy is not, as in Protestant countries, a cloak to be worn on particular days; or a passport which those who do not wish to be railed at carry with them to exhibit; or a gloomy passion for penetrating the impenetrable mysteries of our being, which terrifies its possessor at the darkness of the abyss to the brink of which it has conducted him. Religion coexists, as it were, in the mind of an Italian Catholic, with a faith in that of which all men have the most certain knowledge. It is interwoven with the whole fabric of life. It is adoration, faith, submission, penitence, blind admiration; not a rule for moral conduct. It has no necessary connection with any one virtue. The most atrocious villain may be rigidly devout, and without any shock to established faith, confess himself to be so. Religion pervades intensely the whole frame of society, and is according to the temper of the mind which it inhabits, a passion, a persuasion, an excuse, a refuge; never a check. Cenci himself built a chapel in the court of his Palace, and dedicated it to St. Thomas the Apostle, and established masses for the peace of his soul. Thus in the first scene of the fourth act Lucretia's design in exposing herself to the consequences of an expostulation with Cenci after having administered the opiate, was to induce him by a feigned tale to confess himself before death; this being esteemed by Catholics as essential to salvation; and she only relinquishes her purpose when she perceives that her perseverance would expose Beatrice to new outrages.

I have avoided with great care in writing this play the introduction of what is commonly called mere poetry, and I imagine there will scarcely be found a detached simile or a single isolated description, unless Beatrice's description of the chasm appointed for her father's murder should be judged to be of that nature.[1]

In a dramatic composition the imagery and the passion should interpenetrate one another, the former being reserved simply for the full development and illustration of the latter. Imagination is as the immortal God which should assume flesh for the redemption of mortal passion. It is thus that the most remote and the most familiar imagery may alike be fit for dramatic purposes when employed in the illustration of strong feeling, which raises what is low, and levels to the apprehension that which is lofty, casting over all the shadow of its own greatness. In other respects, I have written more carelessly; that is, without an over-fastidious and learned choice of words. In this respect I entirely agree with those modern critics who assert that in order to move men to true sympathy we must use the familiar language of men, and that our great ancestors the ancient English poets are the writers, a study of whom might incite us to do that for our own age which they have done for theirs. But it must be the real language of men in general and not that of any particular class to whose society the writer happens to belong. So much for what I have attempted; I need not be assured that success is a very different matter; particularly for one whose attention has but newly been awakened to the study of dramatic literature.

I endeavoured whilst at Rome to observe such monuments of this story as might be accessible to a stranger. The portrait of Beatrice at the Colonna Palace is admirable as a work of art: it was taken by Guido during her confinement in prison. But it is most interesting as a just representation of one of the loveliest specimens of the workmanship of Nature. There is a fixed and pale composure upon the features: she seems sad and stricken down in spirit, yet the despair thus expressed is lightened by the patience of gentleness. Her head is bound with folds of white drapery from which the yellow strings of her golden hair escape, and fall about her neck. The moulding of her face is exquisitely delicate; the eyebrows are distinct and arched: the lips have that permanent meaning of imagination and sensibility which suffering has not repressed and which it seems as if death scarcely could extinguish. Her forehead is large and clear; her eyes, which

[1] An idea in this speech was suggested by a most sublime passage in *El Purgatorio de San Patricio* of Calderon; the only plagiarism which I have intentionally committed in the whole piece.

we are told were remarkable for their vivacity, are swollen with weeping and lustreless, but beautifully tender and serene. In the whole mien there is a simplicity and dignity which, united with her exquisite loveliness and deep sorrow, are inexpressibly pathetic. Beatrice Cenci appears to have been one of those rare persons in whom energy and gentleness dwell together without destroying one another: her nature was simple and profound. The crimes and miseries in which she was an actor and a sufferer are as the mask and the mantle in which circumstances clothed her for her impersonation on the scene of the world.

The Cenci Palace is of great extent; and though in part modernized, there yet remains a vast and gloomy pile of feudal architecture in the same state as during the dreadful scenes which are the subject of this tragedy. The Palace is situated in an obscure corner of Rome, near the quarter of the Jews, and from the upper windows you see the immense ruins of Mount Palatine half hidden under their profuse overgrowth of trees. There is a court in one part of the Palace (perhaps that in which Cenci built the Chapel to St. Thomas), supported by granite columns and adorned with antique friezes of fine workmanship, and built up, according to the ancient Italian fashion, with balcony over balcony of open-work. One of the gates of the Palace formed of immense stones and leading through a passage, dark and lofty and opening into gloomy subterranean chambers, struck me particularly.

Of the Castle of Petrella, I could obtain no further information than that which is to be found in the manuscript.

[1819; publ. 1820]

HELLAS

PREFACE

THE POEM of *Hellas,* written at the suggestion of the events of the moment, is a mere improvise, and derives its interest (should it be found to possess any) solely from the intense sympathy which the Author feels with the cause he would celebrate.

The subject, in its present state, is insusceptible of being treated otherwise than lyrically, and if I have called this poem a drama from the circumstance of its being composed in dialogue, the licence is not greater than that which has been assumed by other poets who have called their productions epics, only because they have been divided into twelve or twenty-four books.

The *Persae* of Aeschylus afforded me the first model of my conception, although the decision of the glorious contest now waging in Greece being yet suspended forbids a catastrophe parallel to the return of Xerxes and the desolation of the Persians. I have, therefore, contented myself with exhibiting a series of lyric pictures, and with having wrought upon the curtain of futurity, which falls upon the unfinished scene, such figures of indistinct and visionary delineation as suggest the final triumph of the Greek cause as a portion of the cause of civilisation and social improvement.

The drama (if drama it must be called) is, however, so inartificial that I doubt whether, if recited on the Thespian waggon to an Athenian village at the Dionysiaca, it would have obtained the prize of the goat. I shall bear with equanimity any punishment, greater than the loss of such a reward, which the Aristarchi of the hour may think fit to inflict.

The only *goat-song* which I have yet attempted has, I confess, in spite of the unfavourable nature of the subject, received a greater and a more valuable portion of applause than I expected or than it deserved.

Common fame is the only authority which I can allege for the details which form the basis of the poem, and I must trespass upon the forgiveness of my readers for the display of newspaper erudition to which I have been reduced. Undoubtedly, until the conclusion of the war, it will be impossible to obtain an account of it sufficiently authentic for historical materials; but poets have their privilege, and it is unquestionable that actions of the most exalted courage have been performed by the Greeks—that they have gained more than one naval victory, and that their defeat in Wallachia was signalized by circumstances of heroism more glorious even than victory.

The apathy of the rulers of the civilised world to the astonishing circumstance of the descendants of that nation to which they owe their civilisation, rising as it were from the ashes of their ruin, is something perfectly inexplicable to a mere spectator of the shows of this mortal scene. We are all Greeks. Our laws, our literature, our religion, our arts have their root in Greece. But for Greece—Rome, the instructor, the conqueror, or the metropolis of our ancestors, would have spread no illumination with her arms, and we might still have been savages and idolaters; or, what is worse, might have arrived at such a stagnant and miserable state of social institution as China and Japan possess.

The human form and the human mind attained to a perfection in Greece which has impressed its image on those faultless productions, whose very fragments are the despair of modern art, and has propagated impulses which cannot cease, through a thousand channels of manifest or imperceptible operation, to ennoble and delight mankind until the extinction of the race.

The modern Greek is the descendant of those glorious beings whom the imagination almost refuses to figure to itself as belonging to our kind, and he inherits much of their sensibility, their rapidity of conception, their enthusiasm, and their courage. If in many instances he is degraded by moral and political slavery to the practice of the basest vices it engenders—and that below the level of ordinary degradation—let us reflect that the corruption of the best produces the worst, and that habits which subsist only in relation to a peculiar state of social institution may be expected to cease as soon as that relation is dissolved. In fact, the Greeks, since the admirable novel of *Anastasius* could have been a faithful picture of their manners, have undergone most important changes; the flower of their youth, returning to their country from the universities of Italy, Germany, and France, have communicated to their fellow-citizens the latest results of that social perfection of which their ancestors were the original source. The University of Chios contained before the breaking out of the revolution eight hundred students, and among them several Germans and Americans. The munificence and energy of many of the Greek princes and merchants, directed to the renovation of their country with a spirit and a wisdom which has few examples, is above all praise.

The English permit their own oppressors to act according to their natural sympathy with the Turkish tyrant, and to brand upon their name the indelible blot of an alliance with the enemies of domestic happiness, of Christianity and civilisation.

Russia desires to possess, not to liberate Greece; and is contented to see the Turks, its natural enemies, and the Greeks, its intended slaves, enfeeble each other until one or both fall into its net. The wise and generous policy of England would have consisted in establishing the independence of Greece, and in maintaining it both against Russia and the Turk;—but when was the oppressor generous or just?

Should the English people ever become free, they will reflect upon the part which those who presume to represent their will have played in the great drama of the revival of liberty, with feelings which it would become them to anticipate. This is the age of the war of the oppressed against the oppressors, and every one of those ringleaders of the privileged gangs of murderers and swindlers, called Sovereigns, look to each other for aid against the common enemy, and suspend their mutual jealousies in the presence of a mightier fear. Of this holy alliance all the despots of the earth are virtual members. But a new race has arisen throughout Europe, nursed in the abhorrence of the opinions which are its chains, and she will continue to produce fresh generations to accomplish that destiny which tyrants foresee and dread.

The Spanish Peninsula is already free. France is tranquil in the enjoyment of a partial exemption from the abuses which its unnatural and feeble government are vainly attempting to revive. The seed of blood and misery has been sown in Italy, and a more vigorous race is arising to go forth to the harvest. The world waits only the news of a revolution of Germany to see the tyrants who have pinnacled themselves on its supineness precipitated into the ruin from which they shall never arise. Well do these destroyers of mankind know their enemy, when they impute the insurrection in Greece to the same spirit before which they tremble throughout the rest of Europe, and that enemy well knows the power and the cunning of its opponents, and watches the moment of their approaching weakness and inevitable division to wrest the bloody sceptres from their grasp.

[1821; publ. 1822]

Essays

ON LOVE

WHAT is love? Ask him who lives, what is life? ask him who adores, what is God?

I know not the internal constitution of other men, nor even thine, whom I now address. I see that in some external attributes they resemble me, but when, misled by that appearance, I have thought to appeal to something in common, and unburthen my inmost soul to them, I have found my language misunderstood, like one in a distant and savage land. The more opportunities they have afforded me for experience, the wider has appeared the interval between us, and to a greater distance have the points of sympathy been withdrawn. With a spirit ill fitted to sustain such proof, trembling and feeble through its tenderness, I have everywhere sought sympathy and have found only repulse and disappointment.

Thou demandest what is love? It is that powerful attraction towards all that we conceive, or fear, or hope beyond ourselves, when we find within our own thoughts the chasm of an insufficient void, and seek to awaken in all things that are, a community with what we experience within ourselves. If we reason, we would be understood; if we imagine, we would that the airy children of our brain were born anew within another's; if we feel, we would that another's nerves should vibrate to our own, that the beams of their eyes should kindle at once and mix and melt into our own, that lips of motionless ice should not reply to lips quivering and burning with the heart's best blood. This is Love. This is the bond and the sanction which connects not only man with man, but with everything which exists. We are born into the world, and there is something within us which, from the instant that we live, more and more thirsts after its likeness. It is probably in correspondence with this law that the infant drains milk from the bosom of its mother; this propensity develops itself with the development of our nature. We dimly see within our intellectual nature a miniature as it were of our entire self, yet deprived of all that we condemn or despise, the ideal prototype of everything excellent or lovely that we are capable of conceiving as belonging to the nature of man. Not only the portrait of our external being, but an assemblage of the minutest particles of which our nature is composed;[1] a mirror whose surface reflects only the forms of purity and brightness; a soul within our soul that describes a circle around its proper paradise, which pain, and sorrow, and evil dare not overleap. To this we eagerly refer all sensations, thirsting that they should resemble or correspond with it. The discovery of its antitype; the meeting with an understanding capable of clearly estimating our own; an imagination which should enter into and seize upon the subtle and delicate peculiarities which we have delighted to cherish and unfold in secret; with a frame whose nerves, like the chords of two exquisite lyres, strung to the accompaniment of one delightful voice, vibrate with the vibrations of our own; and of a combination of all these in such proportion as the type within demands; this is the invisible and unattainable point to which Love tends; and to attain which, it urges forth the powers of man to arrest the faintest shadow of that, without the possession of which there is no rest nor respite to the heart over which it rules. Hence in solitude, or in that deserted state when we are surrounded by human beings, and yet they sympathize not with us, we love the flowers, the grass, and the waters, and the sky. In the motion of the very leaves of spring, in the blue air, there is then found a secret correspondence with our heart. There is eloquence in the tongueless wind, and a melody in the flowing brooks and the rustling of the reeds beside them, which by their inconceivable relation to something within the soul, awaken the spirits to a dance of breathless rapture, and bring tears of mysterious tenderness to the eyes, like the enthusiasm of patriotic success, or the voice of one beloved singing to you alone. Sterne says that, if he were in a desert, he would love some cypress. So soon as this want or power is dead, man becomes the living sepulchre of himself, and what yet survives is the mere husk of what once he was.

[1815; publ. 1840]

[1] These words are ineffectual and metaphorical. Most words are so—No help!

ON LIFE

LIFE and the world, or whatever we call that which we are and feel, is an astonishing thing. The mist of familiarity obscures from us the wonder of our being. We are struck with admiration at some of its transient modifications, but it is itself the great miracle. What are changes of empires, the wreck of dynasties, with the opinions which supported them; what is the birth and the extinction of religious and of political systems to life? What are the revolutions of the globe which we inhabit, and the operations of the elements of which it is composed, compared with life? What is the universe of stars, and suns, of which this inhabited earth is one, and their motions, and their destiny, compared with life? Life, the great miracle, we admire not, because it is so miraculous. It is well that we are thus shielded by the familiarity of what is at once so certain and so unfathomable, from an astonishment which would otherwise absorb and overawe the functions of that which is its object.

If any artist, I do not say had executed, but had merely conceived in his mind the system of the sun, and the stars, and planets, they not existing, and had painted to us in words, or upon canvas, the spectacle now afforded by the nightly cope of heaven, and illustrated it by the wisdom of astronomy, great would be our admiration. Or had he imagined the scenery of this earth, the mountains, the seas, and the rivers; the grass, and the flowers, and the variety of the forms and masses of the leaves of the woods, and the colours which attend the setting and the rising sun, and the hues of the atmosphere, turbid or serene, these things not before existing, truly we should have been astonished, and it would not have been a vain boast to have said of such a man, 'Non merita nome di creatore, se non Iddio ed il Poeta.' But now these things are looked on with little wonder, and to be conscious of them with intense delight is esteemed to be the distinguishing mark of a refined and extraordinary person. The multitude of men care not for them. It is thus with Life— that which includes all.

What is life? Thoughts and feelings arise, with or without our will, and we employ words to express them. We are born, and our birth is unremembered, and our infancy remembered but in fragments; we live on, and in living we lose the apprehension of life. How vain is it to think that words can penetrate the mystery of our being! Rightly used they may make evident our ignorance to ourselves, and this is much. For what are we? Whence do we come? and whither do we go? Is birth the commencement, is death the conclusion of our being? What is birth and death?

The most refined abstractions of logic conduct to a view of life, which, though startling to the apprehension, is, in fact, that which the habitual sense of its repeated combinations has extinguished in us. It strips, as it were, the painted curtain from this scene of things. I confess that I am one of those who am unable to refuse my assent to the conclusions of those philosophers who assert that nothing exists but as it is perceived.

It is a decision against which all our persuasions struggle, and we must be long convicted before we can be convinced that the solid universe of external things is 'such stuff as dreams are made of.' The shocking absurdities of the popular philosophy of mind and matter, its fatal consequences in morals, and their violent dogmatism concerning the source of all things, had early conducted me to materialism. This materialism is a seducing system to young and superficial minds. It allows its disciples to talk, and dispenses them from thinking. But I was discontented with such a view of things as it afforded; man is a being of high aspirations, 'looking both before and after,' whose 'thoughts wander through eternity,' disclaiming alliance with transience and decay; incapable of imagining to himself annihilation; existing but in the future and the past; being, not what he is, but what he has been and shall be. Whatever may be his true and final destination, there is a spirit within him at enmity with nothingness and dissolution. This is the character of all life and being. Each is at once the centre and the circumference; the point to which all things are referred, and the line in which all things are contained. Such contemplations as these, materialism and the popular philosophy of mind and matter alike forbid; they are only consistent with the intellectual system.

It is absurd to enter into a long recapitulation of arguments sufficiently familiar to those inquiring minds, whom alone a writer on abstruse subjects can be conceived to address. Perhaps the most clear and vigorous statement of the intellectual system is to be found in Sir William Drummond's Academical Questions.

After such an exposition, it would be idle to translate into other words what could only lose its energy and fitness by the change. Examined point by point, and word by word, the most discriminating intellects have been able to discern no train of thoughts in the process of reasoning, which does not conduct inevitably to the conclusion which has been stated.

What follows from the admission? It establishes no new truth, it gives us no additional insight into our hidden nature, neither its action nor itself. Philosophy, impatient as it may be to build, has much work yet remaining, as pioneer for the overgrowth of ages. It makes one step towards this object; it destroys error, and the roots of error. It leaves, what it is too often the duty of the reformer in political and ethical questions to leave, a vacancy. It reduces the mind to that freedom in which it would have acted, but for the misuse of words and signs, the instruments of its own creation. By signs, I would be understood in a wide sense, including what is properly meant by that term, and what I peculiarly mean. In this latter sense, almost all familiar objects are signs, standing, not for themselves, but for others, in their capacity of suggesting one thought which shall lead to a train of thoughts. Our whole life is thus an education of error.

Let us recollect our sensations as children. What a distinct and intense apprehension had we of the world and of ourselves! Many of the circumstances of social life were then important to us which are now no longer so. But that is not the point of comparison on which I mean to insist. We less habitually distinguished all that we saw and felt, from ourselves. They seemed as it were to constitute one mass. There are some persons who, in this respect, are always children. Those who are subject to the state called reverie, feel as if their nature were dissolved into the surrounding universe, or as if the surrounding universe were absorbed into their being. They are conscious of no distinction. And these are states which precede, or accompany, or follow an unusually intense and vivid apprehension of life. As men grow up this power commonly decays, and they become mechanical and habitual agents. Thus feelings and then reasonings are the combined result of a multitude of entangled thoughts, and of a series of what are called impressions, planted by reiteration.

The view of life presented by the most refined deductions of the intellectual philosophy, is that of unity. Nothing exists but as it is perceived. The difference is merely nominal between those two classes of thought, which are vulgarly distinguished by the names of ideas and of external objects. Pursuing the same thread of reasoning, the existence of distinct individual minds, similar to that which is employed in now questioning its own nature, is likewise found to be a delusion. The words *I, you, they,* are not signs of any actual difference subsisting between the assemblage of thoughts thus indicated, but are merely marks employed to denote the different modifications of the one mind.

Let it not be supposed that this doctrine conducts to the monstrous presumption that I, the person who now write and think, am that one mind. I am but a portion of it. The words *I,* and *you,* and *they,* are grammatical devices invented simply for arrangement, and totally devoid of the intense and exclusive sense usually attached to them. It is difficult to find terms adequate to express so subtle a conception as that to which the Intellectual Philosophy has conducted us. We are on that verge where words abandon us, and what wonder if we grow dizzy to look down the dark abyss of how little we know.

The relations of *things* remain unchanged, by whatever system. By the word *things* is to be understood any object of thought, that is any thought upon which any other thought is employed, with an apprehension of distinction. The relations of these remain unchanged; and such is the material of our knowledge.

What is the cause of life? that is, how was it produced, or what agencies distinct from life have acted or act upon life? All recorded generations of mankind have weariedly busied themselves in inventing answers to this question; and the result has been,—Religion. Yet, that the basis of all things cannot be, as the popular philosophy alleges, mind, is sufficiently evident. Mind, as far as we have any experience of its properties, and beyond that experience how vain is argument! cannot create, it can only perceive. It is said also to be the cause. But cause is only a word expressing a certain state of the human mind with regard to the manner in which two thoughts are apprehended to be related to each other. If any one desires to know how unsatisfactorily the popular philosophy employs itself upon this great question, they need only impartially reflect upon the manner in which thoughts develop themselves in their minds. It is infinitely improbable that the cause of mind, that is, of existence, is similar to mind.

[1815; publ. 1840]

ON A FUTURE STATE

It has been the persuasion of an immense majority of human beings in all ages and nations that we continue to live after death,—that apparent termination of all the functions of sensitive and intellectual existence. Nor has mankind been contented with supposing that species of existence which some philosophers have asserted; namely, the resolution of the component parts of the mechanism of a living being into its elements, and the impossibility of the minutest particle of these sustaining the smallest diminution. They have clung to the idea that sensibility and thought, which they have distinguished from the objects of it, under the several names of spirit and matter, is, in its own nature, less susceptible of division and decay, and that, when the body is resolved into its elements, the principle which animated it will remain perpetual and unchanged. Some philosophers—and those to whom we are indebted for the most stupendous discoveries in physical science, suppose, on the other hand, that intelligence is the mere result of certain combinations among the particles of its objects; and those among them who believe that we live after death, recur to the interposition of a supernatural power, which shall overcome the tendency inherent in all material combinations, to dissipate and be absorbed into other forms.

Let us trace the reasonings which in one and the other have conducted to these two opinions, and endeavour to discover what we ought to think on a question of such momentous interest. Let us analyse the ideas and feelings which constitute the contending beliefs, and watchfully establish a discrimination between words and thoughts. Let us bring the question to the test of experience and fact; and ask ourselves, considering our nature in its entire extent, what light we derive from a sustained and comprehensive view of its component parts, which may enable us to assert, with certainty, that we do or do not live after death.

The examination of this subject requires that it should be stript of all those accessory topics which adhere to it in the common opinion of men. The existence of a God, and a future state of rewards and punishments, are totally foreign to the subject. If it be proved that the world is ruled by a Divine Power, no inference necessarily can be drawn from that circumstance in favour of a future state. It has been asserted, indeed, that as goodness and justice are to be numbered among the attributes of the Deity, He will undoubtedly compensate the virtuous who suffer during life, and that He will make every sensitive being, who does not deserve punishment, happy for ever. But this view of the subject, which it would be tedious as well as superfluous to develop and expose, satisfies no person, and cuts the knot which we now seek to untie. Moreover, should it be proved, on the other hand, that the mysterious principle which regulates the proceedings of the universe, is neither intelligent nor sensitive, yet it is not an inconsistency to suppose at the same time, that the animating power survives the body which it has animated, by laws as independent of any supernatural agent as those through which it first became united with it. Nor, if a future state be clearly proved, does it follow that it will be a state of punishment or reward.

By the word death, we express that condition in which natures resembling ourselves apparently cease to be that which they were. We no longer hear them speak, nor see them move. If they have sensations and apprehensions, we no longer participate in them. We know no more than that those external organs, and all that fine texture of material frame, without which we have no experience that life or thought can subsist, are dissolved and scattered abroad. The body is placed under the earth, and after a certain period there remains no vestige even of its form. This is that contemplation of inexhaustible melancholy, whose shadow eclipses the brightness of the world. The common observer is struck with dejection at the spectacle. He contends in vain against the persuasion of the grave, that the dead indeed cease to be. The corpse at his feet is prophetic of his own destiny. Those who have preceded him, and whose voice was delightful to his ear; whose touch met his like sweet and subtle fire; whose aspect spread a visionary light upon his path—these he cannot meet again. The organs of sense are destroyed, and the intellectual operations dependent on them have perished with their sources. How can a corpse see or feel? its eyes are eaten out, and its heart is black and without motion. What intercourse can two heaps of putrid clay and crumbling bones hold together? When you can discover where the fresh colours of the faded flower abide, or the music of the broken lyre, seek life among the dead. Such are the anxious and fearful contemplations of the common observer, though the popular religion often prevents him from confessing them even to himself.

The natural philosopher, in addition to the sensations common to all men inspired by the event of death, believes that he sees with more certainty that it is attended with the annihilation of sentiment and thought. He observes the mental powers increase and fade with those of the body, and even accommodate themselves to the most transitory changes of our physical nature. Sleep suspends many of the faculties of the vital and intellectual principle; drunkenness and disease will either temporarily or permanently derange them. Madness or idiotcy may utterly extinguish the most excellent and delicate of those powers. In old age the mind gradually withers; and as it grew and was strengthened with the body, so does it together with the body sink into decrepitude. Assuredly these are convincing evidences that so soon as the organs of the body are subjected to the laws of inanimate matter, sensation, and perception, and apprehension, are at an end. It is probable that what we call thought is not an actual being, but no more than the relation between certain parts of that infinitely varied mass, of which the rest of the universe is composed, and which ceases to exist so soon as those parts change their position with regard to each other. Thus colour, and sound, and taste, and odour exist only relatively. But let thought be considered as some peculiar substance, which permeates, and is the cause of, the animation of living beings. Why should that substance be assumed to be something essentially distinct from all others, and exempt from subjection to those laws from which no other substance is exempt? It differs, indeed, from all other substances, as electricity, and light, and magnetism, and the constituent parts of air and earth, severally differ from all others. Each of these is subject to change and to decay, and to conversion into other forms. Yet the difference between light and earth is scarcely greater than that which exists between life, or thought, and fire. The difference between the two former was never alleged as an argument for the eternal permanence of either, in that form under which they first might offer themselves to our notice. Why should the difference between the two latter substances be an argument for the prolongation of the existence of one and not the other, when the existence of both has arrived at their apparent termination? To say that fire exists without manifesting any of the properties of fire, such as light, heat, &c., or that the principle of life exists without consciousness, or memory, or desire, or motive, is to resign, by an awkward distortion of language, the affirmative of the dispute. To say that the principle of life *may* exist in distribution among various forms, is to assert what cannot be proved to be either true or false, but which, were it true, annihilates all hope of existence after death, in any sense in which that event can belong to the hopes and fears of men. Suppose, however, that the intellectual and vital principle differs in the most marked and essential manner from all other known substances; that they have all some resemblance between themselves which it in no degree participates. In what manner can this concession be made an argument for its imperishability? All that we see or know perishes and is changed. Life and thought differ indeed from everything else. But that it survives that period, beyond which we have no experience of its existence, such distinction and dissimilarity affords no shadow of proof, and nothing but our own desires could have led us to conjecture or imagine.

Have we existed before birth? It is difficult to conceive the possibility of this. There is, in the generative principle of each animal and plant, a power which converts the substances by which it is surrounded into a substance homogeneous with itself. That is, the relations between certain elementary particles of matter undergo a change, and submit to new combinations. For when we use the words *principle, power, cause,* &c., we mean to express no real being, but only to class under those terms a certain series of co-existing phenomena; but let it be supposed that this principle is a certain substance which escapes the observation of the chemist and anatomist. It certainly *may be;* though it is sufficiently unphilosophical to allege the possibility of an opinion as a proof of its truth. Does it see, hear, feel, before its combination with those organs on which sensation depends? Does it reason, imagine, apprehend, without those ideas which sensation alone can communicate? If we have not existed before birth; if, at the period when the parts of our nature on which thought and life depend, seem to be woven together, they are woven together; if there are no reasons to suppose that we have existed before that period at which our existence apparently commences, then there are no grounds for supposition that we shall continue to exist after our existence has apparently ceased. So far as thought and life is concerned, the same will take place with regard to us, individually considered, after death, as had place before our birth.

It is said that it is possible that we should continue to exist in some mode totally inconceivable to us at present. This is a most unreasonable presumption. It casts on the adherents of annihilation the burthen of proving the negative of a question, the affirmative of which is not supported by a single argument, and which, by its very nature, lies beyond the experience of the human understanding. It is sufficiently easy, indeed, to form any proposition, concerning which we are ignorant, just not so absurd as not to be contradictory in itself, and defy refutation. The possibility of whatever enters into the wildest imagination to conceive is thus triumphantly vindicated. But it is enough that such assertions should be either contradictory to the known laws of nature, or exceed the limits of our experience, that their fallacy or irrelevancy to our consideration should be demonstrated. They persuade, indeed, only those who desire to be persuaded.

This desire to be for ever as we are; the reluctance to a violent and unexperienced change, which is common to all the animated and inanimate combinations of the universe, is, indeed, the secret persuasion which has given birth to the opinions of a future state.

[1815; publ. 1840]

ON THE PUNISHMENT OF DEATH

A FRAGMENT

THE first law which it becomes a Reformer to propose and support, at the approach of a period of great political change, is the abolition of the punishment of death.

It is sufficiently clear that revenge, retaliation, atonement, expiation, are rules and motives, so far from deserving a place in any enlightened system of political life, that they are the chief sources of a prodigious class of miseries in the domestic circles of society. It is clear that however the spirit of legislation may appear to frame institutions upon more philosophical maxims, it has hitherto, in those cases which are termed criminal, done little more than palliate the spirit, by gratifying a portion of it; and afforded a compromise between that which is best;—the inflicting of no evil upon a sensitive being, without a decisively beneficial result in which he should at least participate;—and that which is worst; that he should be put to torture for the amusement of those whom he may have injured, or may seem to have injured.

Omitting these remoter considerations, let us inquire what *Death* is; that punishment which is applied as a measure of transgressions of indefinite shades of distinction, so soon as they shall have passed that degree and colour of enormity, with which it is supposed no inferior infliction is commensurate.

And first, whether death is good or evil, a punishment or a reward, or whether it be wholly indifferent, no man can take upon himself to assert. That that within us which thinks and feels, continues to think and feel after the dissolution of the body, has been the almost universal opinion of mankind, and the accurate philosophy of what I may be permitted to term the modern Academy, by showing the prodigious depth and extent of our ignorance respecting the causes and nature of sensation, renders probable the affirmative of a proposition, the negative of which it is so difficult to conceive, and the popular arguments against which, derived from what is called the atomic system, are proved to be applicable only to the relation which one object bears to another, as apprehended by the mind, and not to existence itself, or the nature of that essence which is the medium and receptacle of objects.

The popular system of religion suggests the idea that the mind, after death, will be painfully or pleasurably affected according to its determinations during life. However ridiculous and pernicious we must admit the vulgar accessories of this creed to be, there is a certain analogy, not wholly absurd, between the consequences resulting to an individual during life from the virtuous or vicious, prudent or imprudent, conduct of his external actions, to those consequences which are conjectured to ensue from the discipline and order of his internal thoughts, as affecting his condition in a future state. They omit, indeed, to calculate upon the accidents of disease, and temperament, and organization, and circumstance, together with the multitude of independent agencies which affect the opinions, the conduct, and the happiness of individuals, and produce determinations of the will, and modify the judgement, so as to produce effects the most opposite in natures considerably similar. These are those operations in the order of the whole of nature, tending, we are prone to believe, to some definite mighty end, to which the agencies of our peculiar nature are subordinate; nor is there any reason to suppose, that in a future state they should become suddenly exempt from that subordination. The philosopher is unable to determine whether our existence in a previous state has affected our present condition, and abstains from deciding whether our present condition will affect us in that which may be future. That, if we continue to exist, the manner of our existence will be such as no inferences nor conjectures, afforded by a consideration of our earthly experience, can elucidate, is sufficiently obvious. The opinion that the vital principle within us, in whatever mode it may continue to exist, must lose that consciousness of definite and individual being which now characterizes it, and become a unit in the vast sum of action and of thought which disposes and animates the universe, and is called God, seems to belong to that class of opinion which has been designated as indifferent.

To compel a person to know all that can be known by the dead, concerning that which the living fear, hope, or forget; to plunge him into the pleasure or pain which there awaits him; to punish or reward him in a manner and in a degree incalculable and incomprehensible by us; to disrobe him at once from all that intertexture of good and evil with which Nature seems to have clothed every form of individual existence, is to inflict on him the doom of death.

A certain degree of pain and terror usually accompany the infliction of death. This degree is infinitely varied by the infinite variety in the temperament and opinions of the sufferers. As a measure of punishment, strictly so considered, and as an exhibition, which, by its known effects on the sensibility of the sufferer, is intended to intimidate the spectators from incurring a similar liability, it is singularly inadequate.

Firstly,—Persons of energetic character, in whom, as in men who suffer for political crimes, there is a large mixture of enterprise, and fortitude, and disinterestedness, and the elements, though misguided and disarranged, by which the strength and happiness of a nation might have been cemented, die in such a manner, as to make death appear not evil, but good. The death of what is called a traitor, that is, a person who, from whatever motive, would abolish the government of the day, is as often a triumphant exhibition of suffering virtue, as the warning of a culprit. The multitude, instead of departing with a panic-stricken approbation of the laws which exhibited such a spectacle, are inspired with pity, admiration and sympathy; and the most generous among them feel an emulation to be the authors of such flattering emotions, as they experience stirring in their bosoms.

Impressed by what they see and feel, they make no distinction between the motives which incited the criminals to the actions for which they suffer, or the heroic courage with which they turned into good that which their judges awarded to them as evil, or the purpose itself of those actions, though that purpose may happen to be eminently pernicious. The laws in this case lose that sympathy, which it ought to be their chief object to secure, and in a participation of which consists their chief strength in maintaining those sanctions by which the parts of the social union are bound together, so as to produce, as nearly as possible, the ends for which it is instituted.

Secondly,—Persons of energetic character, in communities not modelled with philosophical skill to turn all the energies which they contain to the purposes of common good, are prone also to fall into the temptation of undertaking, and are peculiarly fitted for despising the perils attendant upon consummating, the most enormous crimes. Murder, rapes, extensive schemes of plunder, are the actions of persons belonging to this class; and death is the penalty of conviction. But the coarseness of organization, peculiar to men capable of committing acts wholly selfish, is usually found to be associated with a proportionate insensibility to fear or pain. Their sufferings communicate to those of the spectators, who may be liable to the commission of similar crimes, a sense of the lightness of that event, when closely examined, which, at a distance, as uneducated persons are accustomed to do, probably they regarded with horror. But a great majority of the spectators are so bound up in the interests and the habits of social union that no temptation would be sufficiently strong to induce them to a commission of the enormities to which this penalty is assigned. The more powerful, and the richer among them,—and a numerous class of little tradesmen are richer and more powerful than those who are employed by them, and the employer, in general, bears this relation to the employed,—regard their own wrongs as, in some degree, avenged, and their own rights secured by this punishment, inflicted as the penalty of whatever crime. In cases of murder or mutilation, this feeling is almost universal. In those, therefore, whom this exhibition does not awaken to the sympathy which extenuates crime and discredits the law which restrains it, it produces feelings more directly at war with the genuine purposes of political society. It excites those emotions which it is the chief object of civilization to extinguish for ever, and in the extinction of which alone there can be any hope of better institutions than those under which men now misgovern one another. Men feel that their revenge is gratified, and that their security is established by the extinction and the sufferings of beings, in most respects resembling themselves; and their daily occupations constraining them to a precise form in all their thoughts, they come to connect inseparably the idea of their own advantage with that of the death and torture of others. It is manifest that the object of sane polity is directly the reverse; and that laws founded upon reason, should accustom the gross vulgar to associate their ideas of security and of interest with the reformation, and the strict restraint, for that purpose alone, of those who might invade it.

The passion of revenge is originally nothing more than an habitual perception of the ideas of the sufferings of the person who inflicts an injury, as connected, as they are in a savage state, or in such portions of society as are yet undisciplined to civilization, with security that that injury will not be repeated in future. This feeling, engrafted upon superstition and confirmed by habit, at last loses sight of the only object for which it may be supposed to have been implanted, and becomes a passion and a duty to be pursued and fulfilled, even to the destruction of those ends to which it originally tended. The other passions, both good and evil, Avarice, Remorse, Love, Patriotism, present a similar appearance; and to this principle of the mind over-shooting the mark at which it aims, we owe all that is eminently base or excellent in human nature; in providing for the nutriment or the extinction of which, consists the true art of the legislator.[1]

[1] The savage and the illiterate are but faintly aware of the distinction between the future and the past; they make actions belonging to periods so distinct, the subjects of similar feelings; they live only in the present, or in the past, as it is present. It is in this that the philosopher excels one of the many; it is this which distinguishes the doctrine of philosophic necessity from fatalism; and that determination of the will, by which it is the active source of future events, from that liberty or indifference, to which the abstract liability of irremediable actions ·is attached, according to the notions of the vulgar.

This is the source of the erroneous excesses of Remorse and Revenge; the one extending itself over the future, and the other over the past; provinces in which their suggestions can only be the sources of evil. The purpose of a resolution to act more wisely and virtuously in future, and the sense of a necessity of caution in repressing an enemy, are the sources from which the enormous superstitions implied in the words cited have arisen.

Nothing is more clear than that the infliction of punishment in general, in a degree which the reformation and the restraint of those who transgress the laws does not render indispensable, and none more than death, confirms all the inhuman and unsocial impulses of men. It is almost a proverbial remark, that those nations in which the penal code has been particularly mild, have been distinguished from all others by the rarity of crime. But the example is to be admitted to be equivocal. A more decisive argument is afforded by a consideration of the universal connexion of ferocity of manners, and a contempt of social ties, with the contempt of human life. Governments which derive their institutions from the existence of circumstances of barbarism and violence, with some rare exceptions perhaps, are bloody in proportion as they are despotic, and form the manners of their subjects to a sympathy with their own spirit.

The spectators who feel no abhorrence at a public execution, but rather a self-applauding superiority, and a sense of gratified indignation, are surely excited to the most inauspicious emotions. The first reflection of such a one is the sense of his own internal and actual worth, as preferable to that of the victim, whom circumstances have led to destruction. The meanest wretch is impressed with a sense of his own comparative merit. He is one of those on whom the tower of Siloam fell not—he is such a one as Jesus Christ found not in all Samaria, who, in his own soul, throws the first stone at the woman taken in adultery. The popular religion of the country takes its designation from that illustrious person whose beautiful sentiment I have quoted. Any one who has stript from the doctrines of this person the veil of familiarity, will perceive how adverse their spirit is to feelings of this nature.

[1815; publ. 1840]

SPECULATIONS ON METAPHYSICS

I—THE MIND

It is an axiom in mental philosophy, that we can think of nothing which we have not perceived. When I say that we can think of nothing, I mean, we can imagine nothing, we can reason of nothing, we can remember nothing, we can foresee nothing. The most astonishing combinations of poetry, the subtlest deductions of logic and mathematics, are no other than combinations which the intellect makes of sensations according to its own laws. A catalogue of all the thoughts of the mind, and of all their possible modifications, is a cyclopedic history of the universe.

But, it will be objected, the inhabitants of the various planets of this and other solar systems; and the existence of a Power bearing the same relation to all that we perceive and are, as what we call a cause does to what we call effect, were never subjects of sensation, and yet the laws of mind almost universally suggest, according to the various disposition of each, a conjecture, a persuasion, or a conviction of their existence. The reply is simple; these thoughts are also to be included in the catalogue of existence; they are modes in which thoughts are combined; the objection only adds force to the conclusion, that beyond the limits of perception and thought nothing can exist.

Thoughts, or ideas, or notions, call them what you will, differ from each other, not in kind, but in force. It has commonly been supposed that those distinct thoughts which affect a number of persons, at regular intervals, during the passage of a multitude of other thoughts, which are called *real* or *external objects*, are totally different in kind from those which affect only a few persons, and which recur at irregular intervals, and are usually more obscure and indistinct, such as hallucinations, dreams, and the ideas of madness. No essential distinction between any one of these ideas, or any class of them, is founded on a correct observation of the nature of things, but merely on a consideration of what thoughts are most invariably subservient to the security and happiness of life; and if nothing more were expressed by the distinction, the philosopher might safely accommodate his language to that of the vulgar. But they pretend to assert an essential difference, which has no foundation in truth, and which suggests a narrow and false conception of universal nature, the parent of the most fatal errors in speculation. A specific difference between every thought of the mind, is, indeed, a necessary consequence of that law by which it perceives diversity and number; but a generic and essential difference is wholly arbitrary. The principle of the agreement and similarity of all thoughts, is, that they are all thoughts; the principle of their disagreement consists in the variety and irregularity of the occasions on which they arise in the mind. That in which they agree, to that in which they differ, is as everything to nothing. Important distinctions, of various degrees of force, indeed, are to be established between them, if they were, as they may be, subjects of ethical and economical discussion; but that is a question altogether distinct.

By considering all knowledge as bounded by perception, whose operations may be indefinitely combined, we arrive at a conception of Nature inexpressibly more magnificent, simple and true, than accords with the ordinary systems of complicated and partial consideration. Nor does a contemplation of the universe, in this comprehensive and synthetical view, exclude the subtlest analysis of its modifications and parts.

A scale might be formed, graduated according to the degrees of a combined ratio of intensity, duration, connexion, periods of recurrence, and utility, which would be the standard, according to which all ideas might be measured, and an uninterrupted chain of nicely shadowed distinctions would be observed, from the faintest impression on the senses, to the most distinct combination of those impressions; from the simplest of those combinations, to that mass of knowledge which, including our own nature, constitutes what we call the universe.

We are intuitively conscious of our own existence, and of that connexion in the train of our successive ideas, which we term our identity. We are conscious also of the existence of other minds; but not intuitively. Our evidence, with respect to the existence of other minds, is founded upon a very complicated relation of ideas, which it is foreign to the purpose of this treatise to anatomize. The basis of this relation is, undoubtedly, a periodical recurrence of masses of ideas, which our voluntary determinations have, in one peculiar direction, no power to circumscribe or to arrest, and against the recurrence of which they can only imperfectly provide. The irresistible laws of thought constrain us to believe that the precise limits of our actual ideas are not the actual limits of possible ideas; the law, according to which these deductions are drawn, is called analogy; and this is the foundation of all our inferences, from one idea to another, inasmuch as they resemble each other.

We see trees, houses, fields, living beings in our own shape, and in shapes more or less analogous to our own. These are perpetually changing the mode of their existence relatively to us. To express the varieties of these modes, we say, *we move, they move;* and as this motion is continual, though not uniform, we express our conception of the diversities of its course by—*it has been, it is, it shall be.* These diversities are events or objects, and are essential, considered relatively to human identity, for the existence of the human mind. For if the inequalities, produced by what has been termed the operations of the external universe, were levelled by the perception of our being, uniting and filling up their interstices, motion and mensuration, and time, and space; the elements of the human mind being thus abstracted, sensation and imagination cease. Mind cannot be considered pure.

II—WHAT METAPHYSICS ARE. ERRORS IN THE USUAL METHODS OF CONSIDERING THEM

We do not attend sufficiently to what passes within ourselves. We combine words, combined a thousand times before. In our minds we assume entire opinions; and in the expression of those opinions, entire phrases, when we would philosophize. Our whole style of expression and sentiment is infected with the tritest plagiarisms. Our words are dead, our thoughts are cold and borrowed.

Let us contemplate facts; let us, in the great study of ourselves, resolutely compel the mind to a rigid consideration of itself. We are not content with conjecture, and inductions, and syllogisms, in sciences regarding external objects. As in these, let us also, in considering the phenomena of mind, severely collect those facts which cannot be disputed. Metaphysics will thus possess this conspicuous advantage over every other science, that each student, by attentively referring to his own mind, may ascertain the authorities upon which any assertions regarding it are supported. There can thus be no deception, we ourselves being the depositaries of the evidence of the subject which we consider.

Metaphysics may be defined as an inquiry concerning those things belonging to, or connected with, the internal nature of man.

It is said that mind produces motion; and it might as well have been said, that motion produces mind.

III—DIFFICULTY OF ANALYSING THE HUMAN MIND

If it were possible that a person should give a faithful history of his being, from the earliest epochs of his recollection, a picture would be presented such as the world has never contemplated before. A mirror would be held up to all men in which they might behold their own recollections, and, in dim perspective, their shadowy hopes and fears,—all that they dare not, or that, daring and desiring, they could not expose to the open eyes of day. But thought can with difficulty visit the intricate and winding chambers which it inhabits. It is like a river whose rapid and perpetual stream flows outwards;—like one in dread who speeds through the recesses of some haunted pile, and dares not look behind. The caverns of the mind are obscure, and shadowy; or pervaded with a lustre, beautifully bright indeed, but shining not beyond their portals. If it were possible to be where we have been, vitally and indeed—if, at the moment of our presence there, we could define the results of our experience,— if the passage from sensation to reflection—from a state of passive perception to voluntary contemplation, were not so dizzying and so tumultuous, this attempt would be less difficult.

IV—HOW THE ANALYSIS SHOULD BE CARRIED ON

MOST of the errors of philosophers have arisen from considering the human being in a point of view too detailed and circumscribed. He is not a moral, and an intellectual,—but also, and pre-eminently, an imaginative being. His own mind is his law; his own mind is all things to him. If we would arrive at any knowledge which should be serviceable from the practical conclusions to which it leads, we ought to consider the mind of man and the universe as the great whole on which to exercise our speculations. Here, above all, verbal disputes ought to be laid aside, though this has long been their chosen field of battle. It imports little to inquire whether thought be distinct from the objects of thought. The use of the words *external* and *internal,* as applied to the establishment of this distinction, has been the symbol and the source of much dispute. This is merely an affair of words, and as the dispute deserves, to say, that when speaking of the objects of thought, we indeed only describe one of the forms of thought—or that, speaking of thought, we only apprehend one of the operations of the universal system of beings.

V—CATALOGUE OF THE PHENOMENA OF DREAMS, AS CONNECTING SLEEPING AND WAKING

1. LET us reflect on our infancy, and give as faithfully as possible a relation of the events of sleep.

And first I am bound to present a faithful picture of my own peculiar nature relatively to sleep. I do not doubt that were every individual to imitate me, it would be found that among many circumstances peculiar to their individual nature, a sufficiently general resemblance would be found to prove the connexion existing between those peculiarities and the most universal phenomena. I shall employ caution, indeed, as to the facts which I state, that they contain nothing false or exaggerated. But they contain no more than certain elucidations of my own nature; concerning the degree in which it resembles, or differs from, that of others, I am by no means accurately aware. It is sufficient, however, to caution the reader against drawing general inferences from particular instances.

I omit the general instances of delusion in fever or delirium, as well as mere dreams considered in themselves. A delineation of this subject, however inexhaustible and interesting, is to be passed over.

What is the connexion of sleeping and of waking?

2. I distinctly remember dreaming three several times, between intervals of two or more years, the same precise dream. It was not so much what is ordinarily called a dream; the single image, unconnected with all other images, of a youth who was educated at the same school with myself, presented itself in sleep. Even now, after the lapse of many years, I can never hear the name of this youth, without the three places where I dreamed of him presenting themselves distinctly to my mind.

3. In dreams, images acquire associations peculiar to dreaming; so that the idea of a particular house, when it recurs a second time in dreams, will have relation with the idea of the same house, in the first time, of a nature entirely different from that which the house excites, when seen or thought of in relation to waking ideas.

4. I have beheld scenes, with the intimate and unaccountable connexion of which with the obscure parts of my own nature, I have been irresistibly impressed. I have beheld a scene which has produced no unusual effect on my thoughts. After the lapse of many years I have dreamed of this scene. It has hung on my memory, it has haunted my thoughts, at intervals, with the pertinacity of an object connected with human affections. I have visited this scene again. Neither the dream could be dissociated from the landscape, nor the landscape from the dream, nor feelings, such as neither singly could have awakened, from both.

But the most remarkable event of this nature, which ever occurred to me, happened five years ago at Oxford. I was walking with a friend, in the neighbourhood of that city, engaged in earnest and interesting conversation. We suddenly turned the corner of a lane, and the view, which its high banks and hedges had concealed, presented itself. The view consisted of a windmill, standing in one among many plashy meadows, inclosed with stone walls; the irregular and broken ground, between the wall and the road on which we stood; a long low hill behind the windmill, and a grey covering of uniform cloud spread over the evening sky. It was that season when the last leaf had just fallen from the scant and stunted ash. The scene surely was a common scene; the season and the hour little calculated to kindle lawless thought; it was a tame uninteresting assemblage of objects, such as would drive the imagination for refuge in serious and sober talk, to the evening fireside, and the dessert of winter fruits and wine. The effect which it produced on me was not such as could have been expected. I suddenly remembered to have seen that exact scene in some dream of long[1]——

[1815; publ. 1840]

SPECULATIONS ON MORALS

I—PLAN OF A TREATISE ON MORALS

THAT great science which regards nature and the operations of the human mind, is popularly divided into Morals and Metaphysics. The latter relates to a just classification, and the assignment of distinct names to its ideas; the former regards simply the determination of that arrangement of them which produces the greatest and most solid happiness. It is admitted that a virtuous or moral action, is that action which, when considered in all its accessories and consequences, is fitted to produce the highest pleasure to the greatest number of sensitive beings. The laws according to which all pleasure, since it cannot be equally felt by all sensitive beings, ought to be distributed by a voluntary agent, are reserved for a separate chapter.

The design of this little treatise is restricted to the development of the elementary principles of morals. As far as regards

[1] Here I was obliged to leave off, overcome by thrilling horror.

that purpose, metaphysical science will be treated merely so far as a source of negative truth; whilst morality will be considered as a science, respecting which we can arrive at positive conclusions.

The misguided imaginations of men have rendered the ascertaining of what *is not true,* the principal direct service which metaphysical science can bestow upon moral science. Moral science itself is the doctrine of the voluntary actions of man, as a sentient and social being. These actions depend on the thoughts in his mind. But there is a mass of popular opinion, from which the most enlightened persons are seldom wholly free, into the truth or falsehood of which it is incumbent on us to inquire, before we can arrive at any firm conclusions as to the conduct which we ought to pursue in the regulation of our own minds, or towards our fellow beings; or before we can ascertain the elementary laws, according to which these thoughts, from which these actions flow, are originally combined.

The object of the forms according to which human society is administered, is the happiness of the individuals composing the communities which they regard, and these forms are perfect or imperfect in proportion to the degree in which they promote this end.

This object is not merely the quantity of happiness enjoyed by individuals as sensitive beings, but the mode in which it should be distributed among them as social beings. It is not enough, if such a coincidence can be conceived as possible, that one person or class of persons should enjoy the highest happiness, whilst another is suffering a disproportionate degree of misery. It is necessary that the happiness produced by the common efforts, and preserved by the common care, should be distributed according to the just claims of each individual; if not, although the quantity produced should be the same, the end of society would remain unfulfilled. The object is in a compound proportion to the quantity of happiness produced, and the correspondence of the mode in which it is distributed, to the elementary feelings of man as a social being.

The disposition in an individual to promote this object is called virtue; and the two constituent parts of virtue, benevolence and justice, are correlative with these two great portions of the only true object of all voluntary actions of a human being. Benevolence is the desire to be the author of good, and justice the apprehension of the manner in which good ought to be done.

Justice and benevolence result from the elementary laws of the human mind.

CHAPTER I

ON THE NATURE OF VIRTUE

SECT. 1. General View of the Nature and Objects of Virtue.—2. The Origin and Basis of Virtue, as founded on the Elementary Principles of Mind.—3. The Laws which flow from the nature of Mind regulating the application of those principles to human actions.— 4. Virtue, a possible attribute of man.

WE exist in the midst of a multitude of beings like ourselves, upon whose happiness most of our actions exert some obvious and decisive influence.

The regulation of this influence is the object of moral science.

We know that we are susceptible of receiving painful or pleasurable impressions of greater or less intensity and duration. That is called good which produces pleasure; that is called evil which produces pain. These are general names, applicable to every class of causes, from which an overbalance of pain or pleasure may result. But when a human being is the active instrument of generating or diffusing happiness, the principle through which it is most effectually instrumental to that purpose, is called virtue. And benevolence, or the desire to be the author of good, united with justice, or an apprehension of the manner in which that good is to be done, constitutes virtue.

But wherefore should a man be benevolent and just? The immediate emotions of his nature, especially in its most inartificial state, prompt him to inflict pain, and to arrogate dominion. He desires to heap superfluities to his own store, although others perish with famine. He is propelled to guard against the smallest invasion of his own liberty, though he reduces others to a condition of the most pitiless servitude. He is revengeful, proud and selfish. Wherefore should he curb these propensities?

It is inquired, for what reason a human being should engage in procuring the happiness, or refrain from producing the pain of another? When a reason is required to prove the necessity of adopting any system of conduct, what is it that the objector demands? He requires proof of that system of conduct being such as will most effectually promote the happiness of mankind. To demonstrate this, is to render a moral reason. Such is the object of virtue.

A common sophism, which, like many others, depends on the abuse of a metaphorical expression to a literal purpose, has produced much of the confusion which has involved the theory of morals. It is said that no person is bound to be just or kind, if, on his neglect, he should fail to incur some penalty. Duty is obligation. There can be no obligation without an obliger. Virtue is a law, to which it is the will of the lawgiver that we should conform; which will we should in no manner be bound to obey, unless some dreadful punishment were attached to disobedience. This is the philosophy of slavery and superstition.

In fact, no person can be *bound* or *obliged,* without some power preceding to bind and oblige. If I observe a man bound hand and foot, I know that some one bound him. But if I observe him returning self-satisfied from the performance of some action, by which he has been the willing author of extensive benefit, I do not infer that the anticipation of hellish agonies, or the hope of heavenly reward, has constrained him to such an act.

. . . .

It remains to be stated in what manner the sensations which constitute the basis of virtue originate in the human mind; what are the laws which it receives there; how far the principles of mind allow it to be an attribute of a human being; and, lastly, what is the probability of persuading mankind to adopt it as a universal and systematic motive of conduct.

BENEVOLENCE

There is a class of emotions which we instinctively avoid. A human being, such as is man considered in his origin, a child a month old, has a very imperfect consciousness of the existence of other natures resembling itself. All the energies of its being are directed to the extinction of the pains with which it is perpetually assailed. At length it discovers that it is surrounded by natures susceptible of sensations similar to its own. It is very late before children attain to this knowledge. If a child observes, without emotion, its nurse or its mother suffering acute pain, it is attributable rather to ignorance than insensibility. So soon as the accents and gestures, significant of pain, are referred to the feelings which they express, they awaken in the mind of the beholder a desire that they should cease. Pain is thus apprehended to be evil for its own sake, without any other necessary reference to the mind by which its existence is perceived, than such as is indispensable to its perception. The tendencies of our original sensations, indeed, all have for their object the preservation of our individual being. But these are passive and unconscious. In proportion as the mind acquires an active power, the empire of these tendencies becomes limited. Thus an infant, a savage, and a solitary beast, is selfish, because its mind is incapable of receiving an accurate intimation of the nature of pain as existing in beings resembling itself. The inhabitant of a highly civilized community will more acutely sympathize with the sufferings and enjoyments of others, than the inhabitant of a society of a less degree of civilization. He who shall have cultivated his intellectual powers by familiarity with the highest specimens of poetry and philosophy, will usually sympathize more than one engaged in the less refined functions of manual labour. Every one has experience of the fact, that to sympathize with the sufferings of another, is to enjoy a transitory oblivion of his own.

The mind thus acquires, by exercise, a habit, as it were, of perceiving and abhorring evil, however remote from the immediate sphere of sensations with which that individual mind is conversant. Imagination or mind employed in prophetically imaging forth its objects, is that faculty of human nature on which every gradation of its progress, nay, every, the minutest, change, depends. Pain or pleasure, if subtly analysed, will be found to consist entirely in prospect. The only distinction between the selfish man and the virtuous man is, that the imagination of the former is confined within a narrow limit, whilst that of the latter embraces a comprehensive circumference. In this sense, wisdom and virtue may be said to be inseparable, and criteria of each other. Selfishness is the offspring of ignorance and mistake; it is the portion of unreflecting infancy, and savage solitude, or of those whom toil or evil occupations have blunted or rendered torpid; disinterested benevolence is the product of a cultivated imagination, and has an intimate connexion with all the arts which add ornament, or dignity, or power, or stability to the social state of man. Virtue is thus entirely a refinement of civilized life; a creation of the human mind; or, rather, a combination which it has made, according to elementary rules contained within itself, of the feelings suggested by the relations established between man and man.

All the theories which have refined and exalted humanity, or those which have been devised as alleviations of its mistakes and evils, have been based upon the elementary emotions of disinterestedness, which we feel to constitute the majesty of our nature. Patriotism, as it existed in the ancient republics, was never, as has been supposed, a calculation of personal advantages. When Mutius Scaevola thrust his hand into the burning coals, and Regulus returned to Carthage, and Epicharis sustained the rack silently, in the torments of which she knew that she would speedily perish, rather than betray the conspirators to the tyrant;[1] these illustrious persons certainly made a small estimate of their private interest. If it be said that they sought posthumous fame; instances are not wanting in history which prove that men have even defied infamy for the sake of good. But there is a great error in the world with respect to the selfishness of fame. It is certainly possible that a person should seek distinction as a medium of personal gratification. But the love of fame is frequently no more than a desire that the feelings of others should confirm, illustrate, and sympathize with, our own. In this respect it is allied with all that draws us out of ourselves. It is the 'last infirmity of noble minds'. Chivalry was likewise founded on the theory of self-sacrifice. Love possesses so extraordinary a power over the human heart, only because disinterestedness is united with the natural propensities. These propensities themselves are comparatively impotent in cases where the imagination of pleasure to be given, as well as to be received, does not enter into the account. Let it not be objected that patriotism, and chivalry, and sentimental love, have been the fountains of enormous mischief. They are cited only to establish the proposition that, according to the elementary principles of mind, man is capable of desiring and pursuing good for its own sake.

JUSTICE

The benevolent propensities are thus inherent in the human mind. We are impelled to seek the happiness of others. We experience a satisfaction in being the authors of that happiness. Everything that lives is open to impressions of pleasure and pain. We are led by our benevolent propensities to regard every human being indifferently with whom we come in contact. They have preference only with respect to those who offer themselves most obviously to our notice. Human beings are indiscriminating and blind; they will avoid inflicting pain, though that pain should be attended with eventual benefit; they will seek to confer pleas-

[1] Tacitus.

ure without calculating the mischief that may result. They benefit one at the expense of many.

There is a sentiment in the human mind that regulates benevolence in its application as a principle of action. This is the sense
of justice. Justice, as well as benevolence, is an elementary law
of human nature. It is through this principle that men are impelled to distribute any means of pleasure which benevolence
may suggest the communication of to others, in equal portions
among an equal number of applicants. If ten men are shipwrecked on a desert island, they distribute whatever subsistence
may remain to them, into equal portions among themselves. If
six of them conspire to deprive the remaining four of their share,
their conduct is termed unjust.

The existence of pain has been shown to be a circumstance
which the human mind regards with dissatisfaction, and of
which it desires the cessation. It is equally according to its nature
to desire that the advantages to be enjoyed by a limited number
of persons should be enjoyed equally by all. This proposition is
supported by the evidence of indisputable facts. Tell some un-
garbled tale of a number of persons being made the victims of
the enjoyments of one, and he who would appeal in favour of
any system which might produce such an evil to the primary
emotions of our nature, would have nothing to reply. Let two
persons, equally strangers, make application for some benefit in
the possession of a third to bestow, and to which he feels that
they have an equal claim. They are both sensitive beings; pleasure and pain affect them alike.

·   ○   ·   ·   ·   ·   ·   ·

CHAPTER II

It is foreign to the general scope of this little treatise to en-
cumber a simple argument by controverting any of the trite ob-
jections of habit or fanaticism. But there are two; the first, the
basis of all political mistake, and the second, the prolific cause
and effect of religious error, which it seems useful to refute.

First, it is inquired, 'Wherefore should a man be benevolent
and just?' The answer has been given in the preceding chapter.

If a man persists to inquire why he ought to promote the
happiness of mankind, he demands a mathematical or metaphysical reason for a moral action. The absurdity of this scepticism is

more apparent, but not less real than the exacting a moral reason for a mathematical or metaphysical fact. If any person should refuse to admit that all the radii of a circle are of equal length, or that human actions are necessarily determined by motives, until it could be proved that these radii and these actions uniformly tended to the production of the greatest general good, who would not wonder at the unreasonable and capricious association of his ideas?

The writer of a philosophical treatise may, I imagine, at this advanced era of human intellect, be held excused from entering into a controversy with those reasoners, if such there are, who would claim an exemption from its decrees in favour of any one among those diversified systems of obscure opinion respecting morals, which, under the name of religions, have in various ages and countries prevailed among mankind. Besides that if, as these reasoners have pretended, eternal torture or happiness will ensue as the consequence of certain actions, we should be no nearer the possession of a standard to determine what actions were right and wrong, even if this pretended revelation, which is by no means the case, had furnished us with a complete catalogue of them. The character of actions as virtuous or vicious would by no means be determined alone by the personal advantage or disadvantage of each moral agent individually considered. Indeed, an action is often virtuous in proportion to the greatness of the personal calamity which the author willingly draws upon himself by daring to perform it. It is because an action produces an overbalance of pleasure or pain to the greatest number of sentient beings, and not merely because its consequences are beneficial or injurious to the author of that action, that it is good or evil. Nay, this latter consideration has a tendency to pollute the purity of virtue, inasmuch as it consists in the motive rather than in the consequences of an action. A person who should labour for the happiness of mankind lest he should be tormented eternally in Hell, would, with reference to that motive, possess as little claim to the epithet of virtuous, as he who should torture, imprison, and burn them alive, a more usual and natural consequence of such principles, for the sake of the enjoyments of Heaven.

My neighbour, presuming on his strength, may direct me to perform or to refrain from a particular action; indicating a certain arbitrary penalty in the event of disobedience within his power to inflict. My action, if modified by his menaces, can in no degree participate in virtue. He has afforded me no criterion as to what is right or wrong. A king, or an assembly of men, may publish a proclamation affixing any penalty to any particular action, but that is not immoral because such penalty is affixed. Nothing is more evident than that the epithet of virtue is inapplicable to the refraining from that action on account of the evil arbitrarily attached to it. If the action is in itself beneficial, virtue would rather consist in not refraining from it, but in firmly defying the personal consequences attached to its performance.

Some usurper of supernatural energy might subdue the whole globe to his power; he might possess new and unheard-of resources for enduing his punishments with the most terrible attributes of pain. The torments of his victims might be intense in their degree, and protracted to an infinite duration. Still the 'will of the lawgiver' would afford no surer criterion as to what actions were right or wrong. It would only increase the possible virtue of those who refuse to become the instruments of his tyranny.

II—MORAL SCIENCE CONSISTS IN CONSIDERING THE DIFFERENCE, NOT THE RESEMBLANCE, OF PERSONS

THE internal influence, derived from the constitution of the mind from which they flow, produces that peculiar modification of actions, which makes them intrinsically good or evil.

To attain an apprehension of the importance of this distinction, let us visit, in imagination, the proceedings of some metropolis. Consider the multitude of human beings who inhabit it, and survey, in thought, the actions of the several classes into which they are divided. Their obvious actions are apparently uniform: the stability of human society seems to be maintained sufficiently by the uniformity of the conduct of its members, both with regard to themselves, and with regard to others. The labourer arises at a certain hour, and applies himself to the task enjoined him. The functionaries of government and law are regularly employed in their offices and courts. The trader holds a train of conduct from which he never deviates. The ministers of religion employ an accustomed language, and maintain a decent and equable regard. The army is drawn forth, the motions of every soldier are such as they were expected to be; the general commands, and his words are echoed from troop to troop. The domestic actions of men are, for the most part, undistinguishable one from the other, at a superficial glance. The actions which are classed under the general appellation of marriage, education, friendship, &c., are perpetually going on, and to a superficial glance, are similar one to the other.

But, if we would see the truth of things, they must be stripped of this fallacious appearance of uniformity. In truth, no one action has, when considered in its whole extent, any essential resemblance with any other. Each individual, who composes the vast multitude which we have been contemplating, has a peculiar frame of mind, which, whilst the features of the great mass of his actions remain uniform, impresses the minuter lineaments with its peculiar hues. Thus, whilst his life, as a whole, is like the lives of other men, in detail, it is most unlike; and the more subdivided the actions become; that is, the more they enter into that class which have a vital influence on the happiness of others and his own, so much the more are they distinct from those of other men.

> Those little, nameless, unremembered acts
> Of kindness and of love,

as well as those deadly outrages which are inflicted by a look, a word—or less—the very refraining from some faint and most evanescent expression of countenance; these flow from a profounder source than the series of our habitual conduct, which, it has been already said, derives its origin from without. These are the actions, and such as these, which make human life what it is, and are the fountains of all the good and evil with which its entire surface is so widely and impartially overspread; and though they are called minute, they are called so in compliance with the blindness of those who cannot estimate their importance. It is in the due appreciating the general effects of their peculiarities, and in cultivating the habit of acquiring decisive knowledge respecting the tendencies arising out of them in particular cases, that the most important part of moral science consists. The deepest abyss of these vast and multitudinous caverns, it is necessary that we should visit.

This is the difference between social and individual man. Not that this distinction is to be considered definite, or characteristic of one human being as compared with another; it denotes rather two classes of agency, common in a degree to every human being. None is exempt, indeed, from that species of influence which affects, as it were, the surface of his being, and gives the specific outline to his conduct. Almost all that is ostensible submits to that legislature created by the general representation of the past feelings of mankind—imperfect as it is from a variety of causes, as it exists in the government, the religion, and domestic habits. Those who do not nominally, yet actually, submit to the same power. The external features of their conduct, indeed, can no more escape it, than the clouds can escape from the stream of the wind; and his opinion, which he often hopes he has dispassionately secured from all contagion of prejudice and vulgarity, would be found, on examination, to be the inevitable excrescence of the very usages from which he vehemently dissents. Internally all is conducted otherwise; the efficiency, the essence, the vitality of actions, derives its colour from what is no ways contributed to from any external source. Like the plant, which while it derives the accident of its size and shape from the soil in which it springs, and is cankered, or distorted, or inflated, yet retains those qualities which essentially divide it from all others; so that hemlock continues to be poison, and the violet does not cease to emit its odour in whatever soil it may grow.

We consider our own nature too superficially. We look on all that in ourselves with which we can discover a resemblance in others; and consider those resemblances as the materials of moral knowledge. It is in the differences that it actually consists.

[1815; publ. 1840]

ESSAY ON THE LITERATURE, THE ARTS, AND THE MANNERS OF THE ATHENIANS

A FRAGMENT

THE period which intervened between the birth of Pericles and the death of Aristotle, is undoubtedly, whether considered in itself, or with reference to the effects which it has produced upon the subsequent destinies of civilized man, the most memorable in the history of the world. What was the combination of moral and political circumstances which produced so unparalleled a progress during that period in literature and the arts;—why that progress, so rapid and so sustained, so soon received a check, and became retrograde,—are problems left to the wonder and conjecture of posterity. The wrecks and fragments of those subtle and profound minds, like the ruins of a fine statue, obscurely suggest to us the grandeur and perfection of the whole. Their very language—a type of the understandings of which it was the creation and the image—in variety, in simplicity, in flexibility, and in copiousness, excels every other language of the western world. Their sculptures are such as we, in our presumption, assume to be the models of ideal truth and beauty, and to which no artist of modern times can produce forms in any degree comparable. Their paintings, according to Pliny and Pausanias, were full of delicacy and harmony; and some even were powerfully pathetic, so as to awaken, like tender music or tragic poetry, the most overwhelming emotions. We are accustomed to conceive the painters of the sixteenth century, as those who have brought their art to the highest perfection, probably because none of the ancient paintings have been preserved. For all the inventive arts maintain, as it were, a sympathetic connexion between each other, being no more than various expressions of one internal power, modified by different circumstances, either of an individual, or of society; and the paintings of that period would probably bear the same relation as is confessedly borne by the sculptures to all succeeding ones. Of their music we know little; but the effects which it is said to have produced, whether they be attributed to the skill of the composer, or the sensibility of his audience, are far more powerful than any which we experience from the music of our own times; and if, indeed, the melody of their compositions were more tender and delicate, and inspiring, than the melodies of some modern European nations, their superiority in this art must have been something wonderful, and wholly beyond conception.

Their poetry seems to maintain a very high, though not so disproportionate a rank, in the comparison. Perhaps Shakespeare, from the variety and comprehension of his genius, is to be considered, on the whole, as the greatest individual mind, of which we have specimens remaining. Perhaps Dante created imaginations of greater loveliness and energy than any that are to be found in the ancient literature of Greece. Perhaps nothing has been discovered in the fragments of the Greek lyric poets equivalent to the sublime and chivalric sensibility of Petrarch.—But, as a poet, Homer must be acknowledged to excel Shakespeare in the truth, the harmony, the sustained grandeur, the satisfying completeness of his images, their exact fitness to the illustration, and to that to which they belong. Nor could Dante, deficient in conduct, plan, nature, variety, and temperance, have been brought into comparison with these men, but for those fortunate isles, laden with golden fruit, which alone could tempt any one to embark in the misty ocean of his dark and extravagant fiction.

But, omitting the comparison of individual minds, which can afford no general inference, how superior was the spirit and system of their poetry to that of any other period! So that, had any other genius equal in other respects to the greatest that ever enlightened the world, arisen in that age, he would have been superior to all, from this circumstance alone—that his conceptions would have assumed a more harmonious and perfect form. For it is worthy of observation, that whatever the poets of that age produced is as harmonious and perfect as possible. If a drama, for instance, were the composition of a person of inferior talent, it was still homogeneous and free from inequalities; it was a whole, consistent with itself. The compositions of great minds bore throughout the sustained stamp of their greatness. In the poetry of succeeding ages the expectations are often exalted on Icarian wings, and fall, too much disappointed to give a memory and a name to the oblivious pool in which they fell.

In physical knowledge Aristotle and Theophrastus had already —no doubt assisted by the labours of those of their predecessors whom they criticize—made advances worthy of the maturity of science. The astonishing invention of geometry, that series of discoveries which have enabled man to command the elements and foresee future events, before the subjects of his ignorant wonder, and which have opened as it were the doors of the mysteries of nature, had already been brought to great perfection. Metaphysics, the science of man's intimate nature, and logic, or the grammar and elementary principles of that science, received from the latter philosophers of the Periclean age a firm basis. All our more exact philosophy is built upon the labours of these great men, and many of the words which we employ in metaphysical distinctions were invented by them to give accuracy and system to their reasonings. The science of morals, or the voluntary conduct of men in relation to themselves or others, dates from this epoch. How inexpressibly bolder and more pure were the doctrines of those great men, in comparison with the timid maxims which prevail in the writings of the most esteemed modern moralists! They were such as Phocion, and Epaminondas, and

Timoleon, who formed themselves on their influence, were to the wretched heroes of our own age.

Their political and religious institutions are more difficult to bring into comparison with those of other times. A summary idea may be formed of the worth of any political and religious system, by observing the comparative degree of happiness and of intellect produced under its influence. And whilst many institutions and opinions, which in ancient Greece were obstacles to the improvement of the human race, have been abolished among modern nations, how many pernicious superstitions and new contrivances of misrule, and unheard-of complications of public mischief, have not been invented among them by the ever-watchful spirit of avarice and tyranny!

The modern nations of the civilized world owe the progress which they have made—as well in those physical sciences in which they have already excelled their masters, as in the moral and intellectual inquiries, in which, with all the advantage of the experience of the latter, it can scarcely be said that they have yet equalled them,—to what is called the revival of learning; that is, the study of the writers of the age which preceded and immediately followed the government of Pericles, or of subsequent writers, who were, so to speak, the rivers flowing from those immortal fountains. And though there seems to be a principle in the modern world, which, should circumstances analogous to those which modelled the intellectual resources of the age to which we refer, into so harmonious a proportion, again arise, would arrest and perpetuate them, and consign their results to a more equal, extensive, and lasting improvement of the condition of man—though justice and the true meaning of human society are, if not more accurately, more generally understood; though perhaps men know more, and therefore are more, as a mass, yet this principle has never been called into action, and requires indeed a universal and an almost appalling change in the system of existing things. The study of modern history is the study of kings, financiers, statesmen, and priests. The history of ancient Greece is the study of legislators, philosophers, and poets; it is the history of men, compared with the history of titles. What the Greeks were, was a reality, not a promise. And what we are and hope to be, is derived, as it were, from the influence and inspiration of these glorious generations.

Whatever tends to afford a further illustration of the manners and opinions of those to whom we owe so much, and who were perhaps, on the whole, the most perfect specimens of humanity of whom we have authentic record, were infinitely valuable. Let us see their errors, their weaknesses, their daily actions, their familiar conversation, and catch the tone of their society. When we discover how far the most admirable community ever framed was removed from that perfection to which human society is impelled by some active power within each bosom to aspire, how great ought to be our hopes, how resolute our struggles! For the Greeks of the Periclean age were widely different from us. It is to be lamented that no modern writer has hitherto dared to show them precisely as they were. Barthélemi cannot be denied the praise of industry and system; but he never forgets that he is a Christian and a Frenchman. Wieland, in his delightful novels, makes indeed a very tolerable Pagan, but cherishes too many political prejudices, and refrains from diminishing the interest of his romances by painting sentiments in which no European of modern times can possibly sympathize. There is no book which shows the Greeks precisely as they were; they seem all written for children, with the caution that no practice or sentiment, highly inconsistent with our present manners, should be mentioned, lest those manners should receive outrage and violation. But there are many to whom the Greek language is inaccessible, who ought not to be excluded by this prudery from possessing an exact and comprehensive conception of the history of man; for there is no knowledge concerning what man has been and may be, from partaking of which a person can depart, without becoming in some degree more philosophical, tolerant, and just.

One of the chief distinctions between the manners of ancient Greece and modern Europe, consisted in the regulations and the sentiments respecting sexual intercourse. Whether this difference arises from some imperfect influence of the doctrines of Jesus, who alleges the absolute and unconditional equality of all human beings, or from the institutions of chivalry, or from a certain fundamental difference of physical nature existing in the Celts, or from a combination of all or any of these causes acting on each other, is a question worthy of voluminous investigation. The fact is, that the modern Europeans have in this circumstance, and in the abolition of slavery, made an improvement the most decisive in the regulation of human society; and all the virtue and the wisdom of the Periclean age arose under other institutions, in spite of the diminution which personal slavery and the inferiority of women, recognized by law and opinion, must have produced in the delicacy, the strength, the comprehensiveness, and the accuracy of their conceptions, in moral, political, and metaphysical science, and perhaps in every other art and science.

The women, thus degraded, became such as it was expected they would become. They possessed, except with extraordinary exceptions, the habits and the qualities of slaves. They were probably not extremely beautiful; at least there was no such disproportion in the attractions of the external form between the female and male sex among the Greeks, as exists among the modern Europeans. They were certainly devoid of that moral and intellectual loveliness with which the acquisition of knowledge and the cultivation of sentiment animates, as with another life of overpowering grace, the lineaments and the gestures of every form which they inhabit. Their eyes could not have been deep and intricate from the workings of the mind, and could have entangled no heart in soul-enwoven labyrinths.

Let it not be imagined that because the Greeks were deprived of its legitimate object, they were incapable of sentimental love; and that this passion is the mere child of chivalry and the literature of modern times. This object or its archetype for ever exists in the mind, which selects among those who resemble it that which most resembles it; and instinctively fills up the interstices of the imperfect image, in the same manner as the imagination moulds and completes the shapes in clouds, or in the fire, into the resemblances of whatever form, animal, building, &c., happens to be present to it. Man is in his wildest state a social being: a certain degree of civilization and refinement ever produces the want of sympathies still more intimate and complete; and the gratification of the senses is no longer all that is sought in sexual connexion. It soon becomes a very small part of that profound and complicated sentiment, which we call love, which is rather the universal thirst for a communion not only of the senses, but of our whole nature, intellectual, imaginative and sensitive, and which, when individualized, becomes an imperious necessity, only to be satisfied by the complete or partial, actual or supposed fulfilment of its claims. This want grows more powerful in proportion to the development which our nature receives from civilization, for man never ceases to be a social being. The sexual impulse, which is only one, and often a small part of those claims, serves, from its obvious and external nature, as a kind of type or expression of the rest, a common basis, an acknowledged and visible link. Still it is a claim which even derives a strength not its own from the accessory circumstances which surround it, and one which our nature thirsts to satisfy. To estimate this, observe the degree of intensity and durability of the love of the male towards the female in animals and savages and acknowledge all the duration and intensity observable in the love of civilized beings beyond that of savages to be produced from other causes. In the susceptibility of the external senses there is probably no important difference.

Among the ancient Greeks the male sex, one half of the human race, received the highest cultivation and refinement: whilst the other, so far as intellect is concerned, were educated as slaves, and were raised but few degrees in all that related to moral or intellectual excellence above the condition of savages. The gradations in the society of man present us with slow improvement in this respect. The Roman women held a higher consideration in society, and were esteemed almost as the equal partners with their husbands in the regulation of domestic economy and the education of their children. The practices and customs of modern Europe are essentially different from and incomparably less pernicious than either, however remote from what an enlightened mind cannot fail to desire as the future destiny of human beings.

[1818; publ. 1840]

ON THE SYMPOSIUM,
OR PREFACE TO THE BANQUET OF PLATO

A FRAGMENT

THE dialogue entitled *The Banquet* was selected by the translator as the most beautiful and perfect among all the works of Plato.[1] He despairs of having communicated to the English lan-

[1] The *Republic*, though replete with considerable errors of speculation, is, indeed, the greatest repository of important truths of all the works of Plato. This, perhaps, is because it is the longest. He first, and perhaps last, maintained that a state ought to be governed, not by the wealthiest, or the most ambitious, or the most cunning, but by the wisest; the method of selecting such rulers, and the laws by which such a selection is made, must correspond with and arise out of the moral freedom and refinement of the people.

guage any portion of the surpassing graces of the composition, or having done more than present an imperfect shadow of the language and the sentiment of this astonishing production.

Plato is eminently the greatest among the Greek philosophers, and from, or, rather, perhaps through him, his master Socrates, have proceeded those emanations of moral and metaphysical knowledge, on which a long series and an incalculable variety of popular superstitions have sheltered their absurdities from the slow contempt of mankind. Plato exhibits the rare union of close and subtle logic with the Pythian enthusiasm of poetry, melted by the splendour and harmony of his periods into one irresistible stream of musical impressions, which hurry the persuasions onward, as in a breathless career. His language is that of an immortal spirit, rather than a man. Lord Bacon is, perhaps, the only writer, who, in these particulars, can be compared with him: his imitator, Cicero, sinks in the comparison into an ape mocking the gestures of a man. His views into the nature of mind and existence are often obscure, only because they are profound; and though his theories respecting the government of the world, and the elementary laws of moral action, are not always correct, yet there is scarcely any of his treatises which do not, however stained by puerile sophisms, contain the most remarkable intuitions into all that can be the subject of the human mind. His excellence consists especially in intuition, and it is this faculty which raises him far above Aristotle, whose genius, though vivid and various, is obscure in comparison with that of Plato.

The dialogue entitled the *Banquet*, is called Ἐρωτικός, or a Discussion upon Love, and is supposed to have taken place at the house of Agathon, at one of a series of festivals given by that poet, on the occasion of his gaining the prize of tragedy at the Dionysiaca. The account of the debate on this occasion is supposed to have been given by Apollodorus, a pupil of Socrates, many years after it had taken place, to a companion who was curious to hear it. This Apollodorus appears, both from the style in which he is represented in this piece, as well as from a passage in the *Phaedon*, to have been a person of an impassioned and enthusiastic disposition; to borrow an image from the Italian painters, he seems to have been the St. John of the Socratic group. The drama (for so the lively distinction of character and the various and well-wrought circumstances of the story almost entitle it to be called) begins by Socrates persuading Aristodemus to sup at Agathon's, uninvited. The whole of this introduction affords the most lively conception of refined Athenian manners.

[1818; publ. 1840]

[UNFINISHED]

A DEFENCE OF POETRY

PART I

ACCORDING to one mode of regarding those two classes of mental action, which are called reason and imagination, the former may be considered as mind contemplating the relations borne by one thought to another, however produced; and the latter, as mind acting upon those thoughts so as to colour them with its own light, and composing from them, as from elements, other thoughts, each containing within itself the principle of its own integrity. The one is the τὸ ποιεῖν, or the principle of synthesis, and has for its objects those forms which are common to universal nature and existence itself; the other is the τὸ λογιζεῖν, or principle of analysis, and its action regards the relations of things, simply as relations; considering thoughts, not in their integral unity, but as the algebraical representations which conduct to certain general results. Reason is the enumeration of quantities already known; imagination is the perception of the value of those quantities, both separately and as a whole. Reason respects the differences, and imagination the similitudes of things. Reason is to the imagination as the instrument to the agent, as the body to the spirit, as the shadow to the substance.

Poetry, in a general sense, may be defined to be 'the expression of the imagination': and poetry is connate with the origin of man. Man is an instrument over which a series of external and internal impressions are driven, like the alternations of an ever-changing wind over an Aeolian lyre, which move it by their motion to ever-changing melody. But there is a principle within the human being, and perhaps within all sentient beings, which acts otherwise than in the lyre, and produces not melody alone, but harmony, by an internal adjustment of the sounds or motions thus excited to the impressions which excite them. It is as if the lyre could accommodate its chords to the motions of that which strikes them, in a determined proportion of sound; even as the musician can accommodate his voice to the sound of the lyre. A child at play by itself will express its delight by its voice and motions; and every inflexion of tone and every gesture will bear exact relation to a corresponding antitype in the pleasurable impressions which awakened it; it will be the reflected image of that impression; and as the lyre trembles and sounds after the wind has died away, so the child seeks, by prolonging in its voice and motions the duration of the effect, to prolong also a consciousness of the cause. In relation to the objects which delight a child, these expressions are, what poetry is to higher objects. The savage (for the savage is to ages what the child is to years) expresses the emotions produced in him by surrounding objects in a similar manner; and language and gesture, together with plastic or pictorial imitation, become the image of the combined effect of those objects, and of his apprehension of them. Man in society, with all his passions and his pleasures, next becomes the object of the passions and pleasures of man; an additional class of emotions produces an augmented treasure of expressions; and language, gesture, and the imitative arts, become at once the representation and the medium, the pencil and the picture, the chisel and the statue, the chord and the harmony. The social sympathies, or those laws from which, as from its elements, society results, begin to develop themselves from the moment that two human beings coexist; the future is contained within the present, as the plant within the seed; and equality, diversity, unity, contrast, mutual dependence, become the principles alone capable of affording the motives according to which the will of a social being is determined to action, inasmuch as he is social; and constitute pleasure in sensation, virtue in sentiment, beauty in art, truth in reasoning, and love in the intercourse of kind. Hence men, even in the infancy of society, observe a certain order in their words and actions, distinct from that of the objects and the impressions represented by them, all expression being subject to the laws of that from which it proceeds. But let us dismiss those more general considerations which might involve an inquiry into the principles of society itself, and restrict our view to the manner in which the imagination is expressed upon its forms.

In the youth of the world, men dance and sing and imitate natural objects, observing in these actions, as in all others, a certain rhythm or order. And, although all men observe a similar, they observe not the same order, in the motions of the dance, in the melody of the song, in the combinations of language, in the series of their imitations of natural objects. For there is a certain order or rhythm belonging to each of these classes of mimetic representation, from which the hearer and the spectator receive an intenser and purer pleasure than from any other: the sense of an approximation to this order has been called taste by modern writers. Every man in the infancy of art observes an order which approximates more or less closely to that from which this highest delight results: but the diversity is not sufficiently marked, as that its gradations should be sensible, except in those instances where the predominance of this faculty of approximation to the beautiful (for so we may be permitted to name the relation between this highest pleasure and its cause) is very great. Those in whom it exists in excess are poets, in the most universal sense of the word; and the pleasure resulting from the manner in which they express the influence of society or nature upon their own minds, communicates itself to others, and gathers a sort of re-duplication from that community. Their language is vitally metaphorical; that is, it marks the before unapprehended relations of things and perpetuates their apprehension, until the words which represent them become, through time, signs for portions or classes of thoughts instead of pictures of integral thoughts; and then if no new poets should arise to create afresh the associations which have been thus disorganized, language will be dead to all the nobler purposes of human intercourse. These similitudes or relations are finely said by Lord Bacon to be 'the same footsteps of nature impressed upon the various subjects of the world';[1] and he considers the faculty which perceives them as the storehouse of axioms common to all knowledge. In the infancy of society every author is necessarily a poet, because language itself is poetry; and to be a poet is to apprehend the true and the beautiful, in a word, the good which exists in the relation, subsisting, first between existence and perception, and secondly between perception and expression. Every original language near to its source is in itself the chaos of a cyclic poem: the copiousness of lexicography and the distinctions of grammar are the works of a later age, and are merely the catalogue and the form of the creations of poetry.

But poets, or those who imagine and express this indestructible order, are not only the authors of language and of music, of the

[1] *De Augment. Scient.*, cap. i, lib. iii.

dance, and architecture, and statuary, and painting; they are the institutors of laws, and the founders of civil society, and the inventors of the arts of life, and the teachers, who draw into a certain propinquity with the beautiful and the true, that partial apprehension of the agencies of the invisible world which is called religion. Hence all original religions are allegorical, or susceptible of allegory, and, like Janus, have a double face of false and true. Poets, according to the circumstances of the age and nation in which they appeared, were called, in the earlier epochs of the world, legislators, or prophets: a poet essentially comprises and unites both these characters. For he not only beholds intensely the present as it is, and discovers those laws according to which present things ought to be ordered, but he beholds the future in the present, and his thoughts are the germs of the flower and the fruit of latest time. Not that I assert poets to be prophets in the gross sense of the word, or that they can foretell the form as surely as they foreknow the spirit of events: such is the pretence of superstition, which would make poetry an attribute of prophecy, rather than prophecy an attribute of poetry. A poet participates in the eternal, the infinite, and the one; as far as relates to his conceptions, time and place and number are not. The grammatical forms which express the moods of time, and the difference of persons, and the distinction of place, are convertible with respect to the highest poetry without injuring it as poetry; and the choruses of Aeschylus, and the book of *Job*, and Dante's *Paradise*, would afford, more than any other writings, examples of this fact, if the limits of this essay did not forbid citation. The creations of sculpture, painting, and music, are illustrations still more decisive.

Language, colour, form, and religious and civil habits of action, are all the instruments and materials of poetry; they may be called poetry by that figure of speech which considers the effect as a synonym of the cause. But poetry in a more restricted sense expresses those arrangements of language, and especially metrical language, which are created by that imperial faculty, whose throne is curtained within the invisible nature of man. And this springs from the nature itself of language, which is a more direct representation of the actions and passions of our internal being, and is susceptible of more various and delicate combinations, than colour, form, or motion, and is more plastic and obedient to the control of that faculty of which it is the creation. For language is arbitrarily produced by the imagination, and has relation to thoughts alone; but all other materials, instruments, and conditions of art, have relations among each other, which limit and interpose between conception and expression. The former is as a mirror which reflects, the latter as a cloud which enfeebles, the light of which both are mediums of communication. Hence the fame of sculptors, painters, and musicians, although the intrinsic powers of the great masters of these arts may yield in no degree to that of those who have employed language as the hieroglyphic of their thoughts, has never equalled that of poets in the restricted sense of the term; as two performers of equal skill will produce unequal effects from a guitar and a harp. The fame of legislators and founders of religions, so long as their institutions last, alone seems to exceed that of poets in the restricted sense; but it can scarcely be a question, whether, if we deduct the celebrity which their flattery of the gross opinions of the vulgar usually conciliates, together with that which belonged to them in their higher character of poets, any excess will remain.

We have thus circumscribed the word poetry within the limits of that art which is the most familiar and the most perfect expression of the faculty itself. It is necessary, however, to make the circle still narrower, and to determine the distinction between measured and unmeasured language; for the popular division into prose and verse is inadmissible in accurate philosophy.

Sounds as well as thoughts have relation both between each other and towards that which they represent, and a perception of the order of those relations has always been found connected with a perception of the order of the relations of thoughts. Hence the language of poets has ever affected a certain uniform and harmonious recurrence of sound, without which it were not poetry, and which is scarcely less indispensable to the communication of its influence, than the words themselves, without reference to that peculiar order. Hence the vanity of translation; it were as wise to cast a violet into a crucible that you might discover the formal principle of its colour and odour, as seek to transfuse from one language into another the creations of a poet. The plant must spring again from its seed, or it will bear no flower—and this is the burthen of the curse of Babel.

An observation of the regular mode of the recurrence of harmony in the language of poetical minds, together with its relation to music, produced metre, or a certain system of traditional forms of harmony and language. Yet it is by no means essential

that a poet should accommodate his language to this traditional
form, so that the harmony, which is its spirit, be observed. The
practice is indeed convenient and popular, and to be preferred,
especially in such composition as includes much action: but every
great poet must inevitably innovate upon the example of his
predecessors in the exact structure of his peculiar versification.
The distinction between poets and prose writers is a vulgar
error. The distinction between philosophers and poets has been
anticipated. Plato was essentially a poet—the truth and splendour
of his imagery, and the melody of his language, are the most
intense that it is possible to conceive. He rejected the measure
of the epic, dramatic, and lyrical forms, because he sought to
kindle a harmony in thoughts divested of shape and action, and
he forbore to invent any regular plan of rhythm which would
include, under determinate forms, the varied pauses of his style.
Cicero sought to imitate the cadence of his periods, but with
little success. Lord Bacon was a poet.[1] His language has a sweet
and majestic rhythm, which satisfies the sense, no less than the
almost superhuman wisdom of his philosophy satisfies the intellect; it is a strain which distends, and then bursts the circumference of the reader's mind, and pours itself forth together with
it into the universal element with which it has perpetual sympathy. All the authors of revolutions in opinion are not only
necessarily poets as they are inventors, nor even as their words
unveil the permanent analogy of things by images which participate in the life of truth; but as their periods are harmonious
and rhythmical, and contain in themselves the elements of verse;
being the echo of the eternal music. Nor are those supreme poets,
who have employed traditional forms of rhythm on account of
the form and action of their subjects, less capable of perceiving
and teaching the truth of things, than those who have omitted
that form. Shakespeare, Dante, and Milton (to confine ourselves
to modern writers) are philosophers of the very loftiest power.

A poem is the very image of life expressed in its eternal truth.
There is this difference between a story and a poem, that a story
is a catalogue of detached facts, which have no other connexion
than time, place, circumstance, cause and effect; the other is
the creation of actions according to the unchangeable forms of
human nature, as existing in the mind of the Creator, which is
itself the image of all other minds. The one is partial, and applies
only to a definite period of time, and a certain combination of

[1] See the *Filum Labyrinthi*, and the Essay on Death particularly.

events which can never again recur; the other is universal, and contains within itself the germ of a relation to whatever motives or actions have place in the possible varieties of human nature. Time, which destroys the beauty and the use of the story of particular facts, stripped of the poetry which should invest them, augments that of poetry, and for ever develops new and wonderful applications of the eternal truth which it contains. Hence epitomes have been called the moths of just history; they eat out the poetry of it. A story of particular facts is as a mirror which obscures and distorts that which should be beautiful: poetry is a mirror which makes beautiful that which is distorted.

The parts of a composition may be poetical, without the composition as a whole being a poem. A single sentence may be considered as a whole, though it may be found in the midst of a series of unassimilated portions: a single word even may be a spark of inextinguishable thought. And thus all the great historians, Herodotus, Plutarch, Livy, were poets; and although the plan of these writers, especially that of Livy, restrained them from developing this faculty in its highest degree, they made copious and ample amends for their subjection, by filling all the interstices of their subjects with living images.

Having determined what is poetry, and who are poets, let us proceed to estimate its effects upon society.

Poetry is ever accompanied with pleasure: all spirits on which it falls open themselves to receive the wisdom which is mingled with its delight. In the infancy of the world, neither poets themselves nor their auditors are fully aware of the excellence of poetry: for it acts in a divine and unapprehended manner, beyond and above consciousness; and it is reserved for future generations to contemplate and measure the mighty cause and effect in all the strength and splendour of their union. Even in modern times, no living poet ever arrived at the fullness of his fame; the jury which sits in judgement upon a poet, belonging as he does to all time, must be composed of his peers: it must be impanelled by Time from the selectest of the wise of many generations. A poet is a nightingale, who sits in darkness and sings to cheer its own solitude with sweet sounds; his auditors are as men entranced by the melody of an unseen musician, who feel that they are moved and softened, yet know not whence or why. The poems of Homer and his contemporaries were the delight of infant Greece; they were the elements of that social system which is the column upon which all succeeding civilization has reposed. Homer embodied the ideal perfection of his age in human character; nor can we doubt that those who read his verses were awakened to an ambition of becoming like to Achilles, Hector, and Ulysses: the truth and beauty of friendship, patriotism, and persevering devotion to an object, were unveiled to the depths in these immortal creations: the sentiments of the auditors must have been refined and enlarged by a sympathy with such great and lovely impersonations, until from admiring they imitated, and from imitation they identified themselves with the objects of their admiration. Nor let it be objected, that these characters are remote from moral perfection, and that they can by no means be considered as edifying patterns for general imitation. Every epoch, under names more or less specious, has deified its peculiar errors; Revenge is the naked idol of the worship of a semi-barbarous age; and Self-deceit is the veiled image of unknown evil, before which luxury and satiety lie prostrate. But a poet considers the vices of his contemporaries as a temporary dress in which his creations must be arrayed, and which cover without concealing the eternal proportions of their beauty. An epic or dramatic personage is understood to wear them around his soul, as he may the ancient armour or the modern uniform around his body; whilst it is easy to conceive a dress more graceful than either. The beauty of the internal nature cannot be so far concealed by its accidental vesture, but that the spirit of its form shall communicate itself to the very disguise, and indicate the shape it hides from the manner in which it is worn. A majestic form and graceful motions will express themselves through the most barbarous and tasteless costume. Few poets of the highest class have chosen to exhibit the beauty of their conceptions in its naked truth and splendour; and it is doubtful whether the alloy of costume, habit, &c., be not necessary to temper this planetary music for mortal ears.

The whole objection, however, of the immorality of poetry rests upon a misconception of the manner in which poetry acts to produce the moral improvement of man. Ethical science arranges the elements which poetry has created, and propounds schemes and proposes examples of civil and domestic life: nor is it for want of admirable doctrines that men hate, and despise, and censure, and deceive, and subjugate one another. But poetry acts in another and diviner manner. It awakens and enlarges the mind itself by rendering it the receptacle of a thousand unapprehended combinations of thought. Poetry lifts the veil from the hidden beauty of the world, and makes familiar objects be as if they were not familiar; it reproduces all that it represents, and the impersonations clothed in its Elysian light stand thenceforward in the minds of those who have once contemplated them as memorials of that gentle and exalted content which extends itself over all thoughts and actions with which it coexists. The great secret of morals is love; or a going out of our own nature, and an identification of ourselves with the beautiful which exists in thought, action, or person, not our own. A man, to be greatly good, must imagine intensely and comprehensively; he must put himself in the place of another and of many others; the pains and pleasures of his species must become his own. The great instrument of moral good is the imagination; and poetry administers to the effect by acting upon the cause. Poetry enlarges the circumference of the imagination by replenishing it with thoughts of ever new delight, which have the power of attracting and assimilating to their own nature all other thoughts, and which form new intervals and interstices whose void for ever craves fresh food. Poetry strengthens the faculty which is the organ of the moral nature of man, in the same manner as exercise strengthens a limb. A poet therefore would do ill to embody his own conceptions of right and wrong, which are usually those of his place and time, in his poetical creations, which participate in neither. By this assumption of the inferior office of interpreting the effect, in which perhaps after all he might acquit himself but imperfectly, he would resign a glory in a participation in the cause. There was little danger that Homer, or any of the eternal poets, should have so far misunderstood themselves as to have abdicated this throne of their widest dominion. Those in whom the poetical faculty, though great, is less intense, as Euripides, Lucan, Tasso, Spenser, have frequently affected a moral aim, and the effect of their poetry is diminished in exact proportion to the degree in which they compel us to advert to this purpose.

Homer and the cyclic poets were followed at a certain interval by the dramatic and lyrical poets of Athens, who flourished contemporaneously with all that is most perfect in the kindred expressions of the poetical faculty; architecture, painting, music, the dance, sculpture, philosophy, and, we may add, the forms of civil life. For although the scheme of Athenian society was deformed by many imperfections which the poetry existing in chivalry and Christianity has erased from the habits and institutions of modern Europe; yet never at any other period has so much energy, beauty, and virtue, been developed; never was blind strength and stubborn form so disciplined and rendered subject to the will of man, or that will less repugnant to the dictates of the beautiful and the true, as during the century which preceded the death of Socrates. Of no other epoch in the history of our species have we records and fragments stamped so visibly with the image of the divinity in man. But it is poetry alone, in form, in action, or in language, which has rendered this epoch memorable above all others, and the storehouse of examples to everlasting time. For written poetry existed at that epoch simultaneously with the other arts, and it is an idle inquiry to demand which gave and which received the light, which all, as from a common focus, have scattered over the darkest periods of succeeding time. We know no more of cause and effect than a constant conjunction of events: poetry is ever found to coexist with whatever other arts contribute to the happiness and perfection of man. I appeal to what has already been established to distinguish between the cause and the effect.

It was at the period here adverted to, that the drama had its birth; and however a succeeding writer may have equalled or surpassed those few great specimens of the Athenian drama which have been preserved to us, it is indisputable that the art itself never was understood or practised according to the true philosophy of it, as at Athens. For the Athenians employed language, action, music, painting, the dance, and religious institutions, to produce a common effect in the representation of the highest idealisms of passion and of power; each division in the art was made perfect in its kind by artists of the most consummate skill, and was disciplined into a beautiful proportion and unity one towards the other. On the modern stage a few only of the elements capable of expressing the image of the poet's conception are employed at once. We have tragedy without music and dancing; and music and dancing without the highest impersonations of which they are the fit accompaniment, and both without religion and solemnity. Religious institution has indeed been usually banished from the stage. Our system of divesting the actor's face of a mask, on which the many expressions appropriated to his dramatic character might be moulded into one permanent and unchanging expression, is favourable only to a partial and inharmonious effect; it is fit for nothing but a monologue, where all the attention may be directed to some great master of ideal mimicry. The modern practice of blending comedy with tragedy, though liable to great abuse in point of practice, is undoubtedly an extension of the dramatic circle; but the comedy should be as in *King Lear,* universal, ideal, and sublime. It is perhaps the intervention of this principle which determines the balance in favour of *King Lear* against the *Oedipus Tyrannus* or the *Agamemnon,* or, if you will, the trilogies with which they are connected; unless the intense power of the choral poetry, especially that of the latter, should be considered as restoring the equilibrium. *King Lear,* if it can sustain this comparison, may be judged to be the most perfect specimen of the dramatic art existing in the world; in spite of the narrow conditions to which the poet was subjected by the ignorance of the philosophy of the drama which has prevailed in modern Europe. Calderon, in his religious *Autos,* has attempted to fulfil some of the high conditions of dramatic representation neglected by Shakespeare; such as the establishing a relation between the drama and religion, and the accommodating them to music and dancing; but he omits the observation of conditions still more important, and more is lost than gained by the substitution of the rigidly-defined and ever-repeated idealisms of a distorted superstition for the living impersonations of the truth of human passion.

But I digress.—The connexion of scenic exhibitions with the improvement or corruption of the manners of men, has been universally recognized: in other words, the presence or absence of poetry in its most perfect and universal form, has been found to be connected with good and evil in conduct or habit. The corruption which has been imputed to the drama as an effect, begins, when the poetry employed in its constitution ends: I appeal to the history of manners whether the periods of the growth of the one and the decline of the other have not corresponded with an exactness equal to any example of moral cause and effect.

The drama at Athens, or wheresoever else it may have approached to its perfection, ever co-existed with the moral and intellectual greatness of the age. The tragedies of the Athenian poets are as mirrors in which the spectator beholds himself, under a thin disguise of circumstance, stript of all but that ideal perfection and energy which every one feels to be the internal type of all that he loves, admires, and would become. The imagination is enlarged by a sympathy with pains and passions so mighty, that they distend in their conception the capacity of that by which they are conceived; the good affections are strengthened by pity, indignation, terror, and sorrow; and an exalted calm is prolonged from the satiety of this high exercise of them into the tumult of familiar life: even crime is disarmed of half its horror and all its contagion by being represented as the fatal consequence of the unfathomable agencies of nature; error is thus divested of its wilfulness; men can no longer cherish it as the creation of their choice. In a drama of the highest order there is little food for censure or hatred; it teaches rather self-knowledge and self-respect. Neither the eye nor the mind can see itself, unless reflected upon that which it resembles. The drama, so long as it continues to express poetry, is as a prismatic and many-sided mirror, which collects the brightest rays of human nature and divides and reproduces them from the simplicity of these elementary forms, and touches them with majesty and beauty, and multiplies all that it reflects, and endows it with the power of propagating its like wherever it may fall.

But in periods of the decay of social life, the drama sympathizes with that decay. Tragedy becomes a cold imitation of the form of the great masterpieces of antiquity, divested of all harmonious accompaniment of the kindred arts; and often the very form misunderstood, or a weak attempt to teach certain doctrines, which the writer considers as moral truths; and which are usually no more than specious flatteries of some gross vice or weakness, with which the author, in common with his auditors, are infected. Hence what has been called the classical and domestic drama. Addison's *Cato* is a specimen of the one; and would it were not superfluous to cite examples of the other! To such purposes poetry cannot be made subservient. Poetry is a sword of lightning, ever unsheathed, which consumes the scabbard that would contain it. And thus we observe that all dramatic writings of this nature are unimaginative in a singular degree; they affect sentiment and passion, which, divested of imagination, are other names for caprice and appetite. The period in our own history of the grossest degradation of the drama is the reign of Charles II, when all forms in which poetry had been accustomed to be expressed became hymns to the triumph of kingly power over liberty and virtue. Milton stood alone illuminating an age unworthy of him. At such periods the calculating principle pervades all the forms of dramatic exhibition, and poetry ceases to be expressed upon them. Comedy loses its ideal universality: wit succeeds to humour; we laugh from self-complacency and triumph, instead of pleasure; malignity, sarcasm, and contempt, succeed to sympathetic merriment; we hardly laugh, but we smile. Obscenity, which is ever blasphemy against the divine beauty in life, becomes, from the very veil which it assumes, more active if less disgusting: it is a monster for which the corruption of society for ever brings forth new food, which it devours in secret.

The drama being that form under which a greater number of modes of expression of poetry are susceptible of being combined than any other, the connexion of poetry and social good is more observable in the drama than in whatever other form. And it is indisputable that the highest perfection of human society has ever corresponded with the highest dramatic excellence; and that the corruption or the extinction of the drama in a nation where it has once flourished, is a mark of a corruption of manners, and an extinction of the energies which sustain the soul of social life. But, as Machiavelli says of political institutions, that life may be preserved and renewed, if men should arise capable of bringing back the drama to its principles. And this is true with respect to poetry in its most extended sense: all language, institution and form, require not only to be produced but to be sustained: the office and character of a poet participates in the divine nature as regards providence, no less than as regards creation.

Civil war, the spoils of Asia, and the fatal predominance first of the Macedonian, and then of the Roman arms, were so many symbols of the extinction or suspension of the creative faculty in Greece. The bucolic writers, who found patronage under the lettered tyrants of Sicily and Egypt, were the latest representatives of its most glorious reign. Their poetry is intensely melodious; like the odour of the tuberose, it overcomes and sickens the spirit with excess of sweetness; whilst the poetry of the preceding age was as a meadow-gale of June, which mingles the fragrance of all the flowers of the field, and adds a quickening and harmonizing spirit of its own, which endows the sense with a power of sustaining its extreme delight. The bucolic and erotic delicacy in written poetry is correlative with that softness in statuary, music, and the kindred arts, and even in manners and institutions, which distinguished the epoch to which I now refer. Nor is it the poetical faculty itself, or any misapplication of it, to which this want of harmony is to be imputed. An equal sensibility to the influence of the senses and the affections is to be found in the writings of Homer and Sophocles: the former, especially, has clothed sensual and pathetic images with irresistible attractions. Their superiority over these succeeding writers consists in the presence of those thoughts which belong to the inner faculties of our nature, not in the absence of those which are connected with the external: their incomparable perfection consists in a harmony of the union of all. It is not what the erotic poets have, but what they have not, in which their imperfection consists. It is not inasmuch as they were poets, but inasmuch as they were not poets, that they can be considered with any plausibility as connected with the corruption of their age. Had that corruption availed so as to extinguish in them the sensibility to pleasure, passion, and natural scenery, which is imputed to them as an imperfection, the last triumph of evil would have been achieved. For the end of social corruption is to destroy all sensibility to pleasure; and, therefore, it is corruption. It begins at the imagination and the intellect as at the core, and distributes itself thence as a paralysing venom, through the affections into the very appetites, until all become a torpid mass in which hardly sense survives. At the approach of such a period, poetry ever addresses itself to those faculties which are the last to be destroyed, and its voice is heard, like the footsteps of Astraea, departing from the world. Poetry ever communicates all the pleasure which men are capable of receiving: it is ever still the light of life; the source of whatever of beautiful or generous or true can have place in an evil time. It will readily be confessed that those among the luxurious citizens of Syracuse and Alexandria, who were delighted with the poems of Theocritus, were less cold, cruel, and sensual than the remnant of their tribe. But corruption must utterly have destroyed the fabric of human society before poetry can ever cease. The sacred links of that chain have never been entirely disjoined, which descending through the minds of many men is attached to those great minds, whence as from a magnet the invisible effluence is sent forth, which at once connects, animates, and sustains the life of all. It is the faculty which contains within itself the seeds at once of its own and of social renovation. And let us not circumscribe the effects of the bucolic and erotic poetry within the limits of the sensibility of those to whom it was addressed. They may have perceived the beauty of those immortal compositions, simply as fragments and isolated portions: those who are more finely organized, or born in a happier age, may recognize them as episodes to that great poem, which all poets, like the co-operating thoughts of one great mind, have built up since the beginning of the world.

The same revolutions within a narrower sphere had place in

ancient Rome; but the actions and forms of its social life never seem to have been perfectly saturated with the poetical element. The Romans appear to have considered the Greeks as the selectest treasuries of the selectest forms of manners and of nature, and to have abstained from creating in measured language, sculpture, music, or architecture, anything which might bear a particular relation to their own condition, whilst it should bear a general one to the universal constitution of the world. But we judge from partial evidence, and we judge perhaps partially. Ennius, Varro, Pacuvius, and Accius, all great poets, have been lost. Lucretius is in the highest, and Virgil in a very high sense, a creator. The chosen delicacy of expressions of the latter, are as a mist of light which conceal from us the intense and exceeding truth of his conceptions of nature. Livy is instinct with poetry. Yet Horace, Catullus, Ovid, and generally the other great writers of the Virgilian age, saw man and nature in the mirror of Greece. The institutions also, and the religion of Rome were less poetical than those of Greece, as the shadow is less vivid than the substance. Hence poetry in Rome, seemed to follow, rather than accompany, the perfection of political and domestic society. The true poetry of Rome lived in its institutions; for whatever of beautiful, true, and majestic, they contained, could have sprung only from the faculty which creates the order in which they consist. The life of Camillus, the death of Regulus; the expectation of the senators, in their godlike state, of the victorious Gauls: the refusal of the republic to make peace with Hannibal, after the battle of Cannae, were not the consequences of a refined calculation of the probable personal advantage to result from such a rhythm and order in the shows of life, to those who were at once the poets and the actors of these immortal dramas. The imagination beholding the beauty of this order, created it out of itself according to its own idea; the consequence was empire, and the reward everliving fame. These things are not the less poetry *quia carent vate sacro*. They are the episodes of that cyclic poem written by Time upon the memories of men. The Past, like an inspired rhapsodist, fills the theatre of everlasting generations with their harmony.

At length the ancient system of religion and manners had fulfilled the circle of its revolutions. And the world would have fallen into utter anarchy and darkness, but that there were found poets among the authors of the Christian and chivalric systems of manners and religion, who created forms of opinion and action never before conceived; which, copied into the imaginations of men, become as generals to the bewildered armies of their thoughts. It is foreign to the present purpose to touch upon the evil produced by these systems: except that we protest, on the ground of the principles already established, that no portion of it can be attributed to the poetry they contain.

It is probable that the poetry of Moses, Job, David, Solomon, and Isaiah, had produced a great effect upon the mind of Jesus and his disciples. The scattered fragments preserved to us by the biographers of this extraordinary person, are all instinct with the most vivid poetry. But his doctrines seem to have been quickly distorted. At a certain period after the prevalence of a system of opinions founded upon those promulgated by him, the three forms into which Plato had distributed the faculties of mind underwent a sort of apotheosis, and became the object of the worship of the civilized world. Here it is to be confessed that 'Light seems to thicken,' and

> The crow makes wing to the rooky wood,
> Good things of day begin to droop and drowse,
> And night's black agents to their preys do rouze.

But mark how beautiful an order has sprung from the dust and blood of this fierce chaos! how the world, as from a resurrection, balancing itself on the golden wings of knowledge and of hope, has reassumed its yet unwearied flight into the heaven of time. Listen to the music, unheard by outward ears, which is as a ceaseless and invisible wind, nourishing its everlasting course with strength and swiftness.

The poetry in the doctrines of Jesus Christ, and the mythology and institutions of the Celtic conquerors of the Roman empire, outlived the darkness and the convulsions connected with their growth and victory, and blended themselves in a new fabric of manners and opinion. It is an error to impute the ignorance of the dark ages to the Christian doctrines or the predominance of the Celtic nations. Whatever of evil their agencies may have contained sprang from the extinction of the poetical principle, connected with the progress of despotism and superstition. Men, from causes too intricate to be here discussed, had become insensible and selfish: their own will had become feeble, and yet they were its slaves, and thence the slaves of the will of others: lust, fear, avarice, cruelty, and fraud, characterized a race amongst whom no one was to be found capable of *creating* in form, language, or institution. The moral anomalies of such a state of society are not justly to be charged upon any class of events immediately connected with them, and those events are most entitled to our approbation which could dissolve it most expeditiously. It is unfortunate for those who cannot distinguish words from thoughts, that many of these anomalies have been incorporated into our popular religion.

It was not until the eleventh century that the effects of the poetry of the Christian and chivalric systems began to manifest themselves. The principle of equality had been discovered and applied by Plato in his *Republic*, as the theoretical rule of the mode in which the materials of pleasure and of power, produced by the common skill and labour of human beings, ought to be distributed among them. The limitations of this rule were asserted by him to be determined only by the sensibility of each, or the utility to result to all. Plato, following the doctrines of Timaeus and Pythagoras, taught also a moral and intellectual system of doctrine, comprehending at once the past, the present, and the future condition of man. Jesus Christ divulged the sacred and eternal truths contained in these views to mankind, and Christianity, in its abstract purity, became the exoteric expression of the esoteric doctrines of the poetry and wisdom of antiquity. The incorporation of the Celtic nations with the exhausted population of the south, impressed upon it the figure of the poetry existing in their mythology and institutions. The result was a sum of the action and reaction of all the causes included in it; for it may be assumed as a maxim that no nation or religion can supersede any other without incorporating into itself a portion of that which it supersedes. The abolition of personal and domestic slavery, and the emancipation of women from a great part of the degrading restraints of antiquity, were among the consequences of these events.

The abolition of personal slavery is the basis of the highest political hope that it can enter into the mind of man to conceive. The freedom of women produced the poetry of sexual love. Love became a religion, the idols of whose worship were ever present. It was as if the statues of Apollo and the Muses had been endowed with life and motion, and had walked forth among their worshippers; so that earth became peopled by the inhabitants of a diviner world. The familiar appearance and proceedings of life became wonderful and heavenly, and a paradise was created as out of the wrecks of Eden. And as this creation itself is poetry, so its creators were poets; and language was the instrument of their art: 'Galeotto fù il libro, e chi lo scrisse.' The Provençal Trouveurs, or inventors, preceded Petrarch, whose verses are as spells, which unseal the inmost enchanted fountains of the delight which is in the grief of love. It is impossible to feel them without becoming a portion of that beauty which we contemplate: it were superfluous to explain how the gentleness and the elevation of mind connected with these sacred emotions can render men more amiable, more generous and wise, and lift them out of the dull vapours of the little world of self. Dante understood the secret things of love even more than Petrarch. His *Vita Nuova* is an inexhaustible fountain of purity of sentiment and language: it is the idealized history of that period, and those intervals of his life which were dedicated to love. His apotheosis of Beatrice in Paradise, and the gradations of his own love and her loveliness, by which as by steps he feigns himself to have ascended to the throne of the Supreme Cause, is the most glorious imagination of modern poetry. The acutest critics have justly reversed the judgement of the vulgar, and the order of the great acts of the 'Divine Drama', in the measure of the admiration which they accord to the Hell, Purgatory, and Paradise. The latter is a perpetual hymn of everlasting love. Love, which found a worthy poet in Plato alone of all the ancients, has been celebrated by a chorus of the greatest writers of the renovated world; and the music has penetrated the caverns of society, and its echoes still drown the dissonance of arms and superstition. At successive intervals, Ariosto, Tasso, Shakespeare, Spenser, Calderon, Rousseau, and the great writers of our own age, have celebrated the dominion of love, planting as it were trophies in the human mind of that sublimest victory over sensuality and force. The true relation borne to each other by the sexes into which human kind is distributed, has become less misunderstood; and if the error which confounded diversity with inequality of the powers of the two sexes has been partially recognized in the opinions and institutions of modern Europe, we owe this great benefit to the worship of which chivalry was the law, and poets the prophets.

The poetry of Dante may be considered as the bridge thrown over the stream of time, which unites the modern and ancient world. The distorted notions of invisible things which Dante and his rival Milton have idealized, are merely the mask and the mantle in which these great poets walk through eternity enveloped and disguised. It is a difficult question to determine how

far they were conscious of the distinction which must have sub-
sisted in their minds between their own creeds and that of the
people. Dante at least appears to wish to mark the full extent of
it by placing Riphaeus, whom Virgil calls *justissimus unus,* in
Paradise, and observing a most heretical caprice in his distribution of rewards and punishments. And Milton's poem contains
within itself a philosophical refutation of that system, of which,
by a strange and natural antithesis, it has been a chief popular
support. Nothing can exceed the energy and magnificence of the
character of Satan as expressed in *Paradise Lost.* It is a mistake
to suppose that he could ever have been intended for the popular
personification of evil. Implacable hate, patient cunning, and a
sleepless refinement of device to inflict the extremest anguish on
an enemy, these things are evil; and, although venial in a slave,
are not to be forgiven in a tyrant; although redeemed by much
that ennobles his defeat in one subdued, are marked by all that
dishonours his conquest in the victor. Milton's Devil as a moral
being is as far superior to his God, as one who perseveres in some
purpose which he has conceived to be excellent in spite of adversity and torture, is to one who in the cold security of undoubted triumph inflicts the most horrible revenge upon his
enemy, not from any mistaken notion of inducing him to repent
of a perseverance in enmity, but with the alleged design of
exasperating him to deserve new torments. Milton has so far violated the popular creed (if this shall be judged to be a violation)
as to have alleged no superiority of moral virtue to his God over
his Devil. And this bold neglect of a direct moral purpose is the
most decisive proof of the supremacy of Milton's genius. He
mingled as it were the elements of human nature as colours upon
a single pallet, and arranged them in the composition of his great
picture according to the laws of epic truth; that is, according to
the laws of that principle by which a series of actions of the external universe and of intelligent and ethical beings is calculated
to excite the sympathy of succeeding generations of mankind.
The *Divina Commedia* and *Paradise Lost* have conferred upon
modern mythology a systematic form; and when change and
time shall have added one more superstition to the mass of those
which have arisen and decayed upon the earth, commentators
will be learnedly employed in elucidating the religion of ancestral
Europe, only not utterly forgotten because it will have been
stamped with the eternity of genius.

Homer was the first and Dante the second epic poet: that is, the second poet, the series of whose creations bore a defined and intelligible relation to the knowledge and sentiment and religion of the age in which he lived, and of the ages which followed it: developing itself in correspondence with their development. For Lucretius had limed the wings of his swift spirit in the dregs of the sensible world; and Virgil, with a modesty that ill became his genius, had affected the fame of an imitator, even whilst he created anew all that he copied; and none among the flock of mock-birds, though their notes were sweet, Apollonius Rhodius, Quintus Calaber, Nonnus, Lucan, Statius, or Claudian, have sought even to fulfil a single condition of epic truth. Milton was the third epic poet. For if the title of epic in its highest sense be refused to the *Aeneid,* still less can it be conceded to the *Orlando Furioso,* the *Gerusalemme Liberata,* the *Lusiad,* or the *Fairy Queen.*

Dante and Milton were both deeply penetrated with the ancient religion of the civilized world; and its spirit exists in their poetry probably in the same proportion as its forms survived in the unreformed worship of modern Europe. The one preceded and the other followed the Reformation at almost equal intervals. Dante was the first religious reformer, and Luther surpassed him rather in the rudeness and acrimony, than in the boldness of his censures of papal usurpation. Dante was the first awakener of entranced Europe; he created a language, in itself music and persuasion, out of a chaos of inharmonious barbarisms. He was the congregator of those great spirits who presided over the resurrection of learning; the Lucifer of that starry flock which in the thirteenth century shone forth from republican Italy, as from a heaven, into the darkness of the benighted world. His very words are instinct with spirit; each is as a spark, a burning atom of inextinguishable thought; and many yet lie covered in the ashes of their birth, and pregnant with a lightning which has yet found no conductor. All high poetry is infinite; it is as the first acorn, which contained all oaks potentially. Veil after veil may be undrawn, and the inmost naked beauty of the meaning never exposed. A great poem is a fountain for ever overflowing with the waters of wisdom and delight; and after one person and one age has exhausted all its divine effluence which their peculiar relations enable them to share, another and yet another succeeds, and new relations are ever developed, the source of an unforeseen and an unconceived delight.

The age immediately succeeding to that of Dante, Petrarch, and Boccaccio, was characterized by a revival of painting, sculpture, and architecture. Chaucer caught the sacred inspiration, and the superstructure of English literature is based upon the materials of Italian invention.

But let us not be betrayed from a defence into a critical history of poetry and its influence on society. Be it enough to have pointed out the effects of poets, in the large and true sense of the word, upon their own and all succeeding times.

But poets have been challenged to resign the civic crown to reasoners and mechanists, on another plea. It is admitted that the exercise of the imagination is most delightful, but it is alleged that that of reason is more useful. Let us examine as the grounds of this distinction, what is here meant by utility. Pleasure or good, in a general sense, is that which the consciousness of a sensitive and intelligent being seeks, and in which, when found, it acquiesces. There are two kinds of pleasure, one durable, universal and permanent; the other transitory and particular. Utility may either express the means of producing the former or the latter. In the former sense, whatever strengthens and purifies the affections, enlarges the imagination, and adds spirit to sense, is useful. But a narrower meaning may be assigned to the word utility, confining it to express that which banishes the importunity of the wants of our animal nature, the surrounding men with security of life, the dispersing the grosser delusions of superstition, and the conciliating such a degree of mutual forbearance among men as may consist with the motives of personal advantage.

Undoubtedly the promoters of utility, in this limited sense, have their appointed office in society. They follow the footsteps of poets, and copy the sketches of their creations into the book of common life. They make space, and give time. Their exertions are of the highest value, so long as they confine their administration of the concerns of the inferior powers of our nature within the limits due to the superior ones. But whilst the sceptic destroys gross superstitions, let him spare to deface, as some of the French writers have defaced, the eternal truths charactered upon the imaginations of men. Whilst the mechanist abridges, and the political economist combines labour, let them beware that their speculations, for want of correspondence with those first principles which belong to the imagination, do not tend, as they have in modern England, to exasperate at once the extremes of luxury and want. They have exemplified the saying, 'To him that hath, more shall be given; and from him that hath not, the little that

he hath shall be taken away.' The rich have become richer, and
the poor have become poorer; and the vessel of the state is driven
between the Scylla and Charybdis of anarchy and despotism.
Such are the effects which must ever flow from an unmitigated
exercise of the calculating faculty.

It is difficult to define pleasure in its highest sense; the definition involving a number of apparent paradoxes. For, from an
inexplicable defect of harmony in the constitution of human nature, the pain of the inferior is frequently connected with the
pleasures of the superior portions of our being. Sorrow, terror,
anguish, despair itself, are often the chosen expressions of an
approximation to the highest good. Our sympathy in tragic fiction
depends on this principle; tragedy delights by affording a shadow
of the pleasure which exists in pain. This is the source also of
the melancholy which is inseparable from the sweetest melody.
The pleasure that is in sorrow is sweeter than the pleasure of
pleasure itself. And hence the saying, 'It is better to go to the
house of mourning, than to the house of mirth.' Not that this
highest species of pleasure is necessarily linked with pain. The
delight of love and friendship, the ecstasy of the admiration of
nature, the joy of the perception and still more of the creation of
poetry, is often wholly unalloyed.

The production and assurance of pleasure in this highest sense
is true utility. Those who produce and preserve this pleasure are
poets or poetical philosophers.

The exertions of Locke, Hume, Gibbon, Voltaire, Rousseau,[1]
and their disciples, in favour of oppressed and deluded humanity,
are entitled to the gratitude of mankind. Yet it is easy to calculate
the degree of moral and intellectual improvement which the
world would have exhibited, had they never lived. A little more
nonsense would have been talked for a century or two; and perhaps a few more men, women, and children, burnt as heretics.
We might not at this moment have been congratulating each
other on the abolition of the Inquisition in Spain. But it exceeds
all imagination to conceive what would have been the moral condition of the world if neither Dante, Petrarch, Boccaccio, Chaucer, Shakespeare, Calderon, Lord Bacon, nor Milton, had ever
existed; if Raphael and Michael Angelo had never been born; if
the Hebrew poetry had never been translated; if a revival of the
study of Greek literature had never taken place; if no monu-

[1] Although Rousseau has been thus classed, he was essentially a
poet. The others, even Voltaire, were mere reasoners.

ments of ancient sculpture had been handed down to us; and if the poetry of the religion of the ancient world had been extinguished together with its belief. The human mind could never, except by the intervention of these excitements, have been awakened to the invention of the grosser sciences, and that application of analytical reasoning to the aberrations of society, which it is now attempted to exalt over the direct expression of the inventive and creative faculty itself.

We have more moral, political and historical wisdom, than we know how to reduce into practice; we have more scientific and economical knowledge than can be accommodated to the just distribution of the produce which it multiplies. The poetry in these systems of thought, is concealed by the accumulation of facts and calculating processes. There is no want of knowledge respecting what is wisest and best in morals, government, and political economy, or at least, what is wiser and better than what men now practise and endure. But we let '*I dare not* wait upon *I would*, like the poor cat in the adage.' We want the creative faculty to imagine that which we know; we want the generous impulse to act that which we imagine; we want the poetry of life: our calculations have outrun conception; we have eaten more than we can digest. The cultivation of those sciences which have enlarged the limits of the empire of man over the external world, has, for want of the poetical faculty, proportionally circumscribed those of the internal world; and man, having enslaved the elements, remains himself a slave. To what but a cultivation of the mechanical arts in a degree disproportioned to the presence of the creative faculty, which is the basis of all knowledge, is to be attributed the abuse of all invention for abridging and combining labour, to the exasperation of the inequality of mankind? From what other cause has it arisen that the discoveries which should have lightened, have added a weight to the curse imposed on Adam? Poetry, and the principle of Self, of which money is the visible incarnation, are the God and Mammon of the world.

The functions of the poetical faculty are two-fold; by one it creates new materials of knowledge and power and pleasure; by the other it engenders in the mind a desire to reproduce and arrange them according to a certain rhythm and order which may be called the beautiful and the good. The cultivation of poetry is never more to be desired than at periods when, from an excess of the selfish and calculating principle, the accumulation of the materials of external life exceed the quantity of the power of assimilating them to the internal laws of human nature. The body has then become too unwieldy for that which animates it.

Poetry is indeed something divine. It is at once the centre and circumference of knowledge; it is that which comprehends all science, and that to which all science must be referred. It is at the same time the root and blossom of all other systems of thought; it is that from which all spring, and that which adorns all; and that which, if blighted, denies the fruit and the seed, and withholds from the barren world the nourishment and the succession of the scions of the tree of life. It is the perfect and consummate surface and bloom of all things; it is as the odour and the colour of the rose to the texture of the elements which compose it, as the form and splendour of unfaded beauty to the secrets of anatomy and corruption. What were virtue, love, patriotism, friendship—what were the scenery of this beautiful universe which we inhabit; what were our consolations on this side of the grave—and what were our aspirations beyond it, if poetry did not ascend to bring light and fire from those eternal regions where the owl-winged faculty of calculation dare not ever soar? Poetry is not like reasoning, a power to be exerted according to the determination of the will. A man cannot say, 'I will compose poetry.' The greatest poet even cannot say it; for the mind in creation is as a fading coal, which some invisible influence, like an inconstant wind, awakens to transitory brightness; this power arises from within, like the colour of a flower which fades and changes as it is developed, and the conscious portions of our natures are unprophetic either of its approach or its departure. Could this influence be durable in its original purity and force, it is impossible to predict the greatness of the results; but when composition begins, inspiration is already on the decline, and the most glorious poetry that has ever been communicated to the world is probably a feeble shadow of the original conceptions of the poet. I appeal to the greatest poets of the present day, whether it is not an error to assert that the finest passages of poetry are produced by labour and study. The toil and the delay recommended by critics, can be justly interpreted to mean no more than a careful observation of the inspired moments, and an artificial connexion of the spaces between their suggestions by the intertexture of conventional expressions; a necessity only imposed by the limitedness of the poetical faculty itself; for Milton conceived the *Paradise Lost* as a whole before he executed it in portions. We have his own authority also for the muse having 'dictated' to him the 'unpremeditated song'. And let this be an answer to those who would allege the fifty-six various readings of the first line of the *Orlando Furioso*. Compositions so produced are to poetry what mosaic is to painting. This instinct and intuition of the poetical faculty is still more observable in the plastic and pictorial arts; a great statue or picture grows under the power of the artist as a child in the mother's womb; and the very mind which directs the hands in formation is incapable of accounting to itself for the origin, the gradations, or the media of the process.

Poetry is the record of the best and happiest moments of the happiest and best minds. We are aware of evanescent visitations of thought and feeling sometimes associated with place or person, sometimes regarding our own mind alone, and always arising unforeseen and departing unbidden, but elevating and delightful beyond all expression: so that even in the desire and regret they leave, there cannot but be pleasure, participating as it does in the nature of its object. It is as it were the interpenetration of a diviner nature through our own; but its footsteps are like those of a wind over the sea, which the coming calm erases, and whose traces remain only, as on the wrinkled sand which paves it. These and corresponding conditions of being are experienced principally by those of the most delicate sensibility and the most enlarged imagination; and the state of mind produced by them is at war with every base desire. The enthusiasm of virtue, love, patriotism, and friendship, is essentially linked with such emotions; and whilst they last, self appears as what it is, an atom to a universe. Poets are not only subject to these experiences as spirits of the most refined organization, but they can colour all that they combine with the evanescent hues of this ethereal world; a word, a trait in the representation of a scene or a passion, will touch the enchanted chord, and reanimate, in those who have ever experienced these emotions, the sleeping, the cold, the buried image of the past. Poetry thus makes immortal all that is best and most beautiful in the world; it arrests the vanishing apparitions which haunt the interlunations of life, and veiling them, or in language or in form, sends them forth among mankind, bearing sweet news of kindred joy to those with whom their sisters abide—abide, because there is no portal of expression from the caverns of the spirit which they inhabit into the universe of things. Poetry redeems from decay the visitations of the divinity in man.

Poetry turns all things to loveliness; it exalts the beauty of that which is most beautiful, and it adds beauty to that which is most deformed; it marries exultation and horror, grief and pleasure, eternity and change; it subdues to union under its light yoke, all irreconcilable things. It transmutes all that it touches, and every form moving within the radiance of its presence is changed by wondrous sympathy to an incarnation of the spirit which it breathes: its secret alchemy turns to potable gold the poisonous waters which flow from death through life; it strips the veil of familiarity from the world, and lays bare the naked and sleeping beauty, which is the spirit of its forms.

All things exist as they are perceived; at least in relation to the percipient. 'The mind is its own place, and of itself can make a heaven of hell, a hell of heaven.' But poetry defeats the curse which binds us to be subjected to the accident of surrounding impressions. And whether it spreads its own figured curtain, or withdraws life's dark veil from before the scene of things, it equally creates for us a being within our being. It makes us the inhabitants of a world to which the familiar world is a chaos. It reproduces the common universe of which we are portions and percipients, and it purges from our inward sight the film of familiarity which obscures from us the wonder of our being. It compels us to feel that which we perceive, and to imagine that which we know. It creates anew the universe, after it has been annihilated in our minds by the recurrence of impressions blunted by reiteration. It justifies the bold and true words of Tasso: *Non merita nome di creatore, se non Iddio ed il Poeta.*

A poet, as he is the author to others of the highest wisdom, pleasure, virtue and glory, so he ought personally to be the happiest, the best, the wisest, and the most illustrious of men. As to his glory, let time be challenged to declare whether the fame of any other institutor of human life be comparable to that of a poet. That he is the wisest, the happiest, and the best, inasmuch as he is a poet, is equally incontrovertible: the greatest poets have been men of the most spotless virtue, of the most consummate prudence, and, if we would look into the interior of their lives, the most fortunate of men: and the exceptions, as they regard those who possessed the poetic faculty in a high yet inferior degree, will be found on consideration to confine rather than destroy the rule. Let us for a moment stoop to the arbitration of popular breath, and usurping and uniting in our own persons the incompatible characters of accuser, witness, judge, and executioner, let us decide without trial, testimony, or form, that certain motives of those who are 'there sitting where we dare not soar', are reprehensible. Let us assume that Homer was a drunkard, that Virgil was a flatterer, that Horace was a coward, that Tasso was a madman, that Lord Bacon was a peculator, that Raphael was a libertine, that Spenser was a poet laureate. It is inconsistent with this division of our subject to cite living poets, but posterity has done ample justice to the great names now referred to. Their errors have been weighed and found to have been dust in the balance; if their sins 'were as scarlet, they are now white as snow': they have been washed in the blood of the mediator and redeemer, Time. Observe in what a ludicrous chaos the imputations of real or fictitious crime have been confused in the contemporary calumnies against poetry and poets; consider how little is, as it appears—or appears, as it is; look to your own motives, and judge not, lest ye be judged.

Poetry, as has been said, differs in this respect from logic, that it is not subject to the control of the active powers of the mind, and that its birth and recurrence have no necessary connexion with the consciousness or will. It is presumptuous to determine that these are the necessary conditions of all mental causation, when mental effects are experienced unsusceptible of being referred to them. The frequent recurrence of the poetical power, it is obvious to suppose, may produce in the mind a habit of order and harmony correlative with its own nature and with its effects upon other minds. But in the intervals of inspiration, and they may be frequent without being durable, a poet becomes a man, and is abandoned to the sudden reflux of the influences under which others habitually live. But as he is more delicately organized than other men, and sensible to pain and pleasure, both his own and that of others, in a degree unknown to them, he will avoid the one and pursue the other with an ardour proportioned to this difference. And he renders himself obnoxious to calumny, when he neglects to observe the circumstances under which these objects of universal pursuit and flight have disguised themselves in one another's garments.

But there is nothing necessarily evil in this error, and thus cruelty, envy, revenge, avarice, and the passions purely evil, have never formed any portion of the popular imputations on the lives of poets.

I have thought it most favourable to the cause of truth to set down these remarks according to the order in which they were suggested to my mind, by a consideration of the subject itself, instead of observing the formality of a polemical reply; but if the view which they contain be just, they will be found to involve a refutation of the arguers against poetry, so far at least as regards the first division of the subject. I can readily conjecture what should have moved the gall of some learned and intelligent writers who quarrel with certain versifiers; I confess myself, like them, unwilling to be stunned by the Theseids of the hoarse Codri of the day. Bavius and Maevius undoubtedly are, as they ever were, insufferable persons. But it belongs to a philosophical critic to distinguish rather than confound.

The first part of these remarks has related to poetry in its elements and principles; and it has been shown, as well as the narrow limits assigned them would permit, that what is called poetry, in a restricted sense, has a common source with all other forms of order and of beauty, according to which the materials of human life are susceptible of being arranged, and which is poetry in a universal sense.

The second part will have for its object an application of these principles to the present state of the cultivation of poetry, and a defence of the attempt to idealize the modern forms of manners and opinions, and compel them into a subordination to the imaginative and creative faculty. For the literature of England, an energetic development of which has ever preceded or accompanied a great and free development of the national will, has arisen as it were from a new birth. In spite of the low-thoughted envy which would undervalue contemporary merit, our own will be a memorable age in intellectual achievements, and we live among such philosophers and poets as surpass beyond comparison any who have appeared since the last national struggle for civil and religious liberty. The most unfailing herald, companion, and follower of the awakening of a great people to work a beneficial change in opinion or institution, is poetry. At such periods there is an accumulation of the power of communicating and receiving intense and impassioned conceptions respecting man and nature. The persons in whom this power resides may often, as far as regards many portions of their nature, have little apparent correspondence with that spirit of good of which they are the ministers. But even whilst they deny and abjure, they are yet compelled to serve, the power which is seated on the throne of their own soul. It is impossible to read the compositions of the most celebrated writers of the present day without being startled with the electric life which burns within their words. They measure the circumference and sound the depths of human nature with a comprehensive and all-penetrating spirit, and they are themselves perhaps the most sincerely astonished at its manifestations; for it is less their spirit than the spirit of the age. Poets are the hierophants of an unapprehended inspiration; the mirrors of the gigantic shadows which futurity casts upon the present; the words which express what they understand not; the trumpets which sing to battle, and feel not what they inspire; the influence which is moved not, but moves. Poets are the unacknowledged legislators of the world.

[1821; publ. 1840]

Index of Titles